60/-

568

THE GENESIS OF
PARLIAMENTARY REFORM

" . . . Your political principles at present are as much out of fashion as your clothes." — F. Burdett

" I know it. I have good reason to know it. But the fashion must one day return or the nation be undone." — H. Horne Tooke, 1805

Diversions of Purley II.15.

The Genesis of Parliamentary Reform

BY GEORGE STEAD VEITCH

WITH AN INTRODUCTION BY

IAN R. CHRISTIE

READER IN MODERN HISTORY
UNIVERSITY COLLEGE LONDON

CONSTABLE

LONDON

Published by
Constable and Company Limited
10-12 Orange Street London wc2
First published 1913
Reprinted 1964
Introduction © Ian R. Christie 1964
Printed in Great Britain by
Gilmour & Dean Limited
Hamilton & London

INTRODUCTION

Ramsay Muir, in his introduction to the first impression of this book, marked as its great distinction the attention given to political movements outside the circle of court and parliament. In this break with the dominant trend of writing British history almost exclusively from the view-point of Westminster and Whitehall Veitch was not quite a lone pioneer in his treatment of his theme. It was also taken up by the American scholar, Walter Phelps Hall, whose *British Radicalism, 1791-1797*, appeared a year earlier, in 1912, and again by the Englishman, Philip Anthony Brown, whose book *The French Revolution in English History*, had been largely completed by 1914 although not published till four years later. But of these three works Veitch's is in almost all respects the most valuable. In particular he gave proportionately as much attention to the earlier reform movements associated with Wilkes in London and with Wyvill in Yorkshire as to the radical outbursts which followed the French Revolution. The fullest and most satisfactory treatment of the whole subject from 1760 to 1800, his book has long maintained its position as a standard work. For twenty years after 1918 the subject was left practically untouched. More recently a few scholars have begun to explore aspects of it with which he was not concerned and to challenge some of his conclusions, but his book is far from being superseded.

To some extent the interpretation of the story of parliamentary reform in this period has been modified since Veitch's day in consequence of the displacements in eighteenth-century historical studies arising out of the work of Sir Lewis Namier. Namier's studies have deepened our understanding of the way in which the old representative system, despite its illogical absurdities, had an effective functional role in a society in which politics was the virtually unchallenged preserve of a landed oligarchy. The continuance of such a system depended upon the maintenance of a stable and homogeneous society, homogeneous in the sense that people were for the most part conscious of the direct or not very indirect connection of their fortunes with the 'landed interest' and were, despite diversities of rank and fortune, on the whole satisfied with their niches in society. By the later years of the eighteenth century, when Paley (and others) called attention to the way in which the House of Commons represented the important interests in the nation,[1] the situation was in fact changing (it is usually when systems are breaking down that they evoke methodical definition and defence). Increase of population and industrialization were both disturbing the *status quo*, giving rise to a fair amount of individual hardship—though this was much less in the aggregate than was to be encountered in the years after 1815, and for large sections of the population the standard of living was rising.[2] But in the present state of our knowledge it is in the harmony of the system of representation with the social structure, rather than in other reasons adduced by Veitch,[3] that we find the ground for the complacency with which Englishmen regarded it in the early years of George III's reign.

Apart from this, greater understanding of the unreformed parliamentary system has pointed to the need to make a clearer distinction between the reformers' conceptions of the system and the system as it really was. This level of interpretation was not methodically developed by Veitch. The explanation of his neglect of it is perhaps to be found in the intellectual climate in which his work was done. The assumption that the reform movements in the reign of George III were the first steps on the road towards the more rational democratic system of his own time seems implicit in his treatment. In one

---

[1] pp. 19–20 below.
[2] T. S. Ashton, *An Economic History of England: The Eighteenth Century* (1955), 46, 215, 233.
[3] pp. 18–22 below.

sense this belief was true. But it may have deflected his attention from what now seem important aspects of the subject: the degree to which reformers were misled in their suspicions about the working of the parliamentary system of their day, and the extent to which a good deal (though not all) of their agitation was backward-looking rather than intelligent anticipation of the nineteenth-century rationalization of institutions.

Caroline Robbins, in *The Eighteenth-Century Common-wealthman*, published in 1959, has emphasized the continuity of an intellectual tradition current among parliamentary reformers of the late eighteenth century which runs back to Locke and Sydney and beyond. In this tradition the machinery of representation was seen as the barrier against authoritarianism on the part of the executive—separation of powers was an inherent part of the concept—and its spokesmen were concerned with reforms that would subserve this end. It was in fact the Whig political theory. It spurred its votaries on to the defence of 'Liberty', the rallying cry which Wilkes found so potent, a concept re-echoed in the writings of Major John Cartwright and other reformers through and beyond the period of the great French wars. It gave birth, in a watered-down version, to the Economical Reform programme of the Rockingham party. But the fullest expression of it in political action was the county association movement of the years 1780-1785. The two distinctive demands of the county movement—shorter parliaments and an increase in the number of knights of the shire—were both directed towards the establishment of a greater degree of separation between parliament and the executive. There was no conception here of making parliament more representative in the modern democratic sense. The difference between Wyvill and Burke was one of 'more' or 'less', not a reflection of fundamental disagreements about the basis of state organization; and Wyvill, far from being a pioneer of a 'democratic revolution' might more plausibly be represented as a doctrinaire Whig reactionary. The movement led by

Wyvill had a definition of its own, and this is merely obscured by labelling him as on the right wing of the reformers.[1]

Movements with other definitions are also to be distinguished in this early period of George III's reign, before the onset of the French Revolution. There were at least two tributary head-waters of the liberal democracy of the late nineteenth century the immanence of which insensibly shaped Veitch's treatment of his subject. One was the re-emergence, a hundred years after its earlier airing in a somewhat different guise by the Levellers, of the idea of personality as the basis of political rights. This concept appeared in various writings in the 1770s, and it captured the minds of the little band of intellectuals who came together in 1780 to form the Society for Constitutional Information, but there is little evidence to show that it had any influence on popular political agitation. The other, more material, was the demand of a minority of the commercial community in the metropolis for a larger share of the parliamentary representation, based on the conviction that, as an 'interest' whose stake in the country could be measured in terms of tax burdens, they should have a proportionate strength in spokesmen and voting power. It is impossible however to say to what extent this idea took precedence over Whig political theory in the minds of those who supported reform in the metropolis in those years. It may be observed of this demand for political power on the part of a class or group distinct from the landowners, that the social-economic development which gave rise to it had preceded the 'Industrial Revolution'. And it is significant that it attracted little support in the northern and midland areas where industrialization was already crowding people into the towns.

As Veitch did not see clearly the extent to which parliamentary reform movements before 1789 displayed diversities and a certain degree of constitutional atavism, it is to be expected that his treatment of British radicalism

[1] p. 280 below.

in the period of the French Revolution should show similar limitations. He tended to stress the continuity from the earlier period of the pressures tending towards democratic reform and to give less emphasis than it deserves to the 'commonwealthman' tradition which continued to colour the utterances of many of the reformers. As a result, although he constructed a very full and valuable narrative of the growth, proceedings, and collapse of the corresponding societies of the 1790s, in which for the first time men of the 'working class' engaged in organized political activity, he paid little attention to certain features on which a writer of the present day would perhaps lay more stress, in particular their novelty, the degree to which they represented a change, a discontinuity, in the character of reform agitation in comparison with the years before 1789. The idea of associations had indeed had wide circulation in reform literature during the years of the American revolution, but it is extremely difficult to find any evidence for 'mechanics' engaging in political activity of this kind before 1791. The sense of discontinuity is heightened by the reflection that, in the period before 1789 practically all those who engaged in reforming activity were already within the pale of the constitution, at least having the parliamentary franchise if not (as in many cases) some wider opportunity for political self-expression; whereas the most characteristic section of the reform movement after 1789 drew its strength from men who were not of the 'political nation'. Also Veitch did not probe far into the problem of what kind of men enrolled themselves in the corresponding societies and he showed even less concern with the reasons which led them to do so. It is a weakness in his handling of this part of his theme, that he paid practically no attention to reflections upon social and economic discontent which some pamphleteers of the time clearly linked up with the demand for parliamentary reform—a feature of the movement to which attention had already just been drawn in the work of W. P. Hall. It is true that the corresponding societies never formulated programmes of social change and confined themselves to demands for constitutional reform; for were they not being told in effect by these writers: 'Seek ye first the political kingdom'? But it can hardly be doubted that part of their popular appeal can be traced to the outpourings of hostility towards the material privileges of the propertied classes and to various unsystematized pleas for greater attention to the interests of the poor, which are to be culled from the writings not only (as Veitch mentions) of Mary Wollstonecraft, but also of Paine, Thelwall, Catharine Phillips, and other pamphleteers.[1] It was this note, perhaps, as much as the purely political demands of the societies, that aroused a fear of 'levelling' tendencies in the minds of anti-reformers.

Veitch devoted much attention to the relationships between French revolutionaries and British reformers. On this subject he drew together material from both the British and the French archives, and it may fairly be claimed that his treatment is authoritative and also definitive. The two other most detailed scholarly studies give no ground for questioning his judgments.[2] He concluded that in general the British reformers were both pacific and loyal. The outbreak of the French Revolution undoubtedly stimulated a great deal of interest in Britain and gave a powerful impetus to the movement for reform. There were numerous exchanges of fraternal greetings between British and French societies and between British societies and the French assemblies. These gestures of mutual admiration, however, were not inevitably evidence of a desire on the part of the British to emulate the French. The British attitude was often rather one of somewhat condescending pleasure, that Frenchmen were at last securing political liberties which had long been enjoyed north of the Channel. As for

[1] p. 169 below; W. P. Hall, 139–56.
[2] P. A. Brown, *op. cit.*; W. A. L. Seaman, 'British Democratic Societies in the period of the French Revolution' (unpublished Ph.D. thesis, 1954, University of London).

reform, their own problems were different, their own modes of thinking about them were firmly established, and there was no need for them to borrow from French example. To the extent that Paine's *Rights of Man* overlaid the negative attributes of the universal suffrage preached by John Cartwright with a more positive concept of popular sovereignty derived from revolutionary France, which was incompatible with individual right, it probably lost far more support for the reformers than it attracted, especially among the middle class.[1] Their gladness at the French achievement of 'Liberty' developed naturally and readily into sympathy with the French when the eastern monarchies appeared to league against them to restore Bourbon despotism. But with the onset of republicanism and violence at Paris, the contacts made by the societies were soon broken off, the wave of British enthusiasm for the Revolution lost much of its force, and the few individual Britons who remained in contact with France cannot be regarded as representative of any general body of opinion. Members of the corresponding societies were opposed to the policy of war with France and identified Pitt with the Whig bogey of executive tyranny, just as the North administration had been so identified during the American War of Independence. But very few of them were prepared to go beyond the legitimate bounds of peaceful protest.

On the basis of a thorough examination of Home Office papers Veitch set in proper perspective a few treasonable incidents which were unduly exaggerated in the work of W. P. Hall,[2] rejected the view that there was widespread revolutionary disaffection in the country either before or after the outbreak of war with France in 1793, and presented much evidence to indicate the peaceful intentions of the corresponding societies and their concern to seek reform only by constitutional means. Although Talleyrand assured his principals in 1792, that there was

[1] *The Debate on the French Revolution 1789–1800*, ed. by Alfred Cobban (1960), 14–16.
[2] W. P. Hall, 197–224.

not the slightest likelihood of a revolution in England,[1] successive leaders of revolutionary France did not accept this view, and it would appear as if some continental historians, to the present day, still hesitate to do so. The problems posed by their interpretation merge with those raised by proponents of the view that, from about 1770 onwards, the western world, including Great Britain, was going through a general phase of 'democratic revolution'.[2] The assumptions underlying these interpretations, so far as Britain is concerned, seem to some extent to beg two questions: the nature of the British reformers' intentions and the extent of their numbers.

The work of Veitch and Brown reveals clearly enough that, save for a few exceptions, the British reformers were not revolutionaries. They were themselves fully conscious of the difference between a revolutionary and a reformer. In December 1791, the Sheffield Constitutional Society—a 'working-class' organization—prescribed the following declaration for new recruits:[3]

> I solemnly declare myself an enemy of all conspiracies, tumults, and riotous proceedings, or maliciously surmising any attempt that tends to overturn, or anywise injure or disturb the peace of the people; or the laws of this realm; and that my only wish and design is, to concur in sentiment with every peaceable and good citizen of this nation, in giving my voice for application to be made to parliament, praying for a speedy reformation, and an equal representation in the House of Commons.

In so doing its members were evidently determined to make clear to which category they belonged. Plenty of similar evidence has been adduced by Veitch and Brown

[1] pp. 209–11 below.

[2] Jules Dechamps, *Entre la guerre et la paix: Les Iles Britanniques et la Révolution Française (1789–1803)* (Brussels, 1949); R. R. Palmer, *The Age of the Democratic Revolution: a Political History of Europe and America, 1760–1800:* Volume I, *The Challenge* (1960); Jacques Godechot, *Les Révolutions (1770–1799)* (Paris, 1963).

[3] Cited W. A. L. Seaman, p. 59.

to support this instance. It is therefore confusing the issue when a French historian, to take the most recent example, Jacques Godechot, writes of '*l'opposition révolutionnaire en Grande-Bretagne*'.[1] In their own eyes, as in the eyes of British historians since, these reformers were not revolutionaries: their object was to build up a sufficient body of public opinion to secure a peaceful and generally accepted change achieved through the existing legislative instruments (as was to be effected to a limited extent in 1832).

There is much more ground for placing some sections of the British reform agitation within a general picture of a western trend towards democracy, provided a *caveat* is observed over the term 'revolution', and provided also that the definition 'democratic' is applied with strictness. Little of the reform agitation in Britain before 1789 falls within the definition. After 1789 the outlook of some reformers, Wyvill, for instance, was not 'democratic', and the thinking of others, even of Cartwright, was coloured by concepts of 'constitutional balance' not necessarily identical with democracy in the modern sense of the term.

There remains the problem of the numbers of the British reformers. This subject is a quagmire in which it is all too easy to sink. The evidence appears to be so inadequate, that it is unlikely that any very firm estimates will ever be reached. But figures of two quite different levels of magnitude have emerged in the discussions. Those of the larger magnitude derive from pamphlet literature, scares and rumours. A well-known example is Burke's estimate, that out of a 'political nation' of about 400,000 a fifth (80,000) were 'Jacobins',[2] a figure which in any case had little relevance to the corresponding societies which drew most of their membership from

[1] *Les Révolutions* (1770–1799), 304. Godechot relies on a limited number of secondary works for his treatment of this subject. It is odd that Veitch's book is not among them.

[2] *The Works of Edmund Burke* (Bohn edn. 8 v. 1894–1900), v. 5, 189–90.

lower social strata. But information of this kind (and there seems to be a certain tendency on the part of continental writers to rely on it)[1] cannot be regarded as so valuable as the information to be culled from government investigations at the time and from the records of the societies themselves. Pamphlets were written to create an effect, either confidence among reformers, or on the other side fear and a stronger reaction. Veitch judiciously ignored the propaganda and made what tentative deductions he thought possible from the records. His estimates point to the conclusion that a number of thousands, but still only a small minority, of the British people were involved in the corresponding societies.[2]

The Genesis of Parliamentary Reform remains an admirable one-volume survey of the parliamentary reform movement during the first forty years of George III's reign. Veitch's scholarship was exact, and in the pursuit of those questions which he considered important he ranged broadly and deeply in the manuscript and the printed evidence. At the level of political action—the activities of societies, manifestos, petitions, parliamentary discussions, and the development of the government's policy of repression—his narrative is full and at many points seems likely to be proved exhaustive. For historians turning their attention to aspects of the subject which he did not examine his book is a rock on which they can safely build.

University College London   IAN R. CHRISTIE

Note: An additional bibliography to this edition appears on page 387.

[1] J. Dechamps, 43–4. This work is cited as 'fundamental' by Godechot, *op. cit.*, 305.
[2] pp. 217–18, 321 below. Cf. P. A. Brown, 59 and W. A. L. Seaman, 49, 52, 54.

ADDITIONAL
BIBLIOGRAPHICAL NOTE
TO THE
SECOND IMPRESSION

The following is a short list of monographs and articles dealing specifically with the movement for parliamentary reform which have appeared since 1913. For the constitutional background a good, up-to-date, select bibliography will be found in *The Eighteenth-Century Constitution, 1688–1815: Documents and Commentary*, by E. Neville Williams (Cambridge U.P., 1960).

(The place of publication unless otherwise stated is London)

BIRLEY, ROBERT, *The English Jacobins from 1789 to 1802* (1924)

BLACK, EUGENE CHARLTON, *The Association: British Extra-parliamentary Political Organization, 1769–1793* (Harvard U.P., 1963).

BLEACKLEY, HORACE, *Life of John Wilkes* (1917). Other Lives by Raymond Postgate (1930, 2nd rev. edn. 1956), Owen Aubrey Sherrard (1930), Charles P. Chenevix-Trench (1962).

BROWN, PHILIP ANTHONY, *The French Revolution in English History* (1918).

BUTTERFIELD, HERBERT, 'The Yorkshire Association and the crisis of 1779–80.' *Transactions of the Royal Historical Society*, 4th series, **XXIX** (1947), 69–92.

———————— *George III, Lord North, and the People, 1779–1780* (1949).

CHRISTIE, IAN R., 'Economical Reform and the "Influence of the Crown", 1780.' *Cambridge Historical Journal*, **XII** (1956), 144–54.

———————— 'Great Yarmouth and the Yorkshire Reform Movement, 1782–1784.' *Norfolk Archaeology*, **XXXII**, pt. II (1959), 104–10.

———————— 'The Yorkshire Association: a study in political organization.' *Historical Journal*, **III** (1960), 144–61.

———————— 'Sir George Savile, Edmund Burke, and the Yorkshire Reform Programme, February 1780.' *Yorkshire Archaeological Journal*, **XL** (1959–62), 205–8.

CHRISTIE, IAN R., 'The Wilkites and the General Election of 1774.' *Guildhall Miscellany* II, 4 (1962), 155–64.

———————— *Wilkes, Wyvill, and Reform: The Parliamentary Reform Movement in British Politics, 1760–1785* (1962).

COBBAN, ALFRED (ed.), *The Debate on the French Revolution, 1789–1800* (1960).

KEIR, DAVID LINDSAY, 'Economical Reform, 1779–1787.' *Law Quarterly Review*, L (1934), 368–85.

KEMP, BETTY, 'Crewe's Act, 1782.' *English Historical Review* LXVIII (1953), 258–63.

LINCOLN, ANTHONY, *Some political and social ideas of English Dissent, 1763–1800* (Cambridge, 1938).

MACCOBY, S., *English Radicalism, 1762–1785. The origins* (1955).

———————— *English Radicalism, 1786–1832. From Paine to Cobbett* (1955).

PHILLIPS, N. C., 'Burke and the County Movement.' *English Historical Review* LXXVI (1961), 254–278.

———————— 'County against Court. Christopher Wyvill, a Yorkshire Champion.' *Yorkshire Archaeological Journal*, XL (1959–62), 588–603.

ROBBINS, CAROLINE, *The Eighteenth-Century Commonwealthman* (Cambridge, Mass., 1959).

RUDÉ, GEORGE F. E., 'Wilkes and Liberty, 1768–69.' *Guildhall Miscellany*, no. 8 (1957), 3–24.

———————— 'The Middlesex Electors of 1768–1769.' *English Historical Review* LXXV (1960), 601–17.

———————— *Wilkes and Liberty: A Social Study of 1763 to 1774* (Oxford, 1962).

———————— 'John Wilkes and the Re-birth of British Radicalism.' *Political Science*, XIV (Wellington, N.Z., 1962), 11–29.

SEAMAN, W. A. L., 'Reform Politics at Sheffield, 1791–1797.' *Transactions of the Hunter Archaeological Society*, VII (1957), 215–28. Largely supersedes previous articles by G. P. Jones, *ibid*. IV (1929–30), 57–68, and J. Taylor, *ibid*. V (1940), 133–46.

THOMPSON, E. P., *The Making of the English Working Class* (1963).

PREFACE

THE opportunity to begin this book I owe to the University of Liverpool, which elected me in 1906 to a Research Fellowship, founded in memory of Dr. Charles Beard. Another Fellowship, to which I was subsequently elected, enabled me to continue a part of the work which could be done only in Paris.

My thanks are due to Professor J. M. Mackay for his interest and encouragement; to Professor Ramsay Muir, who has been unfailing in help and suggestion from the sketching of the first plan to the passing of the last proof; to Sir Alfred Dale, Professor Émile Bourgeois and Professor Gonner, through whose assistance I obtained access to important manuscript sources; to Professor MacCunn, for his friendly advice and for the loan of books not otherwise accessible to me; and not least to Professor Aulard, without whose aid some chapters of the book could hardly have been written.

I am deeply indebted to M. Louis Farge of the Archives des Affaires Etrangères at Paris for his courteous assistance; to Mr. J. C. Ledlie for permission to consult the Registers of the Privy Council; and to the archivists of the Archives nationales, our own Record Office, and the Manuscript Department of the British Museum for unstinted aid.

To Mr. G. T. Shaw, Chief Librarian to the City of Liverpool; to Mr. W. Cunningham, Master and Librarian of the Liverpool Athenæum; to Mr. Henry Guppy of the John Rylands Library; to Mr. Francis Jenkinson of the Cambridge University Library; and to the staff of the Department of Printed Books in the British Museum I owe my warmest thanks for unnumbered acts of kindness.

My friends Mr. G. K. Grierson and Mr. D. J. Sloss were good enough to read large portions of the book in manuscript, and I owe to them many useful suggestions. To Miss T. Lightbound, B.A., I am greatly indebted for assistance in the tedious work of preparing the index.

G. S. V.

TABLE OF CONTENTS

CHAPTER I

CHAPTER III

CHAPTER IV

THE REFORM CAMPAIGN IN PARLIAMENT AND IN THE COUNTRY (1782–1789)

TABLE OF CONTENTS

CHAPTER V

THE BEGINNING OF THE FRENCH REVOLUTION, AND ITS INFLUENCE ON THE PARLIAMENTARY REFORM MOVEMENT (1789–1790)

CHAPTER VI

CHAPTER IX

CHAPTER X

CHAPTER XIII

The Political Societies under the Ban (Jan.–Nov. 1794

CHAPTER XIV

The Decline and Fall of the Political Societies (Oct. 1794–July 1799) 321

APPENDICES

THE GENESIS OF
PARLIAMENTARY REFORM

CHAPTER I

THE NEED FOR REFORM

JUDGED according to modern standards of representative government, the English House of Commons as it existed in the second half of the eighteenth century was grievously defective. From the accession of George III in 1760 to the Reform Act of 1832 it grew less and less satisfactory, not so much because the system of representation changed [1] as because it remained unaltered, and because, for a time, it became unalterable when that universal dread of organic change which came with the French Revolution foiled the first generation of parliamentary reformers. The radical defects of the system by which the House of Commons was chosen grew rapidly more apparent as England was transformed from an agricultural to an industrial country, and as the weight of population was shifted from the south and east towards the north and west. The displacement of population which resulted from the industrial revolution changed the balance of representation to such an extent that, ultimately, all but those who had determined to protect a vested interest at any cost were forced to recognise the necessity for readjustment and reform.

In the eighteenth century the representation was already

[1] So far as England and Wales were concerned very few changes were made in the electoral law between 1677 and 1832. See *The Unreformed House of Commons*, by E. and A. Porritt, I. 15, 89. Mr. and Mrs. Porritt give an excellent account of the whole parliamentary and electoral system, and their work, to which I am much indebted, should be consulted for the whole of this chapter.

disproportionate. It was the product, not of plan or principle, but of growth, of custom, even of caprice. It was,
therefore, unequal and inequitable; borough was favoured
as against county, one district as against another; and, to
adopt the phrase of modern politicians, the time was ripe
for a redistribution of seats. The representation of a
county was an indication of its past prosperity rather than
of its actual importance. Cornwall, once busy with thriving seaports, contained 21 parliamentary boroughs, and
in addition to the two knights of the shire, returned 42
members to Parliament. Cornwall, as a whole, had therefore 44 members, or one less than the whole of Scotland.
While this county had 44 out of the 513 representatives
of England and Wales, it was estimated that it paid only
16 out of 513 parts of the land tax.[1] Lancashire, on the
other hand, had been later in its economic development;
when its towns grew to prosperity, custom had already
fixed the representation of the boroughs; and the 12
members for the six ancient boroughs, together with the
two county members, gave only 14 representatives to the
shire as a whole.

There was even greater disparity between the representation of the boroughs of a county and of that portion of a
county which lay outside municipal boundaries. A committee, of which Sheridan was chairman, reported in 1780
to the Westminster Association, presided over by Charles
James Fox, that the total electorate of England and Wales
was 214,000. According to this estimate, 92 county members were returned by 130,000 voters; only 84,000 electors
were represented by the 421 members who sat for cities,
towns and universities.[2]

A remarkable illustration of this inequality is afforded
by the representation of the great county of York. Two
members were returned by the 16,000 extra-burghal voters
of the county;[3] two members were equally returned by
the 50 electors of Thirsk, or by the close corporation of

[1] *Wyvill Papers*, I. 212-218.
[2] *Add. MSS.* (Newspaper Cuttings) 27837, ff. 6 *sqq.*
[3] When Grampound was disfranchised, in 1821, two extra members
were given to the county of York. 1 and 2 Geo. IV, c. 47. See Porritt, I. 86-89.

Scarborough. The city of York had 3000 electors, but the remaining 13 boroughs of the county had just over 4000 all told. Rather more than 7000 burghal voters were therefore able to return 28 members to Parliament. To put the case in another way, in Yorkshire each county member represented about 8000 electors, or more than the whole electorate of all the boroughs; each borough member represented an average of about 250 electors, or, if the city of York be excluded from the calculation, of not more than 160. Anomalies so evident seemed to call for instant reform.[1]

Even such as it was, the representation was shamelessly bought and sold. In 1769 Junius declared, with intentional exaggeration, that the Duke of Bedford had "bought and sold more than half the representative integrity of the nation,"[2] and if this statement was unfair to the duke it was not because he was guiltless, but because his companions in iniquity were many. A petition presented to the House of Commons in 1790 averred that seats "were as notoriously rented and bought as standings for cattle in a fair." The petition was voted scandalous and libellous, yet in 1809, when two ministers were accused of being concerned in the sale of a seat, they were screened from punishment on the plea of "the extreme notoriety of the practice," which many members of Parliament unblushingly defended.[3] A pretence of ignorance was, indeed, idle when seats were openly advertised for sale in the newspapers;[4] when £5000 had been left by will for the purchase of a seat in Parliament; when a seat had been reckoned amongst the saleable assets of a bankrupt; and when a defaulting debtor had paid the market price for a seat in order that, under the protection of parliamentary

[1] *Wyvill Papers*, IV. 233.
[2] *Letter to Grafton*, May 30, 1769. Junius, I. 157.
[3] Cited in a printed sheet called "Resolutions of the Inhabitants, Householders, Electors of the City and Liberty of Westminster, Feb. 9, 1810." *Add. MSS.* 27839, p. 25. For negotiations between Lord Sandwich and J. Robinson, the court borough-monger, about the sale of a seat, see *H. M. C. X.*, App. VI. p. 11.
[4] Advertisements from the *London Courier* and the *London Telegraph* are reprinted in Mrs. Thelwall's *Life of Thelwall*, I. 364. See also one from the *Morning Post*, Carlyle's *Cobbett*, 135.

privilege, he might evade his creditors by escaping from England without arrest.[1] The capital value of a seat can be estimated from the fact that in 1812 the Duke of Bedford sold his "property in the borough of Camelford" for £32,000,[2] and though the price of a seat was rising during the reign of George III, the market rate can be gauged by the knowledge that in 1784 the electors of Wallingford sold the election to the members for £6000.[3] It was not without justification that a critic of the established order declared in 1782 that "the price of a seat in Parliament" was "better known than the price of a horse." [4]

This distortion of the representation by sale and purchase was rendered possible by the state of the 203 English parliamentary boroughs which returned the majority of the members of the House of Commons.[5] With few exceptions they were alike in returning two members,[6] but they were all alike in no other respect. No uniform rule fixed the constitution of the boroughs or the franchise of the electors. Borough differed widely from borough, and each had its own electoral custom, drawn in part, perhaps, from its charter, but more often derived from ancient tradition, or the "last determination" of the House of Commons on the occasion of a disputed election. For convenience, however, the boroughs may be separated into four main divisions, though within each group there was really great variety.

(1) The widest franchise was to be found in what were

---

[1] Petition, May 14, 1814. *Proceedings of the Hampden Club*, p. 6.

[2] Oldfield, *Representative History*, II. 236.

[3] *Ib.* II. 88–90. In one notorious instance the Corporation of Oxford, which was in debt, offered to secure the election of 1766 for the sitting members in return for a loan of £4000 free of interest.—*Parl. Hist.* XVI. 397–402. In Chatham's youth £2000 seems to have been regarded as the normal price of a seat. W. Pitt to Ann Pitt, Nov. 7, 1734 — Rosebery's *Chatham*, pp. 75-6.

[4] Spencer Stanhope at the Yorkshire County Meeting of Dec. 19, 1782.—*Wyvill Papers*, II. 58.

[5] See, for this subject generally, Porritt as cited, and F. W. Maitland, *Township and Borough*. An electoral map showing the enfranchised boroughs before and after 1832 is given in Prof. Muir's *Historical Atlas* (1911), plate 43.

[6] The united boroughs of Weymouth and Melcombe Regis returned four members.—Oldfield, *History of the Boroughs*, I. 265-8. The City of London returned four members, and there were five single-member constituencies.—Porritt, I. 29.

called scot and lot and potwalloper boroughs. The suffrage was so easily acquired in some boroughs of this class that the franchise imposed by the Reform Act of 1832 came rather as a restriction than as an emancipation, for it had the effect of disfranchising a portion of the old electorate. In both the scot and lot and potwalloper boroughs a vote was given either to every resident, or to every resident householder who was not a pauper; they differed mainly in the test of pauperism which custom imposed. In the scot and lot boroughs every one was an elector who had resided for six months in the borough [1] and who had paid scot and lot,[2] that is to say, church rate and poor rate. Sometimes every male resident of full age was a voter, provided he had not been in actual receipt of parish relief during the qualifying period. In the potwalloper boroughs every adult male was an elector if he had control of a separate doorway to his dwelling, if he could provide his own sustenance, and if he had a fireplace at which to cook his meals. Perhaps the original idea had been that a vote should be given to every man who fed at his own table, to every one who lived in no dependence on a lord. It was a rough-and-ready attempt to provide a test of economic independence. In 59 boroughs—populous places like Preston and Westminster, Southwark and Northampton, mere clusters of dwellings like Gatton,[3] decayed towns like Grampound,[4] where all but about 25 of the 200 inhabitants were too poor to pay scot and lot—the members were elected by the potwallopers, by the payers of scot and lot, or in accordance with some analogous custom.

(2) Of a second class of boroughs—the freeman

---

[1] Between 1786 and 1832. This qualification was required in 1786, by 26 Geo. III. c. 100, in consequence of the loose definition of "inhabitant" previously accepted at Preston. Any one who had slept for a night in the borough was admitted to vote at an election on the succeeding day.— Porritt, I. 37.

[2] More properly, paid scot and bore lot, *i. e.* was liable to serve in unpaid offices, etc. But payment of church rate and poor rate was the only test applied in practice.

[3] Oldfield, writing in 1792, said that Gatton consisted of only two houses (*History of the Boroughs*, III. 24), but he was probably representing things as worse than they were, because he states in the *Representative History*, II. 606, that there were six houses in 1816.

[4] Oldfield, *History of the Boroughs*, I. 180.

boroughs—there were 62, including, for example, all the Lancashire boroughs except Preston. The freedom of these boroughs could be acquired, as of right, in certain customary ways—by inheritance, by servitude of apprenticeship, by a fortunate marriage with a freeman's daughter —but it was also possible for the corporation to elect to the freedom of the borough an unlimited number of people who might, or might not, be resident within the municipal boundaries. Whenever, therefore, an election seemed likely to go against the wishes of the majority of the governing corporation, it was always possible to turn a minority into a majority by creating enough freemen of the right political colour to make up the deficiency. This convenient property of elasticity was also possessed by some scot and lot boroughs like Southampton, where the elder Gibbon was elected in 1741 by the sudden creation, on the eve of the poll, of 170 honorary burgesses.[1]

(3) In 39 boroughs, called burgage-boroughs, the franchise was attached to a certain holding or burgage. Residence was not always required: it was not always possible, as the burgage was not in all cases capable of occupation. At Downton, in Wiltshire, for example, one of the burgages was in the middle of a watercourse;[2] at Droitwich the burgages were really shares in a dried-up salt pit;[3] and again, in one Sussex constituency six or eight of the burgages were represented by black stones in a nobleman's park wall.[4] In general the burgage boroughs were small, had few electors, and were easily controllable by some lord or country gentleman near the gates of whose park the little borough lay.

(4) Least popular of all was the constitution of the 43

---

[1] Gibbon, *Memoirs*, pp. 27-8. For the electoral custom of Southampton, see Oldfield, *History of the Boroughs*, II. 67.

[2] Hansard, 3rd Series, VII. 1394, quoted by Porritt, I. 37.

[3] Petitions, April 9, 1783, *C. J.* XXXIX. 361. The burgesses of the corporation of the salt-springs of Droitwich numbered fourteen.—Oldfield, *History of the Boroughs*, III. 239.

[4] Spencer Stanhope at Yorkshire Meeting, December 19, 1782. *Wyvill Papers*, II. 55. There were three burgage boroughs in Sussex, each controlled, partially or completely, by a nobleman. The Duke of Norfolk was joint patron of Horsham, the Earl of Egremont was patron of Midhurst, and the Duke of Dorset of East Grinstead.—Oldfield, *History of the Boroughs*, III. 43, 45, 71.

boroughs where a close corporation elected the members. Tiverton, for instance, with its 5000 inhabitants, had no say in the election of its representatives, who were chosen by the 25 members of the self-elected corporation.[1] At Bury St. Edmunds 37 persons, the alderman, capital burgesses and common councilmen, chose representatives for 6000 inhabitants, of whom 500 were assessed to the poor rate, but none of whom had any voice in the election of their members.[2] Many of these corporations were of no use whatever for purposes of local government. They were merely organisations for the return of members to Parliament; and when some of them were disenfranchised in 1832 they at once ceased to exist, because there was no longer anything to be gained by maintaining the pretence of a real burghal life.[3]

In most boroughs the electorate was extremely small. A committee of the Society of the Friends of the People estimated, in 1793, not perhaps with any very strong desire to make things appear better than they were, that 257 members, or a majority of the representatives of England and Wales, were returned by 11,075 electors.[4] In the same report it is alleged that in 51 constituencies there were less than 50 voters, returning on the average a member of Parliament for every 15 electors. According to this estimate there were, in all, 130 boroughs with less than 300 electors apiece.[5]

Even amongst the boroughs with the wider scot and lot franchise there were constituencies like Wallingford [6] and Penryn,[7] where, if the electorate did not fall below 100, it never rose to 150. Great Grimsby, with its 75 freemen,[8] was respectable in comparison with Hastings, where in

---

[1] Petition of Jan. 31, 1783, *C. J.* XXXIX. 127 ; cf. Oldfield, *Hist. of the Boroughs*, I. 219.

[2] Petition of Feb. 17, 1783, *C. J.* XXXIX. 231.—Oldfield, *Hist. of the Boroughs*, II. 547. The patron of Bury St. Edmunds was the Duke of Grafton.

[3] See Spencer Walpole, *Hist. of England,* IV. 36 ; cf. also 34 and 35.

[4] *Wyvill Papers*, III. App. 195.

[5] *Ib.* 196-7.

[6] Oldfield, *Rep. Hist.* II. 88-90; *Hist. of the Boroughs*, I. 18.

[7] *Ib.* I. 158-9. Protest of Portreeve and 100 electors against reform.—*Wyvill Papers,* II. 130-5.

[8] *Hist. of Boroughs*, II. 218.

1783 there were 22 electors.[1]   Bossiney, a hamlet of a score
of houses in the parish of Tintagel, had not even a dozen
electors,[2] and in 1784, at the first election after the disfranchisement of revenue officers, only one voter, it is said,
was qualified to go to the poll.[3]   At Launceston no new
freemen had been created between 1734 and 1783, and about
a score of people returned the members;[4] whilst at Lyme,
where the right of election resided in the mayor, 15 capital
burgesses and a few honorary freemen, there were said, in
1792, to be no more than 31 electors.[5]

But Old Sarum, which James I would gladly have seen
disfranchised in 1624,[6] is the classic example of the rotten
borough.   It is more famous for its want of inhabitants
than because it was once represented by the elder Pitt.
On the site of what had once been Old Salisbury there
remained, in 1776, one house, whose occupier supplied
curious visitors with punch, wine and tea; but in 1792 this
last remnant of a habitation had been demolished, and it
was necessary to erect a tent to shelter the returning officer
whilst he took the votes of the seven burgage-holders.[7]

Almost as striking was the case of the once thriving
seaport of Dunwich, which was gradually being washed
away by the sea.   In 1792 it still consisted of 38 houses

---

[1] Petition presented to Commons, May 5, 1753, *C. J.* XXXIX. 402.
According to an estimate of 1792, there were then not more than a
dozen electors.—*Hist. of Boroughs*, III., *Cinque Ports*, 47.

[2] Oldfield says that in 1792 there were twenty houses and four or five
electors (*ib.* I. 166); in 1816 there were sixteen houses and nine electors,
eight of whom were of one family.—*Rep. Hist.* II. 209-13.

[3] *Hist. of Boroughs*, I. 163.

[4] Petitions presented to Commons, Jan. 23, 1783, *C. J.* XXXIX. 81
and 82 ; *Hist. of Boroughs*, I. 178-9.

[5] Petitions presented to Commons, Feb. 13, 1783, *C. J.* XXXIX.
191 ; *Hist. of Boroughs*, I. 265.

[6] Porritt, I. 2.

[7] *Hist. of Boroughs*, III. 198-9.   Porritt, I. 35-6.   Thomas Mozley,
tells how once (probably after the Reform Act of 1832, for Mozley did
not take orders till 1831) he took a service for a friend which was
attended by "a bright-looking old fellow, with a full rubicund face and
a profusion of white hair."   "He had been the borough of Old Sarum,"
says Mozley, with some exaggeration, "and had returned two representatives to Parliament for forty years, all honest men and gentlemen, not
the sort of men they were sending to Parliament in these days."—T.
Mozley's *Reminiscences* (1883), II. 13.   Attention is drawn to this curious
passage in Rosebery's *Chatham*, p. 129 note.

and part of a church, and it still had 14 voters;[1] but it seemed probable that in a few years the encroachment would "compel the constituent body to betake themselves to a boat whenever the king's writ" should "summon them to the exercise of their elective franchise."[2]

How farcical the old system was is seen from the account given by Sir Philip Francis of his election for Appleby in 1802. Nominally there were 100 burgage-holders; actually the members were nominated by the Earl of Lonsdale and the Earl of Thanet. ". . . I was unanimously elected by one Elector," says Francis, "to represent this ancient borough in Parliament . . . there was no other Candidate, no Opposition, no Poll demanded, Scrutiny or petition. So I had nothing to do but to thank the said Elector for the Unanimous Voice with which I was chosen. . . . On Friday Morning I shall quit this triumphant Scene with flying Colours and a noble Determination not to see it again in less than seven years."[3] Even if the "one elector" is interpreted as meaning one of the patrons of the borough, the Earl of Thanet, who was the friend and patron of Francis, it is not on that account less true that the member for Appleby could in no sense be called the representative of Appleby.

The electorates were not merely small, they bore no relation to the population of the boroughs. As the voters were often non-resident, the interests of the electors were seldom those of the townsmen at large, and there was, in any case, no necessary correspondence between the size and importance of the town and the number of voters who elected its representatives in Parliament. In Scarborough, where the 44 electors were reduced to 34 by the Act disqualifying revenue officers, 700 people paid the parish rate;[4] and in Winchester, where 650 people out of a

---

[1] Oldfield, *Hist. of Boroughs*, II. 531-4.　　　[2] *Ib.* 531.

[3] Sir Philip Francis to Harriet Francis, July 7, 1802.—*Francis Letters*, II. 493. Francis adds that Appleby is a very rainy place, and makes the inhabitants very melancholy; "insomuch that my Elector intends to hang himself in November, and then I shall elect myself: and that will do as well" (*Ib.* 494).—Oldfield, *Hist. of Boroughs*, III. 111.

[4] *Wyvill Papers*, II. 252-3. Oldfield, *Hist. of Boroughs*, III. 264. Petitions presented to Commons, March 10, 1783, *C. J.* XXXIX. 285.

population of 3400 were assessed to the poor rate, the electorate, according to the highest estimate, was 119,[1] and, according to another, was only half that number.[2] If no borough had been worse than Winchester or Scarborough the case would have been bad enough. But it was still more serious that in growing towns like Derby only about a quarter of the householders had a vote, for it could not seriously be pretended that 400 or 500 electors were a due proportion of the 12,000 inhabitants of the town,[3] any more than it could be maintained that 80 was an adequate number of voters in a growing seaport like Portsmouth, with 20,000 inhabitants.[4]

Cambridge, with a population of 7000, of whom 1200 were assessed to the poor rate, had the ridiculously small number of 180 electors, but it suffered also from the vice of non-residence which was common to most of the English boroughs. About 44 per cent. of its electors lived away from the borough, and could not, therefore, be regarded as satisfactory electors by any active citizen of Cambridge.[5] But it is a misuse of language to speak of representation at all in the case of Lymington, where the resident electors numbered only half-a-dozen,[6] or in the case of a thriving town like Droitwich, where 47 of the 50 electors lived outside its boundaries.[7]

Tiny electorates like those described were manifestly easy to control. It was estimated in 1793 that 71 peers, together with the Lords of the Treasury, could absolutely nominate 90 members of the House of Commons, and could procure the return of 77 more; that 91 commoners could nominate 82 members and procure the return of 57; and therefore that 162 people could, together with the

---

[1] Petition, presented to Commons, Feb. 5, 1783, *C. J.* XXXIX. 149.

[2] Oldfield, *Hist. of Boroughs*, I. 97.

[3] Petition presented to Commons, Feb. 21, 1783, *C. J.* XXXIX. 239; cf. Oldfield, *Hist. of Boroughs*, I. 206.

[4] Petition presented to Commons, April 10, 1783, *C. J.* XXXIX. 363. *Hist. of Boroughs*, II. 66.

[5] Petition presented to Commons, Feb. 10, 1783, *C. J.* XXXIX. 176.

[6] Petition presented to Commons, March 6, 1783, *C. J.* XXXIX. 281.

[7] Petition presented to Commons, April 9, 1783, *ib.* 361.

Treasury, nominate 306 members, or a substantial majority of the House of Commons.[1]

The process was simple though it was not cheap. Control of a borough might be obtained either by purchase or by influence, and probably no single politician would have doubted, at the accession of George III, that influence, at any rate over what were called family boroughs, was perfectly legitimate. Nor is it likely that any one thought it strange when a few years later the *Times* spoke of the borough of Malton as "in the gift" of Earl Fitzwilliam.[2] His right of nomination was no more doubted than his right of presentation to a living.

The process by which influence over a borough was established has been described by Shelburne, who resisted the doctrine that "family boroughs," boroughs which lay "naturally within the reach of cultivation of any house or property," cost nothing to the patron. They cost a great deal because they had to be corrupted gradually, by means of "insensible perspiration," which meant that the patron must pay a little too much for every article he bought; that he must purchase all his goods from a particular set of tradesmen, and sometimes also from their relatives in London; that he must be content to be overcharged and take no notice; that he must give handsomely towards roads and other objects of public subscription; and that rents of houses and lands must be fixed with an eye to the votes of the tenants. The patron must be urgent in obtaining favours from ministers for the electors of his borough,[3] he must consent to be swindled by a local attorney under the name of his agent, and finally he must be free in his hospitality and unceasing in his management of men and things.[4] Sometimes the patron might be robbed of the election in the end by the advent of an open-handed millionaire, but the path was plain and can seldom have

---

[1] Report of a committee of the Soc. of the Friends of the People, Feb. 9, 1793.— *Wyvill Papers*, III. App. 229 ; cf. 238–46.

[2] Quoted from the *Times* in Mrs. Thelwall's *Life of Thelwall*, I. 364.

[3] See Peel's strong protest against this system, as it existed in 1829.— Parker's *Peel*, II. 140.

[4] Undated memorandum by Shelburne, *Life*, II. 363.

been as difficult as Shelburne, in his cynicism, would make it appear.

A borough patron, who was without territorial influence or court favour, had to obtain and secure his position by a lavish expenditure of money. Corruption was not so respectable as family influence, but it was legitimate in moderation, and was regarded with an indulgence which was measured, not in proportion to the bribe, but according to the briber. A venial error in the son of a peer was mortal sin in a nabob. What really excited the resentment of the governing classes was the spectacle of an upstart buying his way into Parliament. "The House," Cavendish tells us, "seemed to set themselves against the admission into Parliament of certain adventurers; men who, having no personal interest anywhere, go about canvassing from borough to borough with their pockets full of money."[1] Such men disturbed existing arrangements and compelled the borough patrons to strain their influence and empty their purses. This accounts for the hatred of the nabobs, or retired servants of the East India Company, whom Chatham denounced because they introduced into England not only Asiatic luxuries, but also Asiatic principles of government. "Without connections, without any natural interest in the soil, the importers of foreign gold have forced their way into Parliament by such a torrent of private corruption as no private hereditary fortune could resist."[2] This speech came oddly from Chatham's lips, for it meant that, in the eyes of the advocate of political purity, a little bribery was a good thing, but that too much was not to be endured, because it threatened the influence of the old family connections.

A public assembly sometimes betrays itself by an incautious laugh. In 1771 Charles Fox had been arguing that it was not his corrupt practices but his expulsion that had incapacitated Walpole to sit in the House during the Parliament of 1712. Sir George Savile at once agreed. "Corruption!" he said. "Did any one ever hear, sir, of

---

[1] *Cavendish Debates*, I. 61.
[2] Debate in the Lords on the State of the Nation, Jan. 22, 1770.—*Parl. Hist.* XVI. 752.

corruption being a bar against sitting in this House?" Members broke out into laughter, which showed at once how widespread and notorious was the practice of electoral corruption.[1]

Huge sums were spent on a single election. A contest at Lincoln in 1808 is said to have cost £25,000 or £30,000,[2] and it is on record that a single candidate spent £30,000 during an election at Liverpool.[3] In some places votes were sold at a fixed market price, varying from five guineas at Boston [4] to forty guineas at Wallingford.[5] But in times of special excitement the market rose. "What," says Shelburne, for instance, "can you say to a blacksmith or to a common labouring man who is offered seven hundred pounds for his vote?"[6]

Sometimes appeal was made to the taste, instead of to the touch. Sheridan corrupted the electors of Stafford with tickets for free beer.[7] Rose, the friend and supporter of that austere reformer, the younger Pitt, was ordered by a court of law to pay a bill of £110 (including a bill for bludgeon-men [8]) for opening the Star and Garter, King Street, Westminster, for the friends of Lord Hood.[9] Even when Horne Tooke, the advocate of parliamentary reform,

[1] Debate of Feb. 7, 1771.—*Cavendish Debates*, II. 250. *Parl. Hist.* XVI. 1357. Occasionally, of course, somebody was punished. In May 1763 a person was fined £200 for bribery at the Evesham election, and committed to prison for three months, and until the fine was paid.—*Ann. Reg.* 1763, *Chron.* 76.

[2] This is the statement in the *Nottingham Journal* of Jan. 23, 1808.

[3] Lord Penrhyn. See Picton's *Memorials*, I. 231. The election of 1780 cost Bamber Gascoyne £8000. After the election Bamber Gascoyne, senior, gave an open-air entertainment to his son's supporters. An ox was roasted whole.—*Ib.* 219.

[4] Nov. 1806.—*Life of Cartwright*, I. 344.

[5] Oldfield, *Rep. Hist.* II. 41.

[6] Undated memorandum by Shelburne. — Fitzmaurice's *Life of Shelburne*, II 363.

[7] See facsimiles, Fraser Rae's *Sheridan*, I. 354, 414.

[8] It was not unusual to supplement persuasion and bribery with violence. As a good example the Coventry election of Sept. 1780 may be cited. The rioting was so bad that only eighty-three voters could be polled in nine days, and the sheriffs decided that they would make no return.—*Early Life of S. Rogers*, 40–41. In 1747 the partizans of one candidate pulled down and destroyed the polling-booth with drag hooks and red-hot chains.—W. Reader, *The History and Antiquities of . . . Coventry . . .* p. 95. The borough records were damaged in an election riot at Leicester in 1790.—T. F. Johnson, *Glimpses of Leicester*, 269–270.

[9] *Add. MSS.* 27814, fo. 32 note.

and the avowed enemy of all corruption, stood in 1796 for Westminster, his supporters, who sang a chorus in which they declared that their votes were unbought and that no bribes would betray them,[1] were nevertheless invited "to Breakfast with an Independent Elector on Cold Beef and strong Beer" at the Robin Hood in Great Windmill Street, and "to go from thence in a Party to assert their Own Freedom."[2]

That the habit of corruption was ingrained is proved most amusingly by the story of two elections at Honiton in 1806, when Lord Cochrane, the sailor, stood as an independent candidate. "I always votes for Mr. Most," one elector told him, but Cochrane refused to bribe, and, at the first election in June, he was defeated. His opponent paid five pounds apiece for his votes, so after the election was over Cochrane sent round the bellman to announce that all his supporters would receive ten guineas on application to his agents. Every man who had voted against Cochrane therefore felt that he had been most wickedly cheated of five pounds ten shillings, and that he had a legitimate grievance against the successful candidate. In October there was a general election; Cochrane stood again, made the same professions, and was elected easily. After the contest his supporters expected to be paid as before, but this time he gave them nothing. Cochrane had achieved his end. He had been elected for Honiton without giving a bribe. But never again did he dare to appear there as a Parliamentary candidate.[3]

Such, then, was the character of the boroughs. The representation of the counties was smaller—there were only

---

[1] *Add. MSS.* 27837, fo. 70.

[2] Advertisement preserved in *Add. MSS.* 27837, fo. 65. In 1741 the Earl of Euston and W. Grove, Esq., were elected to represent Coventry. "One ox and nine sheep were roasted by their friends on the chairing day."—W. Reader, *The History and Antiquities of . . . Coventry . . .* p. 94.

[3] *Auto. of a Seaman*, ed. 1860, I. 179 and 181, 202-4. Doubt has been thrown on this story in *The Trial of Lord Cochrane before Lord Ellenborough*, by J. B. Atlay, 1897, p. 18. But with all due respect to Mr. Atlay, I cannot accept the view that this story is irreconcilable with the version given by Cochrane in the House of Commons, Jan. 29, Feb. 5, May 15, 1817. *Hansard*, XXXV. 92,221 ; XXXVI. 600. See also Carlyle's *Cobbett*, 127-8 ; and *D. N. B.* XI. 166, *Errata*, 72.

92 county members in England and Wales—but it was purer, and the first reformers set their hopes upon it. Early schemes of parliamentary reform all included an addition to the representation of the counties. Apart from a few fancy franchises, held *ex officio*, such as the vote attached to a cathedral prebend, the main qualification was a forty-shilling freehold, assessed to the land tax. This qualification had once been fairly high, but had fallen with the depreciation in the value of money, and in 1785 the capital value of a qualifying freehold was estimated at sixty pounds.[1]

The representation of the counties was better than the representation of the boroughs, but it was not without faults. It was unequal, because a small county like Rutland had the same number of members as a large county like Lancashire; it was inequitable, because, whilst the freeholder voted, the copyholder, whose tenure differed only in form, did not. County elections were difficult to conduct, for there was no electoral register—an act passed in 1788 to provide one was repealed before it became operative [2]—and there was only one polling-place in each county. In consequence county elections were costly, as much money had to be spent in bringing voters up to poll at the county town,[3] and even county electors were not totally insensible to corruption, though the size of the electorate made it more difficult to bribe a county than to corrupt a borough. It was perhaps part of the merit of the system that the great county families exercised a controlling influence over the elections; in spite of all defects,

[1] For the county representation in general see Porritt, I. 20–8.

[2] 28 Geo. III. c. 36. Repealed in 1789. 29 Geo. III. c. 13. See Porritt, I. 26–8.

[3] On Dec. 12, 1774, Mr. Rose Fuller stated in the House of Commons that he resided in the county of Sussex, and that his house was eighty miles from the polling-place. Several freeholders lived 100 miles away, and it cost them £4 to cast a vote. He moved for leave, which was granted, to bring in a bill for preventing expenses attending elections.— *Parl. Hist.* XVIII. 54. The distances given by Rose Fuller may be exaggerated. In Sussex nobody would be 100 miles "as the crow flies" from any polling-place. But then it must be remembered that in Sussex no good main roads crossed the county from east to west, and voters must have been compelled to follow a circuitous route. See the road map in Prof. Muir's *Historical Atlas* (1911), Fig. XXIII, Intro., p. 34.

it was in the counties that there was the best opportunity of persuading the electors to give their votes in accordance with their real political convictions; and, as will presently appear, it was due mainly to the counties that the first step was made in the direction of reform.[1]

The representation of Wales was perhaps rather better, as the representation of Scotland was certainly rather worse, than that of England.[2] In the eighteenth century the Welsh were not yet merged in the main current of the national life, and as they have no part in our story it is unnecessary to describe their electoral customs in detail. Scotland, however, was one of the strongholds of the parliamentary reformers, and Scotsmen played a foremost part in the agitation for organic change. The Act of Union gave to Scotland 45 representatives in the English Parliament; 15 of these were assigned to the counties, 30 to the boroughs. Thirteen of the counties received a member each; the remaining four formed two pairs with a member each. Of the cities and burghs Edinburgh alone had a member to itself; the remainder were arranged in groups of from two to five, each of which returned a single member. The election was indirect. In each burgh the close corporation, which itself filled the vacancies in its own ranks, chose a delegate to a sort of electoral college, in which the delegates met to choose the representative of the group. The election was held at each burgh in turn. The burgh in which the election took place was called "the presiding burgh," its delegate had a casting vote in the election, and its town clerk was the returning officer.[3]

[1] An illustration of the comparative independence of the counties is afforded by calculations made by Sir George Savile in 1780. Taking the lists of a division on the influence of the Crown as a basis for calculation, he estimated that the county members were in favour of the restriction of corruption in the proportion of three to one; the English boroughs, as a whole, were against any interference with the existing system of parliamentary management in the proportion of four to three; the Cornish members were eight or nine to one against, and the proportion was four to one against in the case of the members for the Cinque Ports. Nine or eight to one of the Scots members refused to limit patronage. Savile to Wyvill, July 17, 1780. — *Wyvill Papers*, III. 210.

[2] See Porritt, I. 104–17, especially p. 117.

[3] For the representation of Scotland see Porritt, II. Part V.

Of direct corruption there was little or none in Scotland, but the electorates were so small and restricted that it was there even easier than in England for the dispenser of official patronage to control the representation by the more dignified and cleanly methods of influence and favour.[1] In the burghs the members of the municipal councils were few and changed seldom. In the counties the electors were so few that it was generally possible for a member to be on visiting terms with most of his constituents. Parliamentary management was a matter of nice calculation and could be reduced to a fine art. The representation became "a representation of shadows."[2] "An equal number of elbow-chairs, placed once for all on the ministerial benches," wrote a reformer with bitter exaggeration, in 1792, "would be less expensive to government and just about as manageable."[3] During the political ascendency of the younger Pitt, Scotland was so adroitly managed by his henchman, Henry Dundas, afterwards Lord Melville, that he became "a cement of political strength" to the administration. He declined the highest object of his ambition, the Lord Presidency of the Court of Session, rather than endanger the supremacy of his party by placing the reins of parliamentary management in less capable hands.[4] Dundas did not reach this commanding position without effort. There was scarce a family of gentle blood in Scotland but at some time Dundas contrived to place it in his debt. He spared no effort to obtain every scrap of patronage at home, every nomination to a post of employment abroad, that could be so bestowed as to increase his hold upon the electorate of Scotland. His journeys to Scotland for a vacation were no "jaunt of pleasure," for if he was not composing the differences of great landowners,[5] he was suffering himself to be

[1] But cp. the quotation from the *Caledonian Mercury*, Nov. 16, 1782, given by Hume Brown, *Hist. of Scotland*, III. 377 note.

[2] Mr. Boswell of Auchinleck at Ayr Quarter Sessions.—*Caledonian Mercury*, Nov. 16, 1782 ; cp. Hume Brown, III. 355 note.

[3] J. T. Callender, *The Political Progress of Great Britain*, ap. Porritt, II. 5. See post, p. 253.

[4] H. Dundas to W. W. Grenville, Oct. 18, 1789, *H.M.C.*, Rep. XIII., App. III. 534.

[5] *Ib.* Sept. 2, 1787, *H.M.C.*, Mr. Fortescue's *Dropmore MSS.* III. 421.

pestered with letters about some small office, worth less than forty pounds by the year.[1] In Parliament after Parliament Scots members voted at his nod. They became a byword for subserviency to court and ministry. Ferguson of Pitfour, member for Aberdeenshire and a noted humorist, said he never gave but one vote according to his own opinion in his life, and that was the worst vote he ever gave. When Henry Dundas's cousin, Robert Dundas of Arniston, became Lord Advocate,[2] Ferguson made a complaint against the mean figure of the new law officer which illustrates most aptly the docility of Scots members. "The Lord Advocate," he said, "should always be a tall man. We Scotch members always vote with him, and we need, therefore, to be able to see him in a division. I can see Pitt and Addington, but I can't see the Lord Advocate." [3] The representation of Scotland was, in fact, almost a synonym for political subserviency.

More or less docility in the representatives of Wales or Scotland made little difference, however, to the votes of the House of Commons, for they were greatly outnumbered by the representatives of English rotten boroughs.[4] Even a certain measure of political virtue in Wales or Scotland would not have made any enormous change in the docility of the House of Commons. The ministerial wire-pullers might, perhaps, have been given a little more trouble, but the House would still have been controlled by influence, and not by public opinion.

How did it come about that this unrepresentative system of election was accepted or at least tolerated? In the first place, no doubt, because it was a rough-and-ready but certain means of securing a succession of politicians who could at least carry on the king's Government. As soon as a young man of promise had made the grand tour of Europe, and had thereby completed his education, he could be introduced into Parliament as the representative

[1] H. Dundas to W. W. Grenville, Oct. 19, 1789, *H.M.C.*, Rep. XIII. App. III. 535.

[2] Lord Advocate 1789 ; M.P. for Midlothian 1790.

[3] Related on the authority of Henry Addington, afterwards Lord Sidmouth.—Pellew, *Life of Sidmouth*, I. 153.

[4] It is to be remembered that of the 558 members of the House of Commons, Scotland returned only 45 and Wales only 24.

of a nomination borough, and could begin his political apprenticeship at an age when the men of this generation are only beginning to wonder how they will ever be able to acquire the means of entering Parliament at all. Thus, whilst still a minor, was Charles James Fox brought in for Midhurst,[1] and Jenkinson, afterwards prime minister as Lord Liverpool, for Sir James Lowther's borough of Appleby;[2] thus Henry Brougham was nominated at Winchelsea by Lord Darlington and at Camelford by the Duke of Bedford;[3] and thus was William Ewart Gladstone elected for Newark in 1832 through the influence of the Duke of Newcastle, who was determined, the Reform Act notwithstanding, to do what he liked with his own.[4] The practice, no doubt, converted the representation of the people into the monopoly of a class, and afforded insufficient scope for the political activities of the newer and more progressive classes of the nation. The merchant or the "cottoner" had to buy his way in or stay outside. But at least a race of great statesmen received their political education by means of the nomination system, and there was provided a class of trained amateurs competent, on the whole, to carry on the king's business to the satisfaction of the nation, and moderately, if not sufficiently, adaptable to the changing and varied needs of an island-state during its rapid transformation into a world-wide empire.

The established order was sanctioned, in the second place, because it was believed that, whatever flaws there were in the method by which it was chosen, the House of Commons nevertheless represented the substantial interests of the nation. Amongst its members, wrote Paley, "are found the most considerable land-holders and merchants in the kingdom; the heads of the army, the navy and the law; the occupiers of great offices in the state; together with many private individuals eminent by their know-

---

[1] There is some disagreement as to the exact date of Fox's return. Cf. Russell, *Life and Times of C. J. F.*, ed. 1859, I. 10 ; and Trevelyan, *Early Hist. of C. J F.*, new ed. 1908, p. 137. Trevelyan seems to be right. See *D.N.B.*

[2] Yonge's *Life of Liverpool*, I. 16.

[3] *D.N.B.* VI 455.

[4] Morley's *Gladstone*, I. 88–94.

ledge, eloquence or activity. Now, if the country be not safe in such hands, in whose may it confide its interests? If . . . such men be liable to the influence of corrupt motives, what assembly of men will be secure from the same danger? Does any new scheme of representation promise to collect together more wisdom, or to produce firmer integrity?"[1]

Question-begging was almost a habit with the great Paley, and he ignores the fact that the army and navy, the bench, the bar, and the great offices of State, were all part of the preserve of those same land-holders who stand first in his catalogue. The merchant, sandwiched in between the head of the family and the younger son, cut but a poor figure, whilst the manufacturer did not appear at all. Unless, like the elder Peel, he bought an estate, turned squire, and thereby secured rights of adoption into the territorial aristocracy, the manufacturer stood no chance as a parliamentary candidate till the opening of the nineteenth century, when, in 1802, Horrocks, the great cottoner, broke the spell of the Stanley influence at Preston.

It is plain that during the greater part of the eighteenth century Englishmen were content to be ruled by landlords. England was still an agricultural country, and its welfare depended upon the land. The yeoman was not yet extinct. A large part of the country was still unenclosed, and the smallest holder in the lands of the co-operative village community felt that his interests were, in general, identical with those of the squire. It was no accident that for nearly half a century—from 1784 to 1830—a Stanley and a Blackburne, a Whig and a Tory, the son of a noble house and the leader of the county gentry, were returned to represent the county of Lancaster in Parliament without the challenge of a contest. The country gentlemen were regarded, in the words of Wilberforce, as the very "nerves and ligatures" of the body politic.[2] So long as England remained an agricultural country the existing system survived, because it seemed good to most of those who thought

---

[1] Paley, *Principles of Moral and Political Philosophy*, II. 220-1.
[2] Wilberforce to the Earl of Galloway, Dec. 3, 1800.—*Correspondence*, I 219.

about the matter at all, that where wealth depended upon the land the will of the land-holder should prevail.[1]

A critic of the system of representation said, in 1782, that "the man who bought would sell," and the third reason that electoral customs remained unchanged was that a man who obtained a seat by corruption could be managed by bribery.[2] The minister, whom we now call the leader, was then the "manager" of the House of Commons.[3] It was the golden age of the man who "never thought of thinking for himself at all." The patronage of army and navy, of Church and bench, of customs and excise, of administrative offices and the royal household, of colonial governments and, after 1784, of the East India Company; the revenues of the duchies of Cornwall and Lancaster, and whatever could be spared from a burdened Civil list; all helped to keep a majority at the back of any minister who really possessed the confidence of the Crown. In 1770 there were 192 place-holders in the House of Commons alone.[4] It was estimated that of 190 members who voted, in 1780, in the majority against disclosing the secret part of the Pension list, only 50 were under no visible influence. The rest were either pensioners, placemen, or Government contractors, or the sons of placemen, pensioners, or Government contractors.[5]

In many cases there was a means of controlling votes much easier than the bribery of the individual member, for it was simpler and often cheaper to secure the support of a man who nominated four or five members than to bribe individually the members whose votes he commanded. "It cannot be difficult," said a writer in 1809,

[1] Nevertheless agricultural interests seem, at times, to have received inadequate attention. At a Wiltshire election Henry Hunt asked a question about the malt tax, a matter of painful interest in a barley-growing county. The candidate replied that he had been too old and too ill to attend Parliament for the previous two years and feared he would never attend again. He was nevertheless re-elected.—*Life of Henry Hunt*, I. 342–3.

[2] Spencer Stanhope at the Yorkshire County Meeting, Dec. 19, 1782. —*Wyvill Papers*, II. 58.

[3] Horace Walpole to Sir Horace Mann, Oct. 20, 1762.—*Letters*, V. 263.

[4] *Ann. Reg.* 1770 ; *Chron.* 72. (Note that a sheet paged 65* to 96* has been inserted in this volume of the Register.) See also Porritt, I. 222.

[5] John Cartwright, *Letter to the Duke of Newcastle*, p. 93 note.

"to understand why Lieutenant-General Sir James Pulteney who once reconnoitred Ferrol is Secretary-at-War." [1]   He appointed five members of Parliament.

Except under the pressure of some strong external influence it was not to be expected that such a House of Commons would carry a measure of parliamentary reform. It was not to be expected that the minister who was thus assured of a majority would sacrifice the means of security, and ministers did not disappoint expectations until the younger Pitt rather hesitatingly risked his position for his principles. [2]   But members who voted with the minister on every other question voted against him when he proposed to kick away the ladder by which they had mounted in the hope of ridding himself once for all of the necessity of purchasing their votes.   Not merely would those who bought sell; it was also true that those who bought refused to be deprived of the opportunity of buying lest they should also lose their chance to sell.

But there was a fourth and perhaps a more important reason for the complacency with which the so-called representative system was regarded in the early years of George III.   It was not merely that a system which could not be justified according to abstract theories nevertheless worked tolerably in practice; it was not merely that it secured a succession of trained amateurs with the knack of ruling; it was not merely that men were willing to make a market of the representation, to sell and to be sold; what really guaranteed the permanence of the established order was that Government in all its branches and under all its forms was based on private property instead of being directed by public opinion.

[1] John Cartwright,· *Reasons for Reformation*, p. 16.

[2] In September 1799 Coleridge pictured the relationship of the minister to his majority in "The Devil's Thoughts"—

The Devil—

XIV.	XV.
. . . "Saw a certain minister	The Devil quoted Genesis,
(A minister to his mind)	Like a very learned clerk,
Go up into a certain House,	How ' Noah and his creeping things
With a majority behind.	Went up into the ark.' "

It might have been better for Coleridge's reputation as a poet had he never written this atrocious verse; but bad verse may be useful as historical evidence.

CHAPTER II

THE first half of the eighteenth century was a dead season : a time of material content and political indifferentism. No sharp difference of principle marked off the combatants from each other in the political arena, or divided them into clearly defined and continuously hostile camps. No hotly contested measure of the first public importance, no vital question of national policy, served to divide party from party, to keep alive their mutual hostility, or to feed the fires of their divided zeal.

During the era of consolidation under Walpole and of petty intrigue under his successors political indifference became almost a virtue. It was the day of the materialist in politics, as it was the day of the Erastian in the Church. There was, in the modern sense of the term, no public opinion which could be directed against men who made a market in affairs of State, and, even had there been such an opinion, the political machinery was not invented which was necessary to make it effective. It was not until public opinion began to be more definitely formulated, it was not until the machinery of political change was invented and developed, that there was any hope of a serious measure of parliamentary reform.

From this point of view the elder Pitt was a pioneer. When he began to exercise a commanding influence in affairs of State politics became interesting to the average Englishman. His bold conduct of the Seven Years' War roused men from their apathy, kindled their imagination, and taught them to give free play to their political intelligence. Henceforth it was at least permitted to doubt that

23

the House of Commons was perfect as a representative assembly, for Pitt had been thwarted by the men who controlled it, and had won his battle against them by appealing to the nation. "You have taught me," said George II, "to look for the sense of my people in other places than the House of Commons." Pitt had, in a certain sense, created a new public opinion.

It would be a mistake, however, to over-estimate the permanence of this revival. Pitt stirred the nation, but it stirred rather as a man does in his sleep before he is fully awake. If Pitt won a hearing for himself, he won none for the constitutional reformer, for he created no party, he set up no machinery of political agitation that others might use, and, except when his own magical influence was exerted, the parliamentary managers were still supreme. While the Press was in its infancy, while the post was dear and uncertain, while the communication between one part of the country and another was so bad that in the height of summer a main road might be found "impracticable, from the depth of the clay," [1] the conduct of a national agitation was a task of the greatest difficulty. An interested local agitation, like the revolt of the western counties against the cider tax, might succeed,[2] but inadequate means of communication and want of opportunity for the diffusion of political information made it almost impossible to familiarise the nation, as a whole, with a new idea, or, in the modern phrase, to educate public opinion. France, before the great welding processes of the Revolution, was not "one and indivisible"; neither was the England of George II and George III a political unity. Neither in life nor thought was it a coherent whole, and only in moments of great excitement was there a

[1] *Memoirs and Correspondence of John Wilkes*, IV. 140. Letter of Wilkes, dated July 25, 1773. It is difficult to determine how much is fact and how much is poetic imagination in the interesting passage in which Gray describes the paths over the fells beyond Seathwaite as known only to the dalesmen. If it is to be taken *au pied de la lettre*, it is striking evidence of the isolation of certain districts of rural England.—Gray's Journal enclosed in a letter to Dr. Wharton, Oct. 18, 1769. Mason's *Gray* (ed. 1827), 292.

[2] *Ann. Reg.* 1763; *App. to Chron.* 147-55, 183, 1764; *Chron.* 56. Perhaps the best account of this affair is that given by Stanhope, *Hist.* V. 21-4.

national opinion. Geographical disunity was a serious obstacle to reformers who desired to appeal from the professional politicians to the people themselves. The means of overcoming the difficulty were learnt slowly and painfully, but the existence of such difficulties accounts, to some extent at least, for the prolonged ineffectiveness of the parliamentary reformers. The engineer, who has been in so many ways the revolutionist of the modern world, had to come to the aid of the politician, and the road-makers, Telford and Macadam, were the unwitting co-operators of Cartwright and Hardy.

If the first step in the development of a public opinion, distinct from the views of professional politicians, was due to William Pitt, the second was due to John Wilkes.[1] He, too, excited the public mind, and the agitations associated with his name were useful in several ways.

It was undoubtedly because Wilkes was convicted of seditious libel for reprinting his articles in the *North Briton* that Fox's Act was passed to determine that the judge must leave the jury to decide, not merely whether the accused had published the alleged libel, but also whether the passage complained of was in fact libellous. Without such protection of fair comment as Fox's Act ensured it would have been impossible to make the Press a useful means of political education.[2]

A second essential of a useful Press was that it should be free to give full reports of proceedings in Parliament. But it was a recognised fiction that the Houses met in private, and it was a breach of privilege to publish their debates. The Commons insisted upon the enforcement of this privilege, and its debates were reported by adventurous printers, but their reports were published only at the risk of incurring the displeasure of the House. In 1771, by the adroit management of Wilkes, the privilege of the House was brought into conflict with the privilege of

---

[1] See, for instance, Grafton's *Auto.* 229. In 1769 petitions praying for the dissolution of Parliament were sent from all parts of the country. *Ib.* 238–9.

[2] An act to remove doubts respecting the functions of juries in cases of libel, 32 Geo. III. c. 60 (1792).—Erskine May, *Const. Hist. of England* ed. 1871), II. 262.

London : the privilege of the City was used to protect the printers against the privilege of Parliament. In revenge, two of the City magistrates were sent to the Tower, but the House did not dare to touch Wilkes, the real instigator of the resistance. It was plain that an effective struggle against the reporters would be exhausting, and possibly humiliating. The privilege was not formally abandoned, but it was not afterwards insisted upon, and debates were published with impunity. Wilkes had, therefore, secured to the nation food to nourish that political intelligence which he had helped to stimulate.[1]

In the third place, attention was directed to the constitution of Parliament when, in 1768 and 1769, the House of Commons refused to allow Wilkes to sit for Middlesex, for which he had four times been duly elected.[2] When the House finally disfranchised Middlesex by deciding not only that Wilkes was ineligible, but also that Luttrell, whom he had beaten at the poll by four votes to one, was duly elected, people began to examine the authority of a body that had come to such an astonishing decision; and the Middlesex election was all the more important because it happened at a time when men were being driven by the quarrel with the American colonies to consider seriously what the principle of representation meant.

One indirect result of the Wilkes case was, in its ultimate effect, of even greater importance. Wilkes was in chronic need of money. He had spent first his own fortune and his wife's, and then a sum of £5000 bequeathed to him in 1764 by a wealthy Devonshire farmer, "as an acknowledgment to him who bravely defended the constitutional liberties of his country and checked the dangerous progress of arbitrary power."[3] By April 1768 Wilkes was again deep in debt. He owed at least six thousand pounds; probably he owed more. Some of his friends opened a subscription, and a little over eleven hundred pounds was raised for his private needs, in

[1] See Erskine May, *Const. Hist.* II. 39–49 ; Lecky, III. 476–83 ; Anson, *Law and Custom of the Const.*, 4th ed. vol. i. Parliament, 164.
[2] March 28, 1768 ; February, March and April, 1769. On the Middlesex election see Lecky, III. 228–33.
[3] *Ann. Reg.* 1764, *Chron.* 91.

addition to a separate sum of twelve hundred pounds for his election expenses.[1] But bills came in faster than subscriptions; debts grew instead of diminishing; and the maintenance of the needy agitator was becoming a burden heavier than his friends could bear.

It was on the 3rd of February, 1769, that Wilkes was for the second time expelled from the House of Commons. His debts had by now risen to the alarming sum of fourteen thousand pounds;[2] he was on the eve of a new and expensive election, and there was considerable danger that the cause might be lost through the bankruptcy of its hero. The moment was one of great excitement. Among the most ardent supporters of Wilkes was the incumbent of New Brentford, the Rev. John Horne, better known by the name of Horne Tooke, which he assumed in 1782. Horne was the son of a London poulterer, or, as he preferred to tell his school-fellows, of "a Turkey merchant." He received a fair though desultory schooling, and graduated at Cambridge as Senior Optime. Against his will he was pitchforked into the Church by a determined father, who promptly purchased him a living. Horne became a successful preacher, but from the first he heartily disliked his profession, for which, indeed, he was quite unsuited, for he was unorthodox in opinion, and his private life was not immaculate. The Church could not hold him long. He did not actually resign his living until 1773, but long before that time he had ceased to take his clerical duties seriously. It was not then possible for a priest to renounce his orders; and Horne was thereby debarred from the career, either in law or politics, that he would have chosen for himself. He was refused admission to the Bar in 1792, on the ground that clergymen were not eligible, and his subsequent attempts to secure a call were equally unsuccessful. After several vain endeavours to

[1] Almon, *Corr. of Wilkes*, III. 288-9 and note. The amount subscribed for Wilkes between March or April 1768, and February 20, 1769, was £1116 7s. 7d.; for his election expenses, £1227 3s.—*Mem. of Horne Tooke*, I. 270-1, 274-6. *The Controversial Letters of John Wilkes . . . The Rev. John Horne and their Principal Adherents* (London, 1771), 146-9.
[2] *Mem. of Horne Tooke*, I. 274-6; *Controversial Letters*, 149.

get into Parliament, he was brought in for Old Sarum in 1801 by Lord Camelford. But the same barrier which prevented his call to the Bar also excluded him from Parliament. There was some doubt about the matter, and for a few weeks he was allowed to sit in the House of Commons. But precedent was apparently against him, and a declaratory Act was speedily passed affirming the ineligibility of clerks in holy orders to sit in the Commons. Horne Tooke's parliamentary career therefore came to an untimely end with the dissolution of July 1802.[1]

Lady Holland, who met Tooke in 1801, when he was no longer in full bodily vigour, tells us that he had "a mild, placid countenance, a small, penetrating eye, and a flat, broad forehead." His manners were "those of a remarkably high-bred, old-fashioned man of quality." Horne Tooke belonged, in fact, rather to the middle of the eighteenth century than to its close, and though a fearless politician and an earnest reformer, he never accepted the equalitarian doctrines of the more advanced democrats. In his best-known work he lays it down that there is no such thing as an abstract "right." What is right and just is what is ordered or commanded by the laws of the country; and though he somewhat confuses the argument by admitting that when the laws of a country are bad it may be right to appeal to a higher law, the law of God, he nevertheless revered the "constitution and constitutional LAWS of England" because they were "in conformity with the LAWS of God and nature." "Upon these are founded the rational RIGHTS of Englishmen." This may cover confusion of thought—it is from a philological treatise—but it shows no extravagance of political opinion. Horne Tooke was certainly no extremist. "My companions in a stage may be going to Windsor," he said, explaining his position by a parable; "I will go with them to Hounslow. But there I will get out: no farther will I go, by God!" But his wit and dexterity in conversation and debate; his alertness, his adroitness and his

---

[1] On these points cf. Maitland's *Life of Leslie Stephen* (who had a personal interest in the questions).

judgment in controversy; and, during the years of his greatest vigour, his energy as a political campaigner, were of immense service first to Wilkes and afterwards to the parliamentary reformers.[1]

Framed by nature for the law rather than the Church, Horne found in the defence of Wilkes a cause peculiarly suited to his inclinations and his abilities; and probably it was in Horne's fertile and ingenious mind that there first took shape the plan of an organisation by which the excitement of the moment could be turned to good account. By the aid of a political society the fervour of the Wilkites might be directed to the practical end of providing for the necessities, and even the extravagances, of Wilkes. Only by an organised effort could his friends hope to maintain him, but the task which proved too heavy for a few individuals might not, it was thought, be past the strength of an organised society.

On the 20th of February, 1769, the friends of Wilkes, including the leaders of the popular parties in the city, met at the London Tavern in Bishopsgate Street Within, famed for its dinners and its wine, and formed the Society of the Supporters of the Bill of Rights.[2] Years afterwards the biographer of Horne Tooke maintained that the society was formed "to concentrate the hitherto unheeded resentments and influence of scattered individuals into one formidable mass which . . . should produce all the spirit, zeal and effect of a great corporation."[3] It is true that the society was the school in which the secret of popular organisation was learnt; and in that lies its chief importance. But its founders had no idea that they were inventing an important piece of political machinery.

[1] For Horne Tooke the late Sir Leslie Stephen is the best authority. See his article on Horne Tooke in the *Dictionary of National Biography*; also *The English Utilitarians*, I. 124-30; 137-42. Hazlitt's sketch of Horne Tooke, in the *Spirit of the Age*, is interesting. See also *The Diversions of Purley*, especially the Introduction and Part II, Chapter I; Creevey's *Diary*, I. 60-1; *Table-Talk of Samuel Rogers*, 83, 125-31; *Journal of Elizabeth, Lady Holland*, II. 146; Stephens, *Memoirs of J. Horne Tooke.*

[2] Almon, *Corresp. of Wilkes*, IV. 7; *Ann. Reg.* 1769, *Chron.* 75; *Mem. of Horne Tooke*, I. 161-4, 273; *Controversial Letters*, 148. Stephens gives a list of those whom he calls the original members.—*Mem. of H. T.* I. 163.   [3] *Ib.* I. 161.

Proximately, "supporting the Bill of Rights" meant supporting John Wilkes. "It seems reasonable to us," said the associators, "that the man who suffers for the public good should be supported by the public." They intended to rescue Wilkes from his encumbrances and "to render him easy and independent"[1] by purchasing for him a large annuity.[2] As reasonably might the society have hoped to fill the Serbonian bog as to keep pace with the expenditure of Wilkes, but for a time it was strangely successful. Over £3000 was raised at the first meeting.[3] A year later (April 17, 1770) £7400 had been spent on behalf of Wilkes. The greater part of his debts had been compounded, his election expenses had been paid, one of his fines had been discharged, and Wilkes himself had received £1000 "for his pocket." Before the end of the year (1770) his remaining debts, which by that time had mounted to nearly £17,000, had been paid or compounded.[4]

Some members thought that the society had now amply fulfilled its obligations to Wilkes.[5] Horne and Wilkes had already begun to drift apart. Neither would brook contradiction, and there was no room for two dictators in one society. In November 1770 Horne irritated Wilkes by a report sent anonymously to the newspapers, in which he ridiculed a public meeting over which Wilkes had presided.[6] An acrimonious correspondence in the news-

---

[1] Woodfall's *Public Advertiser,* Feb. 22, 1769; *Ann. Reg.* 1769; *Chron.* 75; *Gent's. Mag.* Feb. 1769, XXXIX. 108; Almon, *Corresp. of Wilkes,* IV. 8; *Controversial Letters,* 170-1.

[2] *Mem. of Horne Tooke,* I. 167-8. This is probably accurate, as Horne Tooke by no means desired to exaggerate the promises which were made to Wilkes.

[3] Almon, *Corresp. of Wilkes,* IV. 7-8; *Mem. of Horne Tooke,* I. 275; *Controversial Letters,* 150; *Ann. Reg.* 1769; *Chron.* 75; Walpole to Mann, Feb. 28 and May 11, 1769, *Letters,* VII. 256, 275-6.

[4] Almon, *Corresp. of Wilkes,* 9; *Ann. Reg.* 1769, *Chron.* 79, 1770; *Chron.* 80, 94; *Mem. of Horne Tooke,* I. 276-7, 280, 281; *Controversial Letters,* 151, 154, 160; Junius, I. 291 note. *Ann. Reg.* 1769, *Chron.* 107 records a legacy of £2000 to Wilkes. Wilkes was constantly in financial difficulties till he was chosen Chamberlain of the City of London in Dec. 1779. Until that date "he was sometimes distressed for a guinea," Almon, *Corresp.* V. 82-6.

[5] See Almon's narrative, *ib.* IV. 13-14.

[6] *Ann. Reg.* 1770; *Chron.* 159-60; *Controversial Letters,* 1-8; *Gent's. Mag.* Nov. 1770, XL. 519-20, 538.

papers [1] was followed by quarrels in the society. Horne held that the society had pledged itself to support the cause of Wilkes only "so far as it was a public cause," and that there were other causes of equal importance to a society professing to maintain and defend "the legal constitutional liberty of the subject." [2] Horne was finally exasperated when Wilkes refused to permit the society to give financial assistance to a printer called Bingley who had got into trouble for printing the works of Wilkes himself. [3] On the 9th of April, 1771, at a large meeting of the society, "a very violent altercation passed as usual between Mr. Wilkes and Mr. Horne." [4] Horne moved that the society be dissolved, but the Wilkites defeated the resolution by the narrow majority of two. [5] Horne and his friends at once left the society in disgust, and withdrew to another room, where they formed a new Constitutional Society "to exist only upon the public ground." [6]

In the opinion of Junius, who was no friend to Horne, [7] it required the utmost dexterity and resolution of Wilkes to get the better of the injury which the secession inflicted upon his cause. [8] He did, however, get the better of it, and the Supporters of the Bill of Rights are best remembered for a series of resolutions which they adopted after the secession, the credit of which has, oddly enough, been claimed for Horne. On the 11th of June, 1771, at a meeting presided over by Brass Crosby, Lord Mayor of the

---

[1] *Controversial Letters*, 8 *sqq.*; *Mem. of Horne Tooke*, I. 179 *sqq.* Neither of these works gives the complete correspondence, but they supplement each other. See also *Ann. Reg.* 1771, *Chron.* 68-9.

[2] Advt. in Woodfall's *Public Advertiser*, signed by the secretary, Feb. 27, 1769.

[3] *Mem. of Horne Tooke*, I. 168-75.

[4] *Ann. Reg.* 1771, *Chron.* 93-4.

[5] *Ib.* 93-4 ; Walpole, *Mem.* IV. 200, 204.

[6] *Ann. Reg.* 1771, *Chron.* 93-4, *Mem. of Horne Tooke*, I. 175.

[7] " He, too, was Mr. Wilkes's friend and as incapable " (as Grafton) " of the liberal resentment of a gentleman . . . It was the solitary, vindictive malice of a monk, brooding over the infirmities of his friend until he thought they quickened into public life, and feasting with a rancorous rapture upon the sordid catalogue of his distresses. Now let him go back to his cloister—the church is a proper retreat for him ; in his principles he is already a bishop."—Junius to Grafton, July 9, 1771 ; *Letters*, I. 360.

[8] Junius to Wilkes, Aug. 21, 1771 ; *ib.* II. 65.

city of London, it was resolved unanimously that "it be recommended by this Society to every County, City and borough in the Kingdom, that every Person who shall from henceforth be a Candidate to serve as a Member in this or any future Parliament shall be required to sign a Declaration and confirm it upon Oath, that in case he is elected he will vote for and use his utmost Endeavours to procure a Bill to shorten the Duration of Parliaments and to reduce the Number of Placemen and Pensioners in the House of Commons and also to endeavour to obtain a more fair and equal Representation of the People and that he will promote to the utmost of his Power an Enquiry into the Causes of the Troubles and Discontents which have distracted this Country during the present Reign."[1] A committee was appointed to draw up this test for parliamentary candidates,[2] but it appears to have been drawn up, in the end, by Dr. Charles Lee, an American who wrote in Woodfall's *Public Advertiser* as "Junius Americanus." According to the test, each candidate was to be called upon to pledge himself to eleven articles. Some of them were of small importance, and in certain cases one article was almost a repetition of another. But the candidate was called upon to promote one Bill to prevent bribery and corruption at elections, and another to exclude placemen and pensioners from the House of Commons; he was to promote to the utmost of his power a full and equal representation of the people; and he was to endeavour to restore annual Parliaments.[3]

These resolutions have been taken to represent the political opinions of the Supporters of the Bill of Rights. But apart from the fact that they were adopted more than three months after a very influential section of its members had seceded from the society, there is reason to believe

[1] Advertisement on the front page of Woodfall's *Public Advertiser*, June 13, 1771; reprinted June 15, 18, 20, 22, 25, 1771.

[2] At a meeting of the society on June 24, 1771, the question was referred to the committee for further consideration.—Advt. on front page of *Public Advertiser*, June 27, 1771; reprinted June 29, July 2, 6, 20, 22, 23, 1771.

[3] Adopted July 23, 1771. Woodfall's *Public Advertiser*, July 25, 1771; *Mem. of Horne Tooke*, I. 164–6. The suggestion that Horne Tooke drew up the articles is, of course, absurd.

that some of the members regarded them as foolish or extreme. The resolutions were adopted rather hastily, and when they were criticised by Junius,[1] Wilkes apologised for them and said that he had wished to amend them, but had been overruled by the majority. "I disliked the extreme *verbiage* of every part, and wished the whole put again upon the anvil." But the assembly was impatient, and Wilkes did not dare to thwart the men upon whose support he depended. Still, Wilkes himself was in favour of parliamentary reform; he defended the right of the legislature to disfranchise rotten boroughs—a right which Junius had questioned—for "a barren mountain or a single farm-house can have no representation in Parliament"; he was in favour of giving additional members to the counties; and, in spite of the arguments of Junius, he insisted that it would be better to make Parliaments annual than to make them triennial.[2]

Whatever the activity of its members individually, the society as a society seems to have done little to propagate its views. It is said to have subsidised three London newspapers.[3] We are told that its publications and donations produced a wonderful effect on the public mind.[4] But its only discoverable publications are a few newspaper advertisements, and its bias was certainly not in the direction of making donations.[5] Wilkes, it has been said, was "the unworthy representative of great causes." As the man and the cause were, in practice, inseparable, the society rendered a great constitutional service when it supported him in his opposition to the errors of the ministry and the usurpations of the House of Commons. But so far as the

[1] Junius to Wilkes, Sept. 7, 1771.—*Letters*, II. 71. See also, in reference to this letter, II. 95, 106.

[2] Wilkes to Junius, Sept. 12, 1771.—*Letters*, II. 84–5.

[3] *Mem. of Horne Tooke*, I. 167.

[4] *Ib.* I. 166.

[5] The Society sympathised with the Americans and the Americans sympathised with Wilkes. In 1770 the Assembly of South Carolina voted £1500 to the Society of the Supporters of the Bill of Rights [*Ann. Reg.* 1770, *Chron.* 71, 224–5 ; *Mem. of Horne Tooke*, I. 281 ; *Controversial Letters*, 156–9]. With careful generosity the supporters of the Bill of Rights voted £500 to the Bostonians in 1775 [Wm. Lee to Josiah Quincey, Jr., Boston, March 17, 1775. *H. M. C. Rep.* XIV. App. X. 280].

politics of the moment were concerned the society was otherwise sterile, and its real importance lies neither in its immediate objects nor in its direct results, but in the fact that it was an experiment in a form of political organisation which has become, in fact though not in form, as essential a part of the English Constitution as Crown or Cabinet.

Other people besides the Supporters of the Bill of Rights were already beginning to think seriously about parliamentary reform. The trend of politics was disquieting. Middlesex was represented by a man whom the electors had rejected; the American colonists were refusing to be bound in matters of taxation by a Parliament in which they were not represented; and during the first decade of his reign George III had been using money and patronage, honours and influence, to build up a parliamentary party of "King's Friends" ready to do his bidding. Hardly any one, as yet, contemplated a comprehensive reform of Parliament, but three partial remedies for existing evils were proposed by men who looked at the problem from rather different points of view. Some would have shortened the life of a Parliament; others would have augmented the representation of the counties; others, again, would have reduced those means of corruption which were at the disposal of Crown and Ministry.

A shortening of the duration of Parliaments was an old scheme which had been patronised, at different times, and according to their political necessities, by both Whigs and Tories. In 1744 leave to introduce a Bill into the House of Commons for calling a new Parliament every year was only refused by a small majority.[1] But in 1758 a motion for leave to bring in "a Bill for shortening the Term and Duration of Parliaments" was not nearly so well supported, and Chesterfield, who calls the proposal "a little popular squib," says it was "a very cold scent."[2] Leave was refused by 190 to 74 votes.[3]

In 1771 the question was revived by John Sawbridge,

---

[1] Jan. 29, 1744. Defeated by 145 votes to 113.—*C. J.* XXIV. 726; *Parl. Hist.* XIII. 1056 *et seq.*

[2] To his son, Feb. 24, 1758.—*Letters,* II. 377.

[3] *C. J.* XXVIII. 97 ; *Parl. Hist.* XV. 870.

a gentleman of moderate fortune and some ability who since 1768 had been member of Parliament for Hythe. Sawbridge was one of the leaders of the popular party in the City, and an original member of the Society of the Supporters of the Bill of Rights; he had shown his courage in the popular cause when, despite the threat of a Bill of Pains and Penalties, he had, as sheriff, persisted in declaring Wilkes duly elected for Middlesex. On the 26th of April Sawbridge, having waited, as he said, and waited in vain, for a better man than himself to undertake the duty, moved for "leave to bring in a Bill for shortening the Duration of Parliaments." Several speakers supported him, but, "to the amazement of most members, not one word was uttered by administration," and the resolution was defeated by nearly two votes to one.[1] Year after year Sawbridge moved the same or a similar resolution : he was always defeated by a considerable majority; there was seldom any debate; and ministers preserved the same uniform silence, being content to answer his arguments by voting him down in the division lobby.[2]

To the doctrine of short Parliaments Sawbridge won some august converts. A few days after his first motion in the Commons, Chatham, who was on terms of friendship with Sawbridge, declared in the Lords "that formerly the inconveniences of shortening the duration of Parliaments had great weight with him; but now it was no longer a question of convenience : the *Summa Rerum* was at stake : the whole Constitution was giving way; and therefore, with the most solemn and deliberate conviction of his understanding, he now declared himself a *Convert to Triennial Parliaments*."[3] Shelburne, the ablest of the

[1] Yeas, 54. Noes, 105.—*C. J.* XXXIII. 357; *Parl. Hist.* XVII. 176–82.

[2] March 4, 1772, *C. J.* XXIII. 353; *Parl. Hist.* XVII. 322–7; Jan. 26, 1773, *Parl. Hist.* XVII. 690–6; Feb. 15, 1774 (C. J. Fox was one of the tellers for the Noes), *C. J.* XXXIV. 461; *Parl. Hist.* XVII. 1050–1; Feb. 1, 1775, *C. J.* XXXV. 90, *Parl. Hist.* XVIII. 216–19; March 6, 1776, *C. J.* XXXV. 633, *Parl. Hist.* XVIII. 1237–8; May 1, 1777, *C. J.* XXXVI. 461; March 11, 1778, *Ib.* 818; *Parl. Hist.* XIX. 873–4; July 14, 1779, *C. J.* XXXVII. 46.

[3] April 30 or May 1, 1771. Report from *Public Advertiser; Chat. Corr.* IV. 174 note; Thackeray, *Life*, II. 244; *Parl. Hist.* XVII. 216–19.

Chathamites in the House of Lords, took the same view as his chief.[1] Junius, who was so much a Grenvillite that he has been identified by some with Earl Temple, the head of the Grenville clan, was naturally a supporter of Chatham whenever Chatham was on good terms with his brothers-in-law; and he insisted that a Triennial Act was the first essential of reform.[2] There was, he held, little difference between a seat in Parliament for seven years and a seat for life. The last session of a septennial Parliament was, indeed, usually employed in courting the favour of the people. But members had "six years for offence and one for atonement. A death-bed repentance seldom leads to restitution."[3] Annual Parliaments, he believed, were a delusion, but triennial Parliaments meant, in effect, "keeping the representative under the rod of the constituent." Without such a change other reforms would be useless. A Triennial Act "ought to be the basis, as it assuredly will be the only support, of every barrier raised in defence of the Constitution."[4]

In practical matters Chatham was easily discouraged, and he never learnt the art of parliamentary management. In August 1771, when Junius was assuring the city politicians that it was unnecessary "to bind Lord Chatham by the written formality of an engagement" to persevere in his support of shorter Parliaments,[5] Chatham had already abandoned all thoughts of proposing such a reform. He had found "a real dislike to the measure in minds very sound about other public matters. The dread of more frequent returns of corruption, together with every dissoluteness which elections spread through the country, strongly indisposes families of all descriptions to an alteration. As I am persuaded that this opinion is genuine

---

There is a disagreement as to dates, and the reports are not identical, though they are in substance the same. In the circumstances I have put the whole in reported speech.

[1] Shelburne to Chatham, April 9, 1774.—*Life of Shelburne*, II. 224.
[2] Junius to the Printer of the *Public Advertiser*, Aug. 13, 1771. *Letters*, I. 391-2. See also, for Junius's views on septennial Parliaments, his letter of Oct. 5, 1771, *ib.* I. 417.
[3] Dedication to the English Nation, *ib.* I. 89.
[4] Junius to Wilkes, Sept. 7, 1771, *ib.* II. 75-7.
[5] Junius to Horne, Aug. 13, 1771, *ib.* I. 391-2.

and very widely extended, I should think it totally in-
advisable to stir it." [1] The truth seems to be that Chatham
found the Rockingham Whigs against him, and hesitated
to do anything that would introduce further discord into
the already divided opposition. [2]

Chatham may or may not have said in 1776 that before
the end of the century "either the Parliament will reform
itself from within or be reformed with a vengeance from
without." [3] But it is clear that he was no violent reformer.
"If England were not properly represented," he is reported
to have said in 1776, "the Representation ought to be
amended. . . . People, however, are apt to mistake the
nature of Representation, which is not of person but of
property; and in this light there is scarcely a blade of
grass which is not represented." [4] In other words, he held
exactly the same theory of the representation as the heads
of the great family connections who thought that political
power should be vested exclusively in those who owned
the land. He went even further. In 1771, in a speech in
the House of Lords, he maintained that "the share of
national burdens" which any part of the kingdom bore
was the only rule by which to judge "the weight that it
ought to have in the political balance." [5] Not only was
property to be represented, it was to be represented in direct
proportion to its taxative value.

Chatham's timidity in the constitutional sphere is
illustrated by his scheme of reform. He will give; but
he will not take away. He will not destroy the rotten
boroughs; but, as the counties are the purer part of the
representation, he is willing to give them three members

[1] To Shelburne, April 22, 1771.—*Chat. Corr.* IV. 156-7.
[2] This I take to be the meaning of Chatham's deference for "minds
very sound about other public matters." The influence is confirmed by
the references to Rockingham in Horne to Junius, July 31, and Junius to
Horne, Aug. 13, 1771.—*Letters*, I. 384-6, and 391-2.
[3] Reported by David Stewart Erskine, Earl of Buchan.—*Essays on
the Lives and Writings of Fletcher of Saltoun and the Poet Thomson,
Biographical, Critical and Political* . . . *London, 1792,* 8vo, pp. 215-16.
Buchan may not be a good witness.
[4] Charlemont to Flood, March 13, 1766.—*Original Letters to Henry
Flood,* 14-15.
[5] Speech on Richmond's motion on the Middlesex election, April 30,
1771.—*Parl. Hist.* XVII. 219 ; *Chat. Corr.* IV. 169 note.

each instead of two. On the 22nd of January, 1770, he spoke of the "notorious decay of the internal vigour of the Constitution." A member was no longer, as had once been intended, the representative of his constituents, and Chatham was ready to admit the necessity for reform. "Let us be cautious, however," he said, "how we have recourse to violent expedients." [1]

"The boroughs of this country have, properly enough, been called the rotten parts of the Constitution. But in my judgment, my Lords, these boroughs, corrupt as they are, must be considered as the natural infirmity of the Constitution. Like the infirmities of the body, we must bear them with patience and submit to carry them with us. The limb is mortified, but the amputation might be death." . . . "Since we cannot cure the disorder, let us endeavour to infuse such a portion of new health into the Constitution as may enable it to support its most inveterate diseases."

"The representation of the counties is, I think, still preserved pure and uncorrupted. That of the great cities is upon a footing equally respectable; and there are many of the larger trading towns which still preserve their independence. The infusion of health which I now allude to would be to permit every county to elect one member more, in addition to their present representation. The knights of the shires approach nearest to the constitutional representation of the country because they represent the soil. It is not in the little dependent boroughs, it is in the great cities and counties that the strength of the Constitution resides, and by them alone, if an unhappy question should ever rise, will the Constitution be honestly and firmly defended. I would increase that strength, because I think it the only security we have against the profligacy of the times, the corruption of the people and the ambition of the Crown." [2]

---

[1] *Parl. Hist.* XVI. 752-3. Thackeray's *Pitt*, 162. *Chat. Corr.* III. 406. Chatham may have considered schemes for the representation of the American colonies in the English Parliament. See an article by Mr. Basil Williams, *E. H. R.* 1907, 756-8.

[2] Jan. 22, 1770.—*Parl. Hist.* XVI. 753-4; *Chat. Corr.* III. 406-7 note; Thackeray's *Pitt*, II. 162-3.

A few weeks later Chatham told the House of Lords that "one or more members ought to be added to the representation of the counties, in order to operate a balance against the weight of the several corrupt and venal boroughs which perhaps could not be lopped off entirely without the hazard of a convulsion." [1] In the spring of 1771 Chatham, Shelburne and Temple were in correspondence on the subject; they were agreed in their opinion; and it seemed as if Chatham were actually going to introduce into the House of Lords measures for the shortening of Parliaments and an addition to the knights of the shire. He seems to have consulted the great men of the Whig party about both projects at the same time. But they hardly gave more encouragement to his scheme for increasing the representation of the counties than they had given to his proposal to shorten Parliaments. "At best," said Chatham, "the thing, in theory, is not quite disapproved, but the execution not much desired by any." [2]

Junius in all these matters supported Chatham, but decidedly he was no enthusiast for parliamentary reform. Here as elsewhere his views have a remarkable and significant identity with those of Temple. For Junius and Temple alike held that it was impossible to abolish corruption; they objected to corruption mainly because it was the means by which "all the leading Whig families" were excluded from the councils of the Crown. [3] Junius, like Temple and his great brother-in-law, was in favour of triennial Parliaments and additional knights of the shire, [4] but he was "startled at the idea of so extensive an amputation" as the cutting away of rotten boroughs, [5] and

[1] *Chat. Corr.* III. 457, note. This appears to be the only report of the debate of Aug. 14, 1770. Reporters were rigidly excluded. A summary, in a few lines, is all that is given of Chatham's speech in the *Parl. Hist.* XVI. 978–9 and note.

[2] Shelburne to Chatham, Feb. 25, 1771.—Fitzmaurice's *Shelburne*, II. 223. Shelburne to Chatham, April 9, 1771. *Chat. Corr.* IV. 146–8. Chatham to Temple, April 17, 1771.—*Grenville Papers*, IV. 534. Temple to Chatham, April 18.—*Chat. Corr.* IV. 155. Belief in the purity of county elections accounts, to some extent, for the fury of Junius's opposition to the incapacitation of Wilkes. Letter to Grafton, April 24, 1769.—*Letters*, I. 150 ; see also I. 174.

[3] Preface. Junius, I. 101.

[4] Junius to Wilkes, Sept. 7, 1771.—*Letters*, II. 77 ; see also 78–9.

[5] *Ib.* 77.

would have refused to grant representatives to the great
trading towns which still had no members.[1] "That the
people are not equally and fully represented is unquestion-
able. But let us take care," he said, "what we attempt.
We may demolish the venerable fabric we intend to repair;
and where is the strength and virtue to erect a better in
its stead?"[2]

Triennial Parliaments and additional knights of the
shire represent the panacea of one section of the Whigs:
of Chatham and his followers, of Shelburne, of Temple
and of Junius. Another section of the Whigs, that remnant of the old Pelham connection which followed the
Marquess of Rockingham, favoured a third expedient: an
attempt to stop the sources of corruption. The question
was taken up by William Dowdeswell, who had been
Chancellor of the Exchequer in the Rockingham administration of 1765. Dowdeswell was a county member of the
better sort, careful in business rather than brilliant in
debate, a plodding, persevering man, hardly capable of
rallying an inert party for a great crusade.

Dowdeswell dealt with but a small part of the problem
which Burke afterwards attempted to solve in more comprehensive fashion; and whereas Burke mainly attempted
to reduce the influence of the Crown over members actually
elected, Dowdeswell concerned himself with the influence
of the Crown over the constituents who returned them. On
the 12th of February, 1770, he moved, in a crowded
House,[3] that the chairman of the committee be directed
to bring in a Bill "for better securing the Freedom of
Elections of Members to serve in Parliament, by disabling
certain officers employed in the collection of his Majesty's
Revenue from giving their votes at such Elections."[4] He
proposed to disfranchise the revenue officers, who were
notoriously under the influence of administration; the
officers of the customs, the excise and the post office, by
the aid of whose votes the ministry of the day could return
their nominees in some counties and many boroughs;

[1] *Letters*, II, 79.   [2] *Ib.* 76-9.
[3] The largest known for several years.—Note in *Cavendish Debates*,
I. 458.
[4] *Ib.* I. 446.

those miserable creatures, whose suffrages, as one speaker said, "were not the franchises of individuals but the accumulated votes of the administration."[1] Almost £600,000 was spent each year in the collection of the revenue, and most of the money went in salaries to men who were forced to do the bidding of the minister. "If there comes a contest," said Dowdeswell, "you will find, from the first officer in the revenue to the last in the customs, they will unite in giving their votes in the way that shall be most satisfactory to the ministers for the time being."[2]

"Those tools of any administration have prevailed over the spoils of the East; over all family connexions and the landed interest," said a Cornish member. "If this question is carried I shall hope to see boroughs a less rotten part of the Constitution. I shall meet," he added significantly, "more of my country neighbours in this House, and the boroughs will more frequently see their members."[3]

The question, as Dowdeswell put it, was "who is for the independence of the electors and who is for the influence of the Crown?"[4] The House decided, in a most emphatic manner, for the Crown, as North carried an adjournment of the committee by 263 votes to 188.[5]

In the course of the debate Dowdeswell had pledged himself that, in or out of office, he would persevere with the question;[6] but soon afterwards he fell ill, and in 1775 he died. His policy of decreasing the illegitimate influence of Crown and Ministry remained, however, the policy of the Rockingham connection, and where he had failed his party, as will be seen, to a certain extent succeeded. That policy was criticised at the time and has been criticised since. Junius, for example, thought it a tactical error to make the extermination of corruption a first object. When the Supporters of the Bill of Rights demanded the exclu-

---

[1] Mr. Frederick Montague.—*Cavendish Debates*, I. 457.
[2] Dowdeswell, *ib.* I. 444 ; *Parl. Hist.* XVI. 834, cf. Geo. Grenville's account of Walpole's views.—*Cav. Deb.* I. 455.
[3] Sir John Molesworth of Pencarrow.—*Cav. Deb.* I. 446 ; *Parl. Hist.* XVI, 835.
[4] *Cav. Deb.* I. 443.
[5] *Ib.* I. 458 ; *Parl. Hist.* XVI. 841.
[6] *Cav. Deb.* I. 445-6 ; *Parl. Hist.* XVI. 834.

sion of place-holders and pensioners from Parliament, he ridiculed the idea. Even if such a "place Bill" could be carried, he argued that it would be evaded. But it was a mistake to "grasp at the impossible"—the extermination of corruption—and "lose the really attainable"—triennial Parliaments.[1] More sincere reformers than Junius have thought that Dowdeswell's policy, afterwards adopted by the "economical reformers," was an unhappy divergence from the main line of attack upon the faults and anomalies of the unreformed House of Commons.

It seemed, nevertheless, as if the current of opinion outside Parliament were setting against ministerial influence. A new spirit manifested itself occasionally at elections. In 1774 Lord North advised a hasty dissolution, lest the growing public opinion should gain the mastery.[2] But hastily as he dissolved he could not prevent "the independent part of the county" of Sussex asserting itself with refreshing vigour, proposing its own candidate, paying his election expenses, and finally returning him to Parliament despite influence and corruption.[3] In the same year Lord Stanhope—Citizen Stanhope of later times —entered the field with some tracts in favour of parliamentary reform;[4] and Granville Sharp, who wrote a defence of the liberties of America and Ireland, asserted, *en passant,* the necessity for equal representation and frequent Parliaments.[5]

There is significance in the opening phrase of the long-winded title which Sharp gave to his pamphlet. It is called "A Declaration of the People's Natural Right to a share in the Legislature . . . ," and is some evidence, perhaps, of the influence which the speculations of

---

[1] To Wilkes, Sept. 7, 1771.—*Letters*, II. 75.

[2] North, quoted in a note to *Corr. of Geo. III and North*, I. 219.

[3] Oldfield, *Hist. of Boroughs*, II. 29-30. H. S. Smith, *The Parliaments of England*, II. 74. A similar opposition to the court candidate at Portsmouth failed only by three votes.—*Hist. of Boroughs*, II. 61 ; Smith, I. 132.

[4] Stanhope to J. Cartwright, Dec. 17, 1815. I have not discovered any of these tracts. Is the reference to an election broadside or "squib"?—*Life of J. Cartwright*, I. 82 note.

[5] A Declaration of the People's Natural Right to a share in the Legislature, which is the fundamental principle of the British Constitution of State. By Granville Sharp. London, 1774, 8vo.

Rousseau, and the discussions of abstract rights which his speculations provoked in Europe and America, had upon the thought of English politicians. English parliamentary reformers had not, as a rule, much taste for spinning theories of the State. They were practical men, impatient of theory, who were seeking practicable solutions for definite problems, and were groping about for the readiest satisfactory means of mending the existing Constitution at the points where they found it most defective. In the characteristic English manner they demanded only practical and immediate reforms, such as an increase of county members or shorter Parliaments, which they considered the proper remedies for specified abuses. But many of the reformers took, also, a warm interest in the fortunes of the American colonists. It was, in fact, the dispute with America which had first led some of them to examine the doctrine of representation upon which that dispute ultimately turned, and which had converted them, almost insensibly, into advocates of a reform of Parliament. Some, no doubt, it led even further. As they followed the political discussions in America, which were influenced by the speculations of the French philosophers, and which led at last, in the Declaration of Independence, to a recital of the rights of man, they, in their turn, fell under the spell of Rousseau and were indoctrinated with the same ideas of abstract right. This seems the best explanation of the way in which zealous friends of the colonists, like the Duke of Richmond, were smitten, in spite of their fundamental conservatism, with a temporary enthusiasm for sweeping programmes of reform and for equalitarian doctrines from which they subsequently recoiled. It would be difficult, if not impossible, to estimate the extent to which the speculations of French thinkers moulded English thought during the 'seventies and early 'eighties. Their influence could easily be exaggerated. But such men as Shelburne, the friend of Morellet, and Stanhope, the friend of the Duc de Rochefoucauld, with others like them, must have been familiar with the current conversational coin of French *salons* and been the means of its transmission to English drawing-rooms. Though it is not very manifest, and though its working is not easy to detect or to describe, the leaven of French influence was nevertheless at work in these years, whilst the English reformers were hammering out their plans for improving the representation and inventing the machinery to make their plans effective.[1]

The first prominent politician to propose a comprehensive reform of Parliament seems to have been John Wilkes. On Thursday the 21st of March, 1776, he moved in the House of Commons that "Leave be given to bring in a Bill for a just and equal Representation of the People of England in Parliament."[2] The representation, he told the House, had become "insufficient, partial and unjust."[3] It was necessary "to find a remedy for this great and growing evil."[4] He told of the disfranchisement, in times past, of decayed boroughs of which not even the names were now remembered. On the other hand, "what a happy fate" had "attended the boroughs of Gatton and Old Sarum. . . . Four respectable gentlemen represent their departed greatness as the knights at a coronation represent Aquitaine and Normandy."[5]

Wilkes tabled no detailed plan, but in the course of his speech he summarised his proposals. He would have given a vote to every free agent;[6] he would have disfranchised the rotten boroughs, and allowed what few electors they had to vote for the representatives of the county; he would have given additional members to the more populous counties; and he would have accorded representation to "rich, populous trading towns" like

---

[1] An example might be cited from a declaration of the Cambridge Constitutional Society which is undated, but which seems to have been adopted in March 1780 ; " . . . Every individual of mankind is born with a natural right to life, liberty and property." The Society further declares that "the British Constitution of King, Lords and Commons is the most perfect theory of government in the world, and may be rendered as perfect in practice," if only the Commons be so reformed as to render it independent of the Crown and the peerage. Shorter Parliaments and a more equal representation were the specific reforms demanded.—*Wyvill Papers*, I. 135-7.   [2] *Parl. Hist.* XVIII. 1297.
[3] *Ib.* 1288.   [4] *Ib.* 1287.   [5] *Ib.* 1288.
[6] There is no reason to suppose that the Wilkite definition of "free agent" covered women. In his letters to his daughter, it may be remarked, Wilkes scarcely alludes to politics.

Sheffield and Birmingham, Manchester and Leeds.[1] He thought shorter Parliaments and a Place and Pension Bill absolutely necessary, but he believed that even those remedies would fail if the representation were not reformed. "Without a true representation of the Commons our Constitution is essentially defective, our Parliament is a delusive name, a mere phantom."[2]

"The disfranchising the mean, venal and dependent boroughs would be laying the axe to the root of corruption and Treasury influence, as well as aristocratical tyranny. We ought equally to guard against those who sell themselves or whose lords sell them. Burgage tenures and private property in a share of the legislature are monstrous absurdities in a free State, as well as an insult on common sense. I wish, sir, an English Parliament to speak the free, unbiassed sense of the body of the English people and of every man among us, of each individual who may justly be supposed to be comprehended in a fair majority. The meanest mechanic, the poorest peasant and day-labourer has important rights respecting his personal liberty, that of his wife and children, his property, however inconsiderable, his wage, his earnings, the very price and value of each day's hard labour, which are in many trades regulated by the power of Parliament. Every law relative to marriage, to the protection of wife, sister or daughter against violence and brutal lust, to every contract or agreement with a rapacious or unjust master, is of importance to the manufacturer,[3] the cottager, the servant, as well as to the rich subjects of the State."[4] Poor as well as rich, men of great estate and men of none, should have a share in making the laws which affected their lives and happiness. All government was for the good of the governed, said Wilkes, for the governed were "the original fountain of power and even of revenue, and in all events the last resource."[5] It was therefore safer that the governed

---

[1] *Parl. Hist.* XVIII. 1295. On the representation of the great towns see also 1292.
[2] *Ib.* XVIII. 1297.
[3] *i. e.* "one who manufactures," whether a master or not.
[4] *Parl. Hist.* XVIII. 1295.
[5] *Ib.* 1296.

should share in it, instead of being excluded till a great decision was asked of them in a moment of crisis.

Such a speech from the lips of an acknowledged orator would not pass without notice even in these days of generous franchises and still more generous hopes. It is wonderful that it should have been spoken at all in 1776, in the unreformed House of Commons, by a man who was himself "never a Wilkite." It is still more wonderful that it should have apparently caused no excitement.

The propositions were coldly received, not in anger, but with contempt. The reply of Lord North is the only speech recorded besides that of Wilkes himself. North refused to take the proposals seriously and "was very jocular," though his jokes are unhappily lost. He spoke of the danger of amputations in general and in particular of the danger of such political amputations as lopping off the rotten boroughs; he showed how dangerous such experiments had proved, and "the risk of overthrowing or dissolving the Constitution such experiments were intended to correct or amend."[1] Wilkes replied,[2] but the House of Commons seemed so little disposed to constitutional surgery that he does not appear to have pressed his resolution to the vote, and it was negatived without a division.[3]

Wilkes made his reform speech in April, 1776. In October of the same year Major John Cartwright began the campaign of a lifetime by publishing his pamphlet *Take your Choice*,[4] which afterwards obtained for him the title of "The Father of Reform." Cartwright was the son of a country gentleman in Nottinghamshire. He inherited a small estate, which appears to have maintained him in comfort but not in luxury. The fact that he was a man of property was not lost sight of even by his opponents, and often secured him a measure of respect which was not always accorded to other advocates of parliamentary reform. This man had "a stake in the country."

---

[1] *Parl. Hist.* XVIII. 1297.　　　　[2] *Ib.* 1298.
[3] *C. J.* XXV. 673.
[4] The frontispiece gives the date of publication as Oct. 14, 1776. See also *Life of Cartwright*, I. 82.

Though interested in both naval and military affairs, Cartwright's advocacy of the colonial cause during the American War put an end to a promising career in the navy, as his sympathy for the French revolutionists was afterwards to cost him his commission in the militia. His pamphlets in favour of American independence and parliamentary reform are able, enthusiastic and, to the modern reader, dull. Doctrinaire and impatient of compromises, Cartwright was constitutionally incapable of playing the party game either of court or opposition, and not infrequently was a sore trial to the more practical politicians of his own school of thought. "He was cheerful, agreeable, and full of anecdote," said one of them, but "in political matters exceedingly troublesome and sometimes exceedingly absurd." [1] His strength lay in the persistence with which he hoped all things of political organisation, and the part which he played in the formation and management of the Constitutional Society, the Society of the Friends of the People, and, still later, of the Hampden Club, is his sufficient title to a place in history. One of his younger brothers, Edmund, was the inventor of the power-loom, and, owing to the influence of his machinery upon the localisation of industry, and the consequent changes in the distribution of population, possibly a greater parliamentary reformer than the Major. John Cartwright lived almost to the eve of the first Reform Act. He was more earnest, perhaps, than interesting, and when once started upon his pet theme of parliamentary reform he probably bored quite as many of his hearers as he converted. But even when, as occasionally happened, he became something of a nuisance to his fellow-reformers, he was respected for his past labours and his unflagging enthusiasm. His statue may be found in a garden opposite to the house in which he used to live in Burton Crescent, recently re-christened Cartwright Gardens, a once respectable but now decayed neighbourhood near the Euston Road. He must have been a curious figure as he sat eating his raisins and drinking his gin and water in Francis Place's back shop. The statue represents him seated in

[1] Francis Place, *Add. MSS.* 27850, fo. 108.

a half-crouching posture which seems to remind one of the statue of Voltaire in front of the Institut at Paris; and indeed there was a Voltairean strain in his character, though he had none of the genius of the sage of Ferney. He had been, he said, of thirty religions, and should, perhaps, be of thirty more.[1]

Cartwright had more consistency in politics than in religion. From the views which he expressed in *Take your Choice* he deviated not a hair to the day of his death. He wrote in moderate language, but his proposals were drastic. He "dwelt long on the nature and excellence of the English Constitution" in order to show that it was worth all the regard and concern that could possibly be felt for it.[2] He would have given much to prove his own criticism of the House of Commons "a libel,"[3] and he claimed that his plans were not revolutionary but restorative. "Making our Parliaments *annual* and our representation *equal* can neither of them in any sense, nor without a direct falsehood, be styled innovations. *Both of them were the antient practice of the constitution.*"[4] Cartwright's constitutional history was unsound, but it is clear that he showed no revolutionary disrespect for the past.

Perhaps he was more radical than these words suggest. He would have made crime the only bar to the suffrage,[5] and would, in certain cases, have paid members of Parliament;[6] he would have introduced the ballot,[7] and would have abolished plural voting.[8] He retained a belief in the property qualification for membership of the House of Commons,[9] but he balanced these last shreds and remnants of conservatism by anticipating the modern argument that the greatest possible "stake in the country" is not wealth and property but wife and children,[10] and he foreshadowed the most familiar and most fertile political device of modern times—the congress or convention—when he proposed,

---

[1] Wilberforce's Diary, Oct. 23, 1789.—*Life of Wilberforce*, I. 245.
[2] *Take your Choice*, 18.   [3] *Ib.* Preface, vii.
[4] *Ib.* 15.   [5] *Ib.* 19.
[6] *Ib.* 72. Cartwright's qualified proposal for payment of members is part of an ingenious scheme for preventing bye-elections.
[7] *Ib.* 70.   [8] *Ib.* 73.   [9] *Ib.* 69.   [10] *Ib.* 19.

with full battery of capital letters, a "GRAND NATIONAL
ASSOCIATION FOR RESTORING THE CONSTITUTION." [1]

This suggestion was brought forward again by Dr.
John Jebb, another pamphleteer on the popular side, in
December 1779, when he took occasion to defend the
representative idea against the perennial heresy of delegation, and at the same time to encourage popular union and
correspondence for the purpose of limiting corruption and
promoting reform. He even dared to outline the plan of
a convention and to use, unrebuked, that very word which,
though not without precedent in British history, was soon
to become the anathema maranatha of loyal citizens. [2]
Before the month was out part at least of Jebb's plan had
already been made matter of experiment by the leaders of
the so-called Economy Campaign.

From George II's first dim realisation that there were
in England men holding strong political opinions to which
the votes and speeches of the members of the House of
Commons were not necessarily a true index, it was a far
cry to the comprehensive schemes of parliamentary reform
so boldly set forth by Wilkes and Cartwright, and to the
conception of a plan like Jebb's for formulating the demand
for reform, educating public opinion and bringing it into
proper focus. Within twenty or thirty years there had
been a remarkable development of opinion. Dissatisfaction with the working of the parliamentary system had
been aroused by the treatment of Pitt. A system stood
self-condemned which was found unworkable by a politician who, in the eyes of the nation, towered head and
shoulders above all his contemporaries. Dissatisfaction
was increased by the treatment of Wilkes. A member was
rejected who had been duly returned by the electors of one
of those county constituencies which were esteemed the
purest and the least subject to improper influence. This

---

[1] *Take your Choice*, 89.
[2] An address to the Freeholders of Middlesex assembled at the Free-
masons' Tavern, in Great Queen Street, upon Monday December 25,
1779, being the day appointed for a meeting of freeholders for the
purpose of establishing meetings to maintain and support the freedom
of election. By John Jebb. See also Jebb to Wyvill, Aug. 7, 1781.—
Wyvill Papers, IV. 505.

was not all. The candidate whom Middlesex had rejected was chosen by the House of Commons and declared the duly elected representative of a constituency which had passed him over as incapable of representing it. This barefaced usurpation of the functions of the electors was a disastrous blunder. It made too obvious the resemblance between the House of Commons and a close corporation. When the fundamental problems of representation, brought into prominence during the dispute with America, were considered; when, at the same time, it was remembered how Pitt had been isolated and rendered politically ineffective by inferior men who were better supported by borough influence; and when it was also recalled how Wilkes, the chosen of Middlesex, had been unseated in favour of a rejected candidate, it is not surprising that the system by which the House of Commons was chosen became the object of scathing criticism.

Dissatisfaction, though widespread, had expressed itself at first in demands for more or less paltry rectifications of the parliamentary system. But as discussion proceeded two schools of thought became distinguishable. On the one hand were the Whigs of the school of Burke, who desired no constitutional reconstruction, but aimed only at restricting, by one device or another, the means of corruption which could be employed by the agents of the court to obstruct the natural parliamentary ascendency of the governing class. On the other hand were the radical reformers, influenced by American doctrines or, to some extent, by French theories, who made much more logical and sweeping proposals, and based their demands for more or less wholesale reconstruction upon doctrines of abstract right which were sometimes expressed but more often only implied. This school of radical reformers may be said to have emerged with Wilkes's proposals of 1776 and the pamphlets of Cartwright and Jebb. The same school had also discovered the mode of propaganda in the foundation of the first political society—the Society of the Supporters of the Bill of Rights—soon to be followed by a crop of others which learnt from it and improved upon what they learnt. Between these two schools—the orthodox official

Whigs and the advocates of sweeping change—there could be no real accord. In the next period they are found for a time joining forces and securing the minimum of reform upon which they were agreed, but once they had obtained these reforms their differences became more and more manifest and forced them at last to part company.

CHAPTER III

ECONOMICAL REFORM *VERSUS* PARLIAMENTARY REFORM

1778–1782

IT was not the sweeping reform of Wilkes or of Cartwright, nor the partial reform of Chatham and Sawbridge, but the plan of the Rockingham Whigs for checking corrupt and illicit influence that first came within the range of practical politics. In 1778 the burden of the war with our American colonists, already heavy, was greatly increased and the area of the contest was enormously enlarged when France declared war against us in March 1778. The opponents of the ministry no longer troubled to say that the war was wicked; they now said that it was ill-managed and ineffective, and that the cost in men and money was more than could be borne.[1] Charles Fox found that the House of Commons "went a good deal with him" when he left the justice of the war alone and confined himself to "the absurdity of it in all its parts and the absolute madness of continuing it."[2] An Opposition which had been spurned when it questioned the justice of the cause found the ear of the nation, and especially of the country gentlemen, when it attacked the shortcomings of the commissariat or the mismanagement of a campaign. North himself was suspected, with some justice, of misliking his task, and, writing of the day appointed for solemn fast and humiliation in 1778, even a Tory like Gibbon pointed to a political significance in the words of the liturgy, "And all the people shall say after the *minister,* Turn us again, O Lord, and so shall we be turned."[3]

In this temper the nation demanded economy of public

[1] Rockingham to Chatham, Jan. 21, 1778.—*Chat. Corr.* IV. 457-8.
[2] C. J. Fox to Fitzpatrick (then in America), Feb. 3, 1778.—*Mem. of C. J. Fox,* I. 168.
[3] Gibbon to Holroyd, Feb. 23, 1778.—*Letters,* I. 329-30.

money, and the politicians of the Rockingham party
cleverly directed the resentment of the taxpayer against
those particular forms of wasteful and corrupt expenditure
which assisted the ministry of the day to maintain its
influence over the members of the House of Commons and
over the constituents who returned them. The first attack
was delivered by Sir Philip Jennings Clerke, of Duddle-
stone Hall, Salop, who had represented the little borough
of Totnes, in Devonshire, since 1768.[1] Clerke's view was
that the support of a member of the House of Commons
might as readily be bought by the grant of a lucrative
Government contract as by a direct payment in hard cash.[2]
On Monday, the 13th of April, 1778, he obtained leave to
bring in a Bill which would have excluded from the
Commons all persons who held Government contracts, or
for whom Government contracts were held in trust, except
when the contracts were made at a public bidding, and
therefore in circumstances which excluded the possibility
of influence or corruption.[3] John Dunning and Edmund
Burke were amongst those charged, with Clerke, to draw
the Bill,[4] which passed the first reading without a division,[5]
and the second reading by a small majority.[6] Then
ministers rallied their forces, and, after a close contest,
destroyed the measure by postponing the consideration of
it for two months.[7] In 1779 Clerke again got leave to
introduce his Bill.[8] It was read a first time,[9] and again
defeated by a postponement.[10]

[1] Philip Jennings. Matriculated Oriel College, Oxford, Nov. 7, 1739,
aged 17. Assumed name of Clerke between 1760 and 1774. Cr. baronet
Oct. 26, 1774, d. Jan. 14, 1788.—*Gent's. Mag.* LVIII. 85 ; H. S. Smith, *The
Parliaments of England,* I. 80 ; G. E. C., *Complete Baronetage,* V. 181.

[2] Cf. Fielding's satirical definition of "job" as "a name which the
English give to all works of a public nature : for . . . nobody ever does
anything for the public, but he is certain to make his fortune by it."
Familiar Letters.—Miscellaneous Works (ed. Saintsbury), II. 237.

[3] *C. J.* XXXVI. 918. [4] *Ib.*
[5] April 15, 1778, *ib.* 933. [6] May 1, 1778 (72–61), *ib.* 946.
[7] May 4, 1778 (113–109), *ib.* 950.
[8] Feb. 12, 1779 (158–143), *ib.* XXXVII. 140.—*Parl. Hist.* XX. 124–6.
In the debate Clerke declared that Alderman Harley, M.P., had made
£37,000 in one year by one contract.
[9] Feb. 26, 1779, *C. J.* XXXVII. 187.
[10] March 11, 1779. House refused (165–124) to commit the Bill, and
postponed it, *ib.* 219.

Late in the year the Duke of Richmond moved in the House of Lords to address the Crown for a reform of the Civil List. The address represents "that before this Country can rise superior to its powerful Enemies, the Waste of Public Treasure requires instant Remedy : that Profusion is not Vigour : and that it is become indispensably necessary to adopt that true Oeconomy which, by reforming all useless Expenses, creates Confidence in Government, gives Energy to its Exertions and provides the Means for their Continuance." To this end, the address continues, every member of the House "will chearfully submit to such Reduction of Emolument in any Office he may hold as His Majesty in his Royal Wisdom may think proper to make." Richmond was not discreet. He was himself out of office, and noble place-holders were indisposed to put the same unbounded trust in the Royal wisdom. The motion was rejected by a majority of over two to one.[1]

A few days later Burke gave notice in the House of Commons of a comprehensive measure which, he claimed, would give £200,000 a year to the Exchequer, cut off influence equivalent to fifty seats in the House of Commons, and withal so temper justice with mercy that none should be "the sacrifice of our penitence."[2] The Rockinghams scarcely hoped for success.[3] Only the increasing strength of public opinion in the country could enable them to force a favourable verdict from a reluctant House. ". . . Any endeavour after reformation which tends to weaken the influence of the Court," said Burke, "will be coldly received here, if it be not very warmly called for out of doors. But to offer is all that those out of power can do. If the people are not true to themselves, I am sure it is not in us to save them."[4]

Burke asked for the stimulus of popular demand.

---

[1] Dec. 7, 1779, *C. J.* XXXVI. 15-16. Rejected 77-36.—*Parl. Hist.* XX. 1293-8 ; 1266.

[2] Dec. 15, 1779, *ib.* XX. 1293-1305. Apparently not entered on the Journals. For Burke's draft plan of economical reform, as tabulated for his own use.—See *Corr.* II. 321-32.

[3] See, for instance, Cavendish's speech, *Parl. Hist.* XX. 1301.

[4] *Ib.* 1297.

Already an unknown general had planned his campaign and was mustering the forces that were to bear Burke and his fellows to victory. Christopher Wyvill belonged to the younger branch of an old Yorkshire family. Born in 1740, he was apparently the Christopher Wyvill of Queen's College, Cambridge, who obtained the degree of LL.B. in 1764.[1] Having no prospect of succession to the family estates, he took orders and was presented to the living of Black Notley, in Essex. In October 1773 he married his cousin Elizabeth,[2] apparently many years his senior, who was the only surviving sister of Sir Marmaduke Asty Wyvill, the head of the family. Sir Marmaduke, who was only thirty-four, died unmarried in February of the next year, and his sister thus unexpectedly succeeded to the family estates.[3] Wyvill had made a marriage lucky both for himself and for posterity. It released him from an uncongenial profession and set him free for the political service which he was particularly fitted to render. He ceased to perform his clerical duties and went to live at Burton Hall, the fine family seat of the Wyvills in the tiny village of Burton Constable, in the North Riding of Yorkshire.[4] There he settled down to the life of a country squire, interesting himself in theology, in politics and in the management of his estate—though the order of interest should perhaps be inverted. Wyvill was no orthodox theologian : if a label must be attached to his views they were Unitarian. But he continued to hold the living of Black Notley till 1806, and, just before he resigned it, he defended himself against a charge of hypocrisy on the curious ground that he had not resided in his parish for over thirty years, and that he had scrupulously paid to his curates the whole income of the benefice.[5] Throughout his

---

[1] *Graduati Cantabrigienses*, 1659–1823, p. 534.

[2] Boswell was a friend of Christopher Wyvill, who apparently read the *Corsican Journal* for him in proof. Mrs. Wyvill is described by Boswell as "very homely indeed."—*Letters of James Boswell to the Rev. W. J. Temple*, 162.

[3] The Baronetcy has remained dormant since Sir Marmaduke's death, Feb. 23, 1774. The rights appears to have passed to the descendants of the fourth baronet, whose grandson had emigrated to Maryland. See *G. E. C.'s Complete Baronetage. Creations under James I.* 104.

[4] S. Lewis, *Topographical Dictionary of England*, I. 449.

[5] *Wyvill Papers*, V. 16–17 note.

long career—he died on the 8th of March, 1822, at the ripe age of eighty-two—Wyvill was a vigorous pamphleteer and an active correspondent.[1] Amongst those whom he knew well and consulted frequently was William Mason, the correspondent of Horace Walpole and biographer of the poet Gray. Mason gave Walpole a good account of his friend, the political parson, but when Wyvill began to agitate against the wasteful and corrupt expenditure of public money, against sinecures, rotten boroughs and electoral abuses, he was talking a doctrine far different from the Whiggism that Horace had learnt from his father Sir Robert; such levity was not to be tolerated by one who had inherited, as part of his fortune, a collectorship in the customs worth £1000 a year, with nothing to collect but the salary. "You told me," Walpole wrote reproachfully to Mason, "that he was a sensible man."[2]

For several reasons, apart altogether from the important fact that Wyvill lived there, Yorkshire was a suitable county in which to begin an agitation for economical reform. In the first place, it was the stronghold of Lord Rockingham, the leader of the party which had professed hostility to waste and corruption as a settled portion of its policy. In Yorkshire Rockingham's influence and estates were alike enormous, and to this day the candidate for a county division of Yorkshire would rather be opposed by any one than a Fitzwilliam—by any one, that is, rather than a member of the family that inherited the estates and influence of the Marquess of Rockingham. Secondly, one of the representatives of Yorkshire was Sir George Savile of Rufford, a leader of the Rockingham connection, distinguished among the politicians of his day for the purity of his political character and his opposition to everything dishonest or unclean. Yorkshiremen had in Savile the ideal spokesman for the cause of economical reform, a man moved by no influence and whom no bribe could tempt. Probably a third reason was that in Yorkshire the land tax

---

[1] The list of Wyvill's works occupies a column in the catalogue of the British Museum.

[2] Walpole to Mason, March 22, 1780.—*Letters*, XI. 146–7 ; cf. XII. 195. For the facts of Wyvill's life, see *D. N. B.* and *G. E. C.'s Baronetage. Creations by James I.* 103–5.

pressed with exceptional severity upon the freeholder. It was collected on an assessment nearly a century old, which already bore little relation to the actual value of the land. Its rate was uniform. But economic development had hitherto been more rapid in the south than in the north, where the means of communication were also extremely bad, and where few populous towns had as yet grown up. As, therefore, the soil was not tilled to the same advantage, as there were few good markets at hand, and as there were not the same facilities for selling the produce of the soil in distant markets, the weight of taxation pressed more heavily upon the freeholder of Yorkshire than upon his more prosperous fellows in the genial agricultural counties of the Midlands and the South. Whether this argument be sound or unsound matters little. What does matter is that it was plausible, and that the Yorkshire freeholder accepted it as true.[1]

Wyvill took advantage of these favouring circumstances to render effective an agitation for economical reform. In days when public meetings were almost unknown, an attempt was usually made to give to such as were held a quasi-legal character. The candidate for parliamentary honours might address the "free and independent" electors from the hustings, or the high sheriff and grand jury might express their political views at the assizes,[2] but public meetings in the modern sense there were hardly any. It was, however, the tradition that the freeholders of a county might meet together to formulate an address or adopt a petition, and that such meetings had a certain legal sanction.[3] This machinery had been revived during the terror of the '45, when the Archbishop of York had called together the freeholders of Yorkshire to vote a loyal

---

[1] See *Wyvill Papers*, III. 131. There are also vague hints elsewhere. I cannot answer for the validity of the argument. That is beside the point. An imagined grievance is politically as effective as a real one.

[2] As they did, for example, at the York Summer Assizes in 1769, when they thanked the county members—Savile and Lascelles—for upholding the rights of electors.—*Wyvill Papers*, Prelim. Pp. I. xi–xii; see also, on the Wilkes case, xiv–xlv.

[3] I cannot say precisely what this sanction was, though I imagine that if Mr. Wyvill had been pressed for the legal justification of a county meeting, he would have maintained that it was a shire moot.

address to the king and to pledge their lives and fortunes
in support of the Hanoverian succession.[1] Wyvill now
proposed to adopt the Archbishop's plan, to call the freeholders of the county to a meeting at York, and to carry
a petition in favour of economical reform. His first supporters were "a few private country gentlemen of the North
Riding, who were totally free from all party influence and
equally unconnected with the leaders of administration and
their opponents."[2] In November 1779 Wyvill began to
seek the support of the county magnates.[3] Their answers
are characteristically English. For the most part they
agree that something must be done, but they do not believe
that anything that is done will be a success. They have
no hope that any good will be achieved by Wyvill's plan,
but they are willing to try it as an experiment. Even Sir
George Savile hoped for no result, but he wisely advised
that the movement should be kept clear of the taint of
party. "It should be your own act and deed."[4] But once
they had insured themselves by these warnings and fore-
bodings against the dreadful possibility of having no
scapegoat to blame in case of failure, the chief landowners
in the county lent Wyvill their aid and influence.

On the 30th of December, 1779, as the result of much
negotiation and correspondence, there assembled at York
a remarkable gathering of "the Nobility, Gentlemen,
Clergy and Freeholders of the County," summoned, on
their own authority, by two hundred and nine gentlemen
of weight and influence.[5] There was some debate. Mr.
Smelt—Fanny Burney's Mr. Smelt—who had been Sub-
Governor to the Princes, was horrified to find that the
intention of the freeholders was to weaken the influence of

[1] Sept. 24, 1745.—*Wyvill Papers*, Prelim. pp. I. i-ii. Speech of
Archbishop, address, and articles of association to protect the king with
lives and fortunes, *ib*. iii-x.

[2] *Ib*. I. 9-10 ; III. 113 note.

[3] Wyvill to General Hale, Nov. 24, 1779, *ib*. III. 107-9 ; to Savile,
Nov. 29, *ib*. 150-2 ; to Sir William Anderson and others, Nov. 29, *ib*.
115-17 ; replies, *ib*. 113, 128-49, 161-72.

[4] Savile to Wyvill, Liverpool, Dec. 11, 1779, *ib*. III. 153-7.

[5] *Wyvill Papers*, I. 1-4, 9. There were present eight peers and
seventeen members of the House of Commons, *ib*. I. 6. *Ann. Reg.* 1780,
Chron. 193. See also Gibbon's account of the economy campaign.—
Mem. 207-8.

the Crown at the very moment when it should have been strengthened, and he argued, with some plausibility, that the Whig oligarchy had been more corrupt and less competent than ministers under royal influence. Mr. Smelt had a case. The political heirs of the Duke of Newcastle could not denounce corrupt influence without being told that the pot was calling the kettle black, and Mr. Turner, member for the city of York, admitted that "a Whig in power was very often like a Tory." [1] It is álso perfectly true that when George III elected to break the Whig connections by outdoing them at their own game of bribe and purchase he had, in effect, tossed carelessly to the Rockinghams the one respectable policy that he should have cherished for his own. Mr. Smelt, therefore, had a case if he had known how to argue it. But he was not tactful. He forgot that there was more than a geographical difference between York and Windsor; and, in consequence, the freeholders reminded him of the distinction by most uncourtly hisses. [2] Smelt had two supporters—his son-in-law Cholmley, [3] and a Mr. Drummond who said, justly, that striking off pensions was "plausible in theory but difficult in practice," and that he "would wish to try one year more." [4] Sir George Savile disposed of the alleged objections to the petition in a few cogent sentences, [5] and the minority seems to have collapsed, for the meeting unanimously adopted a petition to Parliament. [6]

The petition related solely to the pressing question of economy and contained no reference to wider schemes of parliamentary reform. [7] The petitioners complained that the war had resulted in "a large addition to the national debt; a heavy accumulation of taxes; a rapid decline of the trade, manufactures and land-rents of the kingdom." "Alarmed at the diminished resources and growing burthens of this country, and convinced that rigid frugality

---

[1] *Wyvill Papers*, I. 29–32.
[2] *Ib*. I. 13–29. For Smelt, see *D.N.B.*
[3] *Fanny Burney's Diary* (ed. Austin Dobson), I. 333 *et seq.*; *Wyvill Papers*, I. 11.   [4] *Ib*. I. 11.   [5] *Ib*. I. 32–3.
[6] *Ib*. I. 40. Almon, *Anecdotes of Eminent Persons*, I. 358.
[7] In deference, no doubt, to Rockingham. Postscript to Preface.— *Wyvill Papers*, I. xi–xii.

is now indispensably necessary in every department of the State," they observe with grief "that, notwithstanding the calamities and impoverished condition of the nation, much public money has been improvidently squandered, and that many individuals enjoy sinecure places, efficient places with exorbitant emoluments, and pensions unmerited by public services, to a large and still increasing amount: whence the Crown has acquired a great and unconstitutional influence, which, if not checked, may soon prove fatal to the liberties of this country." They appealed to the House of Commons, as the guardian of the public purse, to "withhold further supplies until measures had been taken to inquire into and correct the gross abuses in the expenditure of public money; to reduce all exorbitant emoluments, to rescind and abolish all sinecure places and unmerited pensions; and to appropriate the produce to the necessities of the State in such manner as the wisdom of Parliament shall seem fit."[1]   ". . . Your Yorkshire meeting does not admit of much amendment," was Burke's comment to Rockingham on these proceedings. "It is well, very well. The shade was of as much importance as the lights in your picture."[2]

When it was circulated for signature, between eight and nine thousand freeholders of the county subscribed to the Yorkshire petition, and it was presented to the House of Commons on the 8th of February, 1780, by Sir George Savile, who spoke strongly in support of it.[3] Mr. Turner also presented a similar petition from the city of York "signed by nine hundred and ninety burgesses, almost the whole of his constituents."[4]   Burke presented a petition

---

[1] *Wyvill Papers*, I. 7–9 ; *C. J.* XXXVII. 581 ; *Ann. Reg.* 1780, *Chron.* 194, 338–9 ; *Parl. Hist.* XX. 1371–4.

[2] Burke to Rockingham.—*Corr. of Burke*, II. 314.

[3] *C. J.* XXXVII. 581; *Parl. Hist.* XX. 1374–5. The statue of Sir George Savile in York Minster represents him as bearing in his hand a scroll, on which is written, " The Petition of the Freeholders of the County of York."—*Ann. Reg.* 1789, *Chron.* 271.

[4] *C. J.* XXXVII. 581 ; *Parl. Hist.* XX. 1381. At the contested election of 1774 the number of electors who voted was 1415. Turner headed the poll with 828 votes. These figures were, however, exceptionally small, as the poll seldom fell below 2000. In 1820, when Wyvill's eldest son, Marmaduke, was returned, 2722 voters polled.—H. S. Smith, *The Parliaments of England*, II. 172–3.

from Bristol which expressed the same general views and which he had himself assisted to draft.[1] He deplored the port's declining trade and drew a melancholy picture of its distresses. "The evil that has overtaken that city," he said, "has not come on by slow and gradual approaches, but suddenly and violently; it has not suffered diminution and decay but received blows."[2] The Yorkshire model was adopted by twenty-eight other counties and by at least eleven other cities and towns.[3]

These petitioners, in different parts of the country, entered into correspondence for mutual assistance and advice. The example of the Supporters of the Bill of Rights was not forgotten, for they had taught a lesson in political organisation by which the economical reformers were now able to profit. Wyvill fully realised the necessity for association. Under his capable hands the machinery of common political action invented by the Wilkites was rapidly developed and improved, and its effectiveness was now greatly increased by the joint action of politicians in different parts of the country who were presently to meet together in London for the common consideration of common plans and common objects, in a conference which approached, though as yet distantly, Cartwright's idea of a grand national association for restoring the Constitution, and which approximated still more nearly to the political convention proposed by Dr. Jebb. At the Yorkshire county meeting a committee had been appointed "to carry on the necessary correspondence for effectually promoting the object of the petition and to prepare a Plan of Association on legal and constitutional grounds to support that laudable reform and such other measures as may conduce to restore the Freedom of Parliament."[4]

How the freedom of Parliament was to be restored was a question on which parliamentary reformers were unable to agree for a hundred years to come. Economical reform had alone been mentioned in the Yorkshire petition; all

[1] Burke to Champion, Jan. 24, 1780; *Corr.* II. 316–17; *C. J.* XXXVII. 581.
[2] *Parl. Hist.* XX. 1382–3.   [3] See Appendix II.
[4] *Wyvill Papers*, I. 4–5.

were agreed that it represented the irreducible minimum
of useful improvement; but with that minimum many
would have been content. Wyvill, however, did not
believe that the Rockinghams had any monopoly of
political wisdom; he did not wish the proposals of Chatham
and of Sawbridge to be forgotten. Unhappily, those who
agreed that economical reform alone was inadequate were
not of the same mind as to the way in which the representation ought to be improved, or as to the extent to which
reform should be carried. Rockingham, for whom economical reform alone would have been sufficient, complained
that even when the reformers agreed in their demands for
shorter Parliaments and more equal representation, they
did not all mean the same thing by those convenient
formulæ. Shorter Parliaments according to some should
be annual, according to others triennial, according to
others, again, quinquennial. Some would abolish "what
are called rotten boroughs"; some would give compensation to those who suffered by their abolition; others would
not compensate people for what was not legally theirs. The
right to return the members of whom decayed boroughs
were deprived ought, according to some reformers, to go
to the counties; according to others, to the hundred in
which the decayed borough was situated; according to
another opinion, to the great trading and manufacturing
towns which were growing up in the Midlands and the
north. Extremists, again, were for universal suffrage,
whilst some reformers did not desire any extension of the
franchise at all.[1]

To this difference of opinion were due Wyvill's most
serious difficulties. Though the need for larger reforms
had not been mentioned in the petition, Wyvill himself
firmly believed that they were necessary, and that without
them economical reform would be ineffective. When the
Yorkshire committee met to issue an explanation of its plan

---

[1] Rockingham to Pemberton Milnes, Feb. 28, 1780.—*Rock. Mem.* II.
396–8. Pemberton Milnes was a six-bottle squire, chairman of the West
Riding Quarter Sessions, and a leader of the "dissenting interest," *ib.* II.
395 note. It might be added to the catalogue of various opinions given
above that at a Middlesex county meeting (Feb. 14, 1780), resolutions
were also proposed, though not carried, in favour of the ballot.— *Wyvill
Papers,* IV. 325–51.

"for uniting the independent part" of the county "in a legal and constitutional Association," Wyvill's views prevailed. The association was to promote not merely the objects of the petition, but also the shortening of Parliaments and the more equal representation of the people; and members of the association were to refuse their votes to any parliamentary candidate who declined to pledge himself to these reforms.[1]

Petitioners in other counties and towns formed similar associations and Wyvill succeeded in bringing their representatives together for a conference in London. This plan of conference and association, which has since been so extensively employed for the organisation of political and religious parties, may have been the result of Wyvill's own shrewd appreciation of the facts of the case. But there were both precedents and suggestions : the American committees of correspondence which had been so important when the colonists were organising resistance; the committee of Dissenting Deputies which watched over the interests of the English Protestant Dissenters—Presbyterians, Independents and Baptists;[2] the London Committee of Deputies of British Jews, the organisation of the Hebrew community in England;[3] Cartwright's plan of a "grand national association for restoring the Constitution ";[4] Jebb's more recently published suggestions of a convention;[5] and a direct suggestion, in a letter to Wyvill from one Gamaliel Lloyd, of Leeds.[6] William Cowper, whose fears had been excited by an untimely reading of Clarendon, was sure that the correspondence of the petitioners resembled that of the counties which supported the Parliament during the Great Rebellion, and was quite convinced that hostilities were intended "as the last resource."[7]

---

[1] *Wyvill Papers*, I. 60–8.

[2] Dale, *History of Congregationalism*, 519 note A, pp. 523–4 ; see also pp. 568, 574, 609–10.

[3] S. & B. Webb, *Problems of Modern Industry* (ed. 1902), Historical account of the English Jewish organisation, by Mrs. Webb, in Chapter II ; *The Jews of East London*, p. 21.

[4] Ante, pp. 48–9.   [5] Ante, p. 49.

[6] Gamaliel Lloyd to Wyvill, Jan. 24, 1780.—*Wyvill Papers*, I. 71.

[7] Cowper to Unwin, Feb. 13, 1780.—Southey's ed. of Cowper's *Works*, III. 317.

Whatever the origin of the scheme, Wyvill succeeded, in February 1780, in getting together in London a few members of various county committees, who agreed to invite each petitioning county or association to send two or three delegates to a convention to be held in London in March.[1] On the 11th of March, 1780, the conference began at the St. Albans Tavern.[2] Eighteen counties, cities and towns were represented.[3] The convention advised the local committees to make economical reform, shorter Parliaments and additional knights of the shire the main objects of their associations.[4] But a strong minority would have liked a much less positive recommendation of parliamentary reform,[5] and when Wyvill sent copies of these resolutions to the local committees he felt compelled to add a letter suggesting that where it proved inconvenient to adopt the whole plan, it might be well to postpone the advocacy of annual Parliaments to a more convenient season.[6]

At the end of the month Wyvill was able to return to Yorkshire for the constitutive meeting of the Yorkshire Association on the 28th of March, 1780, when its objects were declared to be the promotion of economical reform, the addition of a hundred members to the representation of the counties, and not annual but triennial Parliaments.[7] Wyvill never obtained all the reforms that he desired, but though he was to that extent unsuccessful, he had planned for his fellow-reformers the sort of organisation by which, in modern England, public opinion must be educated and reforms are to be won. Other counties adopted the Yorkshire plan of association,[8] and it was even suggested that these county associations might be the basis for a " General National Association, for the purpose of public reformation," [9] an organisation more permanent in character than any casual conference or chance convention.

[1] Feb. 24, 1780.— *Wyvill Papers*, I. 109–10, 180–1. Letter of summons, Feb. 28, 1780, *ib*. I. 111–12. Covering letter of Wyvill, Feb. 29, *ib*. 113–15.
[2] *Ib*. I. 116 ; in Pall Mall.—Wheatley's *London*, I. 12.
[3] This can be collected from *Wyvill Papers*, I. 116, 118, 120, 126.
[4] *Ib*. I. 120–1, 426–36.   [5] *Ib*. 127–8.   [6] *Ib*. 440–1.
[7] *Ib*. I. 141–50 ; also Preface, xiii–xvi.
[8] *Ib*. passim, *e.g*. I. 185–8 ; 197–9 ; 201–5.   [9] *Ib*. 271.

The county meetings and petitions had an unfamiliar aspect and they were criticised by different people on various grounds. A solemn protest of the six junior members of the corporation of Nottingham, who dissented from the economical petition of the senior eighteen was too ridiculous to be treated as other than a joke.[1] But Lord Hillsborough was a cabinet minister,[2] and he denounced the campaign as if it were a new '45 calling for a new Culloden. The petition "originated in factious motives merely and those of the very worst complexion. They tended to usurp the powers of Government and to compel Parliament to concessions of the most dangerous and unconstitutional nature." "If not timely suppressed" they would "lead to anarchy and public confusion. . . ." "Cautiously and artfully kept within the verge of the law, they reached to the very brink of rebellion," and he would have crushed—how, he does not explain—the "dangerous, innovating and unconstitutional spirit which had given existence to the county meetings."[3]

Shelburne, the ablest of the statesmen who had drawn their inspiration from Chatham, more than once expressed himself in favour of shorter Parliaments and more equal representation,[4] but the Rockinghams were not so decided. Some of the friends of the economy campaign, therefore, thought it more prudent not to complicate it with an agitation for parliamentary reform. It was wiser for the associators to unite in favour of economy and to succeed, they said, than to attempt organic reform which they might fail to carry on account of divisions in their own ranks. First, the legislature should be purified by economical reform; then the assistance of a purified legislature should be obtained to mend the Constitution.[5] For a time

[1] Feb. 15, 1780. Not on the Journals of the House, as it was not drawn in proper form, and technically, therefore, was not presented.— *Parl. Hist.* XXI. 104-5.

[2] The annoyance of court and ministry is shown by the dismissal of placeholders who were concerned in the county meetings. *Protests of the Lords,* II. 199 ; *Ann. Reg.* 1780, 330 *et seq.*

[3] Debate in the Lords, Feb. 8, 1780.—*Parl. Hist.* XX. 1352 ; cf. *Wyvill Papers,* I. 96-7.

[4] Shelburne to Audrey, March 26, 1780.— *Wyvill Papers,* IV. 131-6 ; also *Paper* XXIX. between pp. 108 and 109.

[5] Sir Cecil Wray to Sir James Norcliffe, March 21, 1780.—*Rock. Mem.*

even Savile hesitated about triennial Parliaments and an increase of county members;[1] Burke was hostile to any sort of constitutional reform. Rockingham himself was still anxious to make out of the campaign all the party capital that could be made, but he was unwilling to pledge himself to any scheme more extensive than Burke's.[2] With his opposition to the proposals of the Yorkshire committee to impose a test on parliamentary candidates it is possible to feel a certain agreement. "The being elected a representative, *if it implies a trust*, is most highly honourable, but if it is to lock up your reasoning faculties," if it is "to tie you up beforehand . . . I think it would be disgraceful bondage. . . ."[3] But there was something disingenuous about the way in which Rockingham first denounced visionary schemes and expedients;[4] then coquetted with proposals, right in principle but not ripe for adoption, such as an increase in the knights of the shire;[5] and finally, either because he could not answer for those who were nominally his supporters, or because he cared nothing for reform himself, abandoned the Yorkshire petitioners to their own devices.[6] The Rockinghams, in sum, were willing to use the associators to carry their own economical reform; they were unwilling to be reciprocally useful to the reformers in promoting any more extensive measures. The Yorkshire committee had "a plain intimation" that "the assistance of the Great Whig Aristocracy in any more effectual Reform than that held out in the economical Petition was not to be expected."[7] Wyvill thought himself betrayed by the Rockinghams, and there can be no doubt that in the half-hearted, partial support which they gave to the economical petitioners is to be

---

II. 400-2.   Spencer Stanhope at the Yorkshire Meeting.—*Wyvill Papers*, I. 156.   Rockingham to Rev. H. C. Zouch, Rector of Tankersley, March 23, 1780.—*Rock. Mem.* II. 402-5, 406. Fitzwilliam to W. Chaloner, March 9, 1780.—*Wyvill Papers*, IV. 127-30.

[1] Debate at Yorkshire County Meeting, March 22, 1780.—*Wyvill Papers*, I. 154.
[2] Rockingham to Pemberton Milnes, Feb. 28, 1780.—*Rock. Mem.* II. 398-400.   [3] *Ib.* 395-6.   Did Rockingham always write his own letters?
[4] *Ib.* II. 398-400.   [5] *Ib.* II. 405-6.
[6] Postscript to Preface, *Wyvill Papers*, I. xvi-xix.   [7] *Ib.* I. xv-xvi.

found one of the reasons why the parliamentary reformers distrusted Fox and clave unto Pitt.

Meantime there were signs that the economy campaign had not been without its effect. On the very day on which the Yorkshire petition was presented to the House of Commons, Shelburne moved in the House of Lords for a committee of both Houses to examine into the public expenditure, especially in respect of contracts and sinecures or cognate offices.[1] For the moment Shelburne was unsuccessful, but a number of lords protested against the rejection of a motion which tended "to narrow the widespreading influence of the Crown."[2] In words which acquire a deeper significance for us who know the history of the succeeding thirty years, they refuted the argument that a time of war was no time for reform. "The present is, for that very reason," they said, "the properest time, because nothing is so essential to the conduct and prosecution of the war as the frugal management of that supply, by which alone it can be carried on with any prospect of success. Nor ought the plan of economy to be any longer delayed at the risk of a general bankruptcy, as from the history of this, as well as other countries, times of necessity have been always times of reform."[3]

A few days later Savile obtained substantially what Shelburne sought, an account of all places for life or lives, and of all existing pensions granted by the Crown.[4] The Bill for disabling revenue officers from voting at elections was revived;[5] another Bill to exclude placemen from the House of Commons got as far as a second reading;[6] and Clerke's Bill for excluding contractors from the House of Commons reached the House of Lords, where it was still unsuccessful but where it received a fair measure of support.[7] A contract, said some peers who protested against

[1] *L. J.* XXXVI. 30; *Parl. Hist.* XX. 1318 *et seq.*
[2] *L. J.* XXXVI. 30; *Protests of the Lords*, II. 95.
[3] *L. J.* XXXVI. 30–2; *Protests of the Lords*, II. 195–6; *Ann. Reg.* 1780, p. 326 *et seq.*
[4] Feb. 15, 1780. *C. J.* XXXVII. 143; *Parl. Hist.* XXI. 83–4, 85, 104; C. J. Fox to the Yorkshire Committee, Feb. 28, 1780.—*Wyvill Papers*, I. 100–1, etc.   [5] *C. J.* XXXVII. 743 (March 21, 1780).
[6] *Ib.* 743, 780–1, 874 (second reading, May 24, 1780).
[7] Leave granted for Clerke to introduce the Bill, Thursday, Feb. 24,

its rejection, was the greatest of all bribes a minister had to bestow—"One Day's Job" might be "worth the Purchase of the Fee of most of the Places and Pensions" held in the House of Commons.[1]

A more famous achievement of the economical reformers was Dunning's great victory [2] in the House of Commons, where he carried, in committee, a resolution "that the influence of the Crown has increased, is increasing and ought to be diminished;" this, with its twin resolution affirming the right of the House to inquire into every branch of public expenditure, arose directly out of the economical petitions, and the moral value of the resolutions was doubtless great.   Mr. Thomas Pitt carried a third and unanimous resolution "to redress the abuses complained of in the economy petitions.[3]   Dunning himself succeeded with a motion for accounts of all payments, pensions and salaries received by members of the House of Commons; [4] and this in face of the astounding assertion of Lord North that "no member of the House received a shilling from Government which either Government ought to be ashamed to pay or the member ashamed to receive." [5]   Dunning's first resolution succeeded, said Sir George Savile, because it was "declaratory and theoretic," for "in general people like well-sounding constitutional maxims" though they fall short in action.   "It is pleasanter to read fighting speeches than to fight." [6]   Moreover, resolutions in committee are a sort of false coin which the House of Commons was then, as now, willing to pass upon the country; they are

---

1780.   *C. J.* XXXVII. 624 ; first reading, Feb. 28, *ib.* 634 ; second reading, March 7, *ib.* 718 ; third reading, March 20, *ib.* 735–6 ; introduced into House of Lords and read first time, March 21, *L. J.* XXXVI. 83 ; rejected on second reading, April 14, *ib.* 100.   Majority 61-41.—*Parl. Hist.* XXI. 414–57.
    [1] *L. J.* XXXVI. 100 ; *Protests of the Lords*, II. 202.
    [2] April 6, 1780.
    [3] *C. J.* XXXVII. 763 ; *Parl. Hist.* XXI. 340, 347, 367.   The first resolution was carried by a majority of 18 ; the house was not divided on the other two.
    [4] April 10, 1780.   Carried 215–213.   *Parl. Hist.* XXI. 376.   Thanks of the Yorkshire Committee to Downing and Pitt.—*Wyvill Papers*, I. 168–9.
    [5] *Parl. Hist.* XXI. 376.
    [6] Savile to Wyvill, Aug. 24, 1781 .—*Wyvill Papers*, III. 328.

useless until the metal of which they are composed is minted into the true money of Acts of Parliament. There was much solemn parade of attending to the demands of the economical petitioners, but the House of Commons could with difficulty be driven to consider specific means of redress.[1]

It was Edmund Burke who "bent the whole force of his mind" to the task of rooting out corruption and who, availing himself of the agitation of the petitioners, achieved the greatest reformation of his time—"the reduction," as he put it, "of that corrupt influence which is itself the perennial spring of all prodigality and of all disorder; which loads us more than millions of debt; which takes away the vigour from our arms, wisdom from our councils and every shadow of authority and credit from the most venerable parts of our Constitution."[2] Burke felt a dread of organic change which grew with age into something very like terror, but bribery and corruption he attacked because they were destroying the Constitution which he reverenced, and the county petitions he regarded not so much as expressions of abstract theory but as arising naturally from distresses which were actually felt.[3] On Friday, the 11th of February, 1780, when he obtained leave to introduce a Bill for economical reform, Lord George Gordon alone dissented;[4] and the speech which Burke then delivered is one of the noblest and most splendid products of his genius.[5] His scheme provided for the abolition of the third Secretaryship of State, and of the third Secretary's department, of the Board of Trade and Plantations, and of numerous unnecessary offices in the royal Household. It included plans for supplying the royal table by contract, for reorganising the Department of Works, and the management of the royal parks, for selling the Crown lands and for reforming the Mint. The subordinate

[1] *e.g. C. J.* XXXVII. 884.
[2] *Works*, II. 55 ; see Pitt's account.—Stanhope, I. 58.
[3] Burke to a member of the Bucks Committee, April 12, 1780 ; to Jos. Harford (Sheriff of Bristol), April 4, 1780.—*Corr.* II. 335-45.
[4] *C. J.* XXXVII. 593 ; *Parl. Hist.* XXI. 73. See also a note in the Appendix to Birkbeck Hill's edition of Gibbon's *Memoirs*, 332-3.
[5] See Prior, 186 ; Gibbon's *Memoirs*, 208 ; Stanhope, I. 30.

jurisdictions of Chester and Cornwall, Wales and Lancaster—"the nurseries of mismanagement"—were to be abolished; and, with certain exceptions for the proper maintenance of a secret service, the Pension List was to be publicly printed.[1] Proposals such as that to abolish the Board of Trade, or the Secretaryship for the Colonies, may now seem absurd. In those days they were not so foolish as they now appear. A secretary was no longer required for colonies that had been lost; and Burke could not, with any show of consistency, maintain a department of Trade and Plantations which had almost ceased to have any business. Burke's plan of reform had some faults, but it was far-reaching, and, in the main, it was wise. For a moment it seemed as if it might be carried in the teeth of the ministry. "The storm, however, blew over for a time;" as Gibbon reports it, "a large defection of country gentlemen eluded the sanguine hopes of the patriots," and "administration recovered their strength and spirit." The Bill was, therefore, rejected.[2]

A few days before Burke's Bill was rejected the Duke of Richmond had introduced into the House of Lords a Bill "for declaring and restoring the natural unalienable and equal right of all the Commons of Great Britain (infants, persons of insane mind and criminals incapacitated by law only excepted) to vote in the election of their representatives in Parliament;" and, secondly, for restoring annual Parliaments. The Bill was rejected without a division.[3] Its sweeping character may even have robbed Burke of some supporters by making timid members of

[1] Prior, 185 ; *Works*, II. *et seq.* ; *Parl. Hist.* XXI. 111–35.

[2] June 23, 1780 : no report ; apparently defeated in committee ; *C. J.* XXXVII. 921.—*Parl. Hist.* XXI. 714 ; Gibbon's *Mem.* 208.

[3] Presented and rejected June 3, 1780. *L. J.* XXXVI. 144 ; *Parl. Hist.* XXI. 686–8 ; Report of the Sub-Committee of Westminster . . . 8, B. M., E. 2101 (17) ". . . The Duke is as violent for annual Parliaments as the Rockinghams are against them." H. Walpole to Mason, June 29, 1780.—*Letters*, XI. 233. Wyvill reports that in later life Richmond declared in a speech in the House of Lords that during the American war he supported the demand for reform "not that Parliament might be reformed, but that the close of the American war might be accelerated." This is one of the cases in which a politician's actions might have been judged more favourably if he had not attempted to explain them.— *Wyvill Papers*, IV. 393 note.

the Commons afraid to vote for a reform that, moderate as it seemed, might yet pave the way for measures more extensive than they cared to contemplate.

There is reason to believe that many of the economical petitioners were concerned much about taxation and little about representation, and that the country gentlemen who were most eager for economy looked on parliamentary reform as a convenient stick wherewith to cudgel ministers into compliance with their wishes, rather than as a principle in the agitation of which anything was to be risked.[1] Nevertheless, side by side with the progress of the economy campaign the larger demand for parliamentary reform had grown and gathered strength. Men like Major Cartwright did not forget, did not allow others to forget, that it was the vital question. In April 1780 a number of members of Parliament and leaders of the reform movement, and a few very respectable gentlemen, established the Society for Promoting Constitutional Information.[2] This society could not by any stretch of imagination be called popular; members were to be elected by ballot and the subscription was not to be less than a guinea.[3] Its first president was Sir Cecil Wray, who had, years before, been elected for East Retford in the teeth of a Newcastle opposition, because he was "a neighbouring country gentleman and a member of the Bill of Rights Society." In 1782 the influence of Charles James Fox secured Wray's election for Westminster,[4] but, alienated from Fox by his coalition with North, he became a supporter of Pitt, and it is as the Pittite hero of the great Westminster scrutiny that he is known to fame.

Major John Cartwright, never happy unless he was organising an association or writing a pamphlet, was the most active promoter of the society. His chief coadjutors were two men of letters, Capell Lofft and John Jebb.[5]

---

[1] Some reformers were sore at this. See *Add. MSS.* 27814, fo. 35.

[2] *Ib.* 27808, fo. 14; 27849, ff. 56-7.

[3] Address of the Society.

[4] "The new minister, not very prudently, I think, named a Sir Cecil Wray, very unknown, as candidate for Westminster." H. Walpole to Mann, June 10, 1782.—*Letters,* XII. 263.

[5] *Life of Cartwright,* I. 134-5.

Capell Lofft, of Troston Hall, near Bury St. Edmunds,[1] had been at Eton and Peterhouse, and had been called to the bar. He "set up author," published translations of Virgil and Petrarch, and lived the life of a scholar-gentleman, active as a justice of his county,[2] but taking also a keen interest in national politics. Jebb, an older man, was also of Peterhouse, a second wrangler and a fellow. He had taken orders, but his views changed, he became a Unitarian, and, resigning his livings, he qualified at St. Andrews as a doctor of medicine, and boldly began medical practice at the age of forty-one. A man of originality and daring, he occupied himself not only with theology and medicine but also with politics, and he had already contributed something to the advocacy of reform.[3] Yet another scholar who warmly supported the society was Sir William Jones, a member of Johnson's Club, the friend of Burke and Gibbon, and the most distinguished orientalist of his day.[4] Amongst the original members of the society [5] were Richmond, the advocate of universal suffrage, and Sawbridge, the champion of shorter Parliaments; John (later Sir John) Sinclair, Arthur Young's chief at the Board of Agriculture, and Sir Joseph Mawbey, the friend and supporter of Wilkes, who served the county of Surrey for fifteen years as its representative in Parliament and for twenty-seven in the then unsalaried office of chairman of Quarter Sessions;[6] George Canning's uncle Stratford Canning and his earliest political preceptor Richard Brinsley Sheridan; the Earl of Effingham, Deputy-Earl Marshal and, in the second Rockingham administration,

[1] Lewis, *Topographical Dictionary of England*, 1849, IV. 393.
[2] S. and B. Webb, *English Local Government:* The Parish and the County. 1906. 551.   [3] Ante, p. 49.
[4] 1746–94. "A staunch Whig, but very wrong-headed." Walpole to Mason, May 1780. Walpole says that he had been tutor to Lord Althorp (*i. e.* the second Earl of Spencer, the book-collector, whose library was afterwards purchased to form the nucleus of the John Rylands Library at Manchester).—*Letters*, XI. 170. See also VIII. 1705 and XI. 383.
[5] Their names are known from an incomplete list in the *Life of Cartwright*, I. 134–5. A later and more complete list of members (undated) is in the Prospectus and List of Members.—B. M., E. 2101 (21).
[6] A wealthy vinegar-manufacturer at Vauxhall, and author of verses published in the *Gentleman's Magazine.—Grenville Corr.* II. 81. See also Almon, *Corr. of Wilkes*, II. 296–7, II. 36 ; *Cav. Deb.* I. 46.

Treasurer of the Household,[1] and Sir James Norcliffe, afterwards Duke of Roxburgh; Lord Sempill, the cousin of Clive, and General Fitzpatrick the crony of Charles James Fox; Mr. Bentley, Wedgwood's partner in his wonderful pottery works, and Thomas Day, author of that reputed delight of a past generation of school-boys, *Sandford and Merton*.[2] There were, besides, Dr. Price, a preacher and pamphleteer of whom we shall have to speak again; Thomas Brand, who had assumed the name of Hollis when he inherited the fortune of the eccentric Thomas Hollis, great-nephew and heir of the early benefactor of Harvard; and Granville Sharp who wrote in favour of parliamentary reform and won an honourable fame by his opposition to the slave trade. Probably no complete list of the original members of the society has survived, but amongst those whose names are known can be counted eight English and Scots peers or heirs of peers, fifteen members of Parliament and several magistrates of the City of London : obviously no irresponsible assemblage of coffee-house politicians.

The least circumspect of all its members was socially one of the most distinguished—Charles Howard of Greystoke, known as Earl of Surrey from 1777 to 1786, when he succeeded to the Dukedom of Norfolk. In the year in which the society was founded he contested Carlisle against the Lowther candidate and robbed the traditional Lowther "cat" of one of its nine tails.[3] Surrey had spent his early life almost without training or education, and he never learnt the lesson of restraint. His enthusiasm—or an extra bottle of wine—was apt to get the better of his

---

[1] From his strange figure and dress, and his two staffs of office, called "The devil on two sticks." Walpole to Mann, April 22, 1782.—*Letters*, XII. 240 ; see also 236 and 282.

[2] Most people will remember how Amelia Sedley sold Mayor Dobbin's shawl in order to buy Georgy the book that all the other fellows were reading. There are lives of Day by John Blackman, *A Memoir of the Life and Writings of Thomas Day*, 1862, and by James Keir, *An Account of the Life and Writings of Thomas Day, Esq.*, 1791. Both are unsatisfactory, but there is an interesting passage on Day's life and writings in Prof. Dowden's *English Literature and the French Revolution*, pp. 20-7.

[3] H. Lonsdale, M.D., *Worthies of Cumberland* (J. C. Curwen), 1867, p. 19.

judgment. At a public dinner in 1798 he proposed "Our Sovereign's Health—the Majesty of the People," and gave such offence at court that he was removed from all his offices.[1] The leaders of the Society for Promoting Constitutional Information were, however, men of sober judgment and wise discretion, and it is remarkable that the least circumspect among its members was the heir to a dukedom.[2]

The declaration of the Society for Constitutional Information was always a source of pride to its author, John Cartwright, and ought, in the opinion of Sir William Jones, to have been written in letters of gold.[3] A political homily on the text, "Law to bind all must be assented to by all," it was, in effect, a defence of electoral rights on the ground of their educative value. All Englishmen, it says, owe it as a duty "thoroughly to inform themselves what the Constitution *is;* what is its present danger; and by what means it may be placed in safety."[4]

Uppermost in the minds of its promoters was the idea of political education, but the society did not seek to the same extent as its successors in France and England to attain its object by holding regular meetings for discussion and debate. Such meetings were held, but the society was analogous rather to the later associations for promoting useful knowledge, and sought to achieve its end by disseminating the literature of reform. Many tracts and pamphlets in favour of annual Parliaments, universal suffrage and vote by ballot were printed by the society for free distribution. According to a practice of the age, large extracts from books and pamphlets were read, approved, and inscribed on the minutes. As might be expected,

---

[1] At a banquet in celebration of Mr. Fox's birthday ; some account of it is given in *Ann. Reg.* 1798, *Chron.* 5–6. See *Journal of Elizabeth, Lady Holland,* I. 177 ; also 190.

[2] The house of Howard had some erratic representatives in the eighteenth century. Horace Walpole's theory was that "so many of their heads were cut off formerly that it looks as if they would never have a head worth wearing on their shoulders again." To the Countess of Upper Ossory, Sept. 29, 1777.—*Letters,* X. 121.

[3] *Life of John Cartwright,* I. 136. Unless the address had existed in MSS. for some years prior to the foundation of the writing the statement in the *Life,* that it was praised by Chatham, must be inaccurate.

[4] Address of the Society, 3 ; *Life of J. C.,* 134–5.

these quotations were not always wise, and, indeed, they do not seem to have always been in strict accordance with the views of the society. Amongst them an extract from an Oxford sermon is remarkable for its frank avowal of the doctrine of the sovereignty of the people. "There is no greatness or dominion on earth so sacred but it must fall before the liberties of the people," said the preacher; and during all the subsequent history of the society it never pledged itself to a more revolutionary opinion.[1]

Whilst the avowed reformers were banding themselves together in an association, want of unanimity was hindering the success of the economy campaign. Economists and reformers found it more and more difficult to run in double harness. Rockingham thought that the abstract principles of the reformers, which might theoretically be right, would "furnish matter for disputation in the schools of Utopia till time was no more." Meanwhile the Constitution suffered for want of those obvious remedies which were slight indeed, but sure in their effects.[2] Burke was disappointed at the failure of his Bill, and declared that it could never become law unless he received more systematic support from the counties.[3] When the Yorkshire committee urged him to make another attempt, he wrote despondently that if he saw a prospect of success he would be happy to yield to their request and "bring again before Parliament a matter which from weariness and despair" he "had entirely abandoned."[4]

The parliamentary reformers, on their side, were disgusted with those who believed that economy alone would cure all the ills of the body politic. Several counties were lukewarm in the cause of parliamentary reform, and the zealots cast the blame for their indifference upon the Rockinghams.[5] Jebb thought Burke's Bill a poor expedient.

---

[1] Preached by the Rev. William Crowe, LL.B., Nov. 5, 1781.—Proceedings of the Society, 3.

[2] To Stephen Crofts, May 18, 1780.—*Rock. Mem* II. 409; to Effingham, May 1, 1780, *ib.* 408. See also Portland's opinion, *ib.* II. 410-15, and Burke to Harford, Sept. 27, 1780.—*Corr.* II. 381-9.

[3] Burke to Viscount Courtenay, July 24, 1780.—*Corr.* II. 363-7.

[4] To Wyvill, Aug. 14, 1780.—*Wyvill Papers*, I. 290-1.

[5] Sir R. Smyth to Wyvill, May 4, 1780.—*Ib.* III. 193. See also 199. See in this connection an article in the *Edinburgh Review*, June 1816, p. 375.

"Moving the People of England to carry so small a Reform would be tempesting the ocean to drown a fly." [1] Wyvill and Mahon agreed that "the official ¬egulations proposed by Burke" were "transient anodynes whose slight and insignificant effect would be overpowered by the deeply vitiated habit of our Representative Body." [2] Horace Walpole, who, Whig though he was, made no secret of his dislike for the economy campaign, rejoiced over these divisions, and insisted that Fox and Shelburne, for example, cared nothing for reform. The whole affair, he said, was "a disastrous project" which had "disgusted many of the opposition" and "delighted the court." [3]

In the autumn of 1780 Parliament was dissolved with the same hot haste as its predecessor had been in 1774. [4] The king exerted all his influence and strained all his resources to enable the ministry to regain the credit that it had lost in the spring. [5] The opposition a few months before had been eagerly discussing the prospects of an election. Now, when the election came, money and influence proved too powerful for the economical campaigners to realise their hopes, [6] but they did gather a few grains of comfort. Sir George Savile, for instance, who did not believe that triennial Parliaments were a cure-all or that much was to be hoped from an addition to the representation of the counties, was by now converted to the belief that these measures were the best that had been proposed and that they ought therefore to receive his support. He proclaimed these opinions in his address to the electors of Yorkshire, [7] and his return was a popular triumph.

[1] Jebb to Wyvill, Dec. 19, 1780.—*Wyvill Papers*, IV. 500.

[2] Mem. of Wyvill, drawn up April 6, 1796, in which he attributes these opinions to Mahon and himself in 1780.—*Wyvill Papers*, IV.

[3] Walpole to Mason, April 17, 1780 (see also the still more vigorous letter of April 13, which was not sent).—*Letters*, XI. 159 (and 157-9).

[4] See the extraordinary resolutions of the Yorkshire committee, May 3, 1780.—*Wyvill Papers*, I. 206-8.

[5] The court spent money lavishly. Geo. III. to North, April 18, 1782. —*Corr.* II. 423.

[6] Dr. Holland Rose thinks that the prevailing disgust at the Gordon Riots was a circumstance favourable to the court and that Geo. III. astutely availed himself of it.—*Pitt and National Revival*, 74.

[7] Address dated from Newcastle-on-Tyne, Sept. 5, 1780.—*Wyvill Papers*, I. 276-86; *Ann. Reg.* 1780, 401-3. Cf. correspondence in *Wyvill Papers*, III. 263-77.

"Hitherto," he said, "I have been elected in Lord Rockingham's drawing-room. Now I am returned by my constituents."[1]

At first the economical reformers received no encouragement from the new Parliament. On the 15th of February Burke reintroduced his old Bill, but it was thrown out on the second reading;[2] and a month later Crewe's Bill for disfranchising revenue officers,[3] and Clerke's Bill for excluding Government contractors from the Commons shared a similar fate on the same day.[4] This must have been a keen disappointment to the economical reformers. In February and March a second convention of the associated counties had been held in London,[5] and had renewed the petition of the previous year, which was presented on the 2nd of April,[6] too late to influence the divisions on the Bills which the reformers desired, and which the House refused so much as to consider in committee.[7] The sympathy and support of the sixteen cities and counties that were faithful to reform[8] can hardly have compensated Wyvill for the discovery that the new Parliament was no more favourable to economy than was the old.

There were, however, signs that the court distrusted the permanence of its victories. Markham, Archbishop of York, betrayed the exasperation of the official classes by a naïve declaration in his visitorial charges that participation in the economy campaign was "foreign to the function of a Clergyman and not the road to preferment."[9] In

---

[1] Stanhope's *Pitt*, I. 162.

[2] Leave to introduce, Feb. 15, *C. J.* XXXVIII. 213; first reading, Feb. 19, *ib.* 218; second reading negatived (233-190), Feb. 26, *ib.* 231.— *Parl. Hist.* XXI. 1223, 1292.

[3] March 14, leave to introduce, *C. J.* XXXVIII. 288; March 16, first reading, *ib.* 298; March 21, negatived in second reading (133-86) *ib.* 312.

[4] Feb. 22, leave to introduce, *C. J.* XXXVIII. 225; March 1, first reading, *ib.* 239; March 21, House refused to go into committee on the Bill, which was, therefore, lost (120-100), *ib.* 312.

[5] *Wyvill Papers*, I. 300-4, 319, 332, 337-8, 384-95. Cf. Walpole to Mason, April 1, 1781.—*Letters*, XI. 425.

[6] *Ib.* I. 332-8; *C. J.* XXXVIII. 331; *Parl. Hist.* XXII. 95.

[7] May 8, 1781. Motion to refer the petition to a committee of the house, negatived 212-135, *C. J.* XXXVIII. 450.

[8] *Wyvill Papers*, I. 381-3.

[9] *Ib.* I. 353-5.

October, despite all its failures, the Yorkshire committee was emboldened to issue a new address to the British electors in which it described economical reform as "a palliative plan," and demanded "some substantial reform of Parliament" as the only real remedy for existing abuses.[1]

Two days after the Yorkshire committee adopted this address Cornwallis capitulated at Yorktown. When the news became known a sense of the hopelessness of our struggle to subdue the American colonists changed the current of opinion. The cry for economy grew more insistent, and from places like London and Bristol came petitions to the House of Commons which represented that declining trade and falling credit required the abandonment of the war and relief to the burdened taxpayer.[2] On the 27th of February, 1782, General Conway carried a motion to address the king against a continuance of the war.[3] A month later North was at last out of office, the Marquess of Rockingham was First Lord of the Treasury (March 27, 1782), Edmund Burke was Paymaster-General, and the turn of the economical reformers had come.

The difference was felt at once. A royal message recommended that in view of the expenses of the war the faithful Commons should take into consideration "an effectual plan of economy through all the branches of the public expenditure."[4] Minor measures of reform were carried first. Clerke's Bill to exclude contractors from the House of Commons at last passed both Houses.[5] Crewe's Bill to disable revenue officers from voting at elections also became law.[6] A speaker in the House of Commons

---

[1] *Wyvill Papers*, I. 355–80. Adopted, Oct. 17, 1781.

[2] From the City, Dec. 6, 1781.—*Ann. Reg.* 1781, pp. 199, 320–3. Cf. 1782, pp. 195-6; Feb. 27, 1782, *C. J.* XXXVIII. 860. Bristol Corporation, Jan. 28, *ib.* 652; Bristol Merchants, *ib.* 783. Westminster, Jebb to Wyvill, Dec. 11, 1781.—*Wyvill Papers*, IV. 514-19.

[3] *C. J.* XXXVIII. 861.   [4] *Ib.* 923.

[5] 22 Geo. III. c. 45. Leave to introduce, March 1, 1782, *C. J.* XXXVIII. 864. Passed the Commons, April 19, *ib.* 937. Passed the Lords, May 17, *L. J.* XXXVI. 503. Royal Assent, *ib.* 537; *C. J.* XXXVIII. 1064; *Parl. Hist.* XXII. 1211-12, 1333-6, 1382; *Ann. Reg.* 1782, 308-9. Cf. Walpole's Letters, XII. 216, 223, 232.

[6] 22 Geo. III. c. 41. Passed Commons, April 25, 1782, *C. J.* XXXVIII. 950; Lords, June 3, *L. J.* XXXVI. 514. Royal Assent, *ib.* 537. See also *Parl. Hist.* XXII. 1336-44; XXIII. 101; *Ann. Reg.* 1782, 308.

estimated that 60,000 electors—perhaps a fifth of the existing electorate—who had voted hitherto a*t* the behest of
ministers were disfranchised by Crewe's Act.[1] Rockingham said that in 70 boroughs the votes of revenue officers
decided the election.[2] Of the 44 electors of Scarborough
10 were disfranchised by the Act,[3] and there is a legend
that in one Cornish borough only a single elector was
qualified to go to the poll at the next election.[4] So far
as they went these small reforms were clearly useful. The
Rockinghams, said Wilkes, "have given us a fair earnest
of their reverence for the Constitution by their support of
two Bills essentially necessary to restore the purity and
independence of Parliament."[5]

In May Burke introduced for the third time his Bill
for economical reform. Its progress was eased by the
jettison of a number of those provisions which excited the
most strenuous opposition, but all the most drastic proposals remained. A dozen offices or sets of offices were
wholly abolished. The Secretaryship for the Colonies
was suppressed, and the duties of the Board of Trade were
transferred to a committee of Privy Council.[6] Clerkships
in the Board of Green Cloth, offices in the Board of Works,
in the Great Wardrobe and in the Jewel Office, together
with other offices in the Household also ceased to be.
Stringent regulations were made to prevent the possibility
of a decrease in sinecures leading to an increase in pensions. Until the Pensions List was reduced to £90,000
no grant of more than £300 a year was to be made to any
one person, and the whole of the grants of a single year—
all of which were to be reported to Parliament—were not
to amount to more than £600 altogether. Once the Pension List fell to £90,000 these conditions were to be slightly
relaxed. No single person, even then, was to receive a
pension of more than £1200 a year, and the total Pension
List was never to exceed £90,000. Proper provision was
made for a Secret Service Fund, but the First Lord of the

[1] *Parl. Hist.* XXII. 1344.
[2] *Ib.* XXIII. 101.
[3] *Wyvill Papers*, IV. 233.
[4] Bossiney in Cornwall.
[5] Letters of Junius, I. 344 note.
[6] " . . . And I was stripped of a convenient salary, after having
enjoyed it about three years."—Gibbon's *Mem.* 213.

Treasury was to take oath that no money paid to an unnamed recipient was used either to corrupt the members of the Commons or to purchase the support of those who elected them.[1] Burke completed his reform by a second Bill to reform his own office of Paymaster-General, and in particular to put an end to the practice which had allowed his predecessors to hold large balances of the national funds in their own name and for their own profit. Burke made a great pecuniary sacrifice in proposing such a measure, a sacrifice as honourable to himself as it was valuable to the nation, a contribution not merely to economical reform but to the purification of parliamentary life.[2]

The great Bill for economical reform seems in the end to have passed through the Commons without a division.[3] In the Lords it was challenged once, but only nine peers could be mustered to vote against it.[4] It was not that the peers as a body really liked the Bill; there are signs that the king's resistance was not overcome without a struggle;[5] but the king was dependent for a few brief months on the assistance of the Rockingham party and had perforce to do their bidding. Burke could have received no higher praise than a disgusted politician gave unwittingly when he complained that "Burke's foolish Bill" had "made it a very difficult task for any set of men either to form or maintain an administration."[6] It was no bad Act that unsettled men who were drawn into public life merely by the attraction of its spoils, who looked upon politics as an adventure, and who bargained for office and patronage like greedy

---

[1] 22 Geo. III. c. 82.

[2] *Ib.* c. 81. Leave to introduce, June 24, 1782, *C. J.* XXXVIII. 1122. First reading in Lords, July 3, *L. J.* XXXVI. 555. Royal Assent, July 11, *ib.* 567.

[3] May 6, leave to introduce, *C. J.* XXXVIII. 988 ; June 13, first reading, *ib.* 1054 ; June 14, second reading, *ib.* 1057 ; June 26, report, *ib.* 1130 ; June 27 (no division except on an amendment for which one person voted), *ib.* 1132.

[4] Introduced and read a first time, June 25, *L. J.* XXXVI. 551. Division on an obstructive motion (9–44), July 3, *ib.* 559. Royal Assent, July 11, *ib.* 567.

[5] See draft of speech to the king prepared by Burke for Rockingham. Burke's *Corr.* II. 468–75. See also 466–8. For the debates in Parliament see *Parl. Hist.* XXIII. 122–3, 139, 147.

[6] *Auckland Corr.* I. 12.

mercenaries insisting upon a share of the booty which lured them to battle.

In later times Burke thought fit to disparage the support of the petitioning counties. "Had the portentous comet of the rights of man" appeared during the distractions of the economy campaign,[1] "nothing human," he said, "could have prevented our being irresistibly hurried out of the highway of heaven into all the vices, crimes, horrors and miseries of the French Revolution. . . . Wild and savage insurrection[2] quitted the woods and prowled about our streets in the name of reform. . . . Many of the changes by a great misnomer called parliamentary reforms . . . went home to the utter destruction of the constitution of this kingdom. . . . There are who remember the blind fury of some and the lamentable helplessness of others; here a torpid confusion, from a panic fear of the danger; there the same inaction from a stupid insensibility to it; here well-wishers to the mischief; there indifferent lookers-on. At the same time a sort of national convention, dubious in its nature and perilous in its example, nosed Parliament in the very seat of its authority; sat with a sort of superintendence over it; and little less than dictated to it not only laws but the very form and essence of legislature itself."[3]

This was in any case an unfair and grotesque exaggeration of the story which has just been told. But Burke himself had not always held such language. "I cannot, indeed, take upon me to say that I have the honour to *follow* the sense of the people," he had said in his great speech on economical reform. "The truth is *I met it on the way*, while I was pursuing their interest according to my own ideas. I am happy beyond expression to find that my intentions have so far coincided with theirs, that I have not had cause to be in the least scrupulous to sign their petition, conceiving it to express my own opinions

---

[1] As a matter of fact it did—at Cambridge ! See the principles and resolutions of the Cambridge Constitutional Society.—*Wyvill Papers*, I. 135-7.

[2] Possibly Burke was thinking of the Gordon Riots, which most of the county associations expressly condemned.

[3] Letters to a Noble Lord.—*Works*, V. 116.

as nearly as general terms can express the object of particular arrangements."[1] Jebb and Savile, Wyvill and Cartwright did not labour in vain.[2] If Burke won the honourable credit that he claimed,[3] in that he had saved his country, he earned that credit, at least in part, because his country was determined to be saved.

With Burke's success, however, hearty co-operation between the two groups of reformers who had fought the economy campaign together came virtually to an end. Burke and his friends, though some of them afterwards coquetted—rather gingerly—with bolder schemes, were on the whole well satisfied to have restricted illegitimate influence and to have stopped up the channels of direct corruption; advanced reformers remained, on the contrary, unsatisfied, and accepted economical reform as no more than a preliminary, though it might be a necessary preliminary, to more drastic measures of constitutional reconstruction. Even during the progress of the economy campaign these differences had become manifest and had tended to crystallise. The orthodox Whigs had shown themselves suspicious of reformers who seemed unpractical and doctrinaire; parliamentary reformers had grown more and more impatient of colleagues who dawdled away their opportunities and merely tinkered with the most obvious defects of the parliamentary system. During the next few years the reformers were to obtain their most influential and persistent support not from the Rockinghams but from the Chathamites, and, for a time, they were to find their ablest leader in Chatham's son.

[1] Speech on Economical Reform.—*Works*, II. 66.
[2] See, for instance, Gibbon's opinion, *Mem.* 207–8.
[3] Letters to a Noble Lord.—*Works*, V. 118.

CHAPTER IV

1782–1789

FROM the point of view of the parliamentary reformers the political situation in 1782 was rapidly improving, and seemed to justify those optimists who anticipated an early and decisive victory. Many leading politicians were now committed, more or less definitely, to parliamentary reform. The Chathamites, powerful neither in numbers nor in borough influence, but the most progressive and, in proportion to their numerical strength, the most capable of the parliamentary groups, took the side of the reformers. Advocates of reform were also to be found amongst the Rockinghams : Savile, a slow convert, but no weathercock, and an earnest reformer throughout the short remainder of his life; Charles Fox, rapidly converted and as rapidly discouraged, frequently lukewarm, but readily redeemed by his gift of easy penitence; and Richmond, whose outright advocacy of sweeping reform may help to explain the cessation, a few months later, of his association with the Rockingham party. As they had now obtained the assistance of politicians of the first rank, the reformers had good reason to hope for the speedy triumph of their cause.

Their hopes rose still higher when they found a new leader in the House of Commons. In 1781 William Pitt, second son of the Earl of Chatham, entered Parliament as member for Sir James Lowther's nomination borough of Appleby, took up the question of reform and made the cause, for a time, his own. The arrival of Pitt meant an immense accession of strength to the reforming party. He brought to its aid not merely the prestige of a great name, though that in itself counted for much, but he brought also

83

a talent for debate, a power of attracting capable lieutenants, and a remarkable gift for political leadership, unusual, if not altogether exceptional, in a politician just entering upon his parliamentary apprenticeship. The reformers were lucky to find so capable a leader, and showed their appreciation of their good fortune by the enthusiasm with which they received and supported him.

In 1782 a number of the friends of reform met at the house of the Duke of, Richmond, decided that the moment had come to raise the question in the House of Commons, and persuaded Pitt to be their spokesman.[1] On the 7th of May he moved that "a Committee be appointed to enquire into the present State of the Representation of the Commons of Great Britain in Parliament, to report the same to the House, and likewise what Steps in their Opinion it may be proper for Parliament to take concerning the same."[2] During the debate ample reasons were brought forward to justify Pitt's demand for inquiry. Sir George Savile told the House that it "might as well call itself the representative of France as of the people of England."[3] Pitt himself tried to frame his speech so as to please the economical reformers, whose bugbear was Crown influence, and he inveighed against the corrupt influence of the Crown—"an influence which has been pointed at in every period as the fertile source of all our miseries—an influence which has been substituted in the room of wisdom, of activity, of exertion and of success— an influence which has grown with our growth and strengthened with our strength."[4] With great dexterity Pitt had spread his rhetorical sails to catch the favouring breeze of political circumstance, but, to the great disappointment of the reformers, his resolution was defeated by twenty votes.[5] "We were bullied outrageously about our poor Parliamentary Reform," wrote Sheridan, "but it will do at last, in spite of you all."[6] Sheridan's was a

---

[1] Stanhope's *Pitt*, I. 58.
[2] *C. J.* XXXVIII. 987 ; *Parl. Hist.* XXII. 1422.   [3] *Ib.* 1429.
[4] Stanhope's *Pitt*, I. 58 ; *Parl. Hist.* XXII, 1416–38.
[5] 161–141. *C. J.* XXXVIII. 987 ; *Parl Hist.* XXII. 1438. There is an account of the debate in *Wyvill Papers*, I. 442–80.
[6] Sheridan to Thomas Grenville.—Fraser Rae's *Sheridan*, I 386.

long prophecy. Strong as their case might be, the reformers did not have so good a division again till 1831, long after Sheridan and his cronies had slipped under the table for the last time.

One direct consequence of the rejection of Pitt's resolution was a meeting of the friends of reform, held on the 18th of May at the Thatched House Tavern, in St. James's Street.[1] The Lord Mayor presided. Lord Mahon and the Duke of Richmond, Sir Cecil Wray and the Earl of Surrey, Wilkes and Cartwright, Wyvill and Jebb, as well as Pitt himself,[2] were amongst those who decided—in words quoted threadbare in the years that followed—that "application should be made to Parliament by Petition from the Collective Body of the People in their respective districts, requesting a substantial Reform of the Commons' House of Parliament." As it was already too late in the session for petitions to make such an impression on the House as would induce it to reconsider its decision, the reformers decided "to take the sense of the people" during the summer, "in order to lay their Petitions before Parliament early in the next Session, when their Proposition for a Parliamentary Reformation (without which neither the liberty of the Nation can be preserved nor the permanence of a wise and virtuous Administration can be secured) may receive the ample and mature discussion which so momentous a question demands."[3] For the rest, the reformers were prudent; they neither endorsed the far-reaching proposals of Richmond —the only minister present—nor promulgated a scheme of their own, about which their friends might have disagreed.[4] Twelve years later, when advocates of reform lay under the ban, and some of them had to stand their trial in a court of law, appeal was made to the Thatched House Tavern resolutions, as if to a charter of reform;

[1] On the Thatched House, see Wheatley, *London Past and Present*, III. 370 ; II. 302.

[2] *Wyvill Papers*, I. 424   Preface to *Wyvill Papers*, vol. i. p. x.

[3] *Wyvill Papers*, I. 424-5. The resolutions were in Pitt's handwriting. *S. T.* XXII. 493. Wyvill's version is that they were drawn by him and approved by Pitt.—*Wyvill Papers*, I. x ; cf. *Add. MSS.* 27849, ff. 65-6.

[4] Brass Crosby to Wyvill, Nov. 27, 1782.—*Wyvill Papers*, II. 23-4 ; Wyvill to Crosby, Dec. 7, 1782.—*Ib.* 25-32.

but Pitt, who was head of the ministry in that hour of unrest, wished to forget, or even to disavow, his youthful indiscretion.

Pitt and his followers had failed to convert the House of Commons to reform, but they had done respectably in a division, and they were not discouraged. There was still much in the political situation which bade them hope. Even though the majority of its members were opposed to constitutional change, the Rockingham administration was nevertheless the first English ministry containing members pledged to any comprehensive scheme of reform. It had carried economical reform, and had thus diminished one of the obstacles to an improvement of the representation, by decreasing constitutional corruption and by reducing the profits to be made out of borough seats. The Rockingham administration could not be expected to carry reform, but neither could it treat Pitt in the contemptuous fashion in which North had handled his predecessors. If the ministry, as a body, could not, in any direct fashion, give help to the reformers, neither could it offer an uncompromising and unanimous opposition to their demands.

This changed position produced greater activity among the reformers because it fostered greater hope. The propaganda of reform was carried on with increased zeal on every hand, but the major share in systematising and directing the efforts of the reformers was taken by the Society for Constitutional Information. Whilst the battle for economy was being fought in Parliament, the society had helped to keep alive in the country an agitation for more drastic measures. It had striven to create and educate a public to whose support the reformers could appeal, by steadily pursuing the policy of selecting, printing and distributing addresses, pamphlets and speeches in support of parliamentary reform.[1] In addition to its own addresses [2] the society reprinted, with comments, the speech which Wilkes had delivered in the House of Commons in 1776 in

---

[1] See the publications of the Society in the British Museum, E. 2101 ; Jebb to Wyvill, Dec. 19, 1780.— *Wyvill Papers*, IV. 50 ; J. Cartwright to Mrs. C., Jan. 1781.—*Life*, I. 142–3.

[2] For instance, *A Second Address to the Public from the Society for Constitutional Information.*—B. M., E. 2101 (13).

support of his proposals of reform.[1] Members ransacked
the English classics for passages which seemed to cor-
roborate' their own views of reform, and they entered in the
Proceedings extracts from the writings of men like Somers [2]
or Swift—such as the passage in a letter from Swift to
Pope, in which he adored "the wisdom of the Gothic
institution" which made Parliaments annual.[3] At the
same time they printed the speeches and pamphlets of
their own members, such as Thomas Day [4] or John Cartwright; [5] or sometimes, if these works were lengthy, a
carefully prepared abstract of their argument. In this way,
for example, they circulated the interesting "Dialogue
between a Scholar and a Peasant," by William Jones, the
Orientalist, in which the scholar proves to the peasant that
he has just as much right to a voice in the affairs of the
nation as to a share in the management of his village
club; [6] and a letter by the same writer, in which he attacks
a "dangerous doctrine" of "the late ingenious Henry
Fielding," who had been so wicked as to suggest that "the
Constitution of this country was nothing fixed, but just as
variable as the weather." [7]

Throughout the year 1782 the reformers carried on an
active campaign. In July the Society for Constitutional
Information issued an address "to the people of Great
Britain of all denominations, but particularly to those who
subsist by honest industry." [8] It is a sign that some of
the reformers were beginning to forecast the probable effect

---

[1] March 29, 1782.—*Proceedings in 1782*, pp. 11–20.

[2] March 8 and 22, 1782.—*Ib.* pp. 4–11.

[3] Entered June 28, 1782.—*Ib.* pp. 33–4,

[4] "Two Speeches of Thomas Day, Esq., at the General Meeting of
the Counties of Cambridge and Essex . . . 1780," printed and distributed
gratis by the S. C. I.—B. M., E. 2101 (18).

[5] Summary by Lofft of Cartwright's treatise, "The People's Barrier
against undue influence ; or the Commons' House of Parliament according to the Constitution."—B. M., E. 2101 (14), pp. 1–4.

[6] The Principles of Government in a dialogue between a Scholar and
a Peasant, written by a Member of the Society for Constitutional Information [Sir William Jones], 1782.

[7] Entered July 5, 1782.—Proceedings in 1782, pp. 34–6. This may
seem a strange view for a reformer like Jones to take, but the explanation
lies in the fact that the reformers appealed constantly to history, and
believed that reform would not involve innovation, but would merely be a
estoration of the ancient Constitution.

[8] *Proceedings of 1782* (large edition), B. M., E. 2101 (23), pp. 41–2.

of that equal representation for which they agitated; a sign, too, that their own ideas were being liberalised. Reform, now and for some time to come, was demanded, not by the tradesman and the artisan, but by the country squire and the professional man. In this address we see them reaching downward in the social scale for encouragement and support. The "mechanic" is told that he ought to share in political power; "therefore, let your condition be ever so humble, when any one tells you that you should mind your own business and not meddle with State affairs, be assured he is either a knave or a fool." "It is entirely owing to your negligence" in the past "that you have so much dirty work to inspect." "However, every one knows that you are yet powerful enough to redress all your grievances, whenever you shall think proper to exert yourselves with unanimity." [1] What might have happened to the authors and publishers of this address between 1792 and 1822, what, indeed, might have been said about them in 1842 or 1848, it would not be pleasant to surmise. For the moment these were honest men and reformers; the age of proscription was not yet.

The society was not content merely to be active itself; it desired to promote activity in others. In August it issued a circular letter to country correspondents, urged them to promote petitions, declared that its object was to distribute "constitutional tracts" in favour of parliamentary reform, which appeared "essentially necessary to our existence as a free people," desired assistance in obtaining the notice of provincial newspapers, suggested the sort of paragraphs which reformers might themselves send to the Press, and finally recommended the formation of parochial societies to petition for parliamentary reform. [2] Constitutional societies had already been founded in Nottingham and Cambridge. [3] There may, very probably, have been others of which we now have no record; and it looked for a moment as if constitutional societies might have become

---

[1] *Proceedings of 1782* (large edition), B. M., E. 2101 (23), 43-4.
[2] Aug. 23, 1782. *Proceedings of 1782* (larger ed.), B. M. 2101 (23), pp. 57-9. See also Proceedings of Aug. 30, *ib.* 59-61, and of Oct. 4, 1782, *ib.* 84-6.   [3] *Wyvill Papers*, I. 249-51,135-7.

instruments of agitation as powerful as Reform Unions and Hampden Clubs became in the early nineteenth century.

During the autumn and winter the machinery of the county associations was again set in motion. Once more the Yorkshire committee met, and agreed to take a plebiscite on parliamentary reform and the extent to which it should be carried. Tentatively the Yorkshiremen suggested that fifty of the worst of the rotten boroughs should be abolished, that the electors of disfranchised boroughs should be given votes in the county, and that they should also be compensated for their lost privileges; that the hundred members taken from the rotten boroughs should be given to the counties; that the Septennial Act should be repealed; that, in counties, votes should be given to copyholders; and that the Scots parliamentary system should be reformed. The letter asked for expressions of opinion on this tentative scheme; it also urged the necessity for harmony, for the sake of which the Yorkshire committee was willing, if necessary, to sacrifice so essential a portion of its plan as the abolition of rotten boroughs.[1]

The circular seems to have been sent not merely to county associations, but to corporations in general, and even, as is shown by the answers received by Wyvill, to important individuals. Pitt, for example, avoided a discussion of reform in detail, but replied that his "general sentiments in favour of substantial and practical Reform of Parliament" were "invariable."[2] Sir George Onesiphorus Paul, a fine specimen of the old county justice,[3] a man who knew his Gloucestershire thoroughly, stated in his reply that the moderate men of the county were alarmed by the publications of the Constitutional Society, the pamphlets of Major Cartwright and of Granville Sharp. The Whigs—in the eighteenth century every one at some

---

[1] *Wyvill Papers*, II. 17-23. Printed also in " A Collection of Letters which have been addressed to the volunteers of Ireland on the subject of Parliamentary Reform . . ." 1782, pp. 1-7 (B. M. 8145, C. 37). Discussions of Reformers, *Wyvill Papers*, IV. 290, 299-300, 316-18; IV. 502, 519-20 note.

[2] Pitt to Wyvill, Nov. 26, 1782.—*Ib*. IV. 1.

[3] S. and B. Webb, *English Local Government:* the Parish and the County, 368-9.

time was tempted to call himself a Whig—were lukewarm. Paul himself is probably representative of the average man who recognised the need for reform, but wished it to be moderate, and disliked the idea of shorter Parliaments and universal suffrage; who wanted, in short, to hasten slowly.[1] If some were afraid that reform might go too far, others feared that it might not go far enough, and the full-fledged reformer expected little good from an increase in the knights of the shire whilst the strength of the boroughs remained undiminished.[2]

From the opponents of reform Wyvill received indignant and amusing letters, some of them letters which to our eyes seem to prove the case of the reformers. For example, the Mayor of Poole, a borough of about a hundred electors,[3] which its inhabitants called "an opulent seaport," reproved Wyvill for meddling with reform as he might have scolded a small boy for an unauthorised raid on the jam-cupboard;[4] and at once there came a letter from the Commonalty to say that the Mayor and Corporation misrepresented the opinion of the townsmen.[5] The close corporation of Leicester, the most corrupt in England, believed that "all Committees and Associations (other than Parliamentary ones) for the purpose of altering the constitution, *to speak favourably of them,* tend to create, *at least,* anarchy and confusion,"[6] and instructed the members for the borough strenuously to oppose "any alterations" "in the present representation of the People in Parliament."[7] The aldermen and freemen of West Looe, with its handful of non-resident electors,[8] were unanimous "that it would be highly improper to make any alteration in the

---

[1] G. O. Paul to Wyvill, Dec. 6, 1782.—*Wyvill Papers,* IV. 241–7. See also letter of Oct. 29, 1782.—*Ib.* 236–40.

[2] Price to Wyvill, Dec. 12, 1782.—*Ib.* IV. 221–2.

[3] Judging by the polls.—H. S. Smith, *The Parliaments of England,* I. 89.

[4] To Wyvill, Dec. 2, 1782.—*Wyvill Papers,* 98–9.

[5] To Wyvill, Dec. 12.—*Ib.* II. 99–101. It was the Commonalty which called Poole an "opulent seaport."

[6] To Wyvill, Dec. 5, 1782.—Jas. Thompson, *The History of Leicester in the Eighteenth Century,* 173; *Wyvill Papers,* II. 108–10.

[7] Jan. 17, 1783.—Thompson, 174.

[8] Oldfield, *Representative History,* 1816, III. 236.

Constitution of this country"; [1] and the mayor wrote that "the most respectable persons in Petersfield" thought that Wyvill and his association would do "much injury to old England." The Portreeve and a hundred electors of Penryn [2] denounced Wyvill's plan as "unjust, unwise and ill-timed"; unjust, that is, because it would involve the abolition of rights which the electors of Penryn regarded as property. They would hear of no compensation for the loss of privileges which they regarded as invaluable. [3] The constables of Manchester reported that the principal inhabitants of the township thought it "by no means proper" "to raise disputes and dissension about altering and amending our excellent Constitution, under which the inhabitants of Great Britain and her colonies have for this last century enjoyed more real liberty and property than any nation upon earth." [4] It is difficult to believe that the constables represented the opinion of Manchester, even in 1782. The political history of the town during the ensuing decade suggests that the letter of the constables proved the need for a measure of municipal as well as of parliamentary reform.

Vastly more impressive are the replies in favour of reform. From York [5] and Westminster, [6] from Moray [7] and Sussex, [8] from Glasgow [9] and Portsmouth, [10] from Southwark [11] and Gloucester, [12] came replies favourable, some to a moderate and some to a drastic reform of Parliament; but because it was not possible to draw a specific plan of reform that, in detail, would be acceptable to everybody, it was agreed to preserve the appearance of

---

[1] The Mayor to Wyvill, Jan. 14, 1783.—*Wyvill Papers*, IV.
[2] *Ib.* II. 97.
[3] To Wyvill, Feb. 22, 1783.—*Ib.* II. 130–5.
[4] George Barton and James Billinge, constables. to Wyvill, Nov. 29, 1782.—*Ib.* 95–6.   [5] *Ib.* II. 111.
[6] Fox to Wyvill, Dec. 4, 1782. *Ib.* II. 104–5. See also note, *ib.* II. 216.
[7] Sheriff of Moray to Wyvill, Nov. 26, 1782.—*Ib.* II. 92–3.
[8] Sir W. Frankland to Wyvill, Dec. 14, 1782.—*Ib.* II. 123–6.
[9] Provost to Wyvill, Nov. 28, 1782.—*Ib.* II. 82–5.
[10] John Carter, Mayor, Jan. 20, 1782, to Wyvill.—*Ib.* IV. 155–6.
[11] *Ib.* II. 74–7.
[12] Mayor to Wyvill, Nov. 30, 1782.—*Ib.* 88–91. For other letters see *Wyvill Papers*, II. 23–4, 78–82, 112–14, 210–12.

unanimity by petitioning for reform in general terms. Such a petition was drawn up by the Yorkshire committee and circulated amongst those who were known to sympathise with its aims.[1] It set forth "that the Petitioners, sensible of the original Excellency of the Constitution of this Country, most ardently wish to have it maintained upon the genuine Principles on which it was founded; and that it is necessary to the Welfare of the People, that the Commons' House of Parliament should have a common Interest with the Nation; and that in the present State of the Representation of the People in Parliament, the House of Commons do not sufficiently speak the Voice of the People: And therefore praying the House to take into their most serious Consideration the present inadequate State of the Representation of the People in Parliament, and to apply such Remedy to this great and alarming Evil as to the House may seem meet."[2]

In 1783 the House of Commons was bombarded with petitions. Over ten thousand freeholders signed the Yorkshire petition,[3] which was also adopted by the city of York.[4] The counties of Kent[5] and Cornwall,[6] Suffolk[7] and Derby[8] adopted petitions in almost identical terms. Sussex,[9] Nottinghamshire[10] and north-west Devon[11] made similar demands in rather different words. Middlesex,[12] Southwark[13] and the corporation of the City of London[14] followed the lead of Westminster[15] and spoke the energetic

[1] *Wyvill Papers*, II. 35–71, 249–51, 236–8.
[2] Presented Feb. 24, 1783, *C. J.* XXXIX. 251 ; *Parl. Hist.* XXIII. 571.
[3] 10,152.—*Wyvill Papers*, II. 249–51 ; *Ann. Reg.* 1783, 197.
[4] *C. J.* XXXIX. 251.
[5] May 1, 1783 (the day and month of presentation is given in each case), *C. J.* XXXIX. 406–7 ; *Wyvill Papers*, II. 138–40.
[6] March 6, *C. J.* XXXIX. 280 ; *Wyvill Papers*, 216–18.
[7] May 5, *C. J.* XXXIX. 401–2.
[8] Feb. 17, *ib.* 230 ; *Wyvill Papers*, II. 36–7.
[9] Jan. 22, *C. J.* XXXIX. 41 ; *Wyvill Papers*, II. 224–33.
[10] April 1, *C. J.* XXXIX. 347 ; *Wyvill Papers*, II. 184–209.
[11] Feb. 14, *C. J.* XXXIX. 197–8.   There were also petitions from Somerset and Essex and the counties of Flint and Carnarvon.—*Ib.* 251, 264. 290–1 ; *Wyvill Papers*, II. 210–12, 219–33.
[12] May 6, *C. J.* XXXIX. 404.
[13] March 5, *ib.* 273 ; *Ann. Reg.* 1783, 198.
[14] May 6, *C. J.* XXXIX. 404.
[15] Petition based on resolutions moved by Cartwright at a Westminster meeting presided over by C. J. Fox, July 17, 1782. Presented

language of Major Cartwright. From Scotland came
petitions setting forth the special electoral grievances of
that misrepresented country,[1] and the House was over-
whelmed with the complaints of English cities and
boroughs, which set forth the local grievances of non-
electors in more specific terms, and demanded a reform
of the representation. From Poole[2] and Launceston,[3]
Portsmouth[4] and Lymington,[5] from Yarmouth[6] and
Tiverton,[7] Scarborough[8] and Gloucester,[9] from Cambridge[10] and Chichester,[11] Lyme Regis[12] and Bury St.
Edmunds,[13] from Derby,[14] Denbigh[15] and Winchester,[16]
from Hastings,[17] Droitwich[18] and Southampton,[19] from
London,[20] Rochester[21] and the Tower Hamlets,[22] came one
unanimous complaint that, whatever the original excellence
of the Constitution, the House of Commons no longer spoke
the voice of the people of England.

Whilst the demand for reform had been growing in the
country, changes had taken place in the cabinet which
seemed at first to favour the prospects of the reformers.
In July 1782 the death of the Marquess of Rockingham
had exposed a cleavage in his ministry. Fox and Shelburne, the strongest men in the cabinet, had scarcely been
able to run in double harness during the lifetime of Rockingham, and it was impossible for them to act any longer
together. Shelburne was called upon to form a ministry
and Fox resigned. These changes seemed favourable to

May 7, 1783, *C. J.* XXXIX. 407 ; *Wyvill Papers*, II. 141–83 ; *Life of
John Cartwright*, I. 145–6.
[1] *C. J.* XXXIX. 391, 405, 408–9. ; *Wyvill Papers*, III. 1–10, 15–17.
[2] Jan. 31, *C. J.* XXXIX. 126 ; *ib.* II. 99–101.
[3] Jan. 23, 1783. *C. J.* XXXIX 81–2.   [4] April 10, *ib.* 263.
[5] March 6, *ib.* 281.   [6] Feb. 3, *ib.* 135.
[7] Jan. 31, *ib.* 127 ; *Wyvill Papers*, II. 106–7, 216.
[8] March 10, *C. J.* XXXIX. 285 ; *Wyvill Papers*, II. 252–3, 240–3 ;
Ann. Reg. 1783, 199.
[9] March 3, *C. J.* XXXIX. 263 ; *Wyvill Papers*, II. 89–90.
[10] Feb. 10, *C. J.* XXXIX. 176.   [11] April 14, *ib.* 371.
[12] Feb. 13, *ib.* 191.
[13] Feb. 17, *ib.* 231 ; *Wyvill Papers*, II. 212–15, IV. 259–65.
[14] Feb. 21, *C. J.* XXXIX. 239.   [15] April 9, *ib.* 360.
[16] Feb. 5, *ib.* 149.   [17] May 5, *ib.* 402.
[18] April 9, *ib.* 361.   [19] April 9, *ib.* 361.
[20] May 7, *ib.* 408. This was from the freeholders of the city and
county ; the one previously cited from the corporation.
[21] March 6, *ib.* 281.   [22] May 7, *ib.* 406.

the reformers for two reasons. The secession of Fox and his friends weeded the ministerial party of the strongest anti-reformers. On the other hand, the reformers in the ministry were strengthened because Shelburne gave the Chancellorship of the Exchequer to Pitt, and the parliamentary leader of the reformers thus entered the cabinet. Though Pitt entered office he did not come into power; his position did not enable him to give much assistance to the cause. Too weak to impose its will upon the king, the cabinet was unable to attempt a reform of Parliament. Shelburne gave assurances that he "meant to act nobly" by the Yorkshire Association, but it soon appeared that "acting nobly" did not mean staking the fate of his ministry on the success of a measure of parliamentary reform.[1] Nevertheless the reformers were not discouraged, and for the most part became supporters of the Shelburne ministry. Shelburne inspired them with more confidence than Fox because he seemed to be the more sincere reformer. Greater things were to be hoped from a professed reformer who had followed Chatham, and who was now followed by Chatham's son, than from a renegade king's friend whose very name recalled the blackest infamies of court corruption.

Shelburne did not command a majority in the House of Commons, but he was safe so long as Fox and his followers could resist the temptation of defeating him by a coalition with their former enemy, Lord North. Together the supporters of Fox and North could outnumber those of Shelburne, and though the two leaders had said bitter things of each other in the past, the conclusion of the American War and the success of the economy campaign had put an end to the chief causes of contention between them and had removed the most formidable obstacles to a reconciliation, which would be mutually profitable as it would enable them to join forces against their common foe, Lord Shelburne. To Fox, therefore, a coalition offered both power and revenge. Even the firmest of politicians might have fallen in the face of such a temptation. Fox

[1] Rev. F. Dodsworth to Wyvill, Aug. 15, 1782.—*Wyvill Papers*, III. 333 ; further explanation, 334-62 ; Cartwright to Mrs. C., July 15, 1782. —*Life* I. 146-7.

yielded to it, coalesced with Lord North, turned out Shelburne, and in April 1783 returned to office with Lord North under a respectable Whig magnate, the Duke of Portland, who was a mere shadow in his own cabinet.

A furious storm of moral indignation broke over the heads of Fox and North. Men raged against the authors of the coalition with a passion which now seems exaggerated, and in the warmth of controversy many strictures were passed upon the conduct of the new allies which were far from just. But the heat with which the coalition was opposed by the reformers can occasion no surprise. For them the coalition was an undoubted setback. In place of Shelburne, who was sympathetic to reform, and Pitt, who was deeply pledged to it, they were confronted by North, who was an open foe, and Fox, who was an uncertain friend. The reformers were as bitter against the new ministry as they had been friendly to the last. Fox, in particular, was the object of scathing attacks. Horne Tooke gave graphic expression to their hostility a few years later when he presented to the electors of Westminster "Two Pair of Portraits," setting out in parallel columns the virtues of the pure and patriotic Lord Chatham and the vices of the venal and corrupt Lord Holland. Like father, like son, he argued. The younger Pitt had inherited the blameless purity of the elder, and the tainted character of Henry Fox had descended to Charles James.[1]

Ministerial changes notwithstanding, the continual stream of petitions for reform could not be altogether disregarded. Fortified by the support of the petitioners, Pitt renewed his attempt to turn the attention of the House of Commons to a reform of Parliament. On the 7th of May, 1783, the anniversary of his first attempt, he brought forward three resolutions for the prevention of bribery; the disfranchisement of corrupt boroughs — the uncorrupt minorities to be thrown into the shire electorates; and an addition to the representation of London and the counties.[2]

---

[1] Two Pair of Portraits presented to all the Unbiassed Electors of Great Britain, and especially to the Electors of Westminster. London. 8vo. 1788.

[2] *Parl. Hist.* XXIII. 834. See also Memorandum of Wyvill's conversation with Pitt, May 5, 1783, communicated to the Yorkshire

But the effect of the petitions was lamentably small, and the House of Commons refused even to vote directly upon the resolutions.[1] Indirectly the debate added to the misfortunes of the reformers. Sir George Savile, their wisest friend and best adviser, was very ill, but refusing to listen to the friends who urged him to stay at Rufford, he came up to town to give his support to Pitt. It was his last appearance in the House of Commons. He fainted whilst speaking and never was well again. On the 10th of January, 1784, he died in the arms of David Hartley, saying, "I have finished—I have finished well."

The reformers were not driven from their course by discouragement. "I am more and more convinced," wrote the Duke of Richmond to Colonel Sharman, one of the leaders of the Irish volunteers, in a letter which became one of the classics of reform, "that the restoring the right of voting universally to every man not incapacitated by nature for want of reason or by law for the commission of crimes, together with annual elections, is the only reform that can be effectual and permanent."[2] Pitt told the Yorkshire Association that he only awaited a seasonable opportunity to renew his propositions.[3] His opportunity was soon to come.

George III had accepted the coalition ministry with the greatest reluctance, and watched eagerly for the occasion to get rid of it. Fox's India Bill destroyed the last remnants of the cabinet's popularity, and the outcry against it showed the king that he might safely dismiss a ministry which he had always detested. After enjoying the fruits of office for little more than eight months Fox and North fell ignominiously from power. The king called upon Pitt to form an administration, and on the 19th of December, 1783, he became prime minister. To many

---

Committee, Oct. 1, 1783.—*Wyvill Papers*, IV. 2-5, and Wyvill to Pitt, May 23, 1783.—*Ib.* 6-7.

[1] 293-149. *C. J.* XXXIX. 409. List of those who voted with Pitt and text of resolutions.—*Wyvill Papers*, II. 253-7.—Debate reprinted. —*Ib.* 636-75.

[2] *S. T.* XXIV. 1048-57. Frequently printed. See a number of other letters to Sharman from English reformers in "A Collection of Letters . . ." 1783. B. M. 8145, C. 37.

[3] Pitt to Wyvill, Nov. 8, 1783.—*Wyvill Papers*, 263-4.

reformers his succession to the office vacated by Portland, the shadow-king of the coalition, seemed to herald the triumph of their principles. His success seemed like their success, and his victory to secure their victory.

The coalition of Fox and North had estranged from one another many of the friends of reform. Pitt's accession to office accentuated their differences. One section of the reformers became Pittite;[1] another section put its trust in Fox. But by far.the larger number, especially of those who cared more for an improvement of the representation than for the maintenance of party ties, had no hesitation in joining Pitt. This cleavage between Pittites and Foxites soon showed itself amongst those who had originally banded themselves together to carry economical reform. The breach was not yet complete; but it widened rapidly. On New Year's Day, 1784, the Yorkshire association met again and, in spite of all differences, renewed the petition to Parliament which it had adopted the year before.[2] But it soon became evident that the association was so sharply divided on the politics of the hour that united action was hardly to be expected again.

To many reformers Fox's India Bill had seemed to portend a revival, under a new name and in a disguised form, of the ministerial corruption against which they had so strenuously fought;[3] the man who desired the tainted wealth of the Indies to be placed at his disposal seemed to be no true reformer.[4] To some, on the other hand, Pitt appeared as the pliant agent of an unconstitutional king. On a balance, the weight of opinion appears to have favoured Pitt, and it soon appeared that amongst the Yorkshire petitioners, at least, his supporters were in a handsome majority.

Despite the opposition of the coalitionists, on the 25th of March, 1784, the Yorkshire association carried an address in favour of the dissolution of Parliament to which

[1] Wilkes, for example.—*Corr.* IV. 343 note.
[2] Adopted Jan. 1, 1784.—*Wyvill Papers*, II. 307-10. Presented Jan. 16, 1784.—*C. J.* XXXIX. 865 ; *Parl. Hist.* XXIV. 347. Pitt declared his adhesion to the principles of the petitioners, *ib.* 349.
[3] *Wyvill Papers*, IV. 9-11, 355-7, 369-72. See Pitt to Rutland, Nov. 22, 1783, in Corr. between Pitt and Rutland.
[4] Mason to Wyvill, Jan. 22, 1784, *ib.* IV. 352 ; Wyvill to Arthington, April 5, 1784, *ib.* IV. 379-80.

the Foxites were bitterly opposed, but upon which depended not merely the success, but the political existence of Pitt. "Imperfect as . . . an appeal to the Constituent Body must ever be, under the present manifold defects of our National Representation," said the addressers, "we still conceive the calling of a New Parliament to be the only true Constitutional Measure."[1] The address was not carried without hot debate. "The House of Commons," said General Hale, one of the coalitionists, "is the political Wife of the People; if my Wife behaves ill, I may correct her.: but shall I suffer another man "—the king—"to correct my Wife "—the House of Commons. "No, sir, he will debauch her."[2] Spencer Stanhope had become a Pittite, and delivered his views with his usual pungency. The coalition, the union of Fox and North, he compared to the embrace of a miller and a chimney-sweep, whereby there was formed a black-and-white, or piebald, administration.[3] Wilberforce made an eloquent speech in support of the policy of his friend Pitt.[4] But the more the associators talked about general politics, the less each section of them liked the other. During the month of March twenty-three coalitionists seceded from the association, and before the end of the year fourteen more of the hundred and fifty-three members of the association had followed their example.[5] Thereafter the association must have consisted almost exclusively of the followers of Pitt. At the general election Wyvill worked hard to secure the return, for the county of York, of Wilberforce and his Pittite colleague.[6] A subscription of £20,000 was raised to pay their election

---

[1] March 25, 1784—the actual day of the dissolution of Parliament.— *Wyvill Papers*, II. 325-7. Pitt attached great importance to this meeting. See his letter of March 23, 1784, to Rutland, in which he says that he anticipates "a hard-fought battle, though I think we shall be victorious." —*Corr. of Pitt and Rutland*, 10. It was evidently in view of this meeting that Pitt wrote the letter to Wyvill, printed from Mr. Broadley's MSS. in *Pitt and National Revival*, by Dr. Holland Rose, p. 197.

[2] *Wyvill Papers*, II. 343.   [3] *Ib.* II. 339.

[4] See debate, *ib.* 328-55.

[5] *Wyvill Papers*, IV. 320, 373-4 note, 381, 383 and note. On Jan. 11, 1786, the debts of the association amounted to £600. Part was collected, the rest paid by individual members of the committee. This looks as if the secessionists left their debts behind them.

[6] Wyvill to Pitt, April 3, 1784.—*Ib.* IV. 11-13 and note.

expenses,[1] and so sure of defeat were the coalition candidates that they did not even venture to demand a poll. In part Pitt's victory in the election of 1784 was, therefore, a reformers' victory.

We have already tried to explain the distrust of the Rockinghams felt by the parliamentary reformers. Every suspicion that they had entertained against them revived with redoubled force against Fox when he bound himself in political alliance with Lord North. In so far as the straiter Whigs had never done more than perfunctory lip-service to the widèr cause of reform, it may be said that the economical associations carried with them from birth the seeds of ultimate decay. More than this, the economical campaign, as some conceived it, had ended in victory. The Bills of Burke, of Clerke and of Crewe had been placed upon the statute book; and the battle had therefore been won. Country gentlemen whose political horizon was bounded by the land tax had nothing more to hope, because they had nothing more to gain, from further agitation. It may well be, therefore, that the vitality of the Yorkshire association was exhausted by its efforts in 1782, and that, in a certain sense, the separation of the followers of Fox from the followers of Pitt served to define an existing division rather than to create a new one.

As Pitt owed some of his success in the general election of 1784 to the support of reformers, he was soon in consultation with Wyvill about a measure of reform. Both Pitt and the reformers seem to have been confident that they were now on the eve of victory. In December 1784 Pitt gave Wyvill to understand that he would "put forth his whole power and credit *as a Man and as a Minister,* honestly and boldly to carry a plan of Reform, by which our liberties will be placed on a footing of permanent security."[2] The hopes of leading reformers began to rise.

---

[1] *Wyvill Papers*, IV. 11–13 note. Dr. Holland Rose says, however, in *Pitt and National Revival*, 170, that the total expenses of the successful candidates were less than £5000.

[2] Wyvill to Rev. Jas. Wilkinson, Dec. 9, 1784.—*Wyvill Papers*, IV. 118–19 ; see pp. 120–3, 390–2. Jebb to Cartwright, Dec. 18, 1784.—*Life of John Cartwright*, I. 161. See also Pitt to Rutland on the relation of English to Irish reform, Oct. 7, 1784.—*Corr.* 47. Wyvill's action in

Wyvill expected a severe conflict, but Pitt was undismayed and hoped to beat down all opposition, "*from whatever quarter*" it might come.[1]   "I really think," he wrote to his friend Rutland, then Lord Lieutenant of Ireland, "that I see more than ever the chance of effecting a safe and temperate plan, and I think its success as essential to the credit, if not the stability, of the present administration, as it is to the good government of the country hereafter. A meeting is summoned in Yorkshire for this business. I wish Mr. Wyvill had been a little more sparing of my name in inviting it; but I am persuaded the friends to reform there are disposed to give every countenance to what I shall bring forward . . . I think it very material, as the question is brought forward, that it should have all possible strength and credit."[2]

In 1785, therefore, it is clear that Pitt and the reformers nerved themselves for a great effort, hoping, and almost assuring themselves, that victory was at last within their grasp. Spurred on by hope, they entered with fresh confidence and enthusiasm upon a new campaign of propaganda, and sought throughout the kingdom to promote petitions to Parliament in favour of the reforms proposed by Pitt.

The meeting of the county of York, for example, to which Pitt had referred in his letter to Rutland, was duly held, and adopted a petition in his support;[3] and the city of York followed the lead of the county.[4]   Strangely enough, neither on this nor on the previous occasion did the great unrepresented towns take any share in the petitioning. Leeds and Manchester, Sheffield and Birmingham, unfortunately showed no zeal for reform.[5]   But from the county of Nottingham,[6] from Newcastle[7] and Hull,[8]

---

making Pitt's intention known was criticised as unauthorised and indiscreet.—*Wyvill Papers*, IV. 14–15 and notes.   This view is adopted by Dr. Holland Rose, *Pitt and National Revival*, 197–8.

[1] Wyvill to Mason, Jan. 1, 1785.—*Wyvill Papers*, IV. 416.   Probably an allusion to the king's dislike of reform.

[2] Pitt to Rutland, Jan. 12, 1785.—*Corr. between Pitt and Rutland*, 84.

[3] *Wyvill Papers*, II. 356–70.   Presented Feb. 14, 1785.—*C.J.* XL. 520.

[4] Feb. 25, 1785, *ib.* 566.   [5] *Wyvill Papers*, IV. 460–1 note.

[6] April 5, 1785.—*C.J.* XL. 764–5.

[7] March 21, *ib.* 747.   [8] March 21, *ib.* 748.

from Norwich [1] and Scarborough,[2] from King's Lynn [3] and from Lyme Regis,[4] from Morpeth,[5] from Yarmouth [6] and from Launceston [7] came petitions for reform. From the middle of February to the middle of April they offered to the House of Commons a constant reminder of popular dissatisfaction with the existing state of the representation.

On Monday, the 18th of April, 1785, Pitt asked leave to introduce a Reform Bill. To some, who harped on the sacred character of the Constitution, he replied by asking if the rotten boroughs that remained were more sacred than the thirty-six which had already been disfranchised.[8] When that useful political figure, the thin end of the wedge, was exhibited to confound him, he replied that "nothing was so hurtful to improvement as the fear of being carried further than the principle on which a person set out." [9]

Pitt himself never made known the details of his plan, put he permitted Wyvill to publish the heads of his proposals.[10] Wyvill called it "a plan of reformation, the most extensive and effectual, and at the same time the most mild and practicable which had been devised." [11] "The general idea of the plan," wrote Camden, "is to purchase out the small boroughs by the consent of the electors, and to add to the present number of the county representatives. But this addition only to take place gradually, as the said boroughs are extinguished by a voluntary disfranchisement." [12] A purchase fund of a million pounds was to be established and to be administered by a committee chosen on the same principle as the Grenville committee on disputed elections.[13] The fund was to accumulate till the bribe became sufficient to induce the owners of borough interests to sell out. In this way Pitt hoped to extinguish thirty-six

---

[1] March 21, *C.J.* XL. 747.   [2] March 18, *ib.* 647.   [3] April 11, *ib.* 829.
[4] March 21, *ib.* 752.   [5] April 11, *ib.* 829.
[6] March 16, *ib.* 642.   [7] March 4, *ib.* 579.
[8] *Parl. Hist.* XXV. 438 ; *i.e.* prior to the Restoration.   [9] *Ib.* 449.
[10] Wyvill's *Mem.* April 6, 1796.—*Wyvill Papers*, IV. 62–65.   Wyvill to Pitt, July 29, 1787.—*Ib.* IV. 31–40.
[11] Wyvill's *Mem.* April 6, 1796.—*Ib.* IV. 60.
[12] Grafton, *Auto.* 379.   See Stanhope's account, *Life of Pitt*, I. 256–9.
[13] *Wyvill Papers*, IV. 103–17.   *S. C. I.* reprint.—*Ib.* II. 518–24.

rotten boroughs, and thus have available seventy-two seats wherewith to increase the representation of London and Westminster, the counties and the great unrepresented towns, in a fixed order and proportion prescribed in a schedule to his Bill.[1]

Not even to this mild abridgement of electoral privileges and abuses would the House of Commons consent, and by a majority of seventy-four leave to introduce the Bill was refused.[2] Pitt never again risked his power and credit as a man and a minister in the cause of parliamentary reform.

If he really intended to adopt the vicious principle of compensation, and thereby to admit that there was, or could be, property in the representation of the people, his failure may not have been an unmixed evil.[3] But it disheartened many of his supporters.[4] Wyvill thought that a new Thatched House Tavern meeting might give new encouragement,[5] but it only revealed the divisions of the reformers. Most of the foremost advocates of reform voted for a resolution declaring that Pitt's plan, as expounded in Wyvill's summary, "would form a substantial improvement of the Constitution." Fox himself voted for the resolution; but his followers could see no good in anything that Pitt had touched, and it was defeated by a large majority.[6]

Many reformers lost heart. At the close of the year, as Wyvill tells us, "the enterprise" of agitating for a reform of Parliament was abandoned by the counties, etc., which had co-operated with the Yorkshire committee, and the dissolution of that body tacitly took place."[7] Discouraged by the failure of their hopes, the members of the Society for Constitutional Information relaxed their efforts, and for three or four years after the defeat of Pitt the

[1] *Wyvill Papers*, IV. 103-17 ; II. 518-24, 533-5 ; *Parl. Hist.* XXV. 446 note.

[2] 248-174.—*C. J.* XL. 863 ; *Parl. Hist.* XXV. 475.

[3] Wyvill defends the principle.—*Wyvill Papers*, II. 524-33. He was probably, I think, the proposer of this remedy, as he had been canvassing the question of compensation for some years.

[4] Surrey Committee, for instance, April 21, 1785.—*Ib.* II. 446-7.

[5] *Ib.* II. 451-3.

[6] May 24, 1785. Wyvill gives the division list.—*Ib.* II. 460-2. See Dr. Parr's querulous criticism of Pitt.—*Mem.* I. 227.

[7] *Wyvill Papers*, V. Advertisement to the Reader.

society sank into inactivity, from which it was only to be roused by a new wave of enthusiasm and emotion.

Nevertheless the reform movement was not dead. Several Scots counties ventured, in 1786, to petition for reform.[1] In 1786,[2] and again in 1787,[3] an inquiry into the state of the representation was moved for in the House of Commons. These proposals were defeated, but they helped to keep alive the question of reform. In 1788 it seemed for a moment as if one small but valuable change had at last been effected in the law governing elections in counties, where much confusion and delay, probably also much trickery and expense, was caused by the simple want of a list of persons qualified to vote. To supply this want Lord Mahon carried a Bill establishing electoral registers in counties.[4] But Parliament repented hastily of its virtue, and before the time at which it was to come into operation the Act was repealed.

Yet even before the French Revolution gave a sudden and powerful impetus to the reform movement, there were signs that the reformers were gradually recovering from the great disappointment of 1785. If the activities of the Society for Constitutional Information were suspended, the reality of public interest was shown, in another direction, by the increased vitality of Revolution Societies under the stimulus afforded by the centenary of the Revolution of 1688. These societies probably existed in most of the principal cities and towns of England. They were much less highly organised than the Society for Constitutional Information, for they had grown up in an informal way,

[1] Ayr, Haddington, Inverness and Linlithgow; also the town of Berwick.—*C. J.* XL. 1109-10; *Wyvill Papers*, III. 27-36. In July 1789, in the debate on a petition for the reform of the Scots burghs, Sheridan said that 52 out of 56 burghs supported it.

[2] May 18, 1786.—*C. J.* XLI. 827.

[3] May 2, 1787, *ib.* XLII. 713.

[4] 28 Geo. III. c. 36. Suspended 1789, 29 Geo. III. c. 13. Repealed 29 Geo. III. c. 18. See *Wyvill Papers*, IV. 533-52. Wyvill to Pitt, Jan. 11, 1787, *ib.* IV. 29-31 and note. The plan was abandoned on the ground of expense. But this must have been an excuse. The registers could have been compiled readily enough, for the most part, from the returns of persons assessed to the land tax and from the returns of free-holders between the ages of twenty-one and seventy, liable to serve on juries, which were already deposited annually with the Clerks to the County Justices.

and though they were, for the most part, supported by men
of popular sympathies, parliamentary reform was not their
immediate object. Up and down the country sets of people
had formed the habit of dining together, year by year, on
the 4th or 5th of November [1] to celebrate the revolution of
1688. These festivals were arranged by the committees
which, in England, arise spontaneously whenever it seems
good to us to celebrate such an occasion by the melancholy
pleasure of a public dinner. But in some places clubs
sprang up to charge themselves with the permanence of
the institution. Such, for example, was the Revolution
Club founded in 1782 at Leicester.

Formed for the purpose of "uniting the independent
interest of the town and county . . . preserving the freedom of election, and maintaining the other rights and
franchises of the burgesses and others," the society was
to defend them against "any oppression or invasion they
might suffer from the undue exertions of misplaced power
or the venal influence of the enemies of freedom." [2] This
was doubtless a manifestation of that sympathy with the
economy campaign, which the close corporation of the
borough, one of the most corrupt in England,[3] did its
best to stifle. Indeed, there followed a harmless rivalry
of political dinners. The seven hundred gentlemen of town
and county who met, in 1788, to celebrate the centenary of
the revolution, and to toast the memory of King William III,[4] carried a resolution "that this town is improperly
represented in Parliament." [5] The Mayor replied with a
civic feast,[6] and in 1789 the "Church and King" party
formed a Constitutional Society and again manifested itself
by a dinner; only to be outdone by those of the "Independent Interest," who dined together in overwhelming
numbers.[7] After the outbreak of the French Revolution

---

[1] According as they chose to celebrate it on William III's birthday
or on the day of his landing at Torbay. It was said that Nonconformists
met on the 4th and Churchmen on the 5th, but this does not appear to be
borne out by the evidence.

[2] Thompson, *Leicester in the Eighteenth Century*, 77-8.

[3] S. and B. Webb, *English Local Government:* The Manor and the
Borough, 475-81.

[4] Thompson, *Leicester in the Eighteenth Century*, 191.

[5] *Ib.* 192.   [6] *Ib.* 193.   [7] *Ib.* 194-7.

the Leicester Revolution Club was reorganised, and subscribed the doctrine of the rights of man; [1] but the discredit into which the revolutionary cause fell during the
succeeding years caused the club to melt away, and it never
met after the year 1792. It is a probable surmise, though
from the badness of local histories nothing more than a
surmise, that the story of the rise and fall of the Revolution
Club at Leicester is typical of the history of many clubs
in other towns and cities. [2]

In Birmingham parties were less acutely divided than
at Leicester. It is evident that the famous Book Club and
the Library had for years furnished in fact, though not in
name, a political association for men of liberal thought. [3]
But in 1788, the centennial year of the revolution, the
celebrations were of a semi-official and non-party character. The advertisement of a great public dinner was
signed by the High Bailiff—usually an Anglican—as well
as by the Low Bailiff — usually a Nonconformist. [4]
Amongst those present at the dinner were the High Sheriff
of the county, the justices of the county Sessions, and the
representatives of the county in Parliament. Most of the
company appeared in blue coats, with orange capes, and
"emblematical buttons," and at least eighteen toasts were
drunk, the full number being veiled by a discreet etcetera. [5]
In consequence of these celebrations an Annual Revolution
Union Club was formed under the auspices of the High
Bailiff, [6] but either on account of its semi-official character,
or, as in the case of Leicester, in consequence of the effects
of the French Revolution, the club does not appear to have
aroused any sustained enthusiasm or to have been of long
continuance.

All over the country the centenary of the Revolution
of 1688 was celebrated "with uncommon festivity." [7] In

---

[1] Thompson, *Leicester in the Eighteenth Century*, 197. Thompson
saw the minute-book, but I have not been able to discover it.

[2] Inference from occasional references to dinners, etc.

[3] J. A. Langford, *A Century of Birmingham Life* (1868), I. 57–8.

[4] The advertisement (Oct. 27, 1788), is printed by Langford, *ib.* I.
421–2.

[5] Newspaper cutting, ap. Langford, I. 422–5.   [6] *Ib.* I. 422–5.

[7] *Ib.* I. 422. Probably a difference of opinion in the matter of chron-
ology accounts for the fact that at Bristol exceptional rejoicings appear

London anniversary dinners were held by seven important clubs and many lesser ones. Chief amongst these was the London Revolution Society,[1] whose members were roused, in the enthusiasm of the moment, to undertake the more adequate organisation of the friends of liberty. The society decided to formulate its principles, and, apparently for the first time, to make a definite enrolment of its members;[2] and it was as a result of this revival that the Revolution Society found itself in a sufficiently organised condition to undertake the task of correspondence which its French admirers were soon to thrust upon it.

Constitution, in the strict sense, the Revolution Society never had. It had officers and a committee, subsequently a committee of correspondence, but it met irregularly, and so little is known about its membership that it is not possible to say with certainty whether the members of one period were, or were not, the members of another. The cardinal article of its political creed was a belief in the sovereignty of the people. The rights of private judgment, liberty of conscience, trial by jury, freedom of the Press and freedom of election were declared sacred and inviolable, whilst the abuse of power was held to justify resistance.[3] This declaration was adopted by the Cambridgeshire Constitutional Society as its own, and a correspondence with the London Revolutionary Society shows that both associations cherished ardent hopes of exerting, during the general election which must soon be upon them, an influence potent for their cause.[4]

It is undeniable, therefore, that the reform movement flagged considerably, and in some respects disastrously, after the failures of Pitt and Wyvill. They had come

to have taken place not in 1788, but in 1789. The 4th of Nov., 1789, "being the anniversary of the Glorious Revolution," was celebrated with unexampled rejoicing by the corporation, and £177 11s. 8d. was expended by the chamberlain, chiefly for liquor.—John Latimer, *The Annals of Bristol in the Eighteenth Century* (1893), 487.

[1] *Ann. Reg.* 1788, p. 220 ; cf. *Add. MSS.* 27837, ff. 47, 76 ; 27839, fo. 110.

[2] *An Abstract of the History and Proceedings of the Revolution Society in London.* The annual subscription was half-a-guinea.

[3] *Ib.* 14-15 ; *Proceedings of Nov. 4, 1789*, p. 8 ; *Corr. of the Rev. Soc.* 1-2.   [4] *Ib.* 34-7.

within a handsbreadth of success, and to their followers the disappointment of defeat was both keen and unexpected. But it is also true that the courage of the reformers speedily revived. It was in a mood of buoyant hopefulness that they celebrated the centenary of the Revolution. Where the Revolution Societies were most clearly identified with the cause of reform, as at Leicester, as in London, there it is plain that they were throbbing with life and energy. At Birmingham, on the contrary, where the celebrations were little more than a civic tribute to Bacchus, and where reforming opinions had probably another and a better outlet, the Annual Revolution Club, unsustained by the enthusiasm for reform, proved neither lasting nor effective. All over England the enthusiasm for the centenary of 1688 was strongest and most genuine amongst those whose zeal for constitutional liberty and constructive reform at home made them ready and eager to welcome a movement such as, in its earlier phases, the French Revolution appeared to be, for extending the same advantages to the people of another land. Men like Cartwright, who still hoped in 1789 that Pitt might do "somewhat great and good"[1] for the reform of the representation in England, had minds prepared for the stir and stimulus afforded by the knowledge that constitutional enthusiasts abroad were looking to England for their models and seeking zealously to improve upon them. If the French constitutionalists sought to borrow experience from England, the English reformers were willing, and indeed eager, to receive a new inspiration from France.

[1] Cartwright to the Rt. Hon. Thomas Steele.—*Life of C.*, I. 180. Cartwright hoped for nothing from the Foxites.

CHAPTER V

ROUSED into new life and activity, after the deep sleep
of a century and three-quarters, the States-General of
France met, for the first time since 1614, on the 5th of
May, 1789. Unlike the princess of the fairy tale who arose
from her long slumber with features unchanged and with
the bloom still fresh upon her cheeks, the States-General
awoke in a changed France and a changed world, to find
itself no longer the same. Its very constitution and mode
of election had been forgotten. Its powers were uncertain.
It had to meet new needs in novel circumstances. From
the weak and broken tradition of the old States-General
there was to be had neither help nor inspiration. The
sound constitutional tradition was of later growth, and it
was not French, but English. In 1614, when the work of
the old States-General was suspended, James I was still
bickering with Parliament and haggling over finance. The
future of parliamentary government in England was still
so far from being secure that almost a quarter of a century
later Clarendon thought a little more restraint and discretion on the part of Charles I and his advisers might
have enabled them to turn unparliamentary government
into a permanent success. The events of the seventeenth
century had brought about a tremendous change. Government in England had been securely settled on a parliamentary basis, and though time had revealed some flaws
in the machinery, and experience had proved the necessity
for an improvement of the electoral system, nevertheless
the representative institutions of England, together with
their American modifications, offered to French legislators

the models which they might adapt, and upon which they might perhaps improve, to meet the needs of their own country. Disputes as to its origin and doubts as to its powers at once involved the States-General in a tangle of difficulties. The Constitution of 1614, even if it could have been accurately ascertained, would have been unworkable in the France of 1789, and new forms of government had to be devised to meet the needs of a new time. On the 16th of June, therefore, the representatives of the third estate, with some of the clergy and a few nobles, formed themselves into a National Assembly, and began to grapple with the task of constitutional reconstruction. For two years, down to the day in June 1791 when the king, declining any longer to be a partner in the enterprise, tried to escape from France to its enemies beyond the frontier, the National Assembly and its successor, the Constituent Assembly, were occupied in a sedulous attempt to hammer out some form of constitutional government under a limited monarchy that might be acceptable both to the people and to the king. The process was more than once influenced and interrupted by scenes of excitement and violence, which some found alarming; but the years, broadly speaking, were years of industrious reconstruction, during which the French tried to walk in the paths of constitutional progress which their English neighbours had trodden out before them. Down to the 21st of June, 1791, Louis XVI was still "the Father of his People," and his people, with England for their example, were framing anew the machinery of government in such fashion as to engage the warmest sympathies of those Englishmen who were most concerned for the improvement of their own constitutional inheritance.

Though the men who were seeking to reconstruct the government of France owed much to England, the French Revolution, in its turn, had a tremendous influence upon English politics. It was, in particular, to transform the whole character of the movement for parliamentary reform. For with it there came a touch of flame, firing the minds both of friends and foes. To the reformers the French example was a new stimulus, stirring them to fresh enthusiasm. A strong practical strain, indeed, runs through all the English advocacy of reform. The reformers were more like the guardians of some venerable cathedral, restoring it stone by stone as it fell into decay, than architects with a new vision, which they were in haste to realise. They never ceased to be guided by this practical sense in formulating their proposals of reform, but the French Revolution led them to base more and more upon claims of abstract right and justice the arguments by which these proposals were defended. They spoke less of convenience and more of justice. And, in this sense, the "practical school" may be said to have suffered temporary eclipse. A section of the governing class, on the Whig side, caught the infection of the new ideas, and was converted to reforming zeal. The Revolution, therefore, brought the reformers an immediate addition to their numerical strength, and gave them a new propagandist doctrine which far excelled the old in dynamic force.

The Revolution brought inspiration to the friends of reform, both old and new. But there was another side to the shield. It also provoked fresh opposition and intensified the alarm of old opponents. Of one section of the governing class the Revolution made zealous reformers; in the rest of the governing class it produced a violent reaction, leading to the repression of the reformers and robbing the movement of its vigour for the space of a generation. Nevertheless, dark as the prospect seemed in the years of repression and reaction, the general effect of the Revolution was healthy. It stirred the minds of men. However severe and prolonged the backwash of reaction, their thoughts could never be again as they were before 1789. When at last a Reform Bill was carried, it was a better Bill than Pitt's. The difference is clearly illustrated by the omission from the Reform Act of one vital provision of the Bill of 1785. The Reform Act provided no compensation for borough-owners. Their claims to a property in the representation were no longer respected, for the ideas which the Revolution had forced, not merely upon its friends, but upon its enemies, had rendered the old demands inadmissible, even in the eyes of the majority of the borough-mongers themselves. This view that, despite all drawbacks, the French Revolution exerted a healthy influence upon political thought, acting as the solvent of bad traditions, clarifying knowledge and stimulating reflection, is set forth by Francis Place in a political retrospect which is interesting and suggestive, even though Place draws too dark a picture of the apathy which preceded the Revolution in order to bring out more clearly its stimulating effect upon political opinion. When Pitt came to power, he says, there was no public, but only politicians. "The French Revolution produced a great change. It induced men to look beyond mere party squabbles. It taught them to despise the jugglery of parties. . . . The numbers, too, which now began to think for themselves in respect to government was increased. Many now saw, or thought they saw, information was necessary to produce good government. They comprehended their own ignorance and they sought for information." Pitt, in so far as he resisted and restrained this impulse, "warred against knowledge." [1] But the appetite for political knowledge and political power is healthy, and had ultimately to be satisfied.

At first, in the period covered by this chapter, the effects of the Revolution upon opinion in England were not, on the whole, unfavourable to reform. The governing class was not yet openly hostile, as appears clearly enough from the first opinions of Pitt and the king. Pitt, who had been but once upon the Continent in his life, viewed the first event of the Revolution with as cold and calculating a detachment as if he had learnt diplomacy at the feet of Kaunitz.[2] He saw France only as a disabled competitor, "an object of compassion even to a rival." [3] Yet even he could not resist a momentary and qualified enthusiasm. "The present convulsions of France," he said, "must sooner

[1] *Add. MSS.* 27809, ff. 41–3 ; cf. 43–5. As the foregoing narrative shows, Place under-estimated the extent of political knowledge and the independence of political thought prior to Revolution.

[2] Pitt to Strafford, Sept. 6, 1788.—Rose's *Diaries*, I. 85.

[3] To Lady Chatham, July 14, 1789.—Stanhope's *Pitt*, I. 349. The French were suspicious that the English ministry might take advantage of France's distractions to do her injury. See dispatches of July 23 and 31, and Aug. 3, 1789, ap. Sorel, II. 30, note 4.

or later terminate in general harmony and regular order."
Once freedom based on good order and good government
had been won, "France would stand forward as one of the
most brilliant Powers in Europe." "Nor can I regard with
envious eyes," he continued, "any approximation in
neighbouring States to those sentiments which are characteristic of every British subject."[1] No one, as Lord Morley
has observed, needs so often as the politician to say the
prayer not to be led into temptation.

George III was at first torn by conflicting feelings :
delight at the disturbance of a rival State, and exasperation
at the difficulties of a king ; with more dexterity than consistency he succeeded in rejoicing at the disaster to the
French monarchy, because it was French, and at the same
time in feeling a certain pity for the woes of the French
king, because he was a fellow monarch.   His opinions
rapidly swung over to the side of the king when he realised
that the interests of monarchy in general were as deeply
involved as the particular interests of the monarch of
France.   But almost the sole sensible remark that is to be
credited to the French ambassador, de la Luzerne, is that,
whatever the private sympathies of the king might be, he
would act in this case on the advice of his ministers.[2] So
far as policy was concerned, Pitt and the king would be
at one.

Cautious and reflecting politicians like Grenville, the
Secretary for Foreign Affairs—afterwards, indeed, to be
swept along unresisting in the race of political reaction—
looked on with the placid content of some petty tradesman
who sees his rival's premises destroyed by fire ;[3] and his
view was typical of the prevailing orthodoxy.[4]   Whilst he

---

[1] Feb. 9, 1790.—Stanhope, I. 357-8.   Pitt realised that foreign inter-
vention would unite the French and check their enemies.—Rapport
de Barthélemy, Sept. 1, 1789 ; ap. Sorel, II. 30. Suspicion of England was
constant.   See dispatches of Sept. 9 and 29, 1789, etc.—*Ib.* II. 29-30 and
notes.

[2] Rapport de la Luzerne, Sept. 22, 1789 ; ap. Sorel, II. 29.   Rapport
de la Luzerne, Jan. 9 and March 5, 1790.—*Ib.* II. 29.

[3] W. W. Grenville to Lord Buckinghamshire, Sept. 14, 1789.—*Courts
and Cabinets of Geo. III*, II. 165.   Lord Mornington (Wellesley) seems
first to have excited Grenville's fear of the French, Sept. 27, 1790.—
H. M. C. Rep. XIII. App. III. 608-9.

[4] *Mem. of Romilly*, I. 404 ; Windham, *Diary*, 184.

bore the Revolution no active ill-will, it was a cause for which he could feel no enthusiasm. Others were shrewder, and, like Pitt, saw further. "Succeed in your Revolution," said Shelburne (now Marquess of Lansdown) to Luzerne, "and you will be strong and powerful enough of yourselves to lay down the law to Europe." [1]

At first, therefore, the ruling class was not greatly alarmed by the Revolution, and was disposed to underrate rather than over-rate its European importance. But it was quite willing to make the disturbances in France an excuse for resisting reform at home. The usefulness of the Revolution as a bogey emerged plainly when new proposals of reform were brought forward in the House of Commons on the eve of the general election of 1790.

Henry Flood, one of the greatest of Irish orators, took up the cause which Pitt had abandoned, and moved that "Leave be given to bring in a Bill for amending the Representation of the People in Parliament." [2] The House, he said, was a useful and honourable council which "in any other Government of Europe would be a great acquisition." But the British Constitution entitled them to expect something better; and better the House of Commons could not be unless "freely and frequently elected by the body of the people." [3] He argued in favour of the representative principle, upon which, however, he put the most cautious interpretation. "I admit that property, to a certain degree, is a necessary ingredient to the elective power; that is to say, that franchise ought not to go beyond property; but at the same time to say that it ought to be as nearly commensurate to it as possible." [4] He desired, therefore, an increase in the number of constituents, subject to two conditions: "one, that they should be numerous enough, because numbers are necessary to the spirit of liberty; the other, that they should have a competent degree of pro-

---

[1] Rapport de la Luzerne, Jan. 15, 1790.—*Corr. d'Angleterre*, ap. Sorel, II. 26–7.

[2] March 4, 1790.—*C. J.* XLV. 226.

[3] *Parl. Hist.* XXVIII. 454; *Original Letters, principally from Lord Charlemont . . . to Henry Flood:* 4to, 1820 (Flood's speech is given as an appendix); 182.

[4] *Parl. Hist.* XXVIII. 455; *Original Letters*, 183.

perty, because that is conducive to the spirit of order."[1]
These ends he hoped to attain by adding to the House of
Commons a hundred members, "to be elected by a
numerous and a new body of responsible electors, namely,
the resident householders in every county,"—those whom
Flood regarded as substantial men.[2] Apparently the
qualification was to extend only to those resident householders who paid a minimum of 50s. per annum in scot
and lot (in church rate and poor rate);[3] and also, it would
seem, though it is not plain, that Flood intended to establish new and distinct constituencies, electing members on
the new franchise, alongside of the existing county constituencies, which were to continue to elect their members
according to the old.

To the objection that an additional hundred members
would make the House too numerous, he replied, "Then
deprive a hundred decayed boroughs of one member each."
Flood did not himself propose such a change, but he was
ready to accept it, if members thought that there was any
reality in the objection that an increased membership
would make the House of Commons unwieldy.[4]

A further reform that Flood proposed, small but not
unimportant, was that instead of having elections lasting
over several days, there should be a polling-place in each
parish, and that, in each constituency, the election should
begin and end on the same day.[5]

It was already objected by some people, especially by
people who were opposed to reform in any case and on any
occasion, that a time of convulsion in France was no time
for reform in England. "It is only from want of a timely
and temperate reform," replied Flood, "that these evils
have come upon France. They could not begin with
reparation in France: there was nothing to repair; they
could not begin the[6] ruin: they found ruin accomplished

---

[1] *Parl. Hist.* XXVIII. 456; *Original Letters*, 184.
[2] *Parl. Hist.* XVIII. 460; *Original Letters*, 189.
[3] Flood hints at this but is not explicit. It appears more plainly
from Pitt's speech.—*Parl. Hist.* XXVIII. 470.
[4] *Ib.* 463; *Original Letters*, 192.
[5] *Ib.* 193; *Parl. Hist.* XXVIII. 464.
[6] Both reports read "begin with ruin": "with" must, I take it, be a
misprint for "the."

to their hands."[1] "I am no friend to revolutions, because they are an evil; I am, therefore, a friend to timely reform, and for this reason, that it renders revolutions unnecessary; whilst those who oppose reform may be enemies to revolution in their hearts, but they are friends to it by their folly."[2]

Perhaps Flood did not expect to gain a direct victory. His proposal seems to have been intended, in part, at least, as a tactical movement to pledge Pitt and Fox to the cause of reform on the eve of the expected election.[3] Flood held that he had succeeded in obtaining the desired pledges.[4] Fox made a wriggling speech, but promised to vote with Flood.[5] Pitt professed to maintain his old opinion still and to intend one day to introduce a new Reform Bill, but he said that the time was not one for reform, that he would vote against his own Bill if it were proposed at that moment, and that, for the present, he would move an adjournment of the question.[6]

It was during this debate that Windham made his famous speech against reform during revolution. "What!" he said, in a foolish phrase which has been quoted with gleeful approbation by modern historians, "Would he recommend you to repair your house in the hurricane season?"[7] "When," it might have been replied, "would there be more temptation to restore a house that had fallen into disrepair than during the hurricane season—assuming, of course, that the occupant had been so improvident and so disregardful of advice as not to overhaul his dwelling earlier?" Would Windham have preferred to nurse his sorrows in inactivity whilst the rain pattered through a broken roof and the wind swayed the creaking timbers? But it mattered little whether arguments were sound or unsound; the House of Commons had prejudged the case and would have none of Flood's Reform Bill. Pitt's motion for an adjournment seems to have been carried without a division.[8]

---

[1] *Parl. Hist.* XXVIII. 455–6; *Original Letters*, 184.
[2] *Parl. Hist.* XVIII. 456; *Original Letters*, 185.
[3] *Original Letters*, 195, 197.   [4] *Parl. Hist.* XXVIII. 474.
[5] *Ib.* 471–2.   [6] *Ib.* 469–70.   [7] *Ib.* 467.
[8] *C. J.* XLV. 226. For the debate, in addition to the authorities cited, see *Wyvill Papers*, II. 536.

The members of the House of Commons made the Revolution in France an excuse for opposing a reform which they wanted, in any circumstances, to reject. In other respects, also, the year 1790, to which the reformers had looked forward with hope, proved a year of disappointment. An attempt to revive the county associations proved unsuccessful.[1] In the middle of a scorching June Parliament was dissolved,[2] and the country was involved in the expected general election. But again the reformers, who had hoped to make some impression, were disappointed by the small number of contested elections.[3] Excitement, nevertheless, rose high : but in was in Westminster, where the electorate was of the most popular kind then known, that it reached high-water mark. Long famous for its association with the name of Charles James Fox, the constituency of Westminster deserves to be remembered, along with Sheridan's at Stafford,[4] as amongst the most bribable in England. A contest there was costly, and Fox was none too rich. To avoid expense he had agreed to compromise the election with Hood, the Tory candidate.[5] "Mr. Fox," said the *Times*, "to do him justice, continues *to give his advice gratis,* but is determined, he says, never to break through the little fortune he has acquired with so much industry, integrity and economy." [6] The witty innuendo was doubtless near the truth; Fox could ill afford to fight.

There was no prospect of a contest until Horne Tooke presented himself as a candidate to prevent what he described as the disfranchisement of Westminster. Factions, he said, were dangerous, but coalitions fatal; he therefore relied on "a public both able and willing to teach its Government that it has other and more important duties

---

[1] *Wyvill Papers,* II. 564-70 ; V. i–iii.

[2] Dissolved by proclamation, June 12, 1790. On the heat of the summer, see *Ann. Reg.* 1790, *Chron.* 209.

[3] Mr. Jephson, in his *History of the Platform,* is inclined to minimise the importance of the election on this account. But this seems to be a Foxite view. It should, in any case, be remembered that the Westminster contest was most important as indicating the line along which progress was to be made.

[4] See Fraser Rae's *Sheridan,* I. 354-5.

[5] *Add. MSS.* 27849, fo. 130.

[6] Cutting from the *Times.—Add. MSS.* 27837, fo. 37.

to perform besides the levying of taxes, creation of Peer-
ages, compromising of Counties and arrangement of
Boroughs." [1] Tooke stood as a parliamentary reformer [2]
and did not buy a vote.

"Now how do I retire?" he asked, after his defeat at
the polls. "With sixteen hundred and seventy-nine
awakened and approving electors who are neither to be
influenced by hope or by fear, by Administration or Opposition." [3] He petitioned against the return, [4] and afterwards
refused to pay the costs, which were so heavy that it would,
he said, have been cheaper to have been impeached—
although acquitted, Hastings had just been ruined by an
impeachment—or to have been convicted of crime. The
attention which the public bestowed, first upon the Westminster election and secondly upon Tooke's defence, when
Fox was obliged to sue him for his costs, is important as
an index of the growth of popular interest in political
questions.

"The trial of the cause," wrote Francis Place long
afterwards, when his own genius for organisation had
enabled reformers to reap the harvest for which Tooke had
sown, "produced a great sensation not only in Westminster, but all over the country, and had another election
occurred previous to the alarm which ministers soon afterwards excited, and before the State Trials of 1794, the
probability is that Mr. Tooke would have broken the power
of the aristocratical conspiracy and would have been
elected free from all expense to him, as Sir Francis Burdett
afterwards, in 1807, was elected." [5] Disappointment, therefore, held a core of promise. Horne Tooke's failure
pointed the way to possible success.

Meantime the influence of the French Revolution was
working transformations among the Whigs. It did not
influence all in the same way, but to many, especially of
the younger men, it seemed like the coming of a new age

[1] *Add. MSS.* 27849, ff. 130-1 ; also 27837, ff. 37-45.
[2] It is claimed that he failed to extract from Fox any pledge in favour
of reform.—*Mem. of Horne Tooke*, II. 92-9.
[3] *Add. MSS.* 27849, fo. 135.
[4] *Mem. of Horne Tooke*, II. 92-9.
[5] *Add. MSS.* 27849, fo. 163.

of hope and promise, and it roused their wildest enthusiasm. Fox himself was deeply stirred. "How much the greatest event it is that ever happened in the world! and how much the best!"[1] he wrote, in a famous phrase, on the capture of the Bastille, which in common with most men, then and since, he regarded not as the strategic movement for the defence of Paris that it really was, but as a symbol of victorious liberty in France, such as the acquittal of the seven bishops had been in England. Romilly, famous for his efforts to repeal the barbarous old criminal code, was then an enthusiastic young barrister. He was as eager to read the foreign gazettes "as if the preservation of our liberties depended upon the recovery of those of France."[2] This first outburst of enthusiasm was very general. All the papers joined in it;[3] and though fervour soon declined, it was enough to excite minds already ardent to hope great things of a time when the day-star of progress seemed to be already high in the ascendant.[4]

It would be easy to put too high an estimate on the value of Whig enthusiasm. Fox, for example, was never a real reformer; nor, as the story of the Westminster election of 1790 plainly shows, was he trusted by those who regarded reform as the first object of sound policy. But other Whigs were influenced, opinion was advancing, and sympathy with the reformers was growing amongst the younger members of the party.

On the other hand, opinion amongst Whigs of the school of Burke was developing in the reverse direction. Their suspicions of the Revolution grew as it progressed, and their distrust of any organic change in our representative institutions was correspondingly increased. At the outset Burke himself seems to have felt an admiration for the revolutionists greater than he quite cared to confess. But from the beginning his admiration was tinged with

[1] To Fitzpatrick, July 30, 1789.—*Mem. of C. J. Fox*, II. 341.
[2] Oct. 14, 1788, *Mem. of Romilly*, I. 338; July 28, 1789, *ib.* I. 356. See 369, 389-90, 400, 409-10.
[3] According to Romilly, *ib.* I. 356.
[4] Oct. 24, 1789, *ib.* 369; Rapport de Londres, Sept. 1, 1789, *Corr. d'Angleterre*, ap. Sorel, II. 27.

doubt. A letter which he wrote to Charlemont a week after
Fox had pronounced the fall of the Bastille to be the
greatest and best event that had ever happened in the
world shows plainly that admiration was still battling with
distrust in Burke's mind, but already he had begun to fear
that the French were unfit for liberty and needed the strong
hand of a master to control them.[1] Fear rapidly mastered
sympathy, and by September 1789 he had probably begun
to work upon the first draft of his *Reflections on the French
Revolution*. He carried with him a considerable section
of his party, which gradually crystallised as a distinct
school of Whiggism, and separated itself from the followers
of Fox. The friends of Burke, though there were important
men amongst them, were not numerous enough to be a
great obstacle to the reformers until the publication of the
Reflections in the beginning of November 1790. The
Reflections won converts to Burke's way of thinking, and
it made definite and irreparable the split in the Whig
party. But the schism was not without advantages to the
reformers. It meant that a substantial section of the
Whigs was freed from the trammels which had been
imposed upon it by its alliance with men who clung to the
traditions of the old Rockingham connection, who were
opposed to organic change and inaccessible to new ideas.
Released from this deadening restraint, the Foxites were
to some extent liberalised, and were free to give more
cordial support to the plans of the reformers.

Outside the ranks of organised parties, the beginnings
of the Revolution were welcomed with glad enthusiasm.
There was a glow of hope amongst the poets.[2] Burns
imperilled his chances of promotion in the excise by the
ardour with which he espoused the cause of the revolutionists. Wordsworth's interest did not fully ripen till
1792, but there can be no doubt as to the direction of his
sympathies. Southey, a school-boy at Westminster, steep-
ing his mind in Rousseau, followed the new opinions with

[1] Aug. 9, 1789.—Prior, 295.
[2] The subject has been treated, from different points of view, by Prof.
Charles Cestre, of Bordeaux, in his *Révolution française et les Poètes
Anglais*, 1789-1809 : Dijon, 1906 ; and by Prof. Dowden in his Lowell
Lectures : *The French Revolution and English Literature :* London, 1897.

ardour. Coleridge, at Christ's Hospital, wrote an ode on the destruction of the Bastille, weak in music, but strong in political enthusiasm. It was natural enough that school-boys and undergraduates should be attracted by the glamour of the Revolution. But its influence on William Cowper, in whom there was no predisposition to revolu-tionary opinions, is really much more striking. The impact of the new ideas must have been tremendous, or they could never have moved as they did the mind of a conservative recluse, well past middle life, like Cowper. He thought, for example, that differences of rank were "of God's appointment, and consequently essential to the well-being of society ";[1] yet to him the time of revolution appeared to be "a wonderful period in the history of mankind," so wonderful that only the special interposition of Providence could account for it. "That nations so long contentedly slaves should on a sudden become enamoured of liberty, and understand, as suddenly, their own natural right to it, feeling themselves at the same time inspired with a resolu-tion to assert it, seems difficult to account for from natural causes."[2] "I have seen the reception of the news of the victory of Waterloo and of the carrying of the Reform Bill," wrote one contemporary, in retrospect, "but I never saw joy comparable in its vivid intensity to that occasioned by the early promise of the French Revolution."[3]

It was only natural that avowed reformers should be delighted at a turn of events which seemed to promise the development of representative institutions in a neighbour-ing country. Cartwright, for example, lost no time before congratulating the States-General on the prospect of con-stitutional government in France; and at once put himself into competition with the constitution-mongers of France

---

[1] Cowper to Lady Hesketh, July 7, 1790.—*Letters*, III. 474.
[2] To Joseph Hill, Dec. 18, 1789.—*Ib.* III. 411.
[3] *Auto. of Mrs. Schimmel Penninck*, I. 217-18. She relates how Harry Priestley broke in upon them one night waving his hat and crying—"Hurrah ! Liberty, Reason, and brotherly love for ever ! Down with kingcraft and priestcraft. The Majesty of the People for ever ! France is free, the Bastille is taken ; William was there and helping."—*Ib.* I. 217. If Harry Priestley ever delivered this domestic oration which, for an impromptu, looks uncommonly well prepared, his opinions were much in advance of those of the French in July 1789.

by offering some observations on constitutional questions in general, and on the necessity for frequent Parliaments and free elections in particular. He cherished the hope that the two nations, France and England, might "run the race of glory" together,[1] but he was no apologist for mob-rule or the abuse of historical "landmarks."[2] Neither was the republican Godwin, the teacher of the poet Shelley,[3] for Godwin abhorred politics that were based upon sentiment and emotion instead of upon reason, as steadfastly as he believed that not even God himself had the right to be a tyrant.[4] But his heart "beat high with great swelling sentiments of liberty."[5] A cautious Scots lawyer like Erskine was, fortunately for the reformers, whom he afterwards defended against the charge of treason, caught up by the same contagious enthusiasm, and a short stay in France converted him into a violent democrat.[6]

Upon the political societies interested in reform the Revolution had an enormous influence. A whole crop of new societies presently sprang up. The old ones revived. The Society for Constitutional Information was galvanised into new life. But first and most notable was the effect produced by events in France upon the Revolution Societies which alone had emerged from the previous period in vigorous activity, and it is in the history of the Revolution Society of London that this influence is most important and can be most plainly traced. Its members were men naturally disposed to welcome the advance of liberty in any country, and the Revolution in France aroused their warmest enthusiasm. When the society met on the 4th of November, 1789, Dr. Price, already celebrated as a divine, as the friend of America, and as the inventor of the famous theory of the sinking fund, gained fresh notoriety

---

[1] May 18, 1789, *Life of Cartwright*, I. 185.   [2] *Ib.* 186.
[3] There is an interesting study of Godwin in Dowden, *The French Revolution and English Literature*, 47–76.
[4] Quoted from the sermons called *Historical Sketches.* Kegan Paul. *William Godwin and his Friends*, I. 100.   [5] *Ib.* I. 61.
[6] *Mem. of Romilly*, I. 408, at the date Sept. 25, 1790. Romilly must be wrong in stating that Erskine threatened to wear the uniform of the Jacobins in the House of Commons. The Jacobins never had a "uniform." If the "bonnet rouge" is meant, that was not in use till 1792.

by moving a resolution in which the French Revolution was hailed as the herald of a better day for European liberty.

"The Society for commemorating the Revolution in Great Britain," ran the address—which was adopted unanimously — "disdaining national partialities and rejoicing in every triumph of Liberty and Justice over Arbitrary Power, offer to the National Assembly of France their Congratulations on the Revolution in that country and on the prospect it gives to the two first Kingdoms in the World of a common participation in the blessings of Civil and Religious Liberty.

"They cannot help adding their ardent wishes of an happy settlement of so important a Revolution, and at the same time expressing the particular satisfaction with which they reflect on the tendency of the glorious example given in France to encourage other Nations to assert the *unalienable* rights of Mankind, and thereby to introduce a general reformation in the government of Europe, and to make the World Free and Happy." [1]

Godwin also composed an address, which apparently was never sent, in which the fact was emphasised that the Revolution Society, being no more than an aggregation of private individuals, spoke only for itself, and could not "pretend to the authority of being the organ of the national sentiment" : [2] nor is there reason to suppose that the society ever made any larger claim for itself.

Price's address to the National Assembly of France was sent, and was accepted as a token of international goodwill. [3] In a personal letter to the Duc de la Rochefoucauld, Price himself insisted on the "zeal in the general cause of public liberty " of the distinguished assembly [4] which had

---

[1] *Proceedings of the Rev. Soc.* Nov. 4, 1789, pp. 10-11 ; *Corr. of the Rev. Soc.* (hereafter *C. R. S.*), p. 3 ; *Procès-Verbaux de l'Assemblée nationale* (hereafter *P.-V.*), Nov. 25, 1789, p. 15 ; *New Ann Reg.* 1789, *Public Papers*, 126-7.
[2] *Godwin and his Friends*, I, 62-3. See also Dr. Joseph Towers, *Thoughts on the Commencement of a New Parliament* (Appendix called " Remarks on the Letter of the Rt. Hon. Edmund Burke on the Revolution in France"), pp. 73-4.   [3] *P.-V.* Nov. 25, 14 ; *C. R. S.* p. 4.
[4] The Lord Mayor of London and several members of Parliament were present.

adopted it. "The representatives of France," he said, "labour for the world as much as for themselves, and the whole world is interested in their success." [1]

Rochefoucauld presented the address on the 25th of November. The National Assembly was deeply touched, and received it with great applause. In reply the president was directed to express the "lively and deep sensibility with which the National Assembly of France receive the Address of the Revolution Society in England which breathes those sentiments of universal benevolence that ought to unite together in all countries of the World the true friends of Liberty and of the happiness of Mankind." [2] Accordingly the Archbishop of Aix replied that "a King whom we may call *the best* of Men and the first of Citizens encouraged by his virtues the hope of the Nation, and now by universal concurrence a durable Constitution is established founded on the unalienable rights of Men and Citizens."

That age of reason and liberty was, he continued, to see the extinction of international hate. "We must not allow the prejudices which disgrace nations to produce wars, those *errors* of government. But the two most enlightened peoples of Europe ought to show, by their example, that the love of their country is perfectly compatible with every sentiment of humanity." [3] These principles of universal benevolence the archbishop discovered in the address of the Revolution Society, and they were characteristic of the international correspondence which ensued.

"It belonged to that great Apostle of Liberty, Dr. Price," wrote Rochefoucauld,[4] "to propose a motion tend-

[1] Retranslated from the French version of the letter, *P.-V.* Nov. 25, 1789, pp. 14-15.

[2] *P.-V.* Nov. 25, 1789, p. 12. The Assembly's printer, Baudoin, sent a copy of the debates and promised to send them regularly thereafter. "This Society," was the reply, "consider the World as interested in these Proceedings, and therefore no present could have been more agreeable to them."—*C. R. S.* 21-3.

[3] Dated Dec. 5, 1789.—*C. R. S.* 7-10; *New Ann. Reg.* 1789; *Moniteur*, Dec. 7, 1789, No. 107, p. 435, where see the speech of M. Martineau.

[4] *C. R. S.* 4-5; *New Ann. Reg.* 1789, *Public Papers*, 127. The society ordered that its thanks be conveyed to Rochefoucauld.—*C. R. S.* 5-6.

ing to pay to Liberty the fairest homage, that of National prejudices." The assembly had seen in the address of the Revolution Society "the dawn of a glorious day in which two nations, who have always esteemed one another, notwithstanding their political divisions and the diversity of their governments, shall contract an intimate union founded on the similarity of their opinions and their common enthusiasm for liberty." This letter to Price, read at a dinner of the Revolution Society, was much admired, and "led to a list of constitutional Anglo-Gallic toasts," which seem, says the correspondent of the *Moniteur*, "to suggest that sooner or later perfect harmony will reign between the two nations. In expectation of that happy moment champagne, burgundy and floods of bordeaux water the germ." [1]

The members of the Revolution Society, charmed by the reception accorded to their address, joined in the pæan to the principles of universal benevolence. "Their hearts," they say, "are warmed with these principles; and they desire nothing so earnestly as that the time may soon come when *they shall so possess every human heart* as to put an end to all jealousies between nations, exterminate oppression and slavery, and cause wars, those dreadful errors of governments, to cease in all the earth. They exult in the prospect of such a time which seems to be opening, and with which the proceedings of the National Assembly of France promise to bless mankind." The Revolution, thought these enthusiasts, might be a salutary instruction to monarchs. They rejoiced that the French had been blessed in their king, "justly crowned with the title of RESTORER OF FRENCH LIBERTY. This elevates him to the highest pinnacle of glory. The despots of the world must *now* see their folly. This example must show them that they can never be so great, so happy or truly powerful as by renouncing despotic power and being placed (like the Kings of *France and England*) at the head of an enlightened people and free constitutions of government." [2]

The interest of this correspondence does not lie only in

---

[1] *Moniteur*, Dec. 26, 1789, No. 128, p. 517.

[2] Undated, but after Dec. 5, 1789.—*C. R. S.* 10–11 ; *New Ann. Reg.* 1789, *Public Papers*, 128–9 ; translation in *Moniteur*, Feb. 5, 1790, No. 36, p. 144.

the reverence for constitutional monarchy and the fair dream of universal peace which it reveals. It also introduced the English democrats to the French revolutionists, and from it their friendly intercourse must be dated. By contemporaries its importance was possibly even exaggerated, for it is said to have had an important influence on the formation of the Jacobin Club, the famous political society which became the pulse of revolutionary Paris.

This correspondence was, later on, to be much misinterpreted. The meaning of the name of the Revolution Society was misunderstood, and the society came to be erroneously regarded, both in France and England, as the Society of the French Revolution.[1] Such a mistake may well be excused in the unenlightened, but it had serious consequences. When the tide of opinion in England turned against the Revolution, people tended to saddle the society with all its errors, and to visit the members of the society with the same condemnation as the revolutionists in France. The cause of reform was discredited in England because reformers were thought to approve of violence in France. How misleading this view was can best be realised by examining the correspondence of the Revolution Society and the known opinions of their French correspondents.

[1] See *Corr. of the Rev. Soc.* 215-16, and Dulaure V. 499-50. In Sampson Perry's *Sketch of the French Revolution* (see pp. 30 *et seq.*) they are called "the revolutionists of England."

CHAPTER VI

THE FRENCH POLITICAL CLUBS AND THEIR RELATIONS WITH THE ENGLISH REFORMERS

MAY 1789—FEBRUARY 1792

WE have seen how the French Revolution had stimulated and revived reforming vigour, and how it had been welcomed by enthusiastic reformers. The London Revolution Society especially had been drawn quite naturally, on celebrating the tepid and sober Revolution of 1688, to express cordial enthusiasm for the promising beginnings of the new Revolution in France. The correspondence thus begun with the National Assembly was naturally carried on with the numerous popular societies which sprang up in France during the first two years of the Revolution. There is something touching about the glow of comradeship and the conviction of the dawn of a new age of brotherhood, between the honest folk of two nations soon to be at grips in the most desperate war of history. These relations unquestionably had a great effect upon the ideas of English reformers in encouraging among them French idealism and planting more firmly the doctrine of right against expediency. As a result the English societies became more doctrinaire and less and less in touch with English feeling. But the more unfortunate consequences of the correspondence appeared later, when revolutionary excesses began in France. Then the duress of the king, the September massacres, the reign of terror, all came to be identified in the popular mind with the French societies, and especially with the Jacobins, with whom the London Revolution Society had been chiefly identified. Jacobin became, not unnaturally, a name of horror in England. Equally naturally the ill reputation of the French societies reacted on popular opinion of their English correspondents;

the mere fact of having been in constant and friendly correspondence with the Jacobins was enough to damn reform societies, however moderate their words and actions. The Englishman of 1793 and 1794 did not remember, and probably did not know, that until the loss of confidence in Louis XVI after the flight to Varennes on the night of the 20th of June, 1791, the Jacobins and most of their auxiliary clubs had been perfectly moderate and constitutional in character and aims; and that the correspondence between them and the English reformers had been of the most innocent kind, an interchange of vague and heady, but perfectly unexceptionable sentiments. Even the Englishman of to-day does not know this. It is therefore essential to study with some care the history, constitution and aims of the French clubs, and especially of the Jacobins, during the first three years of the Revolution, and to examine closely their correspondence with England.

From the first moment of the Revolution political clubs seem to have sprung into existence in various towns of France, stimulated, no doubt, by the gathering of local assemblies to elect representatives to the States-General and to draw up their *cahiers* or instructions. Such, for example, were the Patriotic Union of the Town and Castle-ward of Lille and the Patriotic Society of Dijon. These societies, scattered up and down the length and breadth of France, were throughout to exercise a great influence on the course of the Revolution, and it was their known activity which aroused in England fears as to the influence which such societies might wield. The most famous of the French societies, the Jacobin Club of Paris, does not seem to have been formally constituted till almost the end of 1789, and a strong tradition attributed its foundation to a direct imitation of the London Revolution Society. But recently published evidence enables its evolution to be clearly traced; and it was so manifestly the product of special and local circumstances that it would probably have been different in no essential feature had the London Revolution Society never existed.

The club first arose out of a trumpery local dispute as to the provincial privileges of Brittany, where the noblesse and higher clergy objected to the prescribed method of electing deputies to the States-General as a violation of Breton custom. Relying upon the treaty of Vannes, by which Brittany had been united to France, they refused to elect representatives to the States-General otherwise than in a general assembly of the estates of the province.[1] But each estate had been ordered by the royal summons to elect its own deputies separately, and in defiance of their natural leaders—the nobility and higher clergy of the province—the third estate and the inferior clergy complied with the royal edict. It was not surprising, in the circumstances, that the conforming deputies should feel somewhat acutely the exceptional insecurity of their position. Called upon to defend their election against powerful nobles and influential clerics who were angered at a fancied slight and who made a plausible appeal to provincial prejudice, the Bretons were compelled to act together, and when they reached Versailles they were already a party. From the first they entered upon a regular correspondence with their supporters at home,[2] and from the first they were conscious of their peculiar unity and responsibility.

"We have hired together a room where we can meet," wrote one of them, "as we feel the necessity of consulting before the General Assembly about matters which demand a continuous and settled policy." Other deputies joined them the first evening,[3] amongst whom, for example, was Mounier, the leading spirit of the deputation of Dauphiné.[4] The advantages of their concerted action were evident, and "the salon of the Breton deputation" had by June become "the rallying-point of all good citizens."[5]

---

[1] Duchâtellier, *Histoire de la Rév. dans la Bretagne*, I. 150–5; see interesting remarks in Etienne Dumont's *Souvenirs sur Mirabeau*, 99–100; Dubois-Crancé, *Analyse de la Rév. française.* The authorities on the formation of the Jacobin Club are, for the most part, collected in the introduction to Prof. Aulard's *Jacobins.* For the biographies of individual Breton deputies, see René Kerviler, *Cent Ans de Représentation Bretonne;* 1ʳᵉ partie, États-Généraux.

[2] Duchâtellier, I. 168–9.   [3] April 30, 1789.

[4] Letter of Jean-Pierre Boullé, deputy of Ploërmel, to the municipal officers of Pontivy. Published from the Archives of the Morbihan by M. Albert Macé in the *Revue de la Révolution*, 1887; documents inédits, 2ᵉ partie, 163.

[5] Boullé to the municipality of Pontivy, ap. René Kerviler, *Armorique et Bretagne*, III. 19–20; cf. *Revue de la Rév.*, March 1888, p. 234.

After the "journées" of the 5th and 6th October, and the consequent transference of the National Assembly from Versailles, the meetings of the Breton Club were resumed at Paris. "In the month of November," says one historian of that city, "a society established in London under the name of the *Club of the French Revolution,* having addressed to the National Assembly a letter of felicitation on its labours, the members of the Breton committee conceived the idea of forming, at Paris, a society on the model of that in London," which might be at once more stable and of wider scope than the old committee.[1] The society was formed, and is known to history, under the name of the Jacobin Club, though its real name was more than once changed and, according to the historian whom we have cited, it was first called the Revolution Society.

It is possible, and even probable, that the address of the London Revolution Society was the immediate occasion for the regular organisation of the Jacobin Club, though there is no direct evidence to allege in proof of this conjecture. But the club was not imitative; organically, indeed, there was little in the Revolution Society to imitate. The Jacobin Club was evolved naturally from the political conditions of the moment, and, proving useful, survived.[2]

The address of the Revolution Society to the National Assembly at once excited admiration and gratitude in the popular societies of France. On the morrow[3] of its presentation the Patriotic Union of the Town and Castleward of Lille sent an enthusiastic letter of acknowledgment. "It must be owned, Gentlemen," it said, "that in politics, as in philosophy, you are the instructors and examples of the whole World. It is among you; yes, it is in your

[1] J. A. Dulaure, *Histoire physique civile et morale de Paris,* V. 499–500; *v.* also *Avis aux Français sur les Clubs,* ap. Aulard's *Société des Jacobins* (hereafter *A. J.*), II. 242; cf. 257. It is obvious from the foregoing account that Lady Holland is not accurate in stating, in her *Journal,* [June] 1791, that "the Jacobin Club was then in embryo." It was by then well established.—*Journal of Elizabeth, Lady Holland,* I. 1.

[2] Still, Dulaure's view was sustained by the society of Strasbourg. Possibly the Revolution Society had more influence on the provincial societies than on the Jacobin Club, *vide C. R. S.* 60.

[3] The letter is dated Nov. 26, 1789. The address was no secret, so presumably the intelligence had reached Lille direct from England.

favoured Isle, that Liberty, everywhere attacked and trampled upon by Despotism, has formed a sacred Asylum, and if France should obtain that invaluable blessing, she will perhaps be more indebted for it to your Nation than to herself; for if we had not been encouraged by your examples and enlightened by your experience we might yet, perhaps, have been unable to break those chains under which we are bowed down. . . ." [1] So also thought the Patriotic Society of Dijon, which four days later congratulated the Revolution Society on its freedom from national prejudices. "In securing their own happiness," said the letter, "Englishmen have prepared the way for that of the Universe." [2]

To such friendly addresses some acknowledgment obviously had to be given, and thus the London Revolution Society was drawn on from its address to the National Assembly into a correspondence with the popular societies. In its replies the Revolution Society cordially joined in all the hopes of international brotherhood that its correspondents had expressed. "The spirit and unanimity " of the French "seemed like an inspiration from heaven," but the society returned quietly to the enunciation of its own immediate object, when it said that England would soon lose its pre-eminence amongst free peoples if it were not "provoked by the example of France " to correct abuses that grew daily more evident, and in particular to substitute for its partial and imperfect representation such a pure and equal system as the French were likely to enjoy.[3]

Within the next three years between forty and fifty popular societies in France entered into correspondence with the London Revolution Society. Almost all seem to have been affiliated with the Society of Jacobins, itself the most famous amongst them.[4]

---

[1] *C. R. S.* 17–19.

[2] Nov. 30, 1789.—*C. R. S.* 11–16. Amongst the signatures to the address is that of Maret, probably Jean-Philibert (brother of Hughes-Bernard, future duc de Bassano), later préfet of the Loiret and member of the Conseil d'État (1806).

[3] *C. R. S.* 16–17, 19–20 ; cf. also 37–40, where the society of Lille defends the Revolution Society against the charge, said to have been circulated at Paris of being an "assemblage recruited from the dregs of the people."   [4] See the list in Appendix.

During the period of this correspondence, which ended, so far as is known, early in 1792 and which was therefore outlasted by the French monarchy,[1] the principles of the Jacobins were truly indicated in their official name of Friends of the Constitution, though it is also true that their opinions as a body are frequently a matter of doubt. Their records probably perished when the Communards burned the old Hôtel de Ville. Certainly the minutes have been lost, and it is not possible to reconstruct them from official or semi-official documents, as can be done in the case of some of the more important English societies.

A second feature of the evidence calls for humility in the historian. The Jacobin Club was a platform from which men of all shades of liberalism might express their views, and it is not possible to say that one view more than another represents the opinion of the club. Even in November 1790, when the Jacobins murmured against a letter couched in the language of the old régime, a deputy vindicated the constitutional loyalty of its writers.[2] Of many things to which they were willing to listen the majority of the Jacobins might not approve, and in the existing accounts of their meetings it is often difficult to distinguish report from parody; but the reliable sources are still sufficient to enable us to sketch in its main lines the policy and conduct of the society.[3]

"To write and to speak openly," ran the preamble of the regulations, "to profess their principles clearly, to avow their actions, their opinions, their hopes, will be the open policy by which they will endeavour to earn that public esteem which can alone give them strength and utility." The Jacobins set themselves the task of stimulating and directing public opinion as the first essential

---

[1] The last letter received by the London Revolution Society is dated Dec. 27, 1791, and is from the society of Honfleur, to whom the last known reply was sent on Feb. 6, 1792.

[2] *Corr. de L.-P.-J. d'Orléans*, 229-31. In April 1790, a member attacked Burke for describing the French as fools and fanatics. But at the same time he proposed six resolutions of constitutional conservatism, and he appears to have been heard in both cases.—*A. J.* I. 72-3.

[3] In writing this sketch I have been guided by the essay of M. Aulard in his *Études et leçons sur la Révolution française*, 1ʳᵉ série; IV. *Le Club des Jacobins sous la Monarchie*, 171 et seq.

of constitutional government by free discussion, but fidelity to the Constitution, devotion to its defence, and respect and submission to the powers thereby established, were the fundamental laws imposed upon every member of the society. In other words, they believed in an hereditary monarch, acting within constitutional limits, and ultimately subject to the will of the sovereign people.[1] In those principles they never wavered till the flight to Varennes.

In the first three years of their existence the Jacobins were not, any more than the London Revolution Society, a popular society in the widest sense of that term.[2] The entrance fee was twelve livres and the annual subscription twenty-four livres—prohibitive sums to a poor man. In February 1790 the Duc d'Aiguillon was president; in July Lafayette's cousin, the Vicomte de Broglie.[3] The future king Louis Philippe was an ardent Jacobin, and even undertook to translate for the society the reply which Joseph Towers, Price's coadjutor in his pastorate at Newington Green, wrote to Burke's *Reflections*.[4] The intellectual as well as the titular aristocrats were amongst the members of the club. La Harpe[5] represented letters, in company with the Professor of Literature at the Collège de France, and Choderlos de Laclos, the agent of Orléans, whose *Liaisons Dangereuses* it would have defied the ingenuity of Bowdler himself to bowdlerise. Of scientists there were Lacépède and Bailly, with Monge, the mathematician and future

---

[1] In Oct. 1790, for instance, in the proposals for David's "Oath of the Tennis Court," the States-General are referred to as "called by a good king and oppressed by courtiers."--*A. J.* I. 330-3.

[2] *A. J.* I. 394 ; cf. *Voyage de Halem*, ed. Chuquet, 226. In some provincial societies the subscription was also high enough to exclude the poorer citizens, *v.* rules of the society of Arras, ap. Lecesne, *Arras sous la Rév.* I. 90-2. At Rouen it would appear as if only citoyens actifs were admitted to membership (*v.* Pétition des citoyens actifs, membres de la société . . . de Rouen . . .). At Strasbourg the society consisted of men in a fair social position—bankers, lawyers, professors, and military men, especially officers of the artillery and engineers.— Véron-Réville, *La Rév. dans la Haut-Rhin*, 37.   [3] *A. J.* 714 ; cf. I. 28-31.

[4] *Corr. de L.-P.-J. Duc d'Orléans*, 244-5. This reply was the appendix to *Thoughts on the Commencement of a New Parliament* called "Remarks on the letter of the Rt. Hon. Edmund Burke on the Revolution in France." London, 1790, 8°.

[5] A. J. I. 409 *et seq.*

Minister for War. The arts were represented by Talma the actor and David, who, after painting the "Oath of the Tennis Court," as a commission from the Jacobins, was to win equal renown by painting the "Coronation of Napoleon" and the "Distribution of the Imperial Eagles." There was the noble Rochambeau, who had fought for the liberties of America, and the journalist Brune, who was to win a marshal's bâton in the service of the emperor. Alexandre Beauharnais was there, and Salicetti, the future patron of Napoleon; and amongst these famous and able Frenchmen there was probably an Englishman, famed alike in love and politics, Lord Edward Fitzgerald.[1] Finally Mirabeau, whose fidelity to the monarchy none can question, was a member of the club and was proud to be its president.[2]

The society became the centre of a great system of constitutional societies in different parts of France. In June 1791 there were over four hundred of them,[3] and from time to time the mother society, as it was called,[4] addressed circular letters to its provincial correspondents. "The maintenance of order, the execution of the laws, and respect for property," said a letter of September 10, 1790, were no less the care of the Jacobins than "the discovery of abuses, the defence of the oppressed, and a careful vigilance towards the repositories of power." Troubles had arisen in the army between reactionary officers and revolutionary soldiers. The Jacobins implored the societies in garrison towns to bear their part in soothing the irritated soldiery. "Tell them that an unhappy blindness has distorted their patriotism; that, yielding to the suggestions of the enemies of the fatherland, they are working, without wishing it, to destroy that Constitution which they have sworn to maintain; that whilst good citizens are alarmed by these disorders, the evil-disposed rejoice and congratulate themselves on achieving by the insubordination of the army the

---

[1] List of members (Dec. 21, 1790, and supplement).—*A. J.* lxxxiii—lxxxvi.

[2] *Ib.* I. 302; cf. VI. 684, 685, and I. 398-9.

[3] *Ib.* I. lxxxii–lxxxix. Later the number probably increased to a thousand or more.

[4] Erroneously, it would seem. Some, at least, of the societies affiliated with the Jacobin Club were of earlier or contemporary foundation.

ruin of a Constitution which has been formed under the shelter of *Civisme*." They reminded the officers that, if they had the right to command obedience, it was their duty first to earn it, and then to make it easy; and reminding them of the advantages which the Revolution had conferred upon them, they asked if the constitutional Government was to be worse served for its good offices than the ancient despotism for its bad. "Tell them all," they urged the societies, "that the well-being of the fatherland makes a duty of conciliation and unity; that the nation has its eyes turned towards them, and that it expects from their patriotism that unity of effort and of will which can alone render it tranquil at home and imposing abroad." Discipline is the very breath of liberty, and "respect for the laws," so necessary to maintain the liberty that patriotism had won, was henceforth to be the sign by which Frenchmen and citizens would be known.[1] These wise and constitutional words were explained, a few days later, in a letter to the Society of Brest. "The effervescence of the people, excited or deceived, is to-day the most dangerous enemy of a Constitution which is dear to us and on which depends the happiness of us all."[2]

An English statesman once described himself as "absorbed in working the institutions of his country." The phrase accurately describes the policy of the Jacobins at this period of their history. When the law providing for the election of judges came into operation they addressed the affiliated societies on the importance of a wise choice, of vigilance in watching the elections, and of patriotism at the ballot;[3] and a similar exhortation marked the elections of June 1791.[4] When the taxes proved difficult to collect it was the Jacobins who cried out against the people who had paid without resistance the excessive and arbitrary demands of the old régime and yet refused the just and equal taxes voted by their own representatives. The

---

[1] Adresse de la Société des Amis de la Constitution de Paris aux Sociétés qui lui sont affiliées, ap. *A. J.* I. 283–6; Alexandre Lameth was the author of this address.—*Ib.* 283, note.

[2] Lettre du Président de la Société des Amis de la Constitution de Paris à celle de Brest, Sept. 22, 1790, ap. *A. J.* I. 286–7.

[3] Oct. 10, 1790, ap. *A. J.* I. 322–5.   [4] *Ib.* 520–3.

Jacobins realised that just from this very right and its con-
comitant obligations had sprung the liberties of England
and of the United States of America. "It would have been
a strange error," they said, with perfect justice, "not of
liberty, but of licence, to reckon amongst the privileges of
a free people that of being dispensed from taxation. Taxation, on the contrary, is the basis of security, property and
liberty. . . ." Taxation was the foundation of freedom,
and it would be monstrous indeed if the people were to
refuse to meet their just obligations at the very moment
when they had laid the corner-stone of liberty by winning
the right to tax themselves through their representatives.[1]

The Jacobins consistently appealed for the maintenance
of public order,[2] and a German observer [3] assures us that,
although amongst the Jacobins, as amongst all such bodies
of men, there were some factious spirits, their private
debates showed the same temper as their public utterances.
To indulge in turbulence and faction, it was realised, was
to place weapons in the hands of their enemies. Disrespect
of the law would give the reactionaries a handle against
them, and excessive ardour would alienate moderate and
peaceable supporters. Above all, the Jacobins told their
adherents, they desired peace, "for it is in the midst of
peace that the edifice of our Constitution may be firmly
established; it is ours to maintain the laws, for they have
been made for us and by our desire. Under the reign of
liberty criminals and tyrants have alone an interest in
revolt." [4]

Such was the conduct of the Jacobin Club up to the time
of the king's flight to Varennes on the night of the 20th of
June, 1791, and his disavowal, in the criticism of the Revolution which he left behind him, of all his acts during the
preceding two years. Of republicanism there has been

---

[1] Adresse de la Société des Amis de la Constitution de Paris aux
Sociétés qui lui sont affiliées sur la necessité du paiement de l'impôt.
—*A. J.* I. 338–42 ; *v.* also debate, June 17, 1791, *ib.* II. 310–15, and
another address of July 9, 1791, ap. *A. J.* II. 600–4.

[2] *v.* Lettre des Amis de la Constitution, Jan. 24, 1791.—*Ib.* II. 28–9.

[3] Halem.—*Paris en* 1790 : *Voyage de Halem*, ed. Chuquet, 294–5.

[4] Adresse de la Société des Amis de la Constitution de Paris aux
Sociétés qui lui sont affiliées (March 1791).—*A. J.* II. 185–9.

hitherto no word; the Jacobins had been faithful to their motto—"the Constitution or Death."

When Louis XVI abandoned the government of France the first and almost universal feeling was one of dismay. It was, says M. Aulard, as if he had carried away some mystic talisman upon which depended the fortunes of France. There was no confidence that the nation could be ruled and guided without him. Anarchy and the paralysis of the national activities seemed the only prospect. Yet despite their sense of betrayal the Jacobins received the news soberly and set themselves to deal reasonably with the situation. The mere fact that they represented a great organisation, which neither the presence nor the absence of the king could disturb, lent to them a special importance in the first moment of distress, and their minutes of the 21st of June recall the wise and dignified deliberations of some mediæval burghers, about to prepare their city to resist a siege.[1]

Their language was still strictly constitutional. In the remarkable letter which they addressed to the affiliated societies they avoided, with an exactitude worthy of the men of 1689, any implication of the personal responsibility of the king. "Brothers and friends," they wrote, "the King, misled by criminal suggestions, has left the National Assembly." Their courage and their self-control had been worthy of the occasion. "Every division is forgotten; all patriots are united. *The National Assembly* is our guide and the *Constitution* is our watchword."[2]

New constitutional guarantees were obviously necessary in view of the declaration of war against the Constituent Assembly which Louis XVI had left behind him;[3] and the Jacobins were not unwilling that he should be brought to trial. But when Robert appeared on June 22 with an address to the Jacobins from the republican club, known as the Cordeliers, demanding the destruction of the monarchy, the cries of disapproval were so general and so spontaneous as to leave no doubt that the Jacobins were still far from being

[1] Procès-verbal of the session of June 21, 1791.—*A. J.* II. 531-7.
[2] Lettre de la Société des Amis de la Constitution de Paris aux Sociétés qui lui sont affiliées, June 21, 1791.—*Ib.* II. 538.
[3] See minutes of June 23, 1791.—*A. J.* II. 544-7.

republicans.[1] And in July the storm of disapproval aroused
by an address from the Society of Perpignan demanding
a republic showed their opinion to be unchanged.[2]

Still less, as yet, were they propagandists; though the
address to the neighbouring peoples which they issued on
July 9, 1791, shows, like the correspondence of the French
societies with the Revolution Society of London, the sentiments out of which the doctrine of propaganda grew. The
manifesto was primarily directed against the *émigrés*. "It
is them alone whom we menace with just punishment if
they persevere in their hostile views. To you we declare
peace, confidence, union and fraternity." All nations were
henceforth to be one people, one family;[3] but so far there
was no intention to impose the universal empire of peace
and liberty by force of arms.

On July 15, 1791, the cautious constitutional policy of
the Jacobins was rudely thrust aside, though the extent to
which they were themselves consenting parties is matter
of dispute. A deputation of 4000 citizens invaded their
place of meeting and declared that they were going next
day, on the Champ de Mars, to swear never again to
recognise Louis XVI as king. Thereupon Laclos, the
tool of Orléans,[4] proposed that a petition be circulated for
signature in all the affiliated societies declaring that the
fate of Louis XVI was uncertain and ought to be promptly
resolved; that his flight and declaration constituted a formal
abdication of the crown; and that he ought not to be
accepted as king unless a majority of the nation voted for
his reinstatement.[5]

It is obvious that the resolution was first carried in a
tumultuous assembly which, though it included Jacobins,
was not "the Jacobins," and which cannot be held to have
expressed the views of the club. Further reflection led the

---

[1] *A. J.* II. 538-44 ; *v.* also 572-5.
[2] Session of July 6, 1791.—*A. J.* II. 587-9. There is no trace of
correspondence between the Society of Perpignan and any English
society. As to republicanism, see also *A. J.* III. 10-14, especially a
speech of Robespierre.   [3] *A. J.* II. 605-6.
[4] Orléans had himself been elected to membership of the club
immediately after the flight to Varennes.
[5] *A. J.* III. 14-20.

members to perceive that they had put themselves in direct
opposition to the decree of the Assembly, also adopted on
July 15, whereby the king was indirectly acquitted of blame
for his flight.   They therefore rescinded their resolution,[1]
and declared that they would confine their efforts to constitutional means [2]—words which had occurred even in the
obnoxious petition.

All that could be done to repair the error was done, but
no effort could prevent a schism in the club itself, and the
club known as the Feuillants was formed by the moderate
dissidents.   The petition was, in fact, rather the occasion
than the cause of difference, and every effort of conciliation
failed to restore unity.[3]   The majority of the country
societies stood by those who retained the name of Jacobins.
Addresses of attachment were voted by the dozen, and on
August 8 only four societies had withdrawn from their
affiliation.[4]

No doubt there had been a growing tendency on the part
of the Jacobins to assume a dictatorial attitude; their persecution of a club called the Club Monarchique was a case
in point.   But they deserve every credit for their endeavours
to obtain by moderation and conciliation a reunion with
the Feuillants.   After the schism the club became gradually
more and more declamatory, more and more meddlesome,
till little by little it attained to the intolerable absolutism
of the Terror.   In proportion as the aspect of foreign affairs
grew more gloomy for France the Jacobins, through the
affiliated societies, tightened their hold upon the internal
government of the nation,[5] and sought to impose their will
upon the people.   They constituted themselves the apolo-
gists of the Revolution, in each successive phase,[6] down to
the abolition of royalty on September 21, 1792.   Next day
the Republic was proclaimed.   Two months later—so short
were memories during those eventful days—the Jacobins
declared that since the fall of the Bastille, on July 14, 1789,
they had always been "men truly free and republicans."[7]

[1] *A. J.* III. 30–2.   [2] Adresse of July 20, 1791.
[3] The official Jacobin account is in the "Adresse . . ." of Aug. 7,
1791.—*A. J.* III. 72–9.   For further efforts see *ib.* III. 95–100.
[4] *Ib.* III. 79–81 ; see also III. 137–9.
[5] *Ib.* III. 378–81, 413–18 ; IV. 27–9, etc.
[6] *Ib.* IV. 32–5, 534–40.   [7] *Ib.*

The Jacobins may be taken to express, in broad outline, the opinions of the numerous affiliated societies with which the London Revolution Society corresponded. Any attempt to expound their views in detail is beset with danger. M. Aulard has shown how pliant the Jacobins were to the opinion of the nation. As throbbed the people, so throbbed the Jacobins; through them it is possible, so to speak, to place a finger upon the pulse of France. They were the microcosm of the nation.

But the Revolution was not merely simple and national; it was also local and complex. It must be difficult for any one, and above all is it difficult for a foreigner, to sift the parochial and provincial from the general and national. The Society of Rouen, for example, begins an address with an expression of belief in the general good; but it does so only by way of preface to a petition against the proposed abolition of Rouen's special privilege of a local mint.[1] In many towns, again, there was more than one society, and the same society did not always call itself by the same name. It is occasionally difficult to distinguish one society from another, or to know which of two societies was actually affiliated to the Jacobins, or in correspondence with the London Revolution Society. Local histories of scientific method or exactitude are still unhappily rare, and the writer is unaware of any critical bibliography which might indicate sources and save from error. In the absence of such aids to accuracy, any account of the provincial Jacobins is necessarily tentative.

A number of societies were formed in the provinces before the existence of the Parisian Jacobins was known. Such societies when they became affiliated with the central body seem usually to have adopted its name of Friends of the Constitution,[2] to have been faithful to the name, and sufficiently moderate in opinion. In some cases the affiliated societies were at war with the local administrative authorities,[3] though in general they seem to have fairly

[1] Adresse à l'Assemblée Nationale sur le projet de supprimer plusieurs Hôtels de Monnoies, entr'autres celui de Rouen ; par la Société des Amis de la Constitution à Rouen.

[2] See, for instance, Règlement de la Société des Amis de la Constitution établie à Strasbourg, affiliée à celle de Paris.

[3] *P.-V.* of the Assembly, Oct. 19, 1790, p. 16 ; Adresse de la Société

represented the opinion of their neighbours, and one society —that of Marseille—was even founded under municipal patronage.[1] The Society of Lorient in the Morbihan, to take only one example, was probably in perfect agreement with the official address of the commune as a whole, which prayed the National Assembly "to construct the edifice of the Constitution very slowly in order that it might be the more solid."[2]

Strict rules were framed to prevent irresponsible persons from joining the societies. For admission to the Society of Arras it was necessary to have taken the civic oath, or to be willing to take it;[3] for the Society of Brest it was necessary to be on the active list of the National Guard, which involved the same requirement.[4] Members of the Society of Cognac took an oath "to be faithful to the nation, the law and the king, and to maintain with all their power the Constitution decreed by the Assembly and sanctioned by the King."[5]

Though, in an oath, the nation and the law might take precedence of the king, it was hardly so in fact. "The Restorer of French Liberty" appeared to the Society of Rouen "a Monarch worthy by his virtues of the highest destinies. . . ."[6] In June 1790, when a federation of national guards of the three departments of the Nord, Somme and Pas-de-Calais, was held at Lille, the Society of the Friends of the Constitution proposed that a portion of the oath should be read; ". . . we swear to regard as criminals, and surrender to the rigour of the law, whosoever shall dare to allow himself to fail in his duty to the most just, most popular, most adored of monarchs. . . ."[7] It

---

des Amis de la Constitution séante a Aix, département des Bouches-du-Rhône, à l'Assemblée nationale.—*A. J.* III. 555, cf. *ib.* II. 333 *et seq.*; *Moniteur*, Oct. 29, 1790, No. 302, p. 1250.

[1] Boudin, *Hist. de Marseille*, 487–8 ; Fabre, *Hist. de Marseille*, II. 435 *et seq.*   [2] *Moniteur*, Dec. 15, 1789, No. 115, p. 467.

[3] Le Règlement de la Société des Amis de la Constitution établie à Arras, ap. Lecesne.—*Arras sous la Rév.* I. 90–2.

[4] Levot, *Hist. de Brest*, III. 226.

[5] Gallo, "Les Jacobins de Cognac," *Rév. Française*, XLIII. 238.

[6] Pétition des Citoyens actifs de la Commune de Rouen, Membres de la Soc. des Amis de la Const.; see *Arras sous la Rév.* I. 147 ; *C. R. S.* 221–2.

[7] Dérode, *Hist. de Lille*, III. 38. Another address, considered less

is impossible to doubt that in the beginning the clubs were monarchic to the core.[1]

"The object of this institution," said the Society of Brest, "being to enlighten the people as to their interests, to expose those who deceive them, and to place the new laws in the fullest light, failures in those laws and abuses of all sorts ought to be denounced courageously and without hesitation."[2] To unite "an imposing mass of opinions proper to restrain the enemies of the public good, to repress the temerity of their language, to inspire respect for the laws, to destroy prejudice and to enlighten the people as to its rights and duties,"[3] were the words in which the Orléans Society enumerated its principles.[4] "To instruct in the true principles of the Constitution those who are still ignorant of them, or those whom specious argument may have misled," were the objects professed by the Society of Cognac, in which, moreover, to speak ill of the Constitution was a serious offence, involving a fine of six livres and suspension for a week.[5] They were not without generous

---

monarchic and more constitutional, was substituted for this by the commandant of the guards, Comte St. Aldegonde de Noircarmes.

[1] The society of Bayeux expressed, in 1791, a desire that the people might exercise its sovereignty more directly, as in the ancient republics, and therefore would appear to have desired the abolition of monarchy. But the Society of Melun made a vigorous attack upon this heresy. Though neither society is known to have corresponded with any English society, the following reference to England in the Melun address is interesting. ". . . Public opinion has such force among free peoples that in a neighbouring kingdom whose parliaments are septennial, and whose constitution is most imperfect, whose representation is detestable, and whose upper house is really no more than a complement of royal authority, the prince has, nevertheless, only dared once or twice in a century to employ his absolute *veto*, and the nation, without political liberty has preserved its civic liberty."—Réponse de la Société des Ami-de la Constitution séante à Melun, à une Adresse ou pétition de la soc. d. Bayeux, à l'Assemblée nationale, sur les décrets qui ont éprouvé la réclamation publique ; Envoyés à toutes les sociétés patriotiques du Royaumee Melun [June 21], 1791.—B. n. Lb⁴⁰ 997.

[2] Art. 17 of the Règlement.—Levot, *Hist. de Brest*, III. 226-7.

[3] Statuts et règlements de la société des amis de la constitution d'Orléans. Orléans, 1790, 8vo.—B. n. Lb ⁴⁰ 1048.

[4] See also the declaration of the Society of Bourg (which did not correspond with the Revolution Society). "The principal object of the Societies of the Friends of the Constitution ought to be to enlighten the people and to propagate the principles of the Constitution."—Circulaire de la Société des Amis de la Constitution de Bourg aux sociétés affiliées.

[5] *Révolution française*, XLIII. 239-40.

enthusiasm at Cognac. "I proclaim patriotism," the president could say, ". . . as a holy torch." It was patriotism that had given strength, courage and energy to the friends of the Constitution; that had inspired the enrolment of the National Guard for the defence of the fatherland; and that had broken the chains of aristocracy. "Since it has produced our happiness, let us then maintain it with all our strength." [1] A few months earlier the society had endorsed a letter from Angoulême in which patriotism was defined as "love of the laws, and religious submission to the duties they imposed; " [2] and Burke himself could have expressed no sounder maxim than the epigraph of their minute book : "Free corporations exist only by the union and good order preserved in them." [3]

The Society of the Friends of the Constitution at Bordeaux described themselves as "an association of men entirely devoted to meditation on the Decree of the National Assembly." [4] "The defence of liberty, and the maintenance and establishment of the constitution of the kingdom " were the objects of the Society of Tours, which sought to secure, by every legal and constitutional means, the execution of the law. But perhaps most interesting of all is the preamble to the regulations of the Society of Arras. "The society, in no way desiring to hide its thoughts, declares that, animated by a profound sentiment of love for the interests of the country, the true object of its institution, as well as the dearest of its wishes, is to work with success in spreading the sacred principles of the Constitution. . . . Fidelity to the Constitution, devotion to its defence, and respect and submission to the powers which it has established, will be the first laws imposed on those who desire admission to the society. The titles to present oneself shall

---

[1] *Révolution française,* 244 *et supra;* address delivered, Nov. 18, 1791.

[2] April 19, 1791.—*Ib.* 239.   [3] *Ib.* 238.

[4] Adresse de la Société des Amis de la Constitution à Bordeaux. . . . There were several clubs at Bordeaux, and possibly the London Revolution Society corresponded only with the Club du Café National, which M. Jullian calls demagogic. There was, apparently, a third and worse society, "assez mesquine," and we are not sure that the learned Professor of the Collège de France, heir to Fustel de Coulanges though he be, has quite exhausted the sources. See *Hist. de Bordeaux,* 659.

be, above all, love of equality, and that profound sentiment
of the rights of man which impose instinctive devotion to
the defence of the weak and oppressed, and which values
its own dignity sufficiently to honour its like, independently
of exterior distinctions and titles." [1]

Occasionally the societies outstripped the National
Assembly in democratic zeal. There were some murmurs
against the decree making eligibility for election to the
legislature dependent on the payment of direct taxation to
the value of a *marc d'argent*.[2] The Society of Toulon,
after politely complimenting the Assembly on its virtues,
makes a violent attack on a law which "attaches all the
powers of a citizen to the greater or less amount of metal
which he possesses," and demands the repeal of this
"Plebiscite" decree.[3] But more often the societies
strengthened the Assembly by their support. When it
was found difficult to collect the taxes, the Society of Arras,
like the mother society, did its best to influence public
opinion in the direction of obedience to the law.[4]

The assistance which the societies rendered to the
Assembly is most clear in the case of the civil constitution
of the clergy. Addresses of defence and explanation were
prepared, discussed, printed and finally distributed freely,
in order to win men's adhesion to the new order. The
Society of Tours tried hard to show that the former constitution of the clergy admitted of no good thing that could
not be better done under the new.[5] The Society of Arras
tried to demonstrate that the new law need not wound the
conscience of any priest,[6] and it issued an adroit appeal to
the peasantry in favour of the acquisition of clerical estates.[7]
The Society of Lille showed itself impatient of delay in

---

[1] Lecesne, *Arras sous la Rév.* I. 90; cf. President's speech, *ib.* I. 93;
see also 101-2. This constitution should be compared with that of Strasbourg. "Publicity," it says, "will be the guarantee of all its actions."—
Règlement de la Société des Amis de la Const. établie à Strasbourg,
affiliée à celle de Paris. Strasbourg, 1790 in -18.—B. n. Lb⁴⁰ 1103.
[2] Aulard, *Histoire politique*, 66 *et seq.*
[3] Toulon, département du Var. Vivre libre ou mourir. Les Citoyens
Amis de la Constitution (B. n. Lb⁴⁰ 1109); *A. J.* III. 104.
[4] *Arras sous la Rév.* I. 145-7.
[5] Réfutation de la lettre du ci-devant archévêque de Tours. . . . (B. n.
Lb⁴⁰ 1113).
[6] *Arras sous la Rév.* I. 143-4.   [7] *Ib.* I. 102-4.

expropriation and sale, and obtained the support of other societies in its agitation.[1] Some bishops and priests were on good terms with the Jacobins of their locality.[2] Others, on the contrary, exasperated believers in the new order by their furious opposition.[3] Only too often the societies replied with equal fury and talked too much of compulsion,[4] or demanded special legislation against the priests, whom they called refractory and fanatical.[5] But there were others which tried the better way of persuasion [6] and conciliation; [7] and when it was proposed on the plea of economy— how many crimes had been committed in its name?—to withhold the salaries of the expropriated clergy, there was found at least one society to protest, in the name of justice, against so shameful an act.[8]

The king's flight to Varennes had the same effect upon the departmental societies as upon the Jacobins of Paris—an effect of terror and dismay rather than of anger.[9] Probably the majority of societies remained sincerely royalist, but their faith was now troubled by suspicion. "One feels," says the historian of one of them, "that with this monarchic zeal is mingled a certain defiance with respect to the fugitive king, a precursive sign of its future adhesion to the republican form;" [10] and, with a humour that must have

---

[1] *Les Jacobins au Village*, 17-19.

[2] *A. J.* I. 318-19. Discours prononcé le 20 juin, 1793 . . . à Nismes.

[3] Adresse à l'Assemblée nationale (from the Marseille Society).—*P.-V.* Nov. 22, 1790, p. 23.

[4] *Ib.* Dec. 4, 1790, p. 11 ; *Rév. française, ut supra*, XLIII. 246-9.

[5] *A. J.* III. 299. The Jacobins of Poitiers denounced the "bad faith" of departmental administrators who protected refractory priests and hindered their deportation.—Pétition des Amis de la liberté et de l'égalité de Poitiers, au ministre de l'Intérieur, Nov. 23, 1792. Arch. nat. F¹⁹ 481, quoted in R. Doucet, *L'Esprit public dans le département de la Vienne*, 39. It should, however, be noted that this address was less numerously signed than other petitions and addresses of the society. Cf. pp. 49, 54.

[6] Circulaire de la société des amis de la constitution de Bourg aux sociétés affiliées.

[7] Ducrest de Villeneuve et Maillet, *Hist. de Rennes* (B. n. Lk⁷ 8243), 445.

[8] Les Amis de la liberté et de l'égalité à la Convention nationale.

[9] *C. R. S.* 215-16 ; 221-2. See also Extrait du procès-verbal des amis de la constitution de Brest, tenue . . . le 25 juin, 1791. Hostility to the émigrés and non-juring priests increased after Varennes. See *A. J.* III. 144, 188, 289 ; IV. 147-8, 165, 206 ; *P.-V.* April 5, 1791, p. 9 ; *C. R. S.* 229-30.

[10] A. Gallo, "Les Jacobins de Cognac," *Rév. franç.* XLIII, 242-3.

been unconscious or very grim, they decided that, "owing merely to circumstances," they would omit the words of loyalty to the king from the oath of admission.[1] Whilst the superstition that the king's presence was essential to the continuance of government still held ground, and whilst the news of his return was still unknown, the Society of Arras issued a proclamation of unusual but admirable boldness. In it the crime of those who had carried off the king was denounced in constitutional terms, and the friends of liberty were called upon to unite in support of the Assembly and in obedience to its decrees whether they had received the royal sanction or not. "The Fatherland has nothing to fear, our representatives watch over it."[2]

The Society of Clermont-Ferrand was slightly more indignant and disposed to be more severe. It could not forget the violated oaths of the king or his own boast that he had lied consistently during two years. With the knowledge of his flight, but whilst still in ignorance of his return, its members believed that the phantom of the ancient monarchy had disappeared. They were obviously not yet full-fledged republicans. They discussed projects of a regency, or of an elected executive, and decided in favour of the elective plan.[3] But the discussion had an academic ring; and they pledged themselves, as other societies did, to support their elected representatives in the National Assembly,[4] where there was still a monarchist majority. Another circumstance shows that the societies were not yet republican. Almost without exception the provincial societies remained true to the Jacobins of Paris after the secession of the Feuillants, yet the eagerness and unanimity with which they insisted that no effort should be spared to win back the seceders make it clear that they had little sympathy with the premature attack upon the monarchy which had caused the schism.[5]

[1] A. Gallo, " Les Jacobins de Cognac," *Rév. Franç.* XLIII. 243-4 ; cf. 251.
[2] Lecesne, *Arras sous la Rév.* I. 157.
[3] Motion de J. H. Bancal à la Société des Amis de la constitution de Clermont-Ferrand (B.n. Lb⁴⁰ 952).—*A. J.* IV. 46-7.
[4] *P.-V.* July 7, 1791, p. 31-2 for instance.
[5] *A. J.* III. 56, 61, 64, 66, 69, 71, 79, 81, 82, 83, 86, 90, 98, 102, 104, 108, 109, 119, 123, 125, 127, 134, 144. There probably were a few

Several societies, it is true, appear to have become republican before either the Jacobin Society of Paris or the main body of the nation was prepared to reject monarchy. In two cases, Bayeux and Perpignan, the societies do not appear to have had any English correspondents; the third, Montpellier, corresponded with the London Revolution Society.[1] But whether they believed in republicanism as an abstract proposition or as a practical expedient is now difficult to determine, and as the memory of Lafayette serves to remind us, belief in theoretical republicanism is not incompatible with a practical policy of reactionary monarchism.

The main body of the Jacobins gradually drew nearer to the republicans. "Constitution, liberty . . ." became the watchwords; in January 1792 the Society of Dijon knew "no other rallying cry."[2] Louis was no longer "the Restorer of French Liberty," or the most just, most popular, most adored of monarchs; he was, or seemed to be, in league with the enemies of France. On the 10th of August, 1792, he was suspended from his functions. When the news reached Cognac his name was struck out of the society's oath. Henceforth members swore to be faithful to the Nation and to the Law, and to support with all their power "the principles of Equality and Liberty."[3] To the Jacobins of Poitiers the king's suspension seemed a "necessary catastrophe."[4] When the monarchy was finally abolished on the 21st of September, the republic was quietly accepted by the provincial Jacobins. In October

---

deserters. Sometimes the provincial societies had their own quarrels, analogous to the quarrel of the Paris Jacobins with the Feuillants and the Club monarchique. The club at Poitiers petitioned the National Assembly against the " reptiles aristocratiques" of the Société Littéraire and asked for the suppression of that society.—Adresse de la société des Amis de la Constitution de Poitiers à L'Assemblée Nationale, March 16, 1791. Archives nationales, D. IV. 67, ap. Doucet, *L'Esprit Public dans la Vienne* . . . 52.

[1] Réponse de la Société des Amis de la constitution séante à Melun à une Adresse . . . de la Société de Bayeux.—*A. J.* II. 587–9.

[2] *A. J.* III. 304.   [3] *Rév. franç.* XLIII. 254.

[4] R. Doucet, *L'Esprit Public dans le département de la Vienne* . . . pp. 123–4. Doucet gives as his authority, Adresse de la Société des Amis de la Constitution de Poitiers à l'Assemblée Législative, Aug. 19, 1792.—Arch. nat. G. 161.

1792, for example, the Jacobins of Auxerre, already calling themselves the "Friends of the Republic," declared that they were "no longer the French of 1791 . . . ," and swore to obey not the king but the law.[1] And we know of no protest on the part of any Jacobin society against the proclamation of the republic.[2]

Yet republicanism had been a plant of slow growth amongst the Jacobins, both at Paris and in the country. Down to the flight to Varennes they were all constitutional monarchists, and even afterwards it was only slowly and reluctantly that they became republicans. Their correspondence with the London Revolution Society belongs entirely to the monarchist period. No word of it is incompatible with unswerving loyalty to the English monarchy. On the 27th of December, 1791, the Society of Honfleur wrote the last known letter received by the Revolution Society from a Jacobin Club; the answer to it, written on the 6th of February, 1792, seems to have been the last letter in the whole correspondence. It was not until two months later that France became involved in the war with Austria which provoked the worst excesses of the Revolution; and six crowded months lay between the conclusion of the Revolution Society's French correspondence and the suspension of the King of France. Throughout the correspondence the members of the Revolution Society had therefore every reason to believe that the men to whom they wrote were constitutional monarchists.

Nor can it be for one moment admitted that the correspondence, which we shall presently analyse, of necessity committed the London Revolution Society to all or any of the views of the Jacobins, or of their adherents. This chapter has been written ill if it has not served to illustrate our ignorance rather than our knowledge; and no one at all acquainted with the political and journalistic literature

---

[1] Address to the Convention.—Archives nationales, C. 238 (247). In December 1792, a reporter to the Jacobins of Paris praised a society of "sans-culottes" at Bordeaux as "worthy of the Faubourg Saint-Antoine." —*A. J.* IV. 583.

[2] One society, that of Marseille, showed indecent eagerness for the death of the king.—Fabre, *Hist. of Marseille*, 487–8, 489 and note. A. Boudoin, *Hist. de Marseille*, 509.

of the period will be disposed to believe that the members of the Revolution Society were better informed than we. To-day reports of a debate in the French Chamber can be read in Fleet Street before the lights are out in the Palais Bourbon. In those days telegraph and telephone were unknown, steam navigation was a distant dream, and London might be illuminated for victory in the hour that our armies mourned defeat. Such news of the French Jacobins as reached their friends in England through the medium of the Press was scanty, belated, and none too accurate. There was, therefore, no reliable means of checking the account which the French Jacobins gave of themselves. Their letters were accepted at their face value, without any suspicion of the candour of the writers; and in all probability the English societies did well to receive them in that spirit.

The correspondence between the Revolution Society and the societies of Lille and Dijon, opened in November 1789, languished until after the celebration in London of the anniversary of the fall of the Bastille (July 14, 1790). Meantime Mr. Christopher John William Nesham, a young Englishman studying French at Vernon, had been able, during a bread riot, to save from a hostile mob the superintendent of a grain warehouse belonging to the city of Paris. The freedom of the borough of Vernon was conferred upon Nesham, who received a civic crown and a sword of honour from the commune of Paris.[1] All free people were brethren, declared the president of the commune; "France and England ought to entertain a mutual regard for each other;" and "the object most deserving their emulation" was "the promotion of the Happiness of Mankind."[2] An account of the proceedings was sent to the Revolution Society, which reciprocated these fraternal sentiments and expressed the hope that between Great Britain and France perpetual peace might be established to the remotest ages.[3]

On the 14th of July the anniversary of the fall of the

---

[1] *C. R. S.* 23–9; *Notices sur la Révolution dans l'Eure*, I. 152 *et seq.*, especially 166–7.

[2] *Ib.* I. 167–8; *C. R. S.* 30–3.   [3] *Ib.* 33–4.

Bastille was celebrated at the Crown and Anchor by an enthusiastic assembly of 652 friends of liberty, many of whom were members of the London Revolution Society.[1] Earl Stanhope presided. "The French Constitution," he said, "having become the object of every good man's fair wishes, will be hated only by the ill-intentioned; it will give a lesson to the whole world, and will, perhaps, hasten the day when all men, even kings, will regard each other as brothers, without regard to primogeniture." He toasted "the extinction of all jealousy between France and England," and their future emulation in spreading "the blessings of peace, liberty and virtue throughout the rest of the world."[2] Other toasts were numerous. Even if the diners avoided bumpers and stuck to claret—a puritan restraint of which some of them would certainly not be guilty—we still cannot refrain from admiring our ancestors for their strength of head. They drank to "The Majesty of the People,"[3] a subject for many journalistic sneers during the ensuing decade; "The Nation, the Law and the King," according to the French order of precedence; and "Equal representation of the English people in Parliament." But the climax of the entertainment was reached when a waiter mounted the table and lifted upon his head a block of stone from the ruins of the Bastille—duly authenticated, for was it not the gift of Mademoiselle le Chevalier d'Éon? The faithful rendered homage to the relic with all the ardour of crusaders doing reverence to a fragment of the true Cross.[4]

Price, the veteran of the assembly, waxed warm over the apparent accomplishment of his dream, and toasted an alliance between France and England to preserve universal peace and render the world happy.[5] On Sheridan's motion

---

[1] *Moniteur*, July 25, 1790, No. 208, p. 850. There is a reference to the fact of the meeting in the *New Ann. Reg.* 1790, *Occurrences*, 30.

[2] *Rév. de France et de Brabant*, III. 525–9, ap. Robinet *Danton émigré*, 41–2 ; *Moniteur*, July 30, 1790, No. 211, 867.

[3] It is said, though no authority is given, that Castlereagh presided at a banquet where "Our Sovereign Lord the People" was toasted.— Fitzpatrick, *Secret Service under Pitt*, 9.

[4] Probably in either case the united fragments would suffice to replace the original several times over.

[5] *Rév. de France et de Brabant*, ap. Robinet, 525–9.

it was resolved "that this assembly sincerely rejoices in the establishment and confirmation of liberty in France, and sees with particular satisfaction the sentiments of friendship and goodwill that the French people appears to have conceived towards this country. . . . ." The harmony of France and England "is essential to the liberty and happiness not only of these two nations but of the whole world." [1] Horne Tooke, feeling that from its generality and vagueness the resolution was open to misconstruction, tried to add an amendment declaring that the English nation had only to maintain and improve the Constitution which their ancestors had bequeathed to them.[2]   The meeting was too enthusiastic to permit any tampering with the resolution, but accepted a second and substantive motion, "that thanks to the generous efforts of their ancestors the English have not a task so difficult to fulfil as that with which the French are at present occupied; in a word, that they have only to maintain and perfect the Constitution which has been transmitted to them by their ancestors." [3]   The main resolution, conveyed to the National Assembly by Rochefoucauld, was cordially received and anew stimulated the French Jacobins to correspond with the Revolution Society.[4]

They received a further stimulus a few days later. Spain and England seemed to be preparing to fight, in appearance for a small trading settlement on Nootka Sound, in reality because Spanish statesmen suspected England of a desire to further her commercial interests by assisting the rebellious colonists of·Spain to throw off the yoke of their mother country as, a decade earlier, France and Spain had

---

[1] Archives nationales, C. 42 (379).   See also *Moniteur*, July 30, 1790, No. 211, p. 867.

[2] Horne Tooke's Diary, ap. *Notes and Queries*, 8th series, XI. 104 (Feb. 6, 1897) ; Stephens, *Mem. of Horne Tooke*, II. 113.

[3] *Moniteur, loc. cit.*

[4] Archives Nationales, *loc. cit.*   Reply of Treilhard, President of the Assembly, *C. R. S.* 45–7 ; *P.-V.* July 21, 1790, pp. 9–10 ; see also Gower's *Despatches*, 18.   Race hatred dies hard, as Gower's letter shows ; see *Moniteur*, July 26, 1790, No. 207, p. 854.   La Luzerne, in his dispatches to the French Government, made light of the Revolution Society.   " In the heat of wine," he said, " desires for an alliance were indeed expressed.   Everybody here gibes at the convocation."   Still Luzerne, full of Nootka Sound, feared that the English would make only too good use of the affair " to mislead the people of Paris."—Archives des Affaires Etrangères, *Corr. d'Angleterre*, 574, ff. 54–5.

assisted the thirteen American colonies to throw off the yoke of England. If the French National Assembly accepted the diplomatic obligations of the monarchy it would be compelled, in accordance with the Family Compact, to espouse the cause of Spain. France was anxious, irritable and undecided; the Assembly striving to maintain peace, the nation exasperated almost to the point of supporting war.

At this moment the London Revolution Society rendered a service to the cause of peace. Price delivered an eloquent and pacific speech which served to reassure the National Assembly to whom it was communicated. "The armament in preparation in our ports," he said, "excites no less alarm in generous Englishmen, in the sincere friends of humanity, than in Nations that the armament seems to menace; it compromises at once national prosperity and the world's peace, and sets a term to public credit. We are hurried at great strides towards the precipice. To-day France manifests dispositions towards peace, and soon the wisest nations will have no other thought. Already she has declared that she renounces all idea of conquest.[1] She will go still further. She will provoke an alliance with Great Britain. We have long regarded the French as our natural enemy; we wished to have nothing in common with a people that offered us only a despot and his slaves. The French have broken their chains; it is our example they have followed. But they give us another : they call us, not into the plains where the blood of slaves runs for the pleasure of despots, but towards an altar of peace which shall receive the honours of two great nations who wish to remain free and united. Ah ! May such a compact foreshadow the happiness of the human race ! We shall say to all civilised nations, *peace;* and there shall be peace." There is no apparent trace of a reply. One

[1] This refers to the decree of the Assembly, passed on May 22, by which wars of conquest were renounced. According to La Luzerne, Orléans, who was then in England, believed in the possibility of an alliance which would " elevate the two nations to the highest degree of power to which they could arrive." To the disgust of La Luzerne, Orléans made no secret of this belief, even during the Nootka Sound troubles. — *Corr. d'Angleterre,* 573, f. 205

ill-informed deputy stumbled on the just observation that
the English people were governed by a Parliament and
not by the "Society of the Friends of the French Constitution" (sic), which was not, therefore, "the depository of
the national will." But despite some criticism, it is obvious
from the records of the applause and of the debate that the
address had a soothing effect.[1]

Society after society wrote to ask for correspondence
and affiliation with their English contemporaries. The first
—the Society of Calais—must have written as soon as it
received the accounts of the English celebration on July 14.[2]
"Every heart has leapt at the consoling ideas of Price and
Sheridan," wrote the Society of Montpellier,[3] which desired
by its union with the Revolution Society to forge the first
link in the chain which should unite the two peoples. The
hope was more than once expressed that the Channel might,
in a metaphorical sense at least, become "a mere ditch."[4]
Between free peoples, thought many societies, there might
be intercourse, amity and peace; tyrants were the grand
separators of nations.[5] The English were greeted as the
"apostles of liberty." Now that national barriers had been
broken down there existed "no more foreigners in the
universe but tyrants and their slaves."[6] "You, gentlemen," said the Strasbourgeois, "were the first to realise
that the incipient Constitution of France announced the
preliminaries of universal peace."[7]

The Jacobins themselves hoped all things from a union
of free peoples in the same noble enterprise. "May we
soon see the day . . . when the human race, content with
the precious fruit of Liberty, shall bless the English for
having preserved its beneficent code, our brothers in the
United States of America for having put in greater evidence

---

[1] *Moniteur*, July 31, 1790, No. 212, p. 873-4; *P.-V.* July 29, 1790, p. 9-10.
It is not clear when this address was adopted. Presumably it was at the
meeting of July 20, 1790. If so, the minutes are incomplete in *C. R. S.*
See the letter of July 27, 1790, which also seems to imply the existence
of letters not reprinted in the correspondence. See also Towers,
Thoughts on the Commencement of a New Parliament.
[2] *C. R. S.* 40.
[3] *C. R. S.* 42-3; similar letter from Cherbourg, *ib.* 47-8.
[4] By the Ladies of Lille.—*C. R. S.* 256-7.   [5] *Ib.* 48-9, etc.
[6] *Ib.* 51-2.   [7] *Ib.* 60-1.

the rights of man, and our nation for having effaced the
contradictions which were destroying them, and for having
established and consolidated them for ever." [1] The Society
of Limoges proposed that the Jacobins should issue a manifesto to all the peoples of the earth, declaring the pacific
intentions of the French nation and their hope for the
happiness of the world; and they further suggested that
means should be concerted with the Friends of the Revolution in England for realising the "sublime plan of *universal
peace* so long regarded as chimerical." [2] "You do not
desire Universal Peace more than we do," wrote the Society
of Tours; that of Marseille seemed able to reconcile "open
War against Tyrants" with "Peace and Fraternity with the
whole human race;" [3] the "Young Friends of the Constitution of Toulouse," affiliated with the elder body, enunciated
the unimpeachable maxim that if the youth of the nations
grew up without racial prejudice there would be an end to
discord and rivalry; [4] and the dreams of the Society of
Grenoble seem even to have embraced an organic con-
federation of the world. [5]

This generous dream, in which concord between France
and England was but a prelude to universal peace and the
brotherhood of nations, the members of the Revolution
Society shared with their correspondents. It was the main
theme of their reply. "Convinced that the spirit of freedom
is rapidly advancing throughout England," they wrote,
"we hope one day to become *as one* family, and to find the
golden days when there shall be 'Peace on earth and
general goodwill.'" [6] "Esto perpetua !" they cry, in a letter
to the president of the Jacobins. "May the French as well
as the British Constitution, preserved in their purity and

---

[1] Signed by Louis de Noailles, as president.—*C. R. S.* 52–5. See also
Adresse de la Société des Amis de la Constitution de France à Chalon-
sur-Saône à la Société de la Révolution d'Angleterre à Londres ; and
C. R. S. 68–70, 73–8, 82–3, 84–5, 97, 98–9, 112–3, 133, 135.—*A. J.*
II. 386–8, 185–7, 210–12, etc. In consequence of the separate publication in France of the letter from Chalons, several societies refer to it as
the source of true inspiration. See *C. R. S.* 93–5.

[2] *Les Jacobins au Village*, 24–5 ; Chuquet, *Voyage de Halem*, 227.

[3] *C. R. S.* 144–5.   [4] *Ib.* 158–61.

[5] *Ib.* 177–9 ; see also 194–7, 218–20.

[6] To Calais, *ib.* 40–1 ; see also 113–14, 202–4, 209–10, 235–6.

vigour, be *immortal*." [1] "We . . . agree, sir, with your Society that it would be happy for our countries, and for the Nations around if a sacred Union could be found between them, in support of *Universal* FREEDOM. In the meantime, let this union be established among the Friends of Liberty wherever they may be found." [2] Adapting the famous *mot* of Louis XIV, they promised the Society of Marseille that they would act as if "the Strait between Calais and Dover were no more." [3] In another letter, written doubtless by one of the political divines who wielded such influence in the society, they extended "the Right Hand of Fellowship" to their brethren at Clermont-Ferrand. [4]

The members of the corresponding committee did not wander far from the safe path of generalisation. But they did not omit to flatter the men of Orléans by a compliment to the memory of Jeanne d'Arc. [5] Occasionally an individual member seems to have expressed his own particular views—admiration for Harrington's *Oceana,* or a belief in election in two degrees, [6] the domestic hope of a parliamentary reform [7] or the recognition—the mistaken recognition—that French help to the thirteen revolting American colonies had been an unselfish tribute to liberty. [8] References to the details of French internal politics are few and non-committal. These men, at each stage of its progress, had believed that the Revolution had reached the moderate and constitutional termination. [9] To them it was the successful application in another land of political principles which a century before had been laid down by their own ancestors; [10] they were slow to despair of the Revolution, but they, like their ancestors, were constant in their abhorrence

---

[1] *C. R. S.* 55-60 ; see also 62-4.

[2] *Ib.* 55-60 ; see also 78-81, 96, 109-10, 188-90, 193.

[3] *Ib.* 117-18. In another letter they censured the "Gothic rivalry and enmity" which had hitherto separated the two nations.—*Ib.* 252-3. See also 263-4.   [4] *Ib.* 122-3.   [5] *Ib.* 254-6.   [6] *Ib.* 260-1'.

[7] *Ib.* 270-1. "A reform in the Representation of the People is what we principally want and what we shall peaceably obtain."

[8] *Ib.* 109-10.

[9] *Ib.* 165-6. What appears to have been the last letter which the Revolution Society received from a French society was dated December 27, 1791.—*Ib.* 273.   [10] *Ib.* 71-3.

of anarchy and discord.[1] "The principles of your Constitution," they said, "are only disapproved by those who possess and exercise privileges incompatible with the genuine spirit of our own and their servile dependents who profit by those corruptions which have been introduced by criminal negligence and the lapse of time."[2] "Such a Constitution " must be protected "by a rigid obedience to just and equal laws."[3] "Our society . . . is *not* formed to oppose legitimate government or to interfere in *any* manner with the administration of it, but to preserve ourselves and others from that degeneracy which time is apt to produce; and to maintain inviolate the Constitution not *merely* in form but in substance as it was established in 1688, on the Rights of Man."[4] "By . . . checking tyranny," they told the French, "you have legitimated monarchy." "Woe! therefore to any Country that may endeavour to disturb the Constitution you have established, and shame ! shame ! to our own country should she make the attempt : for surely it is not for England to join in a Conspiracy against Liberty."[5]

With some of its correspondents the Revolution Society was more intimately allied than others. Any one coming in its name—however preposterous his story—received a welcome and a courteous hearing from the Jacobins of Paris.[6] When David was commissioned by the Jacobins to paint his now famous picture of the "Oath of the Tennis Court," only the Jacobins and their affiliated societies were permitted to subscribe towards its cost or to receive a copy of the engraving when it was completed ;[7] but "the society, considering that all free people are brothers, makes honourable exception of . . . the Friends of the Revolution of London and admits it to join in the subscription."[8] Whether the offer was accepted or not we do not know ; that it was made is striking proof of the reverence in which the elder society was held by the junior.

[1] *C. R. S.* 119–20. [2] *Ib.* 270–1.
[3] *Ib.* 273–5. [4] *Ib.* 179–80.
[5] To the Society of Aix, March 20, 1791.—*C. R. S.* 91–3.
[6] See accounts of a certain Gisfly (*sic*) who professed to be a member of the London Revolution Society.—*A. J.* II. 417, 447–9.
[7] *A. J.* I. 330–5. [8] *Ib.* I. 330–5. Prospectus, article IV.

If the Jacobins of Paris were the most famous, the most cordial of all the correspondents of the London Revolution Society was the Society of Nantes. It stands out from the rest and deserves special mention. "The meeting in London on July 14, 1790, to celebrate the French Revolution, gave rise," a pamphleteer tells us, "to the Anglo-Gallic festival at Nantes, on the 23rd August following, to which all the English in that city and in the neighbouring towns were invited. This festival was given by the Société des Amis de la Constitution à Nantes, a society consisting of several hundred members, and from that society M. Français, their president, and M. Bougon were sent as deputies to the Revolution Society of London,"[1] with instructions to stay long enough to establish amicable relations with its members.[2]

The committee of the London Revolution Society assembled specially to hear the deputies under the chairmanship of John Hurford Stone,[3] who afterwards took up his residence in France and became naturalised as a Frenchman. Français, who spoke in English, believed that the new Constitution would be the means of maintaining uninterrupted peace between the two nations, and would prevent offensive war, for "only a free nation ' could ' set a proper value on the lives of men." He presented a stained drawing of a tricoloured banner which had been used at the Nantes fête, inscribed "À l'Union de la France et d'Angleterre," and with the motto "Pacte universel." Bougon, who spoke in his own tongue, rejoiced that ". . . France, in concert with its king," had at last raised "its voice to the throne of Jupiter liberator," and that "the great Family of the human race, more enlightened as to true greatness, walked steadily in the footprints which England had traced for it. . . ."[4]

These expressions of reverence for their ancestors and of

---

[1] Towers, *Thoughts on the Commencement of a New Parliament* . . . 78-80 ; see also Rapport des Députés de la Société des Amis de la Constitution de Nantes, 30-4.

[2] They were also instructed to open communications with other societies holding similar views.— *C. R. S.* 64-5.

[3] Rapport des Députés . . . 19-20.

[4] *Ib.* . . 20-4 ; *C. R. S.* 65-7.

goodwill towards themselves greatly flattered the committee of the Revolution Society, but the reply of their spokesman breathed the ancestral prudence as much as the fervour of the living. He rejoiced that their good wishes for the success of the Revolution had not been in vain. "Although accustomed to struggle ceaselessly for our liberty, and to admire in the pages of our history the character of those who have shed their blood in fighting for it, yet we have been unable to resist a profound admiration, an astonishment going almost to terror, when we have seen this sudden and terrible fall of despotism in France." To their friendship for France they had been obliged to add respect and admiration. "We have everything to hope from a race so brave and so enlightened, above all when we consider that they know how to pursue liberty with circumspection, prudence and wisdom." [1]

On October 4, the society gave a dinner in honour of the Nantais. Price, "at once the Socrates and the Euclid " of England, said grace; and a Mr. Watson, M.P., possibly member for the City, presided.[2] It was proposed to send deputies to France, and specially to Nantes, to the fête of the Federation, to bear assurances of peace and fellowship.[3] The delegates were duly toasted,[4] and took home with them to Nantes an address engrossed on vellum, in which the hope was expressed that "perpetual peace and friendship " might "subsist between England and France." [5]

The Nantes society celebrated the anniversary of the English Revolution of 1688 in almost as many toasts as the Englishmen, and they drank also to the London Society.[6] The delegates were received with the enthusiasm and consideration meted out to men returning from a perilous journey,[7] and they in their turn rejoiced that they

[1] Rapport des Députés . . . 24-7. This is called the address of the president—apparently a mistake for chairman (of the committee). If this conjecture is correct the speech is very remarkable, as coming from John Hurford Stone, whose opinions are generally regarded as far too extreme to be clothed in such moderate language.

[2] Brooke Watson, M.P. for the City, 1784-93 ; baronet 1803 ?

[3] Rapport des Députés, 28-9.   [4] *Ib.* 32-5.

[5] *C. R. S.* 67-8 ; Rapport, 14-6. The action of the Nantes society was sharply criticised in a letter from Nantes printed in the *Moniteur*, Oct. 10, 1790, No. 283, p. 1173 ; cf. *C. R. S.* 105-7.

[6] *Ib.* 103-4.   [7] Rapport, 13-14.

had planted "the olive tree of peace near the walls of West-minster."[1]   At the same meeting "M. Vaughan, an Eng-lishman and a relation of the celebrated Hornes (*sic*) Tooke,"[2] delivered a speech full of expressions of admira-tion for the constitutional exertions of the French, which would "spread over the whole surface of the globe the wholesome light of Legislation, with all the gifts of benevolent humanity."[3]

Price and Mirabeau died almost simultaneously,[4] the one in the ripeness of his honoured age, saying a glad *Nunc Dimittis;* the other prematurely wasted, leaving his tasks unaccomplished.   Diverse as were the men, the English followers of the one and the French supporters of the other were drawn closer together in the comradeship of mourning.   The names of the two men were often linked in reciprocal expressions of sympathy and admiration.[5] French societies decided to wear mourning for Price.[6]   The Jacobins of Paris sent a letter of condolence to the Revolu-tion Society of London,[7] and other societies followed their example.[8]   Some spoke of him as a great man who belonged to no single nation but to the world;[9] others spoke of him as "the torch of Liberty in his age;"[10] and a society in the little capital of the Saintonge rejoiced that "Price had not ceased to live," but that his spirit would still inspire men to serve the cause of freedom.[11]   "Elevated above all local prejudice," wrote those who had been his followers, "and disdaining the narrow and sordid dis-tinctions of party, his generous heart expanded with affection to *all* the human race."[12]

With its letter to Honfleur on the 6th of February, 1792, the correspondence of the Revolution Society with

[1] Rapport, 4–12.
[2] M.P. for Calne and uncle by marriage of Cardinal Manning.   It is not clear that he was really related to Horne Tooke, though he some-times acted as his secretary.   See Alger, *Englishmen in the French Revolution*, 91.   [3] Rapport des Députés . . . 16–18.
[4] Price on March 19 ; Mirabeau on April 2, 1791.
[5] *C. R. S.* 194–7, 167–9, 149–51.
[6] *A. J.* II. 395 ; *C. R. S.* 142, 167–9, 149–51, 164–5, 210–12.
[7] *A. J.* II. 391–5, *C. R. S.* 143–4.   [8] *Ib.* 207–8, 213–14, etc.
[9] *Ib.* 173–4.   [10] *Ib.* 204–5.   [11] *Ib.* 194–7.
[12] *Ib.* 205–7 ; cf. also 99–100, etc.

popular societies in France seems, as we have said, to have come to an end. The later history of the society is, in fact, a little obscure. A faithful remnant of it reappeared in November 1792 to celebrate the Revolution of 1688 and to adopt an address to the National Convention, but its real importance seems to end with the cessation of its French correspondence. Nevertheless, the torch was handed on to others, and its leading members reappeared in the ranks of other societies, such as the Society for Constitutional Information, which were, perhaps, better organised, and of which the aims were more clearly defined.

By its French correspondence, therefore, the society stands or falls, and nothing could well be more harmless than the vague and high-flown sentiments exchanged during the period of French constitutionalism. But meanwhile opinion in England was hardening against the French revolutionists, especially after November 1790, when Burke's *Reflections* were published, and most Englishmen were becoming incapable of forming a just judgment either of events in France or of those in England who looked with a sympathetic eye upon the efforts which Frenchmen were making to hammer out a workable Constitution. While English and French societies were exchanging large and sounding phrases, a fierce pamphlet warfare was going on in England, the result of which was to crystallise opinion on both sides; to provide the popular reformers with a lucid, sweeping, plausible body of doctrine in Paine's *Rights of Man;* to provide the defenders of the *status quo* with fuel for their fears and with a theoretic, and still more an emotional, justification for their resistance to change in Burke's *Reflections*. The result of this pamphlet warfare was, therefore, such a hardening of opinion in England, for and against reform, that though parliamentary reform was not their direct subject, the more important pamphlets must, nevertheless, be examined if first the rise and then the ebb of opinion favourable to reform is properly to be understood.

CHAPTER VII

THE DISCUSSION OF THE FIRST PRINCIPLES OF GOVERNMENT IN ENGLAND

NOV. 1789—FEB. 1792

ON the 4th of November, 1789, on the same occasion as that on which he had carried his motion in praise of the French Revolution, Dr. Price had preached before the Revolution Society of London a sermon on "Love of Country." Fate has not dealt kindly with Dr. Price. During his lifetime men of the same cast of political thought held him the equal of Mirabeau; as a practical economist he was more regarded than Adam Smith or Dean Tucker. Yet unhappily for his later fame his contemporaries preferred his economic to his political opinions; they rejected the theories which may have been right, and accepted those which were certainly wrong. Price is now remembered for a fallacious theory of the sinking fund, adopted by Pitt, and for a political sermon, condemned by Burke.

To Burke's condemnation the sermon on "Love of Country" owes half its fame. It was the prelude to one of the fiercest of our political controversies, and evoked some of our finest political pamphlets. But the sermon was not merely political; it had a distinct ethical value. Price, who took for text the patriotic outburst of a Hebrew poet in praise of Jerusalem,[1] rebuked those shallow and immoral patriots who are comparative in their methods, and who glory in their country only because it outshines its neighbours. Had he not sought grounds rather of difference than of agreement, Burke might himself have echoed Price when he declared patriotism to be an emotion, to be love of country for its own sake, and more than an

---

[1] Psalm cxii. 2-9.

160

intellectual assent to its laws. For Price the patriot was a man who sought to enlighten his country with knowledge and to elevate it by virtue. In order that he might attain these twin ends of virtue and knowledge it followed that the citizen must be free.[1]

So ethics led imperceptibly to politics. According to Price's definition "country" was no mere geographical expression; it was the "community," the sum of the citizens who dwelt together so as to form a political entity. Civil laws were the regulations agreed upon by the community to secure the civic ends of enlightenment and virtue.[2] Throughout, therefore, he regarded the community as the final authority in government. Ultimately the citizens were the governors. The king was no more than the collective majesty of the people : [3] "the first servant of the public; created by it, maintained by it and responsible to it." [4]

It was on these grounds that Price defended the principles of the Revolution Society. Liberty of conscience in religion and resistance to the misuse of power he thought essential "rights" in a free community; and, in a famous sentence, he claimed the "right" of Englishmen to choose their own governors; to cashier them for misconduct, and to frame a Government for themselves.[5] His theory of rights may have been fallacious, he may have pressed abstract propositions to unwarrantable extremes, but Price was moderate enough in his suggestion of reform. He proposed nothing more drastic than to remedy the failures of the English Revolution by the abolition of the test laws,[6] and the removal of inequalities in the parliamentary representation.[7]

As he looked forward in hope to the general amendment of human affairs the aged orator spoke a thankful *Nunc Dimittis.* "I have lived to see a diffusion of knowledge which has undermined superstition and error—I have lived to see the rights of man better understood than ever, and

---

[1] *A Discourse on the Love of Country, etc.* The vital principles were not new, but had been enunciated by Price in his "Observations on the Nature of Civil Liberty" in 1776, when he and Burke fought their political battles on the same side.

[2] *Ib.* 21.   [3] *Ib.* 24.   [4] *Ib.* 23.
[5] *Ib.* 34.   [6] *Ib.* 36.   [7] *Ib.* 39–41.

nations panting for liberty that seemed to have lost the idea of it—I have lived to see Thirty Millions of people, indignant and resolute, spurning at slavery, and demanding liberty with an irresistible voice. . . . After sharing the benefits of one Revolution, I have been spared to be a witness to two other Revolutions, both glorious." [1]

In his *Reflections on the Revolution in France*, published in the beginning of November 1790, Burke made light of the Revolution Society as a club but lately heard of which never entered into the thoughts of any person outside the circle of its members.[2] Burke may have told the truth. But he confessed to an ignorance such as he was seldom willing to acknowledge; and if the political significance of the society was so slight it is difficult, at first, to understand why he should have levelled at it one of the greatest of his pamphlets. "There had been no prosecution against them, nor any charge founded even upon suspicion of disaffection against any of their body," Erskine said later. "*Why, then, make their proceedings the subject of alarm throughout England?*" [3]

The truth lies in the fact that Price's sermon before the Revolution Society was not the cause but the occasion of the outburst of Burke's hoarded wrath against the revolutionists and all their works, an outburst which, in the view of some competent observers, changed the course of European history.[4] In it we see the signs of fierce conflict between the rational and the emotional in Burke's nature; and the rational is not left uppermost.

First he appeals to reason, commending to the French that "spirit of rational liberty" which had so long inspired the conduct of his own life. "I think you bound," he told them, "in all honest policy, to provide a permanent body in which that spirit may reside and an effectual organ by

---

[1] *Discourse on the Love of Country*, 49–50. It is evident that Price was conscious of failing powers, and that the much-criticised *Nunc Dimittis* was no mere figure of speech. The Revolution Society asked him to publish the sermon, together with that part which "for want of time and strength" he did not deliver.—*C. R. S.* 3–4.

[2] *Works*, II. 280.   [3] *S. T.* XXII. 429.

[4] Étienne Dumont, for example. Quoted in Stanhope's *Pitt*, I. 375; cf. Windham's *Diary*, 213.

which it may act." [1] He defended rather than reprobated moderate changes. "A State without the means of some change is without the means of its conservation. Without such means it might even risk the loss of that part of the constitution which it wished the most religiously to preserve;" on this principle, at the Restoration of 1660 and the Revolution of 1688 the English nation "regenerated the deficient parts of the old constitution through the parts that were not impaired." [2] In this regard for the sanctity of institutions he was perfectly consistent with himself. He might have said in 1765, as he said in 1790, that "people will not look forward to posterity who never look backward to their ancestors." [3] In defending the hereditary principle he made use of that organic analogy which is his most fruitful contribution to political theory. [4] "Our political system," he wrote, "is placed in a just correspondence and symmetry with the order of the world, and with the mode of existence decreed to a permanent body composed of transitory parts; wherein by the disposition of a stupendous wisdom, moulding together the great mysterious incorporation of the human race, the whole at one time is never old, or middle-aged or young, but in a condition of unchangeable constancy moves on through the varied tenor of perpetual decay, fall, renovation and progression. Thus by preserving the method of nature in the conduct of the State, in what we improve, we are never wholly new; in what we retain we are never wholly obsolete." [5]

Here, where in one sense he is most practical, he is also most abstract and most mystical—as theocratic in the eighteenth century as the dateless prophets of the Hebrews. He pours forth abuse of the abstract principles of the French revolutionists chiefly because he sees their practical dangers. "Circumstances . . . give, in reality, to every political principle its distinguishing colour and discriminating effect. The circumstances are what render every civil and political scheme noxious to mankind." "Is

---

[1] *Works*, II. 278 ; cf. Morley's *Burke*, 146.
[2] *Works*, II. 295. [3] *Ib*. II. 307.
[4] For an interesting account of his influence on Joseph de Maistre, see Vaughan, *The Romantic Revolt*, 430–5. [5] *Works*, II. 307.

it," he says, ridiculing the abstract rights of man, "because liberty may be classed amongst the blessings of mankind that I am to felicitate a madman who has escaped from the protecting restraint and wholesome darkness of his cell, on his restoration to the enjoyment of light and liberty? Am I to congratulate a highwayman and murderer, who has broke his prison, upon the recovery of natural rights." [1]

Burke's powerful imagination was excited by the wrongs of the French Queen, as it had been by the fictitious miseries of imaginary Rohillas; and while he lamented the pomp and pageantry of ancient France, he dilated also on the practical disadvantages and economic errors of the Revolution. But here, to borrow his own phrase, Burke's passions instructed his reason. [2]

More directly to our purpose is his attack on a "new and hitherto unheard-of Bill of Rights," [3] expounded in "a sort of porridge of various political opinions and reflections," [4] by Dr. Price, from whom Burke uniformly withholds the respect which, from his age, station and abilities, he had the right to expect. [5]

The triple right which Price claimed—the right of Englishmen to choose their own governors, to cashier them for misconduct, and to frame a Government for themselves —Burke, arguing from silence, maintains was unrecognised in the Revolution of 1688 and 1689. "That a king of popular choice was the only legal king " [6] could have been established then if ever. He denounces the "unwarrantable maxim " "that no throne is lawful but the elective," and the assertion, "in direct opposition to one of the wisest and most beautiful parts of our constitution, that the king is no more than the first servant of the public, created by it and responsible to it." [7]

All this it is the fashion to admire, and, fairness of interpretation apart, it is justly admirable. But as a reply to Price it owes most of its effect to the straining of Price's meaning. Price did not say that popular choice was to be

[1] *Works*, II. 282.   [2] See Coleridge, *Table Talk* (ed. 1851), 10.
[3] *Works*, II. 290.   [4] *Ib.* II. 285.
[5] *Ib.* 356.   [6] *Ib.* 291.   [7] *Ib.* II. 303.

interpreted as popular election; nor did he mean it. He was satisfied with the national assent and had no wish to dispossess George III, towards whom, as an individual and a monarch, he was conceivably more tolerant than Burke himself. As he regarded the known fact of assent in the light of a choice, so he looked on the undoubted dismission of James II, to be succeeded by William III, as proof of the fact that the nation had the right to choose or cashier its governor. He had no fantastic visions of an unorganised, acephalous nation for which, *de novo*, an academic constitution had to be evolved and a ruler provided. It was enough for him that, as a matter of history and experience, personal rule had given place to parliamentary government. In reason one could ask no greater constitutional change.[1]

His tripartite axiom, therefore, appeared to Price indisputable because at the Revolution of 1688 it had, as he thought, survived dispute. But no more than Burke himself was he in haste to administer the last "critical, ambiguous bitter potion to a distempered State." "With or without right," he would have agreed, "a revolution will be the very last resource of the thinking and the good." [2]

Whatever the defects of Burke's reasoning, the *Reflections* had a profound influence on the English people. Thirty thousand copies of it were sold, in a few years, as a five-shilling pamphlet : an enormous sale for those days.[3] Burke received at least a thousand pounds as the reward of his labours.[4] The *Reflections* drove the nation to take up an attitude hostile to the Revolution.[5] Barthelémy, the French diplomat, reports that not only has "Mr. Burke's book " "united the whole English nation " against the revolutionists, but that it "has rendered infinitely agreeable at the Court of St. James this very man who was formerly

---

[1] Preface to the 4th ed. of *Love of Our Country*, ix–xii.
[2] *Works*, II. 304.   [3] Prior's *Burke*, 311 ; Morley's *Burke*, 151.
[4] Nicoll, Dodsley's executor, showed Arthur Young one receipt from Burke for £1000 for profits on the *Reflections*. Probably this was not the sole payment.—*Auto. of A. Young*, 428.
[5] See, for instance, Edgeworth in the Irish House of Commons, Feb. 25, 1799.—*Mem.* II. 247.

held there in horror." [1]   On Windham especially amongst
English statesmen Burke laid an irresistible spell; [2] perhaps luckily for him, for had they taken the popular side
both Burke and Windham would inevitably have been
hanged. [3]   Many another public man begged leave, with
Gibbon, to subscribe his assent to Mr. Burke's creed on
the Revolution in France. [4]

Burke had endured severe criticism during the progress
of his work from the only man whom he seems ever to
have permitted to offer it, Sir Philip Francis. [5]   Still more
severe was the criticism of the reformers.   The Revolution
Society rebuked his presumption in pretending to act "as
the Representative Majesty and Collective voice of the
whole people of England," [6] and one reformer maintained
that when there was set aside the parts that were unanswer-
able, not worth answering and no subject for an answer,
his false principle and distorted reasonings required little
exposure at the bar of good sense. [7]   There were, nevertheless, at least thirty-eight formal replies. [8]   Most of them
are no longer read, and probably few of them are worth
reading.   But that one of them has been forgotten is the
world's loss.

---

[1] *Correspondance d'Angleterre* (au Ministère des Affaires étrangères),
576, ff. 121–3.

[2] Nov. 7, 1790.—Windham's *Diary*, 213.

[3] Such is the saying attributed to Fox.—Moore's *Sheridan*, II. 129.

[4] Gibbon's *Memoirs*, 237. See Horace Walpole's *Letters*, XIV. 314,
326, 331, 335, 344–5 ; cf. 316. See also the collection of opinions in
Prior, 313–18.

[5] Francis to Burke, Feb. 19, 1790. Francis's *Letters*, II. 377–80.
Burke to Francis, Feb. 20, 1790.—*Ib.* 380–6.

[6] Introduction to the *Correspondence of the Revolution Society*,
which contains a sort of official reply to Burke. See also Priestley's
Letter to Burke, XXII. 168–73 and 179.

[7] Dr. Aikin to Dr. Haygarth, Dec. 1790, *Mem. of Dr. Aikin*, I.
146–7. In this connection see also Buckle's exposition of the effect of the
Revolution on the mind of Burke.—*Hist. of Civilisation*, I. 424.

[8] Prior, 322. They hindered the publication of Cowper's *Homer*.
"Burke's pamphlet stood in my way when I wrote last ; for every press,
and consequently mine, groaned with answers to it."—Cowper to Clot-
worthy Rowley.—*Letters*, IV. 23. Price replied, briefly and with dignity,
in an introduction to the fourth edition of his sermon. A translation of
the added matter was given by the *Moniteur*, Dec. 6, 1790, No. 340,
p. 1403. His co-pastor, Dr. Towers, replied in "Thoughts on the Commencement of a New Parliament, with remarks on the letter of the Right
Hon. Edmund Burke on the Revolution in France."

Mary Wollstonecraft's was the first,[1] and in some ways the best, of the replies. Though she is remembered as the mother of Mary Shelley and as the first wife of that strange defender of freedom, William Godwin, Mary Wollstonecraft has scarcely received the recognition due to her intellectual powers and literary merit. In recent times the course of political controversy has brought her *Vindication of the Rights of Woman* into the prominence which it deserves, but it is strange indeed that the only reply to Burke which is adequate on the emotional side should have lapsed into obscurity, for Burke's strength was due as much to the intensity of his feelings as to the power of his mind, and the antagonist who was sufficiently sympathetic to meet him on his own ground had manifest advantages over other controversialists.[2]

Mary Wollstonecraft had received the help and enjoyed the friendship of Dr. Price. Her *Vindication of the Rights of Man* was therefore something more than a mere defence of his principles; it was a work of gratitude and a tribute of admiration. She was indignant that the man whom she regarded, perhaps with an exaggerated devotion, as sage and prophet, counsellor and friend, should be loaded with undeserved abuse. "In reprobating Dr. Price's opinions," she said—and she laid herself open to a *tu quoque* for her own treatment of Burke—"you might have spared the man; and if you had had but half as much reverence for the grey hairs of virtue as for the accidental distinctions of rank you would not have treated" him "with such indecent familiarity and supercilious contempt."[3]

Like Burke himself, Mary Wollstonecraft made great parade of an appeal to reason, and denounced the "sophisticated arguments" that he advanced "in the questionable shape of natural feelings and common sense."[4] "I know," she said, "that you have a mortal antipathy to reason;

---

[1] Dr. E. R. Clough, *Mary Wollstonecraft and the Rights of Woman*, 72.

[2] For the life of Mary Wollstonecraft, and a study of her works and influence, see Dr. Emma Rauschenbosch Clough's *Mary Wollstonecraft*.

[3] *A Vindication of the Rights of Man*, 34; cf. Priestley, *Mem*. II. 99, 102.

[4] Preface to the *Vindication*, cf. p. 6,

but if there is anything like argument or first principles in your wild declamation, behold the result : that we are to reverence the rust of antiquity, and term the unnatural customs, which ignorance and mistaken self-interest have consolidated, the sage fruit of reason and experience." [1]

"The birthright of man," she said in a definition which, sound or unsound, cut at the very roots of Burke's ridicule of natural rights, "is such a degree of liberty, civil and religious, as is compatible with the liberty of the other individuals whom he is united with in a social compact." [2] But granting, for the sake of argument, his theory of pre-scription, "Will Mr. Burke be at the trouble to inform us how far we are to go back to discover the rights of man, since the light of reason is such a fallacious guide that none but fools trust to its cold investigation ? " [3]   "And is Magna Carta to rest for its support on a former grant . . . till chaos becomes the base of the mighty structure ? " [4]

How, she asks, on his prescriptive principles, could Burke defend the American Revolution or justify the Reformation ? [5] "To go further back;—had you been a Jew, you would have joined in the cry, Crucify Him !— Crucify Him ! The promulgation of a new doctrine and the violation of old laws and customs that did not, like ours, melt into darkness and ignorance, but rested on divine authority, must have been a dangerous innovation, in your eyes, particularly if you had not been informed that the Carpenter's Son was of the stock and lineage of David." [6]

Burke was always haunted—quite needlessly, as Mr. Gladstone maintained—by the delusion that property is sluggish and inert. [7] Mary Wollstonecraft touched on a real weakness when she branded him as "the champion of property, the adorer of the golden image which power has set up." [8] "Security of property ! Behold, in a few words, the definition of English liberty. . . . But softly—it is only the property of the rich that is secure ; the man who lives by the sweat of his brow has no asylum from

[1] *Vindication*, 9.   [2] *Ib.* 7.
[3] *Ib.* 12.   [4] *Ib.* 13.
[5] *Ib.* 22.   [6] *Ib.* 20–1.
[7] *Works*, II. 324.   [8] *Vindication*, 19, cf. 47.

oppression.[1] . . . Misery, to reach your heart . . . must
have its cap and bells. . . ."[2]

In this reference to the poor she struck the true emotional
note which revealed her as sensitive and apprehensive
beyond the measure of her times on questions of social
welfare. The poor, Burke had said, "must respect that
property of which they cannot partake. They must labour
to obtain what by labour can be obtained; and when they
find, as they commonly do, the success disproportioned
to the endeavour, they must be taught their consolation
in the final proportions of eternal justice."[3] It was unlike
Burke, as it was also unworthy of him, to treat religion
as part of a system of police, and Mary Wollstonecraft
was justifiably indignant. "This," she said, "is contempt-
ible, hard-hearted sophistry in specious form of humility
and submission to the will of Heaven."[4]

"Why cannot large estates be divided into small farms?
These dwellings would indeed grace our land. Why are
huge forests allowed to stretch out with idle pomp and all
the indolence of Eastern grandeur? Why do the brown
wastes meet the traveller's view, when men want work?
But commons cannot be enclosed without Acts of Parliament to increase the property of the rich. Why might
not the industrious peasant be allowed to steal a farm
from the heath?" She indulged herself in a fair vision of
peasant homesteads, but had to abandon it with a sigh.[5]
"Domination blasts all these prospects; virtue can only
flourish amongst equals, and the man who submits to a
fellow-creature because it promotes his worldly interest,
and he who relieves only because it is his duty to lay up
a treasure in heaven, are much on a par, for both are
radically degraded by the habits of their life."[6] "It is,
sir, *possible* to render the poor happier in this world
without depriving them of the consolation which you
gratuitously grant them in the next."[7]

It was James Mackintosh, a young Scots lawyer, who

[1] *Vindication*, 23.   [2] *Ib.* 25.
[3] *Works*, II. 514, cf. V. 321.   [4] *Vindication*, 136.
[5] *Ib.* 140–1 ; cf. Thelwall's *Peripatetic*, I. 31, 133, 136.
[6] *Vindication*, 141.   [7] *Ib.* 136.

made the official reply to Burke on behalf of his former
political associates, in a pamphlet called *Vindiciæ Gallicæ*,
which established the reputation of the author.[1] Mackintosh apprehended the mystical basis of all Burke's reasoning. He realised how his splendid imagination at times
overcame his reason altogether, and blunted his sense of
proportion, so that "the sensibility which seems scared by
the homely miseries of the vulgar is attracted only by the
splendid sorrows of royalty."[2] Unlike Mary Wollstonecraft, Mackintosh never abandons the cool and persuasive
language of reason to give play to a passing fancy or a
fleeting emotion; and what it gains in argument his work
loses in intrinsic interest and literary merit. The pamphlet
is now almost unreadable, but when it was originally issued
its sale, though not comparable for a moment with that of
the *Reflections*, was sufficient to induce the publisher to
pay Mackintosh several times the contract price;[3] and it is
evident from the references of the time that the pamphlet
was generally read and frequently applauded.

Much of it is filled with a detailed examination of
Burke's specific criticisms of the work of revolution.
Mackintosh then attacks Burke on more general principles.
It was absurd, he argued, to call for the authority of the
National Assembly; like that of the Convention of 1689,
the validity of its acts must depend on subsequent approval.
The former institutions of France were incorrigible. The
excellences attributed to them by Burke were imaginary.
"These institutions would have destroyed liberty before
liberty had corrected their spirit."[4] To preserve liberty
inviolate there was, indeed, "a necessity of frequently
recalling Governments to their first principles."[5] Suppose
the miseries of France exaggerated. By what principle of
reason or justice were the French precluded from forming
a Constitution less imperfect than other countries had

---

[1] *Life of Mackintosh*, by R. J. Mackintosh, 1835. Mackintosh is the
"Man of Promise" of Sir Henry Bulwer's *Historical Sketches*. See also
Hazlitt's sketch in *The Spirit of the Age*, and the references in Macaulay's
review of Mackintosh's *History of the Revolution of* 1688.

[2] *Vindiciæ Gallicæ*, iii.

[3] *Life of Mackintosh*, I. 58 and note.

[4] *Vindiciæ Gallicæ*, 46.   [5] *Ib.* 47.

acquired by accident?[1] "EXPERIENCE," said Mackintosh, "was still THE BASIS OF ALL. Not the puny and trammelled experience of a *Statesman by Trade,* who trembles at any change in the TRICKS . . . but an experience liberal and enlightened which hears the testimony of ages and nations, and collects from it the general principles which regulate the mechanism of society."[2] France had at her disposal the experience not of one, but of all countries, and a nation in which the discussion of political and constitutional questions was at least a hundred years old[3] was surely entitled to exercise its own judgment on the evil and the good.

Burke pointed to the excesses of the revolutionists. But the sacred Revolution of 1688 had also had its attendant evils and, were transient distresses to stand in the way of permanent good, there would be no possible improvement. "They are never the *many*," he said, in words that sound like an echo of Burke's own, "whose interest is at stake : they cannot judge, and no appeal to them is hazarded. They are the *few* whose interest is linked to the perpetuity of oppression and abuse."[4]

Finally Mackintosh defended Dr. Price. The "right" to choose governors was not, he said, materially affected if we elected to choose a race rather than an individual.[5] If this was allowed, the three claims that Price had made had already been admitted in the course of our history, and were a fair basis for the "tranquil and legal reform"[6] desired by those whom Burke had seen fit to traduce. "The Briefs of the Pope and the pamphlets of Mr. Burke, the edicts of the Spanish Court and the mandates of the Spanish Inquisition, the Birmingham rioters[7] and the Oxford graduates," he cried in a parting sarcasm, "equally render to liberty the involuntary homage of their alarm."[8]

James Mackintosh and Mary Wollstonecraft represent distinct types of the opponents of Burke. Yet another

---

[1] *Vindiciæ Gallicæ*, 48.   [2] *Ib.* 50.
[3] *Ib.* 51-2.   [4] *Ib.* 101.
[5] *Ib.* 139 ; cf. Priestley's Letter to Burke, III., *Works*, XXII. 165-73.
[6] *Vindiciæ*, 163.   [7] See below, p. 183-8.
[8] Not in the first edition : the last paragraph of the *Vindiciæ* as printed in Mackintosh's *Miscellaneous Works*, 1851.

group of thinkers found their prophet in Thomas Paine, whose *Rights of Man*, in Horace Walpole's estimation, earned him a putrid fever.[1] Paine was certainly a republican.[2] All government, in fact, appeared to him as "the badge of lost innocence." "Society is produced by our wants," he had said in 1776, in a phrase which might have come from Godwin, "and Government by our wickedness."[3] But while his theoretical republicanism led him to speak with sufficient contempt of the Crown as "a *metaphor*, shewn at the Tower for sixpence or a shilling,"[4] it is to be remembered also that he believed the English Constitution to be in fact republican,[5] and that George III was therefore put in no bodily fear by the advocacy of Paine's opinions. In practice he was no root-and-branch politician, disposed to disregard facts, but rather condemned those who, turning their eyes from the reality to the pageantry of life, pitied, with Burke, "the plumage, but forgot the dying bird."[6]

The immediate objects of his attack were the constitution and the corruption of the English House of Commons, which, though the guardian of the public purse, received individually the supplies which it voted collectively. Its members were themselves accountable to themselves : "like a man being both mortgager and mortgagee."[7]

He saw a paradox in Burke's preposterous contention that the men of the great and glorious Revolution of 1688 did—or even could—bind themselves and their heirs for ever; for while it vitiated the claim that Price's three principles were established by the practice of 1688, it set up, by assumption, the still more astounding claim that the men of 1688 were entitled to "control posterity to the end of time." "The vanity and presumption of governing

---

[1] Walpole to Mary Berry, April 14, 1791.—*Letters*, XIV. 405.

[2] I worked originally from the earliest editions of Paine's Pamphlets which were accessible to me, but as M. D. Conway's edition of Paine's *Writings* is now the edition most commonly used, I have made all the references to it.—*Rights of Man*, Pt. I, *Writings*, II. 382.

[3] *Common Sense*, *Writings*, I. 69 ; cf. *Rights of Man*, Part II ; *ib.* II. 409, etc.

[4] *Rights of Man*, Part I, *Writings*, II. 316, 366.

[5] *Ib.* 367-8.   [6] *Ib.* 288.

[7] *Ib.* 315.

beyond the grave is the most ridiculous and insolent of all tyrannies. Man has no property in man; neither has any generation a property in the generations that are to follow." [1]

"If any generation of men ever possessed the right of dictating the mode by which the world should be governed, it was the first generation that ever existed; and if that generation did not do it, no succeeding can shew any authority for doing so, or set up any." [2] Burke's theory of prescription set up the authority of a maze of contradictions. Each succeeding generation had reversed some of the judgments of its predecessors. [3] To which saint, then, must man vow himself?

Thus the same theocratic belief which drove Burke to his reverence for prescriptive rights and established institutions drove Paine to find his ultimate authority in the natural rights of man. [4] These "natural, unprescriptible, unalienable rights," though indefensible in so far as they rested on no basis of proof, were far from being the revolutionary maxims that Burke described. "Men are born, and always continue free and equal in respect of their rights," [5] namely, "Liberty, Property, Security and Resistance of oppression," which it is the end of all political associations to preserve. [6] "The Nation," continues this catalogue of rights, "is essentially the source of all sovereignty . . ." [7] and "Political Liberty consists in the power of doing whatever does not injure another . . ." [8] so that Burke's caveat against the natural rights of criminals and madmen was, at best, a cudgel stolen from those opponents against whom he wielded it. A member of the French National Assembly had suggested that a Declaration of Duties should be added as a corollary to the Declaration of Rights. Paine showed clearly that he interpreted the Declaration

---

[1] *Rights of Man*, Part I, *Writings*, II. 277. See also 331 and 366.
[2] *Ib*. 304.   [3] *Ib*. 303.
[4] *Ib*. 303–5. It is hardly necessary to state that Paine's unbelief is a vulgar error.
[5] *Right* I, *ib*. 351.   [6] *Right* II, *ib*. 351.
[7] *Right* III, *ib*. 351.
[8] *Right* IV, *ib*. 351–2. It does not affect the present argument that this involves the fallacy developed in Mill's theory of self-regarding acts.

of Rights in no anti-social sense when he replied by anticipating Mazzini's maxim that every right implies a duty.[1]

The second part of the *Rights of Man* was published some months after the first,[2] but it is convenient to consider it here. It was in some degree provoked by Burke's arrogant suggestion that the only necessary reply to Part I was a criminal prosecution;[3] "as a substitute," said Paine, "for not being able to refute it."[4] "It is better," he said, "that the whole argument should come out, than to seek to stifle it. It was " Burke "himself that opened the controversy, and he ought not to desert it."[5] The case was too general in its application to lay before any jury, for the decision of one jury would be reversed by the next. "The only effectual jury would be a convention of the whole nation fairly elected; for in all such cases the whole nation is the vicinage."[6]

In the second part of the *Rights of Man* Paine's republicanism was more uncompromising than in the first. "All hereditary government is in its nature tyranny," he said;[7] "hereditary succession " is "a burlesque upon monarchy ";[8] and he was unsparing in his attacks on the expense of monarchical as compared with republican government.[9] Monarchies squandered their resources in wasteful war. Then, "wearied with war and tired with human butchery," old governments "sat down to rest and called it peace."[10] But the rights of man involved "a system of universal peace " that was due to a "moral theory,"[11] and was not the mere quiescence of exhaustion.

Perhaps Paine's Quaker blood conquered here, for not the brightest luminary of Clapham could have been more pacific. He desired a revolution, a constitutional revolution, a revolution such as might be accomplished "without convulsion or revenge " in every country in Europe.[12] He

[1] *Rights of Man*, Part I, *Writings*, II. 354-5.   "A Declaration of Rights is, by reciprocity, a Declaration of Duties also.   Whatever is my right as a man is also the right of another : and it becomes my duty to guarantee as well as to possess."—Cf. Pt. II, *ib*. 432.

[2] It is dated Feb. 9, 1792.

[3] *Appeal from the New to the Old Whigs.*—*Works*, III. 75.

[4] *Rights of Man*, Pt. II, Preface, *Writings*, II. 395-6.

[5] *Ib*. 398.   [6] *Ib*. 399.   [7] *Ib*. 415.

[8] *Ib*. 417.   [9] *Ib*. 427, cf. 455, 462, 474.

[10] *Ib*. 404.   [11] *Ib*. 404, cf. 455.   [12] *Ib*. 399.

believed the law and Constitution of England to be defective, and he laboured to establish his belief; but he preferred to obey a bad law rather than endanger by its violation the force of those which were good.[1] His specific plea is for representative government, for that representative system which "places government in a state of maturity. It is . . . never young, never old. It is subject neither to nonage nor dotage. It is never in the cradle nor on crutches. It admits not of a separation between knowledge and power,"[2] and is in all these respects superior to monarchy. "Representation is of itself the delegated monarchy of a nation."[3]

Even criticism of Paine's general political theory is somewhat disarmed by the frank admission—an admission difficult, it is true, to reconcile with his theory of the origin of the rights of man—that man is essentially a gregarious animal. "As nature created him for social life, she fitted him for the station she intended. In all cases she made his natural wants greater than his individual powers; . . . and those wants, acting upon every individual, impel the whole of them into society, as naturally as gravitation acts to a center."[4] "Government is nothing more than a national association acting on the principles of society."[5]

The pamphlets of Edmund Burke and James Mackintosh, of Mary Wollstonecraft and Tom Paine, all crystallise distinct political theories, and each serves to illustrate a distinct phrase of English opinion on the French Revolution.

[1] *Rights of Man*, Pt. II, *Writings*, II. 397.
[2] *Ib.* 424.　　[3] *Ib.* 425.　　[4] *Ib.* 406.　　[5] *Ib.* 411.

CHAPTER VIII

CHANGING OPINIONS AND THE GROWTH OF POPULAR ORGANISATION

1791–1792

IN 1791 Frenchmen were still sincerely monarchist. Before the flight to Varennes, in June 1791, they had not, in fact, realised the possibility of carrying on an orderly government without the king's aid. Unluckily for the king, the attempted flight taught France that it could govern itself, and paved the way for the later triumph of republicanism. But as yet France was loyal to the monarchy. When the king was brought back from Varennes to Paris he was closely watched, but he was restored to his functions, and in September he accepted in its completed form the moderate, middle-class Constitution of 1791, which codified the attempts of the National Assembly at constitutional reconstruction. In his heart the king was not reconciled to the new order. He still resented bitterly the hard necessity which had constrained him to accept the Civil Constitution of the Clergy, and to assent to the reorganisation of the Church on a basis of popular election. But to all outward seeming the king and his people were again at one.

Almost all Englishmen took a partial and one-sided view of the progress of events in France. Each found in those events materials out of which he could construct an image of the Revolution that accorded with his own preconceptions of it. The friends of the Revolution, and in particular the parliamentary reformers, saw only the gradual and orderly accomplishment of moderate and constitutional change. Men whose fears had been aroused by the fulminations of Burke saw, on the contrary, nothing

but the wanton violence of a disorderly and excited people,
who had pulled down the Church, threatened the monarchy,
and placed the king under restraint. A few weeks after
the appearance of the *Reflections* the National Assembly
had wrung from the king a reluctant assent to the Civil
Constitution (December 26, 1790), which drove from
their cures many sincere and hard-working priests, to
whom the Civil Constitution was an act of sacrilege and a
thing of horror. The finances of France, although eked
out by the sale of Church lands, grew daily more embarrassed. The country was on the verge of bankruptcy, if
not bankrupt already. A Government which ignored the
rights of property, whether of individuals or the Church,
which appeared to be rushing to financial disaster, which
seemed hostile to religion, was, to crown all, so wanting in
energy and strength as to be incompetent to maintain civil
order, and even incapable of protecting the king against
the insults of a Paris mob. In April 1791 the king set out
to spend Easter at St. Cloud, where it was believed that
priests who had refused to accept the Civil Constitution of
the Clergy would celebrate the Easter services. A mob of
Parisians, angry that the king should give his countenance
to recalcitrant priests, stopped the royal party. In the eyes
of anti-revolutionary Europe the action of the Paris mob
demonstrated not merely that the king was no longer free
to worship as he chose, but also that he was to all intents
and purposes a prisoner in Paris. It was then that the
Emperor began to threaten war. It was then that Louis,
deprived at the beginning of April of the guiding hand of
Mirabeau, began to prepare for flight to the frontier. His
unsuccessful attempt to escape to Metz, his arrest at
Varennes, and the ignominious fashion in which he was
dragged back to Paris seemed but a renewed demonstration
of his helplessness, and but another proof of the closeness
of his captivity.

In England passion was rising on both sides. Inflamed by events in France, the partisans of Burke
became daily more incensed against the incapable politicians who were removing constitutional landmarks,
ruining their country, and heaping insults on their captive

king. Friends of the Revolution in France and of reform
in England thought that Louis, although misled by the
bad advice of the queen and others about the court, was
personally friendly to the Revolution, and was the partner
of his people, as represented by the National Assembly,
in the attempt to give to France a free but moderate Constitution. Based, as it was, upon property, there was little
in the Constitution of 1791 to alarm the moderate advocates
of reform in England; and the more extreme reformers
probably did not fully realise how far the Constitution fell
short of any attempt to put into effective practice the
doctrines of the rights of man. Whilst, therefore, the
progress of the Revolution served only to increase the
ardour of the reformers, it fed the fears of their opponents.
The passionate hatred of the Revolution which had been
excited by Burke seemed to be justified by experience and
grew daily more intense. And as feeling against the
Revolution abroad gathered force, the position of the
reformers at home grew first difficult and then dangerous.

The era of proscription did not have a definite beginning in England till the year 1792, but by some it had
been fully anticipated months before whilst public opinion
was still undergoing the changes which made it possible.
In an anonymous letter to Sheridan, sent in March 1791,
Godwin exhorted that unstable politician to have the
courage of his liberal opinions during the storm which
he foresaw was about to break. But "if you speak out,"
he warned him, "you must be contented to undergo a
temporary proscription," though "the period of the obloquy
which the true friend to mankind must endure" would,
as Godwin thought, "be very short." [1]

But despite all the vigour and ability of those who
replied to it, Burke's great pamphlet was doing its work.
To every fearful and apprehensive mind the progress of
the Revolution in France seemed to afford daily illustration of the clarity of Burke's vision and the accuracy of
his prognostications. In proportion as his predictions were
verified abroad his opinions were adopted about affairs at

---

[1] William Godwin to Sheridan, April 29, 1791.— *Wm. Godwin and
his Friends*, I. 75-6.

home. Horace Walpole's anger against the reforming party seems almost to mount before our eyes. With Price, for example, he gets angry and still more angry, till he passes the bounds of decency. In July 1790 Price is compared to Bishop Bonner.[1] In November Burke's pamphlet is declared to have turned Price's head, and his proceedings at a meeting of the Revolution Society are rancorously burlesqued.[2] Later in the month Walpole explained that Price "had whetted his ancient talons" to no purpose in the previous year, and had "had them all drawn by Burke." The Revolution Club, he added, was "as much exploded as the Cock Lane Ghost."[3] Still later Price's answer to Burke is "sneaking" and "equivocal," and his words are counted lies.[4] Finally, in April 1791, it is "good news" to Walpole that Mirabeau is dead, and a fortunate omen "for those who hope to die in their beds" that Price also lies dying.[5] When Walpole had so far departed from the traditions of English political life as to rejoice over the approaching end of a controversialist from whom he dissented, no room is left for wonder at his extravagant denunciations of Paine's *Rights of Man,* "the most seditious pamphlet ever seen but in open rebellion."[6]

On the 6th of May, 1791, in a debate on the Quebec Act, in which Quebec was scarcely mentioned except when some stickler for order pointed out how completely it had been forgotten, Burke and Fox quarrelled about the Revolution in France, and broke for ever the close friendship of eighteen years. The glowing word and hot retort light up again the dull pages of the *Parliamentary History,* and from that cramped, imperfect record there seem to flame the fires of a controversy as quenchless as the embers on the vestal altar.[7]

---

[1] To Hannah More, July 25, 1790.—*Letters,* XIV. 275.

[2] To Mary Berry, Nov. 11, 1790.—*Ib.* XIV. 316.

[3] To the same, *ib.* XIV. 323. How much the Cock Lane Ghost was exploded can most conveniently be learnt from Birkbeck Hill's *Boswell's Johnson,* I. 406-8 and notes ; III. 268.

[4] To the Misses Berry, Nov. 28, 1790.—*Letters,* XIV. 326.

[5] To Mary Berry, April 4, 1791.—*Ib.* XIV. 404-5.

[6] To the same, May 4, 1791.—*Ib.* XIV. 428.

[7] *Parl. Hist.* XXIX. 364-401. According to one account of this debate, Burke charged Fox and Sheridan with abetting rebellion. (Dr.

The quarrel of Fox and Burke divided the Opposition. But it was not at once clear how decidedly the country was taking the side of Burke. Romilly believed that Burke lost and Fox gained by their speeches on the Revolution.[1] Even Windham was for some weeks estranged from Burke, and only gradually abandoned an attitude of cautious criticism.[2] Pitt still spoke as a distant "spectator" of French affairs,[3] and his calculating watchfulness seems to have been imitated by his political associates.[4] Even an English traveller in Switzerland, who had no great love for reformers, condemned the absurd talk of the English abroad on questions of French politics. "They are for marching into France, cutting the throats of all the National Assembly, and restoring the poor, good king, as they are pleased to call him, to *all* that he has lost. I should be extremely sorry to see such an unqualified restoration."[5]

In England the mob decided more quickly than its betters. The change of opinion, the displacement of sympathy by mistrust, showed itself in July 1791 when men of popular sympathies proposed to celebrate the taking of the Bastille. In London several anniversary celebrations were at first projected. The Society for Constitutional Information, now revived, made arrangements for an anniversary dinner. As early as the 29th of May Français of Nantes, now a deputy to the French National Assembly, urged Danton to send French envoys—perhaps he had in mind a particular French envoy—to the intended celebrations. The number of subscribers to the fête, he says, "is

---

Parr to Mrs. Sheridan.—Moore's *Sheridan*, II. 128.) Such a construction can scarcely be put upon any passage in the *Parl. Hist.*, though Parr's version may well be accurate. On the other hand, Parr's script was so bad that it is just as likely that Moore misread the letter.

[1] May 20, 1791.—Romilly's *Mem.* I. 427.

[2] Windham's *Diary*, April 22 to Aug. 12, 1791, pp. 223-33. May 6, was "fatal day of rupture with Burke."—*Ib.* 225.

[3] Pitt to Lady Chatham, July 2, 1791.—Stanhope, I. 418.

[4] Dundas to R. Burke, Sept. 20, 1791.—*Mem. of C. J. Fox*, III. 9-10 ; Grenville, in *Courts and Cabinets of George III*, II. 196. See also Dr. Burney to Arthur Young, Sept. 21, 1791.—*Auto. of A. Young*, 198-9.

[5] C. B. Wollaston to his Mother, Mrs. Frampton, from Lausanne, Aug. 23, 1791.—*Journal of Mary Frampton*, p. 70, cf. 71.

already so great that no tavern can contain them."[1] But in June the London correspondent of the *Moniteur* told another story. "The Constitutional Society of London proposed to celebrate the anniversary of the French Revolution; but as it has already been the object of the most atrocious calumnies, and as it fears that malevolence will wish still to place an unfavourable interpretation on its intentions, it has declared them in the following resolution which it has just published "—

"The sole object of this assembly being to celebrate, as a legitimate ground for rejoicing, the fall of despotism, and the establishment of civil and religious liberty in France, all those who are present at it are asked not to propose any motion and not to discuss any question relative to the particular interests of that country."[2]

Despite disclaimers such as this, opposition to the celebration of the Revolution was already strong. Several societies seemed to have planned a joint meeting at Vauxhall, and to have been somehow prevented from hiring the room.[3] It even seems as if the Constitutional Society abandoned its proposed banquet altogether,[4] and it is clear that the celebrants in London had to brave hostility and menace.

Nevertheless the friends of liberty met, a thousand strong, at the Crown and Anchor, and celebrated the fall of the Bastille "in a manner as peaceable as solemn." Mr. George Rous, whose reply to Burke's *Reflections* was in its fourth edition, was elected president, and "easily maintained that order and propriety which all desired." The toasts—there were twenty of them—were like those of the preceding year, save that Burke was toasted "in gratitude for his having provoked the great discussion which occupies every thinking person," and that whereas Price had spoken in 1790, now his admirers could but toast the memory of that "apostle of liberty" and "friend of the human race."[5]

---

[1] Français to Danton, May 29, 1791.—Robinet, *Danton Émigré—Pièces Justificatives*, 195.

[2] *Moniteur*, June 10, 1791, No. 161, p. 662.　　[3] *Ib.* June 30, 1791.

[4] Cf. *S. T.* XXV. 115, and *C. J.* XLIX. 682, with *C. R. S.* 229–30.

[5] *Moniteur*, July 21, 1791, No. 202, p. 833.

At the Jacobin Club it had been proposed to send representatives to the dinner, but there is no trace of their presence; probably they were never sent.[1] But a representative of the Nantais was there,[2] and a letter from the society of Nantes which seems also to have been written for the occasion, hailed the celebration of the Revolution in London as "a happy augury for the Revolution of the Universe." "The decrees which have secured French Liberty have been like the Trumpet which sounds the Resurrection of the World!" England and France were to form a holy coalition to "avenge the Human Species against the unpunished outrages" which had "galled it for centuries."[3]

In order to "rob the ill disposed of every pretext" and confound the calumniators who had sought to alarm the Government and the people as to the object of the assembly, the diners dispersed quietly at nine o'clock.[4] "The same order, the same decency prevailed in all the places—and they were many—where the anniversary of the Revolution was celebrated."[5] At Dublin and Belfast, at Edinburgh and Glasgow, at Liverpool and Manchester the anniversary was celebrated without disturbance.[6]

But the same order and decency was not everywhere preserved by those who claimed to have decency and order under their special protection. At Norwich the house and library of Dr. Parr, a sort of Dr. Johnson of the Whigs, one of the intellectual dictators tolerated in that day as in our own, was marked for destruction, and during three days and three nights he had to stand siege against the mob.[7] Parr knew how to take his revenge when he found the

---

[1] *A. J.* II. 515, 524, 538-9.

[2] A Monsieur Ducouëdic, possibly the person referred to in a letter of Chauvelin, May 26, 1791. He appears to have been a party to litigation in England, and the minister had recommended him to the good offices of the ambassador, Chauvelin, to give him the desired help, whatever that may have been.—Archives Étrangères, *Corr. d'Angleterre*, 581, fo. 76; *Moniteur*, July 21, 1791, No. 202, p. 833. See also *C. R. S.* 223.

[3] *C. R. S.* 229-30. Other societies in France wrote to thank the Revolution Society for the celebration.—*C. R. S.* 231-5, 239.

[4] *Moniteur*, July 21, 1791, No. 20, p. 833.   [5] *Ib.*

[6] *New Ann. Reg.* 1791, *Occurrences*, p. 27 *et seq.*; *Moniteur* as above.

[7] *Mem. of Dr. Parr*, I. 306. See reference to approaching celebrations at Norwich in a letter of July 12, *C. R. S.* 224.

opportunity. Forced once to drink against his will to Church and king, he cried, "Church and king.—Once it was the toast of the Jacobites; now it is the toast of incendiaries. It means a Church without a gospel—and a king above the law." [1]

At Manchester great pains were taken to render the celebration inoffensive to the self-styled constitutional party; but a handbill was distributed saying that "if Englishmen had the spirit they used to have" they would, on the 14th of July, pull the house in which the popular society assembled over the heads of its members; and that "the brains of every man who dined there would much be improved by being mingled with brick and mortar." No such brutal invitation to violence and murder as this manifesto of men who called themselves the friends of law and order was ever, during the whole course of their history, traced to the English popular societies. Fortunately riot was avoided. Walker, the leader of the Manchester reformers, was borough-reeve for the year; he controlled what apology for a police force the unincorporated town could boast; and in consequence he was able to take effective precautions against riot and disorder. [2]

At Birmingham equal care was taken by the celebrants, but not with equal success. There Priestley was the most famous in a group of able men, liberal in politics, opposed to the established orthodoxy in religion, and exasperatingly clever in religious controversy or political debate. To dispute with Priestley was almost a recognised road to ecclesiastical preferment, and the natural opposition of Churchmen and Dissenters was exacerbated by continual controversy. So sharp was the contention that a metaphorical passage in one of Priestley's works was ludicrously misinterpreted as a proposal to blow up the Church with gunpowder. [3] In quieter times such an imputation against a peaceful scholar would instantly have been laughed to scorn; but there are times and places when men are deserted by their sense of proportion, and in

---

[1] *Mem. of Parr*, I. 309.

[2] Walker, *A Review of Some Political Events*, pp. 22–4.

[3] See an analysis of the causes of the riots in Langford, *A Century of Birmingham Life*, I. 472–6.

Birmingham, in 1791, no charge against Priestley was too foolish to find believers.

Birmingham was already excited, therefore, when, on the 11th of July, 1791, "any Friend of Freedom" was invited, through an advertisement in *Aris's Gazette*, the local newspaper, to celebrate the fall of the Bastille by the "temperate festivities" of a five-shilling dinner.[1] The very next paragraph in the newspaper was a warning of evil to come; for it advertised a halfpenny pamphlet which was to be published on the day following the dinner, and was to contain an authentic list of all the diners;[2] or, in other words, a list of the proscribed. The "Vivant Rex et Regina" with which this advertisement concluded, showed that the *soi-disant* "Church and King" party was thirsting for battle, and had already prejudged the loyalty of the celebrants. To make matters worse, either a foolish friend, or a malignant enemy, of the cause of liberty issued a handbill which was certainly indiscreet and possibly seditious. It suggested that "the crown of a certain Great Personage" was becoming too heavy for the head that wore it, and anticipated the day when the majority of the nation should say "the peace of slavery is worse than the war of freedom."[3] This handbill was denounced by the promoters of the dinner,[4] and though the magistrates offered a hundred guineas for the discovery of the writer or the printer, the publisher or the distributor of it,[5] the responsibility was never brought home to a single person. One good witness, Hutton, the historian of Birmingham, believed that a few copies had been brought down from London and scattered under the table at an inn.[6] But whatever the origin of the obnoxious document, there can be no doubt that it helped to excite the anger of the mob against those who met, on Thursday the 14th of July, to celebrate the fall of the Bastille.

About eighty people assembled for the dinner, which

---

[1] *Aris's Gazette*, July 11, 1791, ap. Langford, I. 478.
[2] *Ib*. I.   [3] Reprinted by Langford, *ib*. I. 478.
[4] *Birmingham and Stafford Chronicle*, July 14, 1791, ap. Langford, I. 479.
[5] *Ib*. I. 479. A loyalist reply to the handbill is also given.
[6] Hutton's Narrative.—*Life*, ed. 1816, p. 162 note.

had purposely been arranged for the early hour of three in the afternoon. A crowd hustled them as they entered the hotel in Temple Row, but they drank their eighteen toasts with dispatch, and between five and six in the evening departed quietly to their homes.[1] Presently the crowd gathered again. The magistrates acted foolishly. They had dined together at a neighbouring tavern and inflamed the already excited people with huzzas for "Church and King "[2]—a dangerous watchword, as the sequel proved, to put into the mouth of a mob. Towards eight o'clock the crowd forced an entrance to the hotel and broke the windows. Gathering courage from this preliminary demonstration, the people began to riot with an earnestness and deliberation which makes it difficult to believe that they were without the guidance of men of superior intelligence.[3] Their anger was directed mainly against the Unitarians : their houses, their chapels and the property of their friends. One party of rioters set fire to the New Meeting House; another party, armed with rails and crowbars, demolished the Old Meeting House, which could not be burnt without endangering the property that surrounded it. Next an attack was made on Priestley's house at Fair Hill. The windows were broken, the doors battered in, and manuscripts, books and furniture thrown into the garden. The rioters rewarded themselves for their exertions with the contents of the doctor's cellar, and "there was reason for some time to hope that the Elaboratory (a little distance from the house) would have been saved; nor did it appear to have been noticed as long as the liquor in the cellar lasted "; for the drunken rioters had grown quarrelsome, and were for a time sufficiently occupied by the nine private battles which were in simultaneous progress in different parts of the grounds. When the

---

[1] *Aris's Gazette*, July 25, 1791, ap. Langford I. 481 ; Hutton, *History of Birmingham*, 3rd ed. 1795, p. 390. The list of toasts is given by Hutton, *Life*, ed. 1816, pp. 209-11. Priestley, it should be noted, was not present at the dinner.—*Ib.* 172.

[2] Hutton's Narrative.—*Life*, ed. 1816, p. 172.

[3] This is the opinion of Langford, who has made, perhaps, the most complete survey of the evidence, and it is difficult to accept any other conclusion. Hutton blamed " a hungry attorney "and "a leading justice." —*Life*, p. 163 note.

liquor was exhausted and the rioters had concluded their disputes, they turned to sack the laboratory and destroy the almost priceless collection of scientific instruments which Priestley alone amongst living men could have made or gathered.

Next day—Friday—the rioters opened the gaols, paraded the streets with bludgeons, crying "Church and King," and attacked house after house. The inhabitants had to protect their homes by chalking "Church and King" upon the walls. A mob of boys and prostitutes destroyed or looted the house and shop of Hutton, the bookseller and historian, whose activities as a member of the local Court of Requests had embittered many of the less reputable inhabitants against him. On Saturday his house at Washwood was destroyed by fire, and in two days Hutton lost a large proportion of the property which he had toiled laboriously to acquire during the fifty years of his residence in Birmingham.

The magistrates did nothing till Saturday the 16th, when they issued an appeal for order : the appeal of men who did not expect to be obeyed. The riots, they said, "must injure the Church and King they were intended to support," and they implored the rioters to return to their businesses "as the only Way to do Credit to themselves and their Cause, and to promote the Peace, Happiness and Prosperity of this Great and Flourishing Town." [1] This proclamation had no appreciable effect. Citizens of every political colour or religious faith were now at the mercy of thieves and scoundrels. "There was scarcely a housekeeper that dared refuse them meat, drink, money or whatever they asked." [2] "Then was the sovereignty of the people established in full authority for three days and three nights," wrote Watt, the engineer, to a French correspondent. "Quiet subjects were panic-stricken; and after some feeble efforts to establish peace, people submitted quietly to their fate." [3] "The greatest sufferers," said Romilly, "were persons particularly distinguished for their benevo-

---

[1] Reprinted by Langford, I. 480.
[2] *Aris's Gazette*, July 25, 1791, ap. Langford, I. 484.
[3] Watt to M. de Luc, July 19, 1791.—Muirhead's *Life of Watt*, 395-6.

lence and charity, and who had most contributed to the
prosperity of Birmingham by their industry." [1]

Birmingham, in those days, had no municipal institutions and no proper police force. There was no adequate
machinery whereby the overgrown town, still governed
through the forms of the old manorial organisation, could
be brought to order in such a moment of crisis. All that
the magistrates could do was to swear in special constables,
and these proved ineffective. As a last resort they sent
for troops. Meanwhile, during Sunday, the rioters had
burnt a chapel and two houses, and were preparing to
sack Edgbaston Hall, from which they had several times
been bought off by largesses from the cellars. In the nick
of time came the news that a troop of light horse had
galloped in from Nottingham. Mere rumour did the work
of force; most of the rioters sneaked quietly away, and the
few who remained were easily dispersed. There was still,
here and there, an isolated case of pillage, but the four
days' carnival of insensate violence and wanton destruction
was at last at an end. [2]

Ill-feeling remained and was shamefully fostered. It
was not enough that Priestley's private letters were bandied
about the town. [3] Forged ones were circulated purporting
to show that the Dissenters, Priestley at their head, had
formed a treasonable design to overthrow the Constitution,
and had appointed a day for assembling "to burn the
Churches, blow up the Parliament, cut off the head of the
King and abolish all Taxes." [4]

Of the twelve rioters who were brought to trial for

---

[1] Aug. 2, 1791.—*Mem. of Romilly*, I. 431–2 ; cf. 444–5.

[2] A good general account of the riots is quoted by Langford, I.
481–6, from *Aris's Gazette* of July 25, 1791. Hutton's Narrative, written
a few days after the riots, is printed in his *Life*. See also: *New Ann.
Reg.* 1791, *Occurrences*, p. 27 : *Ann. Reg.* 1791, pp. 29–32 ; *Mem. of
Priestley*, II. 132, etc. ; *Life of Rowland Hill*, I. 33 ; Gibbon's *Memoirs*
(Birkbeck Hill's edition), 320 ; *Moniteur*, July 25, 1791, No. 206, p. 851 ;
July 28, No. 209, p. 863 ; July 30, No. 211, p. 871 ; Aug. 8, No. 220, p. 909 ;
Aug. 20, No. 232, p. 959. Cf. Mary Frampton's *Journal*, 65–6 ; *C. J.*
XLIX. 709–10 ; *S. T.* XXIV. 410–11. The French Chargé d'Affaires
suspected the Government of fomenting the riots from motives of its own
—which are not, for all that, too evident.—*Affaires Étrangères, Corr.
d'Angleterre*, 578, ff. 284–5, and 579, fo. 35.

[3] *Mem. of Priestley*, II. 132, etc.

[4] Advertisement reprinted by Langford, I. 496.

their share in the disturbances only four were convicted, and even one taken *flagrante delicto* was acquitted.[1] Hutton tells us that some time afterwards a gentleman in the hunting-field was so sure of killing the fox that he cried, "Nothing but a Birmingham jury can save him!"[2] The partiality of Birmingham juries had passed into a proverb.

Various estimates have been made of the losses sustained during the riots. On the fourth day the magistrates dolefully exclaimed that more than £100,000 would have to be paid by the ratepayers in compensation.[3] Hutton says that the actual losses of the sufferers amounted to over £60,000;[4] but they did not receive nearly that sum in the courts, where fifteen claimants sued for more than £35,000 and received just under £27,000.[5] In some cases the damages paid did not meet the costs of the action.[6] Hutton's own costs amounted to about an eighth of his claim, and to almost a sixth of the sum which he received.[7] Even when the damages had been awarded, the inhabitants of Birmingham held their responsibilities so lightly that for over two years they delayed the payment of their debt to the victims of riot and disorder.[8]

In Paris, where Priestley's eminence as a scientist was perhaps more clearly recognised than in Birmingham, more sympathy was felt for him. On behalf of the Academy of Sciences, Condorcet wrote to express grief at his persecution, and regret for the loss to science in the destruction of his property;[9] and a subscription was opened on his behalf, apparently by his fellow-scientists.[10] "You are the victim," said the Jacobins in a letter similar to that of Condorcet, "of the interest that you have taken in the

---

[1] Langford, I. 496–7 ; Hutton, *Life*, ed. 1816, p. 205.
[2] *Ib.* 207 note.
[3] Address issued by the magistrates, July 17, 1791, ap. Langford.
[4] *Hist. of Birmingham*, 3rd ed. 1795, p. 392.
[5] Claims, £35,095 13s. 6d. ; damages allowed, £26,961 2s. 3d.—*Life of Hutton*, ed. 1816, p. 219 ; *Hist. of Birmingham*, 471.
[6] *Life of Hutton*, 220.
[7] *Ib.* 220.   [8] *Ib.* 220.
[9] July 30, 1791.—Robinet, *Danton Émigré*, pp. 71–2.
[10] This seems to be the implication of a letter to the Jacobins, July 29, 1791.—*A. J.* III. 59.

cause of humanity, triumphant in the greatest Revolution ever accomplished amongst men." [1]

The spice of opposition must somehow give an edge to political appetites, for the English reformers seem to have been stimulated by hostility. At Manchester the supporters of Church and king had petitioned in March 1790 against the repeal of the Test and Corporation Acts : a repeal which even Pitt thought would open "a dangerous door" "to the absolute ruin of the Constitution." [2] A "Church and King" club, nicknamed "Tythe and Tax Club," had been formed to resist the relief of Dissenters from political disabilities. [3] But the line which separates political parties tends very often to coincide with that which divides men who differ in opinion on matters of religion. It was so at Birmingham; it was so at Manchester. Broadly speaking, Churchmen feared revolution abroad and reform at home, whilst Dissenters rejoiced at the progress of constitutional reform in France, and hoped for constitutional reform in England. In October 1790, by way of opposition to the Church and King Club, the Manchester reformers set up a Constitutional Society to obtain shorter Parliaments and more equal representation. [4]

When it had been in existence about a year and a half the Manchester Constitutional Society leapt into sudden fame by venturing to send an address to the Society of Jacobins at Paris. On the 13th of April, 1792, Robespierre presented to the Jacobins the deputies of the Manchester Constitutional Society—Thomas Cooper, a pamphleteer of some note who was taking a holiday in Paris, and James Watt, junior, son of Watt the engineer, who was there on

---

[1] *A. J.* III. 82. Priestley's Reply, III. 182. For evidence of the sympathy of French clubs in provincial towns, see their letters to the London Revolution Society.—*C. R. S.* 241-50.

[2] March 2, 1790.—*Parl. Hist.* XXVIII. 387-452.

[3] March 13, 1790.—Walker, *A Review of Some of the Political Events* . . . 11-16 ; Prentice, 2-5.

[4] Oct. 5, 1790. The members were to pay an annual subscription of half-a-guinea, and to meet monthly at the Bridgewater Arms. Rules and Orders of the Manchester Constitutional Society.— *Wyvill Papers*, II. 570-5 ; Walker, *A Review of some Political Events*, 16-17 ; Prentice, 5. It was not long before other reforming societies were formed at Manchester. Samuel Shore to Wyvill, May 1792.— *Wyvill Papers*, V. 50.

the business of his firm.[1] Unlike his father, who was a Tory, Watt was a reformer. He had commercial connections in Manchester, and had made acquaintance there with men of the reforming party, who took advantage of the presence in Paris of Cooper and himself to present, through them, an address to the Jacobins. "At this very moment, when an alliance of the despotic powers of Europe is being formed to crush the cause of liberty and annihilate the rights of man, we hope," said the addressers, "that we give you pleasure in informing you that there are men everywhere (even amongst the people that the intrigues of kings and of courtiers have too often presented in the guise of enemies) who take a deep interest in your cause, the cause not only of the French, but of the human race.

"The light that you have just shed on the true principles of politics and of the natural rights of man (lights which, as yet, no more than glimmer in England amidst the gloom of civic ignorance) ought to make us feel that the time is come to abolish all national prejudices, and to embrace freemen as brothers, to no matter what country they belong." The Mancunians asked for a friendly correspondence between themselves and the Jacobins. "Our society will think itself happy," they concluded, "to join its efforts to yours to spread the important principles of universal liberty, which alone can establish the empire of peace and the happiness of man on a solid and immovable basis."

"English and French, reunited henceforth and for ever by the bonds of justice, humanity and the tenderest fraternity," replied the president, "will fight together for the maintenance of their common liberty and the perfecting of their respective governments." The Jacobins, "in their own name and in the name of all the patriotic societies of the French Empire, bind themselves by an inviolable oath to the Constitutional Society of Manchester."[2]

---

[1] *A. J.* III. 496, Cooper's *Reply to Burke's Invective*, 7. Cooper will appear again. For a biography of Watt, see Alger, *Englishmen in the French Revolution*. On Aug. 14 Watt and three other Englishmen presented 1315 livres to the National Assembly for the widows and children of the patriots who had fallen on Aug. 10. — *P.-V.* Aug. 14, p. 222.

[2] Société des Amis de la constitution séante aux Jacobins à Paris. Discours de M.M. Cooper et Watt, députés de la société des amis de la constitution, séante à Paris, le 13 avril, 1792, et imprimé avec la réponse du Président par ordre de la société, in·8 de 5 pp.—*A. J.* III., 499-502.

Though this communication between a society of Englishmen and a society of Frenchmen may now seem harmless and innocent, the Manchester Constitutional Society had nevertheless to explain to the public that its only object was parliamentary reform and that whilst rejoicing in the French revolution, it neither stood pledged to a defence of all its measures, nor saw the necessity for a similar revolution in England.[1]

Nevertheless it was furiously denounced by Edmund Burke in the House of Commons and Thomas Cooper answered him in *Cooper's Reply to Burke's Invective,* in which he mocked at the artificial importance bestowed upon two obscure persons like himself and Watt [2] who had never pretended, as Burke thought they had pretended, to be representatives of the British people,[3] nor, indeed, had they even committed the Manchester society to responsibility for all their acts.[4] "If a wish to reform the manifest abuses in the representation be the same with an intention to overthrow the British Constitution," he said, explaining his own view, "I most certainly admit the charge; *but I am sincerely and decidedly of Opinion that in present Circumstances of this Country, no Man can be justified in going any further than a complete and effectual reform in the Representation of the people and in the duration of Parliament."* [5]

In London the zealous pamphleteering of the reformers in general and of the Constitutional Society in particular was not lost.[6] It led, at the end of 1791 and the beginning of 1792, to the formation, under the guidance of Thomas Hardy, of a new and vigorous society to promote reform of Parliament. Hardy, an honest, straightforward Scotsman of forty years of age, was a master shoemaker and kept a shop in Piccadilly, where he employed five or six journeymen.[7] He became convinced of the necessity for

---

One of the delegates carried the English flag in the procession to honour the released soldiers of Château-Vieux.—*Ib.* 503–4 ; Cooper's *Reply to Burke's Invective*, 85–9.

[1] Walker, *A Review of Some Political Events*, 26–30.
[2] Cooper's *Reply*, 4.   [3] *Ib.* 7.   [4] *Ib.* 5.   [5] *Ib.* 16.
[6] *Mem. of Hardy*, 102 ; *Add. MSS.* 27814, fo. 18.
[7] Examination of Hardy, May 12, 1794.—*Privy Council Register* (hereafter *P. C. R.*), 33 Geo. III. 43.

parliamentary reform and, in 1791, he conceived the plan of a new society to promote it. His first notion was to form a society of the unrepresented, but he soon saw that if he interpreted the word in its strictest sense such a basis would be too narrow : "for it is as clear as a Mathematical Axiom that the whole Mass of the people are unrepresented or misrepresented." Ultimately the society was established on the broadest possible basis, only the physically or morally unfit being excluded from it,[1] and Hardy hoped to enrol "another class of the people " than could be induced to join the Constitutional Society.[2] Afterwards, when the society had become famous to some and infamous to others, Hardy undertook to write its history. His unfinished manuscript was handed to Francis Place, who added to it, and had hopes of publishing a complete history of the society. But the manifold avocations of that great political organiser never allowed him to fulfil his hope.[3] The manuscript collections of Hardy and Place, together with Place's own manuscript autobiography, furnish, however, the greater part of our information as to the interior history of the London Corresponding Society.

Apparently in October 1791 Hardy arranged a meeting with three friends at the sign of the Bell, Exeter Street, Strand—a hostelry which no longer exists.[4] He submitted to them a draft constitution, and his pet scheme for a subscription of a penny a week.[5] This scheme for weekly payments was a stroke of genius, for it admitted into the society hundreds of men who were excluded from other societies by their heavy subscriptions. A formal constitutive meeting was held on January 25, 1792, at which eight friends were present. After some conversation on the hardness of the times and the dearness of all the necessaries of life,[6] his scheme was adopted for the formation of a society, to be called the London Corresponding

[1] *Add. MSS.* 27814, ff. 18–20 ; cf. 27811, fo. 2.
[2] *Mem. of Hardy*, 103 ; *Mem. of Horne Tooke*, II. 182–3 note.
[3] See Hardy's plan for the History, *Add. MSS.* 27814, fo. 7.
[4] I have been unable, at least, either to discover it, or to identify its site with any certainty.
[5] *Add. MSS.* 27814, ff. 22–9 ; *Mem. of T. H.* 13–16, 103–4 ; *Recollections of J. Binns*, 41.   [6] *Mem. of Hardy*, 13.

Society, which was to aim at effecting a radical reform and obtaining an honest Parliament.[1] The new society was to correspond with other societies having the same object in view, as well as with "public-spirited individuals," [2] and it took for its watchword, "Unite—Persevere—and be Free." [3]

"I was," Hardy told the Privy Council, in 1794, "one of the first of the Society which was originally formed for the purpose of Parliamentary Reform—that was my only object then and is my only object now." [4] "If an attempt of this sort," he wrote in his Memoirs, "was either treason, or sedition : I certainly was very culpable; probably our rulers thought so; for they had many secret agents, or in other words spies and informers, employed to report to them what was going on, and the Society was very open in all its measures; indeed, their object was publicity, the more public the better." [5]

Every member was required to signify his belief in the necessity for a parliamentary reform and universal suffrage ; and to promise that he would "endeavour by all justifiable means" to promote these ends.[6] It was a rule of the society that no person be admitted a member unless he be recommended by one member and the recommendation be supported by another.[7] Even when proposed and seconded in this way a member was not duly elected until he had been chosen by a ballot of the society, which, curiously enough, seems at one time to have been against the ballot in parliamentary elections because it was "degrading to Englishmen."

In a long preamble to its rules the society explained its principles. Inequalities in the representation were

[1] *Mem. of Hardy*, 99-101 ; *Add. MSS.* 27814, fo. 14. Hardy counted this the first meeting of the society.—*P. C. R.* 33 Geo. III. 243.

[2] *Add. MSS.* 27808, fo. 3, cf. 27814, fo. 22 ; 27811, ff. 2-3, etc.

[3] *Ib.* 27814, ff. 8, 37.

[4] Hardy's Examination, May 12, 1794.—*P. C. R.* 33 Geo. III. 45.

[5] *Mem. of Hardy*, 99. With slight variations *Add. MSS.* 27814, ff. 10-11.

[6] Address to the Nation at Large, p. 2. Reprint, p. 4. *Add. MSS.* 27814, fo. 37. *S. T.* XXIV. 379.

[7] *Add. MSS.* 27814, fo. 22. This rule is said to have subsequently been struck out (*S. T.* XXIV. 374). But though it may have been modified I scarcely think that it can ever have been completely rescinded.

shown to be an injustice which pressed with peculiar
weight on the great industrial towns of recent growth;[1]
and the society announced its adhesion to the Duke of
Richmond's plan of universal suffrage and annual elections. "As Providence has kindly furnished men in every
station with facilities necessary for judging of what con-
cerns themselves, it is somewhat strange that the Multitude
should suffer the *few*, with no better *natural* intellects than
their own, to usurp the important power of governing
them without their control.

"The views and intentions of this society are to collect
the opinions of all the people, as far as possible. They
certainly are apparently much aggrieved. Therefore they
have the greatest reason to stand up like men and claim
their rights and privileges—and if they are united and
firm and will persevere, who are they who dare oppose
them in their just demands, with any hope of success."[2]

The London Corresponding Society at once justified
its name by opening correspondence[3] with the Constitutional Society which had been founded at Sheffield in 1791
by four or five mechanics of good character.[4] "To allay
. . . the heat of party, to prepare the *public mind* for
deliberate investigation, and to prove that our *Liberties*
may be renovated without destruction of the Constitution
or personal sacrifice, is the immediate purpose, endeavour
and intent of this Society, for which the patronage of all
parties is solicited."[5] The society pursued none but the
peaceful end of parliamentary reform, and wished to pursue
it by none but the peaceful means of petition to Parliament.[6]

[1] Compare the estimates of population in *Add. MSS.* 27814, fo. 20,
with 27811, fo. 2, and *Mem. of Hardy*, 15.
[2] Jan. 25, 1792.—*Add. MSS.* 27814, fo. 20, and, with slight differences,
S. T. XXIV. 373-4.
[3] *Mem. of Hardy*, 15; *Add. MSS.* 27814, ff. 26-7, 29; 27811, ff. 4-5,
7-8; *C. J.* XLIX. 698.
[4] Examination of William Broomhead, May 28, 1794.—*P. C. R.* 33
Geo. III. 244. Memorandum based on information collected from friends
at Sheffield by Shore for Wyvill and enclosed in a letter of May 11-14,
1792.—*Wyvill Papers*, V. 47-50.
[5] Dec. 19, 1791.—*Ib.* III. 576.
[6] Shore's memorandum, already cited.—*Ib.* V. 47-50. "The grand
and only object of these Institutions is a fair and equal Representation of
the People in Parliament." Quoted from a Sheffield newspaper. Shore
to Wyvill, May 4, 1792.—*Ib.* V. 43.

Every member had solemnly to declare himself "an enemy to all conspiracies, tumults and riotous proceedings," or "to any attempt that tends to overturn or in any wise injure or disturb the peace of the People or the Laws of the Realm," and that his sole design was to concur "with every peaceable and good Citizen of this Nation" in giving his voice for an application to Parliament, "praying for a speedy Reformation and an equal Representation in the House of Commons." [1]

At first the society consisted of about a dozen members who "met at the Cock in the Square." [2] But Sheffield was a town reputed to be republican, and a stronghold of dissent. [3] A growing and prosperous industrial population had no legitimate outlet for its political activities, and it is, therefore, not surprising to find that in a comparatively short time the society numbered two thousand four hundred members. [4] The society had made a business-like attempt to prevent confusion and disorder by dividing into separate groups—a plan also adopted, as it increased in numbers, by the London Corresponding Society—and the members were anxious to revive one of the methods of the economy campaigners, and to call a "Convention in London by Deputies from each County or District, by which means the sentiments of the nation may be obtained without any confusion or disorder." [5]

Correspondence with this vigorous body gave encouragement to Hardy and his friends during the infancy of the London Corresponding Society, which, before many months had passed, was in correspondence with twenty or thirty popular societies in different parts of England and Scotland. [6] They entered into friendly relations with the Society for Constitutional Information in particular; and

---

[1] Dec. 19, 1791.—*Wyvill Papers*, II. 577–8.

[2] Examination of Wm. Broomhead, May 28, 1794.—*P. C. R.* 33 Geo. III. 245.

[3] This appears from Wyvill's correspondence with Shore, Dec. 1792—Jan. 1793.—*Wyvill Papers*, V. 118–25.

[4] *Proceedings of the Friends of the People*, 35–46.—*S. T.* XXIV. 1026–30.

[5] *Proceedings of the Friends of the People*, 41–2.

[6] *C. J.* XLIX. 603; *S. T.* XXIV. 375–6; *Add. MSS.* 27811, ff. 7, 9, 16–17.

one division of the Corresponding Society opened a subscription for Tom Paine, who was a member of the Society for Constitutional Information.[1]

Though not the first to be born, the political society advocating parliamentary reform which was most closely allied with the regular opposition, and perhaps on that account the first to wane, was the Society of the Friends of the People. On the 20th of March, 1792, a meeting of the electors of Westminster was held to consider the propriety of impeaching Pitt's henchman, George Rose, who had been ordered by a court of law to discharge a debt of £110 which he owed to a publican for the traditional services of his class during the Westminster election.[2] "Mr. Philip Francis, M.P., there openly declared that he now saw the necessity for a parliamentary reform."[3] A proposal to form at once a society to promote reform was negatived; but, in consequence of a manifesto signed by a hundred and forty-seven gentlemen, of whom twenty-three were members of the House of Commons,[4] the constitutive meeting of the Friends of the People was held on the 11th of April, 1792.

The society has been denounced as an "after-dinner folly" promoted by the Earl of Lauderdale,[5] and though this account is manifestly false, it reflects the opinion of Holland House. "Grey," says Lady Holland, "had contracted a great friendship with Lord Lauderdale, who is one of those active, bustling spirits that will rather engage in perils, and even mischiefs, than remain in a state of insipid tranquillity. At a dinner at Lord Lauderdale's, after having drunk a considerable quantity of wine, they pledged themselves to bring forward the reform of Parliament. Lord Lauderdale, Grey, Maitland, Francis, Courte-

---

[1] *C. J.* XLIX. 667–8, 697; *Add. MSS.* 27811, fo. 6.

[2] See the parliamentary proceedings on this subject, *Parl. Hist.* XXIX. 1014–33, 1171; and Hirsinger's report to the French Government in Pallain, *La Mission de Talleyrand à Londres*, 300–1 note. Hirsinger observes that Fox was not present at the meeting.

[3] *Add. MSS.* 27814, fo. 32.   [4] *Ib.* 27808, fo. 15.

[5] See the hysterical article in the *Encyclopædia Britannica*, New ed. XII. 586, by Mr. Payne, who apparently bases his account on a rather unsatisfactory passage in Lord Holland's *Memoirs of the Whig Party*, I. 13–14.

nay, Piggott and others were of the party. This was the origin of the *Friends of the People* or *Association*." [1] Late in life Grey declared that "one word " from Fox would have kept him out of "all that mess of the ' Friends of the People,' but he never spoke it." [2] Fox, on the other hand, complained at the time that "the Association seemed determined *not to have any advice*, and particularly not to *have his*." Fox cannot have been ignorant of what was proceeding, but it is true that the associators determined not to consult him "until they saw the probability of success, in order that he might not be involved if they failed." [3] Grey may, therefore, have done Fox an injustice. His later judgments certainly did an injustice to himself and his friends. When reminded that the Friends of the People only advocated the reforms which he himself carried in 1832, he replied that all that might be true, "but there were men joined with them in that Society, whose views, though he did not know it at the time, were widely different from his own, and with whom it was not safe to have any communication." [4]

A vague charge of this sort is, after all, of small weight compared with the known fact that the society professed parliamentary reform for its sole object, and defined the reforms which it desired as freedom of election, more equal representation and shorter Parliaments. [5] Correspondence with cognate bodies was to be a part of its business; and it set up friendly relations with such associations as the Society for Constitutional Information and the Sheffield Constitutional Society. [6] But the society was no more democratic than the Yorkshire association. A large proportion of its members were Members of Parliament, peers, baronets, or the sons of peers; and the

[1] *Journal of Elizabeth, Lady Holland*, I. 101.

[2] *Life and Opinions of Charles, second Earl Grey*, p. 11.

[3] Thomas Pelham to Lady Holland, June 15, 1792, recounting a conversation with Fox. Holland House MSS.—Lady Holland's *Journal*, I. 15 note ; see also 14-15.

[4] *Life and Opinions of . . . Earl Grey*, as cited above, 11.

[5] *Proceedings of the year 1792*, pp. 3-10 ; *Wyvill Papers*, III. App. 128-35 ; *Life of Cartwright*, I. 191 ; II. 343-6 ; *Add. MSS.* 27805, ff. 14-15.

[6] *Proceedings*, pp. 35-46 ; *S. T.* XXIV. 1026-30 ; *Wyvill Papers*, III. 149-58, 161-9 ; *C. J.* XLIX. 684 ; *Life of Cartwright*, II. 348-50.

remainder seem to have been men of the same social stand-ing.[1] Moreover, an annual subscription of two guineas and a half can hardly be considered distinctive of a popular society of the kind usually considered dangerous.[2]

Its address, the composition of which has been variously attributed to James Mackintosh and Philip Francis,[3] described parliamentary reform as a restoration rather than a change.[4] Those who indiscriminately praised the con-stitution were "too lavish to be sincere." "They will not innovate, but they are no enemies to gradual decay," ignoring the Baconian maxim that "time is the greatest innovator."[5] It was just this silent, cumulative, unresisted growth of abuses that made the French Revolution neces-sary or possible; and the sensible inference was that we should reform now in order to escape revolution hereafter.[6] Between anarchy and despotism they could make no choice:[7] their object was to avoid both. They disputed the validity of any analogy between the cases of England and France, and "utterly disclaimed the necessity" of resorting in England to remedies similar to those which had been necessary in France.[8]

It was at the request of the Friends of the People[9] that Charles Grey took up, in one period of revolution, the task that he was at last to accomplish in another, and on the 30th of April he gave notice in the House of Commons of a motion in favour of parliamentary reform.[10] Fox, Sheridan and the members of the official opposition lent him but a cold and insincere support.[11] Only Erskine amongst its regular leaders had any enthusiasm for the

---

[1] *Proceedings . . . in 1792*, pp. 4-6; *Wyvill Papers*, III. App. 129-31; *Life of Cartwright*, II. 346-7.

[2] *Proceedings*, pp. 9-10; *Wyvill Papers*, III. App. 134-5.

[3] Compare the catalogue of the British Museum with the *Life of Mackintosh*, I. 79. Mr. Stuart Reid appears to claim that it was written by W. H. Lambton, M.P., father of the first Earl of Durham.—*Life and Letters of Lord Durham*, 1906, I. 19.

[4] *Proceedings . . . of 1792*, p. 14.

[5] *Ib.* 15; Bacon, *Essay* XXIV, Of Innovations.

[6] *Proceedings . . . of 1792*, pp. 16-17.   [7] *Ib.* 18.

[8] *Ib.* 16. For this address see also *Wyvill Papers*, III. App. 135-43.

[9] *Proceedings . . . of 1792*, p. 19, cf. 20-4.

[10] *Parl. Hist.* XXIX. 1300 *et seq.*

[11] Moore's *Sheridan*, II. 181-3; Carlisle to Fox, July 23, 1792.—*Mem. of C. J. Fox*, III. 22-3.

society or its cause.[1] Grey himself was never of the extremest sect of reformers. "I was opposed to these men in 1792," he said later of the wilder spirits, "and I am opposed to them now."[2] Lady Holland, who disliked him, attributed his reforming zeal, rather unjustly, to his ambition and to his dislike of Pitt: he only raised the question of reform, she says, "because it would be more peculiarly distressing to Pitt than any other that he could bring forward."[3] No matter what his motive may have been, Grey fully endorsed the proceedings of the Friends of the People, and had no title to shift his responsibilities to other shoulders.[4] His retrospective desire to rob himself of the credit due to him for proposing an unpopular reform shows a strange perversity of mind, and may, indeed, give a clue to the reasons for his weakness as the head of a cabinet.

In 1792 reform was unpopular. It was an act of political courage to stand forth as its advocate against the furious opposition of ministerialists who had the countenance of the king himself. "The most daring outrage to a popular Government committed by the New Society who yesterday published its Manifesto in several of the News Papers could only be equalled by some of its Leaders standing forth the same day to avow their Similar Sentiments in the House of Commons," wrote the king to Pitt, "and I cannot see any substantial difference in their being joined in debate by Mr. Fox and his not being a Member of that society; but if Men are to be found willing to overturn the Constitution of this Country it is most Providential that they so early cast off the Mask and I am most happy it has given Mr. Pitt so fair an opportunity of avowing Sentiments that must endear him to all lovers of good order and our Excellent Constitution; it is also very material that so many Speakers on the side of Opposition have pledged themselves to co-operate in opposing these Reformers as well as so respectable a list of the friends of

---

[1] Thomas Erskine to his brother, the Earl of Buchan, April 27, 1792.—*Henry Erskine : His Kinsfolk and Times*, 340-1.
[2] *Life of Grey*, 8.
[3] *Journal of Elizabeth, Lady Holland*, I. 101.
[4] *Life of Grey*, 19.

Government." [1] Strong as were the king's opinions, and strongly as they were expressed, George III does not seem, in this case, to have misrepresented the opinion of the people. "Administration was strong and popular," says Lady Holland, "and the extravagance of the French patriots had alarmed all English ones." "Pitt became as popular in resisting Grey's motion for reform as he had been some years before in proposing one himself." [2]

Moderation was the watchword of the Friends of the People; in the debate on Grey's notice of motion members of the society were careful to disclaim any subscription of the doctrines of the *Rights of Man*. [3] In their anxiety to be dissociated from Tom Paine they took the Society for Constitutional Information severely to task for amusing their fellow-citizens with "the magnificent promise of obtaining for them the ' Rights of the People ' in their full extent." This was "the indefinite language of delusion which, by opening unbounded prospects of political adventure, tends to destroy that public opinion which is the support of all Free Government, and to excite a spirit of innovation of which no wisdom can foresee the effect, and no skill direct the course." [4]

If the Society for Constitutional Information strayed from the path of wisdom it was not from any want of chastening criticism. Burke, who had no good word for the reforming societies, reserved his severest condemnation for the Society for Constitutional Information, which appeared to him as a charitable contrivance to disperse bad books, a sort of benevolent corporation to relieve book-sellers of their surplus stock. He set himself in direct opposition to the experience of Hardy and Place, whose political interests had been quickened by the publications of the society, by declaring that he had "never heard a man of common judgment or the least degree of informa-

---

[1] George III to Pitt, May 1, 1792.—Chatham MSS. 103 in Record Office.

[2] *Journal of Elizabeth, Lady Holland*, I. 102.

[3] See *Parl. Hist.* XXIX. 1339.

[4] May 12, 1792. *Proceedings of 1792*, pp. 25–34 ; *Wyvill Papers*, III. App. 149–58 ; Shore to Wyvill about May 12, 1792, *ib.* V. 46 ; Wyvill to Batley, May 24, 1792, *ib.* V. 8–10. Cf. *Life of Cartwright*, I. 192–3 ; *Mem. of Horne Tooke*, II. 324.

tion speak a word in praise of the greater part of the publications circulated by that society"; nor, said he, had their proceedings "been accounted, except by some of themselves, as of any serious consequence."[1]

The society retorted with spirit on their accusers. "It was never in our contemplation," they said in reply to the charge of disaffection, "to destroy any Branch of the Legislature, nor to expend a reform beyond the manifest curruptions of that part of it which the People at large has an undoubted right to create. If this is sedition we are at issue with our accuser."[2] They resolved that the thanks of the society be given to their fellow-member, Mr. Thomas Paine, for the first part of "his most masterly Book, intituled *The Rights of Man*, in which not only the malevolent sophistries of hireling Scribblers are detected and exposed to merited Ridicule, but many of the most important and beneficial political Truths are stated, so irresistibly convincing as to promise the Acceleration of that not very distant Period when usurping Borough Sellers and profligate Borough Buyers shall be deprived of what they impudently dare to call their Property—the Choice of the Representatives of the People."[3]

In this approbation of Paine's writings their correspondents joined heartily.[4] The Manchester society thought Part II of the *Rights of Man* "a Work of the highest Importance to every Nation under Heaven, but particularly to this,"[5] and made special mention of the valuable suggestions for the reduction of taxation which that work contained.[6] From Norwich, where many societies were federated, there came the proposal also for a united society; a national union, it would seem, of the friends of liberty, who ought to be strongly and indissolubly united.[7] Disregarding the criticism of the Friends

---

[1] *Reflections.—Works*, II. 279.
[2] May 28, 1791.—*Wyvill Papers*, V. iv–v; cf. Wyvill to Batley, April 4, 1792, *ib*. V. 1–2.
[3] Resolution of March 23, 1791.—*C. J.* XLIX. 664-5, 681; *S. T.* XXV. 112-13.
[4] *C. J.* XLIX. 682-3, 665, 668, 697, 699; *S. T.* XXV. 135, 137-8, 139.
[5] March 13, 1792. *C. J.* XLIX. 682.
[6] Paine held that Pitt's next budget was a plagiarism.
[7] March 24, 1792.—*C. J.* LXIX. 698-9, 668.

of the People, the Society for Constitutional Information continued sedulously to promote the distribution of Paine's works; [1] and in this they were to a certain extent assisted by the London Corresponding Society. [2] But when Paine offered them a gift of copyright they wisely refused to undertake so dangerous a trust. [3] As it was, staunch friends like Wyvill began to doubt whether they could have complete confidence in the society's discretion. Unlike some of his old associates, Wyvill did not lose faith in the cause of reform during the period of its eclipse. He was no alarmist, and perhaps his evidence should be taken as strong proof of the reality of the alarm which the writings of Paine and the activity of the popular societies were spreading amongst sober people. "If Mr. Paine should be able to rouse up the lower classes," he wrote, "their interference will probably be marked by wild work, and all we now possess, whether in private property or public liberty, will be at the mercy of a lawless and furious rabble." [4]

The toast-list of a dinner which the society held on the 13th of April, 1792, is an odd admixture of folly and of caution—the best possible proof, perhaps, that it was the work not of the disaffected, but of the innocent; not of sneaking conspirators, but of frank enthusiasts. "May liberty threaten every throne by which it is threatened!" and "May revolutions be rendered useless by a radical reform!" reveal an epigrammatic gift which some people might think dangerous; others might catch a *sous-entendu* in "Obedience to equal laws!" though it would be straining justice to send a man to Botany Bay for an inflection of the voice. But no one can object to "An essential reform in the representation of the people to secure for ever public tranquillity!" or "May Liberty establish itself universally by the pen, and not by the sword!" or "May the sun in its course light only upon freemen or men

---

[1] March 24, 1792.—*C. J.* LXIX. 601, 685-7 ; *S. T.* XXV. 152-4, 156, 158-9, cf. 166-7 ; *Add. MSS.* 27814, fo. 87.
[2] *C. J.* XLIX. 687 ; *S. T.* XXV. 159-60, cf. 161.
[3] *Ib.* XXIV. 490-1.
[4] Wyvill to James Martin, April 28, 1792.—*Wyvill Papers*, V. 22-6, especially p. 23.

worthy of freedom!" The last, indeed, shows a nice
appreciation of the finer shades of discretion. "To the
rights of man!" was drunk twice, but this was balanced
by a nobler toast, "May men be not less mindful of their
duties than of their rights!"[1]

Watt and Cooper gave the Constitutional Society some
account of their reception in Paris, which led the society
to send an address to the Jacobins congratulating them on
the success of the Revolution. The argument is that wars
of ambition are the fruit of despotism. "To feed the
Avarice or gratify the Wickedness of Ambition, the
Fraternity of the Human Race has been destroyed: as if
the several Nations of the Earth had been created by rival
Gods. Man has not considered man as the work of One
Creator. . . ." Instead of being taught that all men were
brothers, he had been taught to believe that man was the
natural enemy of man, and "to describe Virtues and Vices
by a Geographical Chart."[2]

The members of the Constitutional Society believed
that many shared their views, but they regretted that the
principles of the Revolution had not been accepted by the
neighbours of France. "We have beheld your peaceable
principles insulted by despotic Ignorance: We have seen
the right Hand of Fellowship which you held out to the
World rejected by those who riot on its Plunder: We now
behold you a Nation provoked into Defence; and we can
see no Mode of Defence equal to that of establishing the
general freedom of *Europe*. In this best of causes we wish
you success. Our Hearts go with you: and in saying this
we believe we utter the Voice of Millions."[3]

In other words, the society set the seal of its approval
on the revolutionary propaganda which was spreading
throughout Europe, and gave a sanction to the new crusade
in defence of liberty which it withheld from wars of

[1] *Moniteur*, April 29, 1792, No. 120, p. 493. Cartwright was toasted
and said, in reply, that if he had the glory of being regarded as the
father of the faithful, he flattered himself that one day his race would not
be less numerous than that of Abraham.

[2] Burke himself once coined a more concise phrase—"geographical
morality."

[3] Adopted May 11, 1792.—*C. J.* XLIX. 685-6, 601, 666; *S. T.* XXV.
150-1; Appendix to Cooper's *Reply to Burke's Invective*, 90.

ambition waged under the banner of despotism. There was nothing in the letter which could be construed as sedition, but it appeared to associate the society with the proselytism of the Revolution. What seemed harmless in May of 1792 became regrettable in September, when Paris was stained with bloodshed, and took on a sinister appearance in 1793, when, nine months after the adoption of the address, England and France were at war. Still more objectionable in the eyes of ministers was the fact that the address and a letter of Paine were printed as one pamphlet and freely distributed. "This single circumstance," said the Committee of Secrecy in 1794, "would, in the Judgment of your Committee, leave little Doubt of the real Nature of the Designs entertained by the Society." [1]

The Jacobins do not seem, however, to have accepted the address without discussion, though the reasons for their hesitation are obscure.[2] It was read ultimately by Watt, to whom the president replied that England had given "an example of the hatred that reasonable men should bear to tyrants." "Free peoples," he said, "will give peace to the world and death to tyranny howsoever it may be veiled." [3] After Watt and Cooper had been denounced in Parliament the Jacobins were urged to send a letter of sympathy to Manchester. Collot d'Herbois advised them not to disregard "the political considerations proper to be observed between two great nations," and finally, after much discussion, the party of caution prevailed.[4]

Nothing is more characteristic of the English popular societies than a determination that all their actions should be open and above-board; that nobody should be able to reproach them with secret plottings or subterranean disaffection, or to allege against them that they loved darkness rather than light because their deeds were evil. They courted publicity, and in all probability it was their anxious eagerness to avoid even the suspicion of concealment that brought down upon them at last the weight of the Government's displeasure.

[1] *C. J.* XLIX. 601, 686 ; *S. T.* XXV. 152-4, 156, 158-9, cf. 166-7 ; *Add. MSS.* 27814, fo. 87.
[2] *A. J.* III. 618-20.   [3] May 27, 1792, *A. J.* III. 623.
[4] June 4, 1792, *A. J.* III. 653-6.

After deep consideration [1] the London Corresponding Society decided, in March 1792, to claim public notice by issuing an address, "declaring publicly their political principles and opinions. They had not printed anything before. And it being the first there were four Addresses prepared by four different Members. When they were all read in the Committee they were all pronounced good. But that short and comprehensive Address and Resolutions by Margarot was preferred." Margarot was a man of brilliant social and intellectual gifts who was later to fall a victim to the repressive policy of Pitt, and though not without faults of character he was, in many ways, a source of strength to the society. "The Committee," continues Hardy, "ordered me to enclose a copy" of his address "to the Society for Constitutional Information for their approbation before it was sent to the Press. Expecting an answer from them it was not signed either by Chairman or Secretary, but the letter that enclosed it was written and signed by me. That society," the Society for Constitutional Information, "had just revived and met at the house of their secretary, Mr. Adams, after it had ceased to meet for nine or ten years. Mr. Tooke, Sheridan, Barlow, Frost, Captain Perrey (*sic*), etc., were then in the room when the letter and Address were read to the company present; they highly approved of it and, without acquainting the London Corresponding Society, Horne Tooke wrote the name of Thomas Hardy, secretary, to the Address and gave it to Captain Perrey to publish in the *Argus* Newspaper next morning. . . ." [2] This is not, however, the whole story. There had been much debate about signing the address, and Margarot, the author, had definitely refused to set his name to it. Now Hardy had kept himself a good deal in the background, hoping that the society would gain members more influential than himself and better calculated to give it consequence with the public. [3] But nobody else dared set his name to a

---

[1] Thomas Hardy to J. H. T. (John Horne Tooke), March 27, 1792.— *Add. MSS.* 27811, fo. 6.

[2] Hardy to Place, July 7, 1831. MS. letter prefixed to John Richter's copy of the Trust Report from the Committee of Secrecy, etc.—B. M. c. 61, b. 16 (1).   [3] *Add. MSS.* 27814, ff. 29-30.

public manifesto, and even in Hardy's case it may have been the precipitation of Horne Tooke which put an end to his hesitation.[1] When the address appeared as a separate publication of the society it was certainly signed with Hardy's name. This manifesto led to the formation of many societies, and was, it is said, the cause of Burke's description of the London Corresponding Society "in one of his mad rants in the House of Commons" as "the Mother of all Mischief."[2]

The address attempted a harmony of the doctrines of natural right and the social contract in order to prove man's right to a share in the government of his country, which fraud or force, under the sanction of custom, withheld from the majority of the people of England. "The few with whom the right of elections and representation remains abuse it, and the strong temptations held out to electors sufficiently prove that the representatives of this country seldom procure a seat in Parliament from the *unbought* suffrages of a free people." The society advocated universal suffrage and "a fair, equal and impartial Representation of the people in Parliament." They deemed it "no less the *right* than the *duty* of every citizen to keep a watchful eye on the government of his country; that the laws by being multiplied do not degenerate into Oppression; and that those who are entrusted with the Government do not substitute *Private Interest for Public Advantage.*" Withal they expressed their "*abhorrence* of tumult and violence." They aimed at "Reform, not anarchy." "Reason, firmness and unanimity" were their only weapons.[3]

As Hardy mentions in his letter, the address was published in the newspapers by the Society for Constitutional Information.[4] The London Corresponding Society had it printed as a sort of handbill, of which, by the aid of the penny-a-week subscription, thousands were given away.[5] The plan and address of the society were sent to Dundas.

[1] *Add. MSS.* 27814, ff. 29–30.
[2] *Ib.* 27808, fo. 4, cf. 17 ; *Mem. of Thomas Hardy*, 109.
[3] April 2, 1792.—*Add. MSS.* 27811, ff. 2–3 ; *Mem. of Thomas Hardy*, 19; *S. T.* XXIV. 378.
[4] *Add. MSS.* 27811, fo. 19 ; *C. J.* XLIX. 686–7.   [5] *Ib.* 27814, fo. 31.

In a covering letter his protection was claimed and he was told that, unless he specifically withheld it within ten days, it would be assumed. Dundas never replied to the letter : in all probability he never read it. Two years later, when the papers of many of the reformers were seized, plenty of copies of this letter were taken by the authorities, but it was evidently thought damaging to the case of the prosecution, as no allusion was made to it during the course of the State trials.[1] In April 1792 it was not of affording protection to parliamentary reformers that Dundas was thinking, but of repressing their activities as dangerous to public order.

[1] See Mrs. Thelwall's *Life of Thelwall*, I. 112–13.

CHAPTER IX

THE BEGINNING OF REPRESSION

MAY 1792—FEBRUARY 1793

THE progress of events in France tended more and more to convince the powers of Europe that the Revolution was an international danger. On the 7th of February, 1792, the Emperor Leopold and the King of Prussia formed an alliance, with the object of securing order in France as the only possible pledge for the maintenance of order in Europe. But just as they were alarmed by events in France, so, in their turn, Frenchmen were dismayed by the menacing attitude of these powerful princes, who not merely threatened war themselves but gave their countenance and support to the *émigrés* who were mustering their forces at Coblentz, and whose hostility to the existing Government in France was not concealed. In France itself the Girondists lent their powerful support to the growing demand for war, and such pressure did they bring to bear upon the king that on the 20th of April they were able to force him into a declaration of war against Austria. This policy of aggression seemed like a challenge to Europe. It excited alarm in England as well as on the Continent. It fanned the fears of the English official classes, and was speedily followed by an attempt to impose a check upon the expression of advanced opinions.

On the 21st of May, 1792, ministers so far gave way to alarm as to issue a proclamation against "seditious meetings and publications;"[1] an act, as a journalist wrote later, "ever memorable as the commencement of the struggle between the House of Commons and the People."[2]

---

[1] *Ann. Reg.* 1792, p. 192.
[2] *Add. MSS.* 27809, fo. 268; cf. *Life of Paine*, I. 323.

It was, no doubt, the fruit of reform manifestos and of addresses to the Jacobins; but neither the ministry nor the nation was yet decidedly hostile to France. Talleyrand was in London hoping to secure the goodwill of England; not even without hopes of an alliance, or at least of some friendly compact. "Believe me," he had written in January, "an understanding with England is not a chimera." [1]

These hopes were due not to the progress in England of revolutionary opinions but to their comparative want of support; not to the insecurity but to the stability of English political institutions. "Mon opinion," wrote Talleyrand, "est toujours que votre meilleur terrain est l'Angleterre. Dans nos circonstances, ce n'est même que là que je vois de la terre-ferme." [2] Talleyrand had already acquired the prudent habit of dictating his own instructions, [3] and those which he received on his departure for England show that, even before he left France, he thought that "the spirit of innovation already manifested in England and Scotland" was "probably exaggerated." [4] A long dispatch signed by Chauvelin, but usually attributed to Talleyrand, and sent to the French Minister for Foreign Affairs two days after the proclamation against sedition, gives us at once the most complete and the most impartial account that we have of the state of English opinion in May 1792.

"Those curiously deceive themselves," it said, "who regard England as on the eve of revolution; who believe that they see the elements of it prepared, and who, on this account, would desire to attach the people to our cause by testifying the warmest interest in theirs. As nothing is worse founded than this opinion, nothing, also, would be more imprudent than such conduct, or more likely to

---

[1] To Delessart, Jan. 27, 1792.—Pallain, *Mission de Talleyrand à Londres*, 49. Talleyrand was twice in London ; first, "to buy horses," Jan. 24 to the beginning of March.—Sorel, II. 387–93. He left Paris the second time April 21, 1792.—*Ib.* 439.

[2] To Delessart, Jan. 31, 1792.—Pallain, 56. See also Talleyrand to Delessart, March 2, 1792.—*Ib.* 137.

[3] In this case he also nominated the ambassador whom he was to serve.—Sorel, II. 391, 419.

[4] Instructions to Chauvelin and Talleyrand, April 20, 1792.—Pallain, 231.

alienate from us every mind; of this we have soon convinced ourselves." [1] "One cannot too often repeat these words : *ministry* and *opposition* have not here the sense attributed to them in our public papers. To read them, one would believe that on one side were ranged the king and all the partisans of privilege and royal prerogative; on the other, all the friends of the people, ceaselessly striving, the former for authority and the latter for liberty. If this view be accepted, it can be understood that a revolution would here be, if not very near, at least very easy. The truth is that the mass of the nation is generally indifferent to all those political discussions which cause so much stir amongst us; attached to its Constitution by ancient prejudices, by habit, by continual comparison of its lot with that of the people of other states, and finally by prosperity, it does not imagine that anything could be gained from a revolution of which, moreover, the very history of England makes it fear the dangers. . . ." The country is solely occupied with questions of material prosperity. "The opposition is, in general, regarded as an ingredient as essential to the Constitution as the ministry itself, but that is all, and however much they appear to struggle with each other for whatsoever opinions may be formed of their respective operations, liberty is believed to be secure." [2] Opposition is "more anti-ministerial than popular." It "rivals and keeps watch upon administration, much more than it defends liberty," and has actually been weakened by the formation of the Society of the Friends of the People and by the attempt to revive the question of parliamentary reform. "It is pretended that beneath the mask of a reform, long demanded by justice and reason, there can be seen the intention of destroying a Constitution equally dear to the peers whose privileges it consecrates, to the rich whom it protects, and to the entire body of the nation to whom it assures all the liberty that a people, methodical and slow by character, can wish to enjoy, a people which is occupied without intermission by its commercial interests,

---

[1] Chauvelin (Talleyrand) to the French Minister for Foreign Affairs, May 23, 1792.—Pallain, 290-1.
[2] Dispatch of May 23.—*Ib.* 292-3.

and does not wish to turn aside from them to occupy itself with public affairs." "It is not, then, in the people that the strength of the opposition normally resides, but in the mass of the great proprietors who form an alliance to maintain it; and as these great proprietors are for the most part great lords, by menacing them with the ruin of the Constitution which distinguishes them, and by arousing their vanity, they have been thrown into the arms of the Court." The old Whigs—the Bentincks and the Cavendishes—would give no support to the movement for reform. Fox refused to agitate for it. Pitt believed in it, but could not venture to carry it. The cry had been raised that the Constitution was in danger, and a great majority of the nation was against organic change. "In vain have the friends of reform protested their attachment to the Constitution; in vain have they said they ask for nothing more" than parliamentary reform, "nor to obtain it by other than legal means; they are persistently disbelieved," for "Paine only is seen in their every action." [1]

It was the general belief that the proclamation against sedition was directed more particularly against the Friends of the People.[2] The society repudiated with indignation the republican opinions imputed to it. Pitt was charged with giving the unnecessary "sanction and incentive" of the proclamation to those "corrupt interests and malignant passions" that were opposed to reform. The Friends of the People were not republican, but, said Mackintosh, "it is certain that . . . your Proclamation is as effectual in irritating some men into Republicanism as Mr. Paine's pamphlets have been in frightening others into Toryism." [3]

---

[1] Dispatch of May 23.—Pallain, 297–303.

[2] All sorts of dreadful things have been said about the society. Lewis Goldsmith, who was none too veracious a historian, says, in his *Secret History of the Cabinet of Bonaparte* (1810), p. 19, that the French enlisted in their cause "*false Patriots*, who, under the name of Reformers and Friends of the People, have received and still do receive a regular stipend from the eternal enemies of England and of liberty." On the same evidence —namely, none—Bland Burges believed the same story about the London Corresponding Society. By way of compensation, the equally absurd story that the popular outbreaks of the revolutionists were assisted by Pitt's gold, was commonly believed in Paris.

[3] Mackintosh. A Letter to the Right Hon. Wm. Pitt, ap. *Life of M.* I. 80–1.

The society published as its manifesto the resolutions passed at the Thatched House Tavern before Pitt became a minister and learned to fear reform.[1] Lord John Russell and a few others, nevertheless, took fright at the growing hostility to the society, and making the membership of Major Cartwright and the proposed, though never completed, election of Cooper the ground of their action, they seceded on the 9th of June, 1792.[2]

Showing a bold front to its traducers, the society issued a second address in favour of parliamentary reform, the advocacy of which it refused to abandon, for reform was an admitted necessity, and opinion only differed as to the scope of a Reform Bill or the time at which it was wise to propose one.[3] It was absurd—almost disloyal—to accuse members of the society of disaffection, "as if a real Representation" were "incompatible with the security of a limited monarchy." If such people as republicans and levellers did exist in England they found no associates amongst the Friends of the People. Abuses could be remedied in a regular parliamentary way, and the friends of reform would do well to try no other, lest they played into the hands of arbitrary power.[4] "Instances are not wanting to prove that, under the specious pretence of strengthening the hands of Government, a design may be formed of destroying the liberty of the press, of calling in the military power, and finally annihilating the Civil Government of the country."[5]

The Friends of the People refused to meddle with the affairs of Ireland, which were outside their proper sphere;[6] they addressed to the more democratic London Corresponding Society "a friendly Admonition" to abstain

---

[1] *Proceedings*, 68–9; *Wyvill Papers*, III. App. 187–9; cf. Watson's *Anecdotes*, 266.

[2] *Proceedings*, 47–52; *Wyvill Papers*, III. App. 165–73; Cartwright's Letter to the Duke of Newcastle, 148–57. Wyvill's correspondent, Shore, who was not an extremist, had a good opinion of Cooper. "He was a warm Friend to Parliamentary Reform and totally denied any evil intention against the Constitutional Government of this Country." Shore to Wyvill, after Dec. 13, 1793.—*Wyvill Papers*, V. 153 note; cf. also Shore to Wyvill, Dec. 4, 1793, *ib.* 150–1; Wyvill to Shore, Dec. 13, 1793, *ib.* 153.

[3] Dec. 15, 1792.—*Proceedings*, 54–5.

[4] *Ib.* 55–6.   [5] *Ib.* 56–7.   [6] *Ib.* 58–67.

from "the Intermixture of Foreign Correspondence and domestic Reform."[1] Addresses to the national Convention of France were, in their view, also dangerous in a time when "the most venial Indiscretion of the Friends of Reform" was converted into an argument against it. The caution of the Friends of the People exasperated their opponents; and the wisdom with which they refrained from putting forward any specific plea of reform[2] is proved by the annoyance which such reticence caused their enemies.[3]

The society had its satellites in plenty—unauthorised imitators, perhaps, who borrowed the sanction of its name. Record survives of such a society in the Borough,[4] and of another at Royston in Hertfordshire.[5] A third, the Aldgate Society of the Friends of the People, which met at the Mitre Tavern, in Mitre Court, demanded universal suffrage and annual Parliaments. It seems to have been the only society that dared to celebrate in 1792 the anniversary of the fall of the Bastille, and in November of that year it sent to the Convention an address of congratulation on the success of the French arms in Belgium.[6]

A previously existing but otherwise unknown Society of Constitutional Whigs adopted the additional name of Friends of the People.[7] This society may be the same as the "Grand Lodge" of the Constitutional Whigs of England meeting in Frith Street,[8] which adopted an address

---

[1] *Add. MSS.* 27812, fo. 30.   [2] *C. J.* XLIX. 704-5.
[3] See, for instance, *Remarks on the Proceedings*, 14.
[4] *Add. MSS.* 27814, fo. 34.
[5] Newspaper cutting of letter, Oct. 1, 1792.—*Ib.* 27837, fo. 46.
[6] Several papers of this society are preserved in the French Archives. Resolutions of May 28, 1792. Resolutions of July 9, 1792. Account of the celebrations of July 14, 1792. Address to the Convention, Nov. 12, 1792. Archives nationales, C. 242. See Robinet, p. 373, where they are said to be in the *Correspondance d'Angleterre* au Ministère des Affaires étrangères, T. 583, pièce 150. I certainly found them, not at the Foreign Office, but in the Archives. On the Aldgate Society see also " A Thing of Shreds and Patches," by an Association against Levellers and to procure the Restoration of the Rights of the People, March 11, 1793.
[7] Address and Declaration of the Society of Constitutional Whigs, Independent and Friends of the People, united for obtaining Equal Liberty by a Parliamentary reform, Nov. 5, 1792.
[8] *Moniteur*, Nov. 13, 1791, No. 317, p. 321. In his examination before the Privy Council Hardy was asked about a Society of Constitutional Whigs in Long Acre. He said that he knew the president, Mr. Puller, a leather-cutter, and the secretary, Mr. James Bligh. The

to the Constituent Assembly on October 25, 1791. The address was presented to the Legislative Assembly on December 6, 1791, and, with the President's reply, circulated by the Assembly's order to the eighty-three departments.[1] The London correspondent of the *Moniteur* openly rebuked the Assembly for acting so lightly as to accept an insignificant address in the apparent belief that it came from the Whig Club of England, and from a society, therefore, which contained "the direct descendants of the founders of our liberty, as well as its most illustrious defenders." He also dwelt on the unconstitutional nature of a direct communication from an English club to the National Assembly.[2] There can be no doubt that the Assembly did render itself ridiculous by its excessive eulogies of a number of obscure individuals whom it hailed as "the ancient Society of Whigs," and by its enthusiasm for the innumerable defenders of liberty, who numbered precisely a hundred and twenty-three.[3]

The delegates of the hundred and twenty-three nevertheless became, for a few brief hours, the heroes of the Society of Jacobins, and Carlyle has described[4] the scenes of enthusiasm amidst which they were presented with an "Ark of Alliance" by the "citoyennes habituées aux tribunes."[5] But if the hundred and twenty-three were one and the same with the "Constitutional Whigs, Independent and Friends of the People," then they had improved both in sense and style before the 5th of November, 1792, when they published their "Address and Declaration."

London Corresponding Society had had no correspondence with this society for over a twelvemonth.—Exam. of Hardy, May 14, 1794 ; *P. C. R.* 33 Geo. III. 68.

[1] *P.-V.* Dec. 6, 1791, pp. 287–9 ; Archives nationales, C. 140 (119–21).

[2] *Moniteur*, Dec. 30, 1791, No. 364, p. 1521.

[3] *P.-V.* Dec. 7, 1791, pp. 298–9 ; Archives nationales, C. 140 (125).

[4] In the essay called "Parliamentary History of the French Revolution," written for the *Westminster* in 1837 as a review of Buchez et Roux.

[5] Dec. 18, 1791.—*A. J.* III. 290–1 ; see earlier proceedings, *ib.* 257–8, 272–4, 289, Société des Amis de la Constitution séante aux Jacobins à Paris. Extrait du procès-verbal . . . Paris, 1792, in –8, p. 2. Discours des citoyennes françaises prononcé à la société des amis de la constitution séante aux Jacobins à Paris in-8° de 3 pp. 1791. See also Buchez et Roux, XII. 339–76. There is trace of a correspondence between the Constitutional Whigs and the Friends of Freedom at Cherbourg.—*C. J.* LXIX. 688.

More important, perhaps, than the Constitutional Whigs was the Society of the Friends of the People at Southwark, founded in 1792 by John Cartwright. John Thelwall, the friend of Coleridge and, in some ways, the most brilliant of the English reformers, soon became a member of this society. It adopted the arrangement into divisions, characteristic of the London Corresponding Society, and in the warmth of its popular sympathies it seems to have approached more nearly to that society than to the Friends. of the People.[1] Loud were its protests against ministerial representation. "The People also," it said, "have their Prerogatives." [2]

Yet another interesting society met at Holborn. It asked for a simpler and more equal government, in which all could share, which all would be interested to maintain, and which would be less costly and less burdensome to support. These reformers desired a "National Convention " to accomplish these ends; but in order to rebut the charge of republicanism they adopted, in words of their own, Bentham's distinction that men have equal rights but not to equal things.[3] The Friends of the People at Holborn deserve to be remembered for the mental elasticity which enabled them, almost in a breath, to chorus Jean Jacques Rousseau and Jeremy Bentham.

Like the Friends of the People, the Society for Constitutional Information felt that the proclamation against sedition was intended, however unjustly, to apply to its publications. It issued its reply and defence in the form of an address. Long Parliaments, place-holders in the House of Commons, the size of the national debt, oppressive taxes, proprietary boroughs, "expensive armaments and menacing Proclamations and encampments in time of profound peace," were denounced in a formal and lengthy catalogue of objections to the existing political order. The

---

[1] Formed April 19, 1792.—*Proceedings*, ap. *Add. MSS.* 27812, ff. 12–13; Cestre's *Thelwall*, 75; cf. *S. T.* XXV. 139 *et seq.*

[2] Mrs. Thelwall's *Life of Thelwall*, 76, where a passage is quoted from a protest against the proclamation.

[3] Address headed "Holborn Society of the Friends of the People, instituted, Nov. 2, 1792, for the purpose of Political Investigation." Another copy of the same address is headed "Universal Society of the Friends of the People."

weapon wherewith the society proposed to scatter this host of evils and to inaugurate the reign of millennial virtue was parliamentary reform.[1]

During the weeks that followed the proclamation the members of the London Corresponding Society, strong in the persuasion that their agitation for reform was perfectly legal, carried on an active propaganda.[2] Hardy was hopeful that the people were awaking "out of their lethargy and standing up for the Rights of Man."[3] "*The Aristocracy*," he wrote—and his letter, it should be remarked, was to a lord—"*is trembling in every joint for their exclusive privileges.*"[4] Withal the society exhorted fellow-reformers to unite "*in guarding against all Attempts aiming at the Subversion of wholesome and regular Government, and repress to the utmost of their Power all Proceedings tending to produce Riots and Tumults.*"[5]

From the very beginning it had been arranged that as soon as the members of the society became too numerous to form a mutually educative circle of friends they should be separated into divisions, and that as each division became, in its turn, unwieldy, it should again divide and a new branch of the society should be established. In January 1792, the first month of the society's existence, there were about two hundred members.[6] By about July the membership had so much increased that the society was split up into ten divisions.[7] In the same month "two more colonies" were planted, the eleventh and twelfth divisions;[8] and within six· months of the first establishment of the branch system, Hardy's own division split up five or six times.[9] In the same way each branch

[1] May 25, 1792.—*C. J.* XLIX. 686, ap. *Add. MSS.* 27814, fo. 87.

[2] *Add MSS.* 27814, fo. 23 ; 27811, ff. 9–10 ; 27812, ff. 4–6, 7–9 ; *S. T.* XXIV. 380–2.

[3] June 4, 1792.—*Add. MSS.* 27811, fo. 12.

[4] Hardy to Lord Daer, July 14, 1792.—*Ib.* 27811, ff. 14–5.

[5] London Corresponding Society to Society for Constitutional Information, May 31, 1792.—*C. J.* XLIX. 687 ; *S. T.* XXV. 155–7 ; cf. *Add. MSS.* 27812, ff. 9–10.

[6] Hardy's Examination, May 12, 1794.—*P. C. R.* 33 Geo. III. 47.

[7] *Ib.*

[8] Hardy to Horne Tooke, July 24, 1792.—*Add. MSS.* 27511, fo. 15 (see also 27814, fo. 32) ; *S. T.* XXV. 178.

[9] Exam. of Hardy, May 12, 1794.—*P. C. R.* 33 Geo. III. 47.

"swarmed" as it became too big for a well-regulated hive, and ultimately there were about thirty branches,[1] each sending delegates to a central committee which directed the general policy of the whole society.

The original intention was that each section should consist of about thirty members.[2] But this rule was not strictly kept. The society increased in membership so rapidly that it would have been unwise, if not impossible, to adhere to the letter of the law. For some weeks prior to November 1792 three or four hundred members are said to have been admitted weekly,[3] though if the membership was augmented at the same rate for many weeks either the estimate must be exaggerated or the admissions must have been balanced by numerous secessions. In Hardy's own division—division two—there were six hundred members in May 1794.[4] In the sixth division there were thirty or forty; in others a hundred or a hundred and twenty;[5] and Hardy believed that some of the other branches had as many members as his own.[6] It would be difficult, if not impossible, to trace the branches in detail; they were constantly changing their place of meeting; and probably several of them were more than once abandoned and revived. Hardy told the Privy Council that the divisions did not always meet in one place. "There are various reasons for this moving—sometimes the Landlords of the Houses where they met have been threatened to have their licenses taken away if the Meeting is continued there."[7] But on the most important point the witnesses agree. They fix the number of the branches at thirty.[8] In May 1794 about six hundred was evidently the maximum reached by the membership of a single branch, and

[1] Exam. of Hardy, May 12, 1794.—*P. C. R.* 33 Geo. III. 37 ; Exam. of Metcalfe, who gives a list, May 15, 1794.—*P. C. R.* 33 Geo. III 85-6.

[2] Hardy explains that the rule was not strictly kept. Exam. of May 12, 1794, *ib.* 47.

[3] Hardy's estimate.—*Add. MSS.* 27814, fo. 40.

[4] Hardy's Exam. May 12, 1794.—*P. C. R.* 33 Geo. III. 40.

[5] Metcalfe's Examination, May 15, 1794, *ib.* 83.

[6] Hardy's Exam. May 12, 1794, *ib.* 47.

[7] Exam. of May 12.—*P. C. R.* Geo. III. 38.

[8] *Ib.* 37, Exam. of Metcalfe, May 15, 1794, *ib.* 85-6. Metcalfe was, I suspect, a spy. He said that the divisions so often changed their place of meeting that he could not pretend to say that his list was accurate.

it is equally evident that such a membership was exceptional. It is therefore manifest that Hardy exaggerated the strength of the society when he estimated its total membership at twenty thousand.[1] In May 1794 it did not, in all probability, exceed five or six thousand, and, even if it be admitted that the high-water mark was then past, it may well be doubted whether there were ever more than ten thousand members of the London Corresponding Society.[2]

In August 1792 the society issued a new address, demanding "annually elected Parliaments, unbiassed and unbought Elections, and an equal Representation of the Whole Body of the People." It was disgraceful for men to suffer themselves to be disposed of "like cattle in a fair, as irrational beasts in a market, to the highest bidder." Though the new address made a greater appeal to the gallery than the first, it was yet studiously moderate;[3] so moderate as to anger the Stockport Society, which always expressed its views with a vigour that sheds an interesting light upon the keen political excitement which prevailed in that town.[4]

The English popular societies faced difficulty with courage, but changing opinions on both sides of the Channel were rapidly narrowing their sphere of action. In London, for example, it was judged unwise to celebrate the 14th of July.[5]   But even after the "suspension" of

---

[1] His estimate is of the membership in Nov. 1792.—*Add. MSS.* 27814, fo. 40.   J. Binns arrives at a similar estimate—eighteen to twenty thousand—by another calculation.—*Recoll. of J. Binns*, 45-6.

[2] If it were allowed that, between the arrangement in divisions, in July 1792, and the month of November, there were 400 new members each week, that would only give about 6000 new members, and it does not seem to be suggested that there were 4000 members in July.   On Oct. 16 there were, moreover, only 19 divisions.   On Hardy's estimate there would have been about a thousand members in each.—*Add. MSS.* 27812, fo. 24 ; cf. fo. 23 for membership in Sept. 1792.

[3] Address from the London Corresponding Society to the Inhabitants of Great Britain.—*S. T.* XXIV. 380-7 ; *Add. MSS.* 27812, ff. 14-19.

[4] *C. J.* XLIX. 668-9, 700 ; *S. T.* XXIV. 388-9, etc. ; cf. *C. J.* XLIX. 669-700 ; *S. T.* XXIV. 389 ; *Add. MSS.* 27812, fo. 24.

[5] Archives nationales, C. II (Carton 58), 242 ; cf. *C. J.* XLIX. 688. There seems to have been one dinner at the Mitre, Aldgate.   In October, Noël reported that French victories had been celebrated in several English towns.—Archives étrangères, *Corr. d'Angl.* 553, fo. 95.

Louis XVI on the 10th of August, 1792, and the consequent recall of the British ambassador from Paris, friendly
relations between the English reformers and the French
revolutionists were, for a time, maintained. On the 26th,
French citizenship was conferred upon Priestley [1] and
Paine, upon Bentham and Clarkson, upon James Mackintosh and David Williams, and even upon that loyal
follower of Pitt, William Wilberforce. [2] A few days later
it was known that Priestley and Paine had been elected
deputies to the Convention. [3] "Tom Paine," said one
English critic, "is just where he ought to be—a member
of the Convention of Cannibals." [4]

Priestley considered "these marks of confidence"—the
citizenship and his election as a deputy—"the two greatest
honours France could bestow on a foreigner." He
accepted the citizenship, which he did not think incompatible with his loyalty as an Englishman, for he hoped
that France and England would be "for ever united in the
bonds of fraternity." But he did not think that he could
serve usefully as a deputy. His letters are remarkable
for their insistence on good order as the only security for
liberty. "Let not barbarous conspirators, crowned bri-
gands, affright you. Liberty is imperishable so long as
you repress the illegal violences which dishonour it, and
all internal dissensions." [5]

David Williams [6] accepted the honour of the citizenship, a "precious title" which could add nothing to the
ardour of his desire to see the establishment of that

---

[1] Priestley's son, W. Priestley, was granted letters of naturalisation
by the French National Assembly on June 13, 1792. "Go and live
among this brave and hospitable people," his father had said. "Learn
from them to detest tyranny and to love liberty."—*Ann. Reg.* 1792,
Chron. 25.

[2] *Moniteur*, Aug. 28, 1792, No. 241, pp. 1020-1. The list is curious.
Guadet proposed the motion. Probably the honour was conferred on
these seven Englishmen as opponents of the slave trade.

[3] Monro to Grenville, Sept. 8, 9, and 17, 1792.—Gower's *Despatches*,
237, 238, 250, 260.

[4] Lord Fortescue to Miles, Sept. 1792.—W. A. Miles, I. 334.

[5] Sept. 21, 1792. Read to the Convention, Sept. 28. Also Priestley
to Roland, Sept. 21.—*Moniteur*, Sept. 30, 1792, No. 274, p. 1162.

[6] Founder of the Royal Literary Fund ; writer, schoolmaster and
dissenting preacher. It was to his chapel at Highgate that the father
of John Wilkes is said to have driven in a coach and six.

French Constitution "with which, probably, will be bound up the interest and happiness of the human race." "All the friends of order, of humanity and of that perfect justice which is the chief end of all political labours," had their eyes fixed upon the Convention, for France had the advantage of being the first nation to be placed "in the circumstances in which philosophy" could "insert into the elements of a political constitution the true principles of reason and virtue." [1]

Paine accepted his new responsibilities with zest. "I come not to enjoy repose," he declared in an address to the French. "Convinced that the cause of the French is the cause of all mankind, and that liberty cannot be purchased by a wish, I gladly share with you the dangers and honours necessary to success." "In entering on this great scene, greater than any nation has yet been called upon to act in," he continued in words which show that, with all his self-sufficiency, Paine still retained some of the wisdom that had inspired *Common Sense*, "Let us say to the agitated mind, be calm. Let us punish by instructing rather than by revenge." [2]

Paine's letter was printed and distributed gratis by the London Corresponding Society. [3] For some time, certainly since the 15th of September, [4] the society had been considering the advisability of sending an address of friendship and encouragement to the French. Brunswick's manifesto of the 25th of July, in which he threatened to sack every town that resisted his invading army, had aroused a sympathy for the French such as some had never felt before, and had excited the ire of the most moderate men. [5] The foolish expression of brutality into which

---

[1] Oct. 26, 1729. Re-translated from the French translation, Archives nationales, C. 239 (261). Transmitted to the Convention by the Minister of the Interior, Nov. 13.—*Moniteur*, Nov. 14, 1792, No. 319, p. 1354. Noël, the French agent, subscribed, in the name of the Bibliothèque nationale, to an edition of Hume's *History* by Williams, whom he praised warmly.—*Affaires étrangères, Corr. d'Angl.* 583, ff. 124-5. The edition did not appear. The contract was cancelled owing to the odium which his French sympathies brought upon Williams.

[2] Sept. 25, 1792.—*S. T.* XXIV. 495-7.   [3] *Ib.* 495.

[4] M. M. (Maurice Margarot) to Horne Tooke, Sept. 15, 1792.—*Ib.* 180, cf. 81.

[5] See, for example, a paragraph from its Brussels correspondent which

Brunswick had been misled by the fury of the French *émigrés* was, in all probability, the cause of the remarkable addresses of sympathy from the English reformers to the French Convention. The address of the London Corresponding Society was prepared for presentation to the Legislative Assembly, but five days before its final adoption, on the 27th of September, the Republic had been proclaimed by the Convention. Three weeks later was issued the decree offering assistance to the peoples of other nations against their despotic rulers, which was the cause of so much panic in England. In consequence, the London Corresponding Society acquired a retrospective ill-fame. Attempts were made to charge it with approval of all the later excesses of the Convention. But it is always dangerous to read history backwards. The society could judge of the Convention, with its history still to make, only by the record of the Assembly that had made history. It is well to remember Balzac's caution that it was an age in which clothes wore longer than parties. Men better qualified by information and experience than the members of the London Corresponding Society to forecast the trend of politics made bad mistakes and misjudged the great transitions.

The address, which was also subscribed by the Manchester Constitutional Society, the Norwich Revolution Society, and the London Constitutional Whigs, Independent and Friends of the People,[1] began with a reference to the invading hosts of Brunswick as "foreign robbers" who were ravaging French territories "under the specious pretext of justice." The French cause, said the addressers, was closely blended with their own. "Frowned upon by an oppressive system of control whose gradual but continual encroachments have deprived this nation of nearly all its boasted liberty and brought us to that abject state of slavery from which you have so gloriously emerged, a few thousands of British citizens, indignant, manfully

---

even the anti-Jacobin *Public Advertiser* printed, Sept. 3, 1792 ; Jenkinson, afterwards Earl of Liverpool, thought it unobjectionable, however. —*Life of Lord Liverpool*, I. 22.

[1] *Ann. Reg* 1792, App. to *Chron.* 70.

step forth to rescue their country from the opprobrium brought upon it by the supine conduct of those in power : they conceive it to be the duty of Britons to countenance and to assist to the utmost of their power the champions of human happiness, and to swear to a nation proceeding on the plan which you have adopted, an inviolable friendship." The beautiful dream of perpetual concord between France and England charmed the members of this society as it had charmed all their fellow-reformers. Freedom, for them, was the herald of peace.

"Information," they said, "makes rapid progress among us. Curiosity has taken possession of the public mind; the conjoint reign of ignorance and despotism passes away. Men now ask each other, What is Freedom ? What are our rights ? Frenchmen, you are already free, and Britons are preparing to become so." "Warm as are our wishes for your success, eager as we are to behold freedom triumphant and man everywhere restored to the enjoyment of his just rights, a sense of our duty, as orderly citizens, forbids our flying in arms to your assistance; our Government has pledged the national faith to remain neutral. . . . We, therefore, must obey; our hands are bound but our hearts are free, and they are with you." [1]

This prudence was, however, a vain precaution against the excesses of foolish friends. An Englishman called Oswald, who was a member of the Jacobin Society, had quite misconceived the character of the English "clubbists," whom he wished to encourage to throw off all restraints. "Rid of its tyrants," England might "lend a strong arm to uproot aristocracy and royalty in France," and to "complete . . . the revolution in Europe." [2] Oswald openly advocated the encouragement of a revolution in England. [3]

---

[1] Published separately as a pamphlet.—*Ann. Reg.* 1792, App. to *Chron.* 70–2 ; *C. J.* XLIX. 688–9 ; 603 ; *S. T.* XXIV. 522–3, 390–1, 525 ; *Mem. of Thos. Hardy*, 20–3 ; *Add. MSS.* 27812, fo. 24, cf. 27814, ff. 22, 23. It is referred to apparently by Noël, Archives des Affaires Étrangères, *Corr. d'Angleterre*, 583, fo. 13. Another version, re-translated into English from the French, and not in all passages faithful to the English original, is in *A Collection of Addresses* . . . 6–8 [B. M. 681, e. 28 (3)].

[2] Aug. 22, 1792.—*A. J.* IV. 230–1.   [3] Sept. 30, 1792, *ib.* 347.

Upon his persuasion the Jacobins did consent, in October, to send an address to the English societies.[1] They bade the English rejoice with them over the fall of royalty, and the complete emancipation of the French. Lying newspapers, in the pay of the English Government, had, they complained, misrepresented their conduct, and they offer explanations of it in the form of a narrative of the Revolution in which Providence is always on the side of the Jacobins. Louis XVI is compared to Louis XI and the tyrant of Syracuse, and Englishmen are invited to join in rejoicing over the birth of the French republic, an event which "advances universal liberty by several centuries."[2] There is no evidence to show that this monument of unwisdom ever reached its destination. Had the English societies been in possession of it there is no likelihood that so many addresses would have been sent to the Convention during the succeeding weeks. At the end of the month the Friends of the People at Newington—where Price had been a minister—added their tribute to that of the London Corresponding Society. Their object, they said, was parliamentary reform at home, but they sympathised with men struggling for liberty abroad. "Illustrious Senators, Enlightened Legislators and dear Friends!" they said. "With unfeigned satisfaction we are enabled to inform you that the unnatural Enmity, so long and basely cherished in the Breasts of a generous people towards the *French Nation,* by the insidious Arts and secret Engines of Court Despotism and Intrigue, is now entirely dissipated except among those who benefit by the abuses; and we Hail with Joy the Auspicious Hour that shall join the two Nations in an indissoluble Bond of Union as the precursor of Universal Peace and Concord."[3]

The address of the London Corresponding Society was

[1] It is only just to say at once that I have not found an English version of this address.

[2] Debates on the subject, Sept. 30 and Oct. 1. Adopted Oct. 3, 1792. —*A. J.* IV. 350, 354, 356-9.

[3] Oct. 31, 1792. The original is in the Archives nationales, C. 240 (275). A French version was printed as a pamphlet : "Convention nationale. Adresse des Amis du Peuple de la Grande Bretagne, de la ville de Newington, à la Convention nationale de la République française. Also reprinted in *A Collection of Addresses,* 1-2.

presented to the Convention on the 7th of November;[1] that of the Newington Society on the 10th;[2] and Hérault de Séchelles, the President, was ordered to send the same reply to both societies. Gravely and with dignity he thanked them for their sympathy, and approved the constitutional moderation of the Corresponding Society. "Their respect for a Constitution which they know how to judge is no longer the old superstition which guaranteed the Government in impunity for its errors; it is rather the effect of a prudent and politic gravity which, knowing how to moderate its strength, seems to force upon the Government that same neutrality, and to warn it to be just, or at least prudent, like the nation. Believe, generous Englishmen, that in preserving that attitude you none the less join with us in the work of universal liberty." The time was not, he hoped, far distant "when the interest of Europe and of the human race will call the two nations to hold out to each other a fraternal hand."[3]

In November, the Society for Constitutional Information followed the example of the Corresponding Society. It had already sent an address of brotherhood and goodwill to the Jacobins;[4] and the Friends of Liberty on the Loire had sent a similar address "to the noble sons of liberty on the happy shores of Thames."[5] The Constitutional Society had approved the spirit of the Corresponding Society's address,[6] and had even considered for some time the advisability of adopting it. It was ultimately decided that separate addresses would serve the purpose better.[7] The members of the Constitutional Society congratulated the French on the victories of liberty and rejoiced that here in England "the Hand of Oppression" had "not yet ventured completely to ravish the *Pen* from us, nor openly to point the Sword at *you*." Their cause was sacred, a bond of union "to the Human Race, in which Union our

---

[1] *P.-V.* Nov. 7, 1792, 2–6; *Moniteur*, Nov. 8, 1792, No. 313, p. 1328.

[2] *P.-V.* Nov. 10, 1792, pp. 105–6.

[3] Copy engrossed on parchment.—Archives nationales, A. F. III. Carton 57 (Dossier 221); *Moniteur*, Nov. 12, 1792; *P.-V.* Nov. 10, 1792, pp. 106–7; Translation, *Ann. Reg.* 1792, App. to *Chron.* 72.

[4] May 11, 1792; *C. J.* XLIX. 601; 606, *S. T.* XXV. 150–1.

[5] July 14, 1791, *ib.* XXV. 115.

[6] *C. J.* XLIX. 666, 688–9, etc.   [7] *Ib.* 689.

own Nation will surely be one of the first to concur;"
this, indeed, they believe to be the sentiment of the English
people, if not of the English Government.[1]

Joel Barlow, a pretentious and shallow American, whose
pamphlet on the vices of the Constitution of 1791 had been
presented to the Convention by Tom Paine and accorded
honourable mention,[2] and John Frost, the intimate friend
of Horne Tooke, were sent to Paris to present the address
to the Convention.[3] They did so on the 28th of November,
when a like address was received from a society of the
English, Scotch and Irish resident in Paris, over which
John Hurford Stone presided.[4] One or other of the
delegates passed beyond the letter of his instructions, and
delivered a most unwise speech to the assembly. Innumerable societies of the sort which he represented were forming, he said, "in all parts of England. . . . Reason will
make rapid progress, and it will not be extraordinary if,
in a shorter time than we dare say, there will arrive from
the continent addresses of solicitation to an English
National Convention." [5]

This speech was unfortunate. Grégoire, who presided
at the session, was a great educationalist, but not a ready
diplomat. He returned to the unhappy subject of an
English convention, and these speeches, little known in
England at the time, afterwards gave a handle to the
Committee of Secrecy, and made it more plausible than it
would otherwise have been to interpret the word convention in the French sense when it was employed by English
reformers. "Brave children of a nation which has already
both made worlds illustrious and given examples to the
Universe," said Grégoire, "you bring us more than wishes,

---

[1] Nov. 9, 1792. Archives nationales, C. 241 (278); Adresse des
Anglois, des Écossois, et des Irlandois . . . 5–7.—B. M. 440 l. 11 (5);
C.J. XLIX. 666, 691 ; *S. T.* XXIV. 526–8; XXV. 183 ; *A Collection of
Addresses* . . . 12–14 ; Horne Tooke wrote the address.

[2] P.-V. Nov. 7, 1792, p. 2 ; *Moniteur*, Nov. 8, 1792, No. 313, p. 1327.

[3] Arch. nat. C. 241 (278) ; *Add. MSS.* 27809, fo. 273.

[4] Arch. nat. C. 241 (278) ; *Moniteur*, Nov. 27, 1792, No. 334, pp. 1414–
15; P.-V. Nov. 28, 1792 ; pp. 379–80 ; *E. H. R.* XII. 672–5.

[5] *Moniteur*, Nov. 29, 1792, No. 334, p. 1415 ; *C.J.* XLIX. 666; Adresse
des Anglois, des Écossois, et des Irlandois, 4–5 ; *A Collection of
Addresses*, 17.

since the lot of our soldiers has merited your solicitude : *the defenders of our liberty will one day be the defenders of yours.* . . . The shades of Pym and Hampden and Sydney hover over your heads; and doubtless the moment approaches when the French will felicitate the National Convention of Great Britain. . . . Generous republicans, your appearance amongst us prepares the materials of history : it will name the day when the citizens of a nation long its rival, in the name of a host of compatriots, appeared in the bosom of the Assembly of the French people : it will relate that all our hearts throbbed at your appearance." [1]   Though it does not appear, in fact, that history has occupied itself much with this episode, or that hearts have since throbbed at the recollection of it, we may permit ourselves to admire the honest warmth of a man who, without being free from all the absurdities of his day, yet preserved his ideals and went on steadily with his appointed task of reorganising the educational system of his country, whilst his fellows were saying many foolish things and doing few wise ones.   In French politics Grégoire was a moderate, and he was betrayed into his indiscreet reply only by his generous enthusiasm; but for his friends, the English democrats, the speech was sadly maladroit.

On the same day the envoy of the Constitutional Society announced that he was charged to inform the Convention that the society which he represented had sent a thousand pairs of shoes as a patriotic gift to the soldiers of liberty.   These shoes had already arrived at Calais, and more were to follow; a thousand pairs each week, for at least six successive weeks. [2]   The true story of these shoes seems irrecoverable.   The treasurer appointed by the

---

[1] *Moniteur*, Nov. 29, 1792, No. 334, p. 1415 ; Adresse des Anglois, etc. 7-8 ; *A Collection of Addresses*, 14-15 ; *Ann. Reg.* 1792, App. to *Chron.* 74-5.   It was resolved that a report of these proceedings should be printed and sent to the departments and to the armies.   The report was to be "translated into all languages to be proclaimed by the General in all the countries where the armies of the Republic should penetrate. . . ." *P.-V.* Nov. 28, 1792, p. 381.

[2] *Moniteur*, Nov. 29, 1792, No. 334, p. 1415 ; Adresse des Anglois, etc., 4-5 ; *A Collection of Addresses*, 11-12 ; Pache to the Convention.— *P.-V.* Nov. 28, 1792, p. 381.

Constitutional Society to collect the subscriptions told the Privy Council that he returned the money to the subscribers.[1] Frost said that he took one pair in his pocket and presented it to the Convention. The shoes were deposited on the bureau, and were much admired.[2] It is very doubtful whether the gift was ever completed. On Talleyrand's authority, Lewis Goldsmith asserts that the shoes were actually paid for by the French Government. This may be true,·though one suspects the evidence of men so accomplished in the art of false-witness as Goldsmith and Talleyrand.[3]

It is just possible that the mystery arises from a confusion of the private and corporate capacities of the same person. More than one subscription had been opened on behalf of the French.[4] In September a meeting for the purpose of opening such a subscription was convened at the house in Portland Square of a Dr. Maxwell,[5] who belonged to the same group of reformers as Horne Tooke, the leading spirit of the Constitutional Society. On the day fixed for the meeting a courtier called Colonel Glover arrived at Maxwell's house and succeeded in intimidating him—according to one picturesque account, by threatening to cut off his nose and ears. A crowd was gathering, and, influenced perhaps by memories of Birmingham as much as by a very natural concern for the integrity of his features, Maxwell fled. Next month a warrant was issued

---

[1] Exam. of Christopher Hull, May 30, 1794.—*P. C. R.* 33 Geo. III. 271.

[2] Exam. of John Frost, May 31, 1794.—*Ib.* 281.

[3] See Alger, *Englishmen in the French Rev.* 56. Mr. Alger says that the boots were seized in the Channel by the British Government. I have been unable to trace the reference given by Mr. Alger to Lewis Goldsmith's *Secret History of the Cabinet of Bonaparte*, II. 152. The British Museum possesses no edition of this work in *two* volumes. The French agent, Noël, mentions proposals for the sale of shoes to the French, which he seems to think worth consideration, Oct. 30, 1792.— Archives étrangères, *Corr. d'Angleterre*, 583 fo. 125 ; see also p. 155.

[4] *Moniteur*, April 27, 1792, No. 120, p. 491 ; Walker, 42–3 ; Prentice, 7–8 ; *A. J.* IV. 347.

[5] Maxwell afterwards entered the French service. "Doctor Maxwell has at last obtained a company in the French service. I understand is soon to leave" Paris "to join the army." Monro to Grenville, Dec. 17, 1792; Gower's *Despatches*, 260. According to Mr. Alger he may have been the Dr. Maxwell who fell in the Vendée.—*Englishmen in the French Rev.* 77–8.

for his arrest—on what ground is unknown; by that time he was in France.[1]

Intending subscribers arrived to find, instead of a hospitable doctor and an open door, a deserted house and a howling mob. On guard was the truculent colonel, who owed such celebrity as he had to his quarrels with Elizabeth Chudleigh, the famous or infamous Duchess of Kingston. Horne Tooke arrived, and found his friends at the mercy of the mob. Tooke had impudence equal to that of Miss Chudleigh's adversary. He challenged the colonel, who proved to be a very Captain Bobadil, and beat a retreat. Horne Tooke then conducted the party to his own house in Soho Square, where the meeting was held and the subscription opened.[2] It appears soon to have amounted to £1000, and Tooke asked Pétion to name an agent in London to whom it might safely be paid. Pétion promised to do so in a letter which Tooke appears to have received on the 1st of October.[3] We have found no sequel to the correspondence. It may be, though this, it must be repeated, is mere conjecture, that Pétion, who was obviously a very busy man, forgot to nominate an agent, and so threw back the English democrats upon the expedient of the shoes.[4]

Addresses to the Convention continued to flow in: some remarkable, one at least both interesting and reprehensible. On the 22nd of November the Convention received an address which the *Moniteur* attributed to the Revolution Society, and which one careful scholar thought to have emanated from the Society for Constitutional Information. Though it came from some London society, it came from neither of these. In some ways it resembles the address of the London Corresponding Society. It denounces Brunswick, and promises to use every legal

[1] *Moniteur*, Oct. 25, 1792, No. 299, p. 1263.

[2] *Ib.* Sept. 25, 1792, No. 269, p. 1139; *A. J.* IV. 346. See also Mr. Alger's article in *E. H. R.* (1898), XII. 685.

[3] Draft letter from Tooke to Pétion. Reply of Pétion, endorsed Oct. 1, 1792, *S. T.* XXIV. 538–9.

[4] In any case Noël, who on Oct. 30 had suggested the purchase of shoes in England, had asked on Sept. 10 for letters of introduction to Pétion's friends in London.—Archives étrangères, *Corr. d'Angleterre*, 583, fo. 125; and 582, fo. 117.

means to prevent England from joining in war against the French.[1]

There were probably more addresses, of which we now know nothing.[2] The most mischievous of all came from the Society Established at Rochester for the Propagation of the Rights of Man. It is neither more nor less than an attack upon Lindsay, the English agent who acted as chargé d'affaires at Paris after the recall of an ambassador, Lord Gower. In expressing personal hostility to a diplomatic agent, the members of the society represented nobody but themselves, and it is so hard to see how such an address could serve even themselves that it is difficult to believe that it was wholly spontaneous.[3]

John Thelwall wrote an address for the Southwark Friends of the People; but the address, if adopted, was not sent.[4] The faithful remnant of the Revolution Society met on the 5th of November, 1792, under the presidency of Dr. Towers, and celebrated the Revolution of 1688. With their wonted fortitude the members drank forty toasts, beginning with the "Rights of Man."[5] They also adopted an address to the Convention. They denounced the invasion of France, anticipated with pleasure the establishment of a wise and equitable government by the National Convention, and hoped that France and England would henceforth be rivals only in promoting the liberty and happiness of mankind.[6]

Lastly, on the 3rd of December there was read to the Convention an address from the Society of the Friends of

---

[1] *Moniteur*, Nov. 23, 1792, No. 328, p. 1392. Dr. Robinet attributes it to the Society for Constitutional Information.—*Danton émigré*, 53-4.

[2] Lebrun's letters of Nov. 29, 1792, seems to imply this.—*Moniteur*, Nov. 30, 1792, No. 335, p. 1420.

[3] *Ib.* The address is in the Archives of the French Foreign Office. La Chesnaye, a Frenchman, married to an Englishwoman who conducted a boarding-school for young ladies, writes a covering letter as president of the society, which has 327 members.—*Corr. d'Angleterre*, fo. 263. The French were several times urged to tamper with the English clubs, and did consider the question; but apparently there was no result.—*Ib.* 582, ff. 133-6, 182.

[4] *Circa*, Nov. 10, 1792.—Mrs. Thelwall's *Life of Thelwall*, I. 102-4.

[5] *Moniteur*, Nov. 23, 1792, No. 328, p. 1389.

[6] Presented Dec. 1, 1792.—*P.-V.* Dec. 1, 1792, p. 5; *A Collection of Addresses* . . . pp. 3-4; *Ann. Reg.* 1792, App. to *Chron.*, 72-3.

the People at Aldgate, which was accorded honourable mention and ordered to be printed. Like the Society for Constitutional Information, this society had for its primary object the diffusion of political knowledge. The French were hailed as "Citizens of the Universe," "Protectors of the Great Family of the Human Race," whose task was "to give to Men Political Life, Health and Strength in every quarter of the Globe." They expressed a touching faith in French renunciations of the right of conquest—a matter in which only those are righteous who have never been tried. As they wrote came the news of Dumouriez's successes, and they rejoiced in the prospect that the blood of brave citizens would produce "an abundant Harvest of Peace and Freedom throughout the World." [1]

Monro, the English agent, referred, on the last day of December, to addresses from Manchester and Derby, the latter of which, he said, has been brought by Redhead Yorke, "a very violent man," who deserved, if possible, to be punished. No trace of these addresses has been found, and though it is neither impossible nor improbable that they were sent, it has to be confessed that Monro's despatches seem more picturesque than reliable. His belief was, however, that the Convention had found out the insignificance of some of the addresses presented, and was "tired of such nonsense." [2]

During the months that followed the proclamation against sedition a host of loyal addresses, spontaneous and forced, had poured in upon the king. Almost every city, town and county in the kingdom returned thanks for the proclamation.[3] John Reeves, the historian of English law, in company with Charles Philip Yorke, elder son of the ill-fated Charles Yorke, founded, in November 1792, "An Association for protecting Liberty and Property against

[1] *P.-V.* Dec. 3, 1792, p. 39 ; Archives nationales, C. II. (carton 58), 242.

[2] Monro to Grenville, Dec. 31, 1792 ; Despatches of Earl Gower, 269. An English Society of the Rights of Man asked permission to present an address on Jan. 23, 1793. I have not found the address and I know nothing more of the society.—*P.-V.* Jan. 22, 1793, p. 353.

[3] On Sept. 1, 341 addresses had been received.—*Ann. Reg.* 1792, *Chron.*, p. *37 ; Paine, *Address to the Addressers*, 23 ; *Anecdotes of the Life of Bishop Watson*, 266–7.

republicans and levellers." [1] Evil rumour said that for a time the society consisted of about ten people.[2] But it issued an address against levellers, set government dependents to "ring the alarm-bell," and soon spread its net over the whole of England.[3] The nation was so evidently and so overwhelmingly loyal that it is difficult to understand why repressive measures were thought necessary. "For my own part," wrote one wise observer, "I would earnestly recommend good humour and gentleness to all well-meaning persons. Foolish or wicked persons will not be brought to reason by invective and reproaches; and I believe much more mischief is done by hard language and illiberal accusations of ill designs than is generally imagined. I really believe that the number of those who wish for mischief and confusion is very small. Though there may be many of weak judgment and consequent indiscretion, I flatter myself that these will be restrained by men of more sense and prudence." [4]

Ministers were outrun by their supporters in zeal for repression. In London a division of the London Corresponding Society was driven from its place of meeting, the Blue Posts in the Haymarket, by threats that the landlord would be deprived of his licence.[5] The Lord Mayor suppressed a debating society in Cornhill, "where people went to buy treason at sixpence a head; where it was retailed to them by the glimmering light of an inch of candle; and five minutes, to be measured by the glass, were allowed to each traitor to perform his part in overturning the State." [6] This was probably the old Coachmakers' Hall Debating Society, a non-party organisation, at whose meetings John Thelwall had begun his oratorical career as a sturdy defender of Church and King.[7] It was

---

[1] *Mem. of Hardy*, 24. [2] *Add. MSS.* 27814, fo 40. [3] *Ib.* fo. 40.
[4] James Martin, M.P.—a member of the Constitutional Society, though he had not recently attended its meetings—to Wyvill, May 24, 1792 ; *i. e.* three days after the proclamation.—*Wyvill Papers*, V. 26–8.
[5] Information given to the Committee by James Black, delegate of Division 8, on Sept. 20, 1792.—*Add. MSS.* 27812, fo. 22.
[6] Nov. 27, 1792, *ib.* 27809, fo. 268 ; Moore's *Sheridan*, II. 222.
[7] *Life of Thelwall*, I. 48. See also Introductory Narrative to Thelwall's lecture on the Moral Tendency of Spies and Informers. For the Coachmakers' Hall, see Wheatley, I. 430.

there that a hesitating speaker had suddenly, in the excitement of debate, hit upon that splendid description of
Thurlow as a man "with the Norman Conquest in his
eyebrow and the feudal system in every feature of his
face!"[1]   The landlord of the Coachmakers' Hall had
been frightened into breaking up the club, which had
migrated to Cornhill, only to be broken up once more by
the Lord Mayor.[2]   Thereupon Thelwall, who held strongly
the view that a free expression of public opinion was
essential to the maintenance of public order,[3] issued an
advertisement offering twenty guineas, to be paid in
advance, for the use, during one night, of a room holding
five or six hundred people.   No licensee or other owner
of a public room in London dared accept his offer.[4]   "The
proclamation and other means resorted to, to create alarm,
succeeded to such an extent as to depreciate the value of
all property."[5]

In Manchester the three reforming societies never
ceased to protest, though they protested in vain, against
the charge of disaffection.   "Instead of endeavouring to
excite sedition," said one, "we are solicitous, by a timely
and well-directed reform of abuses, to remove all pretences
for it."[6]   "Reformation and not revolution . . . is our
object," said another.   "The arms of reason are our only
weapons."[7]   "We are far from countenancing anything
that leads to anarchy and confusion," said the third.
"*Reason and Truth* are the only arms that we will unitedly
wield against those who oppose us, and with them we shall
in the end prevail."[8]   Most preposterous doctrines were
attributed to them, but their repudiations were all in vain.
It was still believed that they intended to reject all rights
of property and establish equality of goods.[9]

Every licensee in Manchester closed his door against

[1] *Life of Thelwall*, I. 50.   [2] *Ib.* 52 ; cf. 107–10.
[3] For Thelwall's dislike of violence, see his lecture on Spies and
Informers, 15–16.
[4] *Life of Thelwall*, I. 98–9 ; cf. also Address to the Addressers, 25.
[5] *Add. MSS.* 27809, fo. 268.
[6] Manchester Constitutional Society, May 15, 1792.—Walker, 26–30.
[7] Manchester Patriotic Society, May 24, 1792.—*Ib.* 33–6.
[8] Manchester Reformation Society, June 6, 1792.—*Ib.* 36–7.
[9] *Ib.* 46-8.

them. When the reformers resorted to a private house the landlord of it [1] did his best to prevent them meeting there. A sort of proclamation in which the licensed victuallers announced their policy of exclusion is something of a curiosity. "We," the publicans of Manchester and Salford, it ran, "*justly* alarmed at the *treasonable* and *seditious* conduct of a *well-known* set of daring MISCREANTS, who have called a public meeting to be held at the *Bull's Head Inn*, in *Manchester*, for the *avowed* purpose of *assisting the* FRENCH SAVAGES, as well as with a SINCERE DESIRE of *introducing similar calamities* to the *inhabitants* of this *Happy and Prosperous Country* as those that now *exist* in *France*, take this very *necessary* opportunity of publishing . . . our *detestation* of such *wicked and abominable* PRACTICES." [2]

Mob-law ruled. The cry against Jacobins and Presbyterians led to a Church and King riot. The office of the *Manchester Herald* and a house where the Reformation Society met were utterly wrecked. All applications to the magistrates for assistance were made in vain. In consequence, at the third attack on Thomas Walker's house he prepared to defend himself. When the mob approached a few charges of powder were blown into the air, and the crowd dispersed.[3] But in consequence of this persecution the societies withdrew from public notice, and their joint address of the 20th of December was not only a defence, it was a valediction.[4]

The long train of revolutionary excesses that followed upon the Duke of Brunswick's manifesto (July 25), and culminated in the September massacres, served to wound the friends and disgust the enemies of liberty,[5] but in England nobody, as yet, desired war with France. In September, if we may believe the French agent, "No war with France" was chalked in large letters on the very walls

[1] Mr. Egerton of Tatton.
[2] *Circa*, Sept. 13, 1792.—Walker, 42–3 ; Prentice, 7–8.
[3] Dec. 11 (? 10), 1792.—Walker, 54–70 ; Prentice, 9–10.
[4] Walker, 92–137.
[5] Fox to Holland, Aug. 20, 1792 ; *Mem. of C. J. F.* II. 366–7, cf. 369 ; Fox to Holland, Sept. 1792, *ib.* II. 370–1, cf. 372–5 ; Romilly, Sept. 10, *Mem.* II. 4–5, 10 ; Grenville to the Neapolitan minister, Sept. 20, 1792. —*Courts and Cabinets*, II. 217.

of St. James's.[1] The opinion of an anonymous chalker—
a sportive dustman, perhaps, or a whimsical crier of hot
rolls, amusing himself on his rounds before the town was
quite awake—mattered little.   The opinion of ministers
mattered much, and their one anxiety was to avoid war.
Grenville wanted to keep wholly and entirely aloof from
continental politics; but "to nurse up in the country a real
determination to stand by the Constitution when it is
attacked, as it most infallibly will be if these things go on ;
and above all," to try "to make the situation of the lowest
orders among us as good as it can be made."[2]   It must
not be understood that Grenville was in any state of panic
even about the condition of England.   Stories about
riot and sedition, he says, "are all much exaggerated
where they are not groundless."   Properly understood,
they are an evidence, not of danger, but of security.   "It
is not unnatural, nor is it an unfavourable symptom, that
people who are thoroughly frightened, as the body of
landed gentlemen in the country are, should exaggerate
these stories as they pass from one mouth to the other."[3]
Pitt seems to have hoped for the opportunity to act as
mediator and negotiate a peace, leaving France, as he
thought it should be left, "to arrange its own internal
affairs as it can."[4]

Ministers were, therefore, in a mind neither for war
with France, nor for violent measures of repression at
home, when, on the 19th of November, the Convention
issued a decree promising help and fraternity to all peoples
struggling for liberty.   This decree, in effect a general
invitation to revolt, could not fail to cause anxiety to the
responsible ministers of an established government.   At
the same time English statesmen were disquieted by the
attempt of France, acting in support of the interests of
Belgium, to open the navigation of the Scheldt in defiance

[1] Noël, Archives des Affaires étrangères, *Corr. d'Angleterre*, 582,
fo. 123.

[2] Nov. 7, 1792, *Courts and Cabinets*, II. 224 ; *Mem. of C. J. Fox*,
III. 9.

[3] Grenville to his brother, Nov. 14, 1792.—*Mem. of C. J. Fox*, III.
28–9.

[4] Pitt to Stafford, Nov. 13, 1792.—Rose's *Diaries*, I. 114–15, cf.
116–17.

of the treaty rights of Holland, our ally.[1] Dundas, who had made up his mind to foreign politics being as bad as possible, still could not believe that France would take any step to create a quarrel with England. He doubts, he continues, "the Propriety of our abusing the French Nation. It gives them a fair Pretence to retaliate and I think the strength of our Cause consists in maintaining that we have nothing to do with the internal politics of Foreign Nations, that We have already undergone all the Consequences of Civil disturbances which were terminated by a Revolution which has rendered us happy for more than a Century and We will not submit to or countenance any other revolution in this Country."[2]

Ministers were determined that no revolution should be encouraged in England by any appearance of weakness. On the 25th of November Grenville issued a circular letter to the Lords Lieutenant asking them to see to the strict enforcement of the proclamation against sedition issued in May.[3] On December 1, 1792, a second proclamation was made. It deplored the ineffectiveness of the first and ordered the embodiment of the militia, owing to the danger to the Constitution from "evil-disposed persons . . . . acting in concert with persons in foreign parts."[4] A certain effect was produced by these proclamations; the publisher of Paine's *Rights of Man* thought that they sensibly impeded its sale.[5] With or without the proclamation, Paine was one of the best-hated men in England. In June his books were burnt at Exeter, and a man supposed to be Paine was hounded out of Manchester.[6] In November 1792 he seems to have been in a fair way to supersede even the immortal Fawkes;[7] and in January

---

[1] Fox was as distrustful of French intentions with regard to Holland as any one in power. Fox to Holland, Nov. 23, 1792.—*Mem. of C. J. Fox* II. 379–80.
[2] Henry Dundas to Nepean, Nov. 25, 1792.—H. O. Scotland, $\frac{102}{8}$.
[3] *Add. MSS.* 27809, fo. 273.
[4] *Ann. Reg.* 1792, pp. 196–7 ; *Add. MSS.* 27809, fo. 268.
[5] Opinion of Richard Carlile, quoted in *Life of Paine*, I. 346.
[6] Quoted from the *Moniteur* of June 17, 1792, *ib.* 347.
[7] See the instances culled by Conway, *Life of Paine*, I. 369–71. See also Charlotte Poole's *Diary*, Dec. 17, 1792, *Tom Poole and His Friends*, I. 35.

1793 he afforded the citizens of Coventry the excuse for a novel celebration of New Year's Day. "The effigy of Tom Paine, with the *Rights of Man* fastened upon his breast, was placed in a cart (with a chimney-sweeper as his companion) and drawn through all the principal streets" of the city of Coventry; "he was taken to Cross Cheaping, where a gibbet had been previously erected for his reception; where, after hanging the usual time, a fire was lighted under the gallows, which consumed him instantly to ashes, amidst the acclamations of a loyal multitude of surrounding spectators, who all joined heartily in the chorus of *God save the King*." [1]

In spite of all impediments, the *Rights of Man* had an enormous sale. When he wrote the preface to Part II, Paine himself estimated the sale of Part I in the British Isles at forty or fifty thousand copies.[2] In July 1792 a thousand pounds, which he ordered to be paid to the Society for Constitutional Information, stood to his credit at his printer's.[3] In 1793 the sale was estimated at 200,000,[4] and, in one edition or another, is said finally to have reached the almost incredible figure of a million and a half. There is, therefore, having regard to the multitude of cheap editions, nothing improbable in the attorney-general's assertion that "even children's sweetmeats" were wrapped up with parts of the *Rights of Man*, though nothing is more preposterous than his assumption that it was thus "delivered into their hands in the hope that they would read it." [5] He had too generous a faith in the prevalence of elementary education.

Paine had aggravated his fault—the fault of instilling into the minds of the poor and wretched the idea of the Rights of Man—by publishing, in September 1792, his "Letter addressed to the Addressers on the late proclamation" of the 21st of May; the more so because, in the first words of it, he claimed that the proclamation, "and the numerous rotten Boroughs and Corporation Addresses

---

[1] *The History and Antiquities of the City of Coventry* . . . by W. Reader, 106.
[2] Preface to Part II, *Rights of Man*, X.
[3] *Life of Paine*, I. 346.   [4] *Ib.* I. 346.
[5] *S. T.* XXII. 381. On Paine's influence, cf. *Wy*

thereon," had stimulated interest in politics, and especially in the Rights of Man.[1] It contained a sufficiently audacious skit on Grenville and other "pocket-felt" revilers of the Rights of Man,[2] and warned the Government that it was dangerous to say to any nation "thou shalt not read."[3] "It is error only, and not truth, that shrinks from enquiry."[4] Paine made a vigorous attack upon monarchical government and the Constitution established by the Bill of Rights; and now he seemed to have lost faith in the adequacy of a parliamentary reform.[5] Only a National Convention to revise and codify the existing law could be of any use.[6] On minds already prone to fear of revolution, and ready to see a manifestation of it in the imitation of its outward forms, such words could have no other influence than that of terror and dismay.

For Part I of the *Rights of Man* Paine had hoped to be prosecuted, but had been disappointed.[7] But official influence appears almost to have prevented the publication of Part II;[8] and his enemies, led, as Paine believed with some colour of reason, by Burke, were now intent on his prosecution.[9] Sampson Perry, printer of the *Argus*, had already been found guilty of publishing a libel for stating that the members of the House of Commons were not the real representatives of the people.[10]

One night in September Paine had been repeating some "inflammatory eloquence" that he had poured forth the preceding evening at a popular society—according to the legend, a society called the Friends to the Liberty of the Press, of which Erskine was the leading member.[11] William

---

[1] *Address to the Addressers.—Writings*, III. 45.
[2] *Ib.* 48 *et seq.*   [3] *Ib.* 58.   [4] *Ib.* 59.   [5] *Ib.* 81–2.
[6] *Ib.* 87 *et seq.*   [7] *Life*, I. 329.   [8] *Ib.* 328.   [9] *Ib.* 341.
[10] *Add. MSS.* 27809, fo. 273 ; Knight Hunt, *The Fourth Estate*, I. 255.
[11] Parts of the Proceedings of the Society were published in pamphlet form. "The Resolutions of the First Meeting of the Friends to the Liberty of the Press, Dec. 19, 1792. Also the Declaration of the Second Meeting, Jan. 22, 1793, written by the Hon. Thomas Erskine ; to which is added a Letter to Mr. Reeves, Chairman of the Association for Preserving Liberty and Property, by Thomas Law, Esq., late one of the committee of the society. Also, Proceedings of the Friends to the Liberty of the Press on Dec. 22, 1792, and Jan. 19, and March 9, 1793." If the first meeting was really on Dec. 19, 1792, Paine must either have spoken at a preliminary meeting or at some other society. He set out for Paris on Monday, Sept. 17, 1792, according to *Ann. Reg.* 1792, *Chron.* Sept. 22.

Blake, who, despite his admirers, seems to have been sane enough at times, saw that this would be the signal for Paine's prosecution, and packed him off to Dover in the nick of time.

He was tried, in absentia, on the 18th of December, and was defended by Erskine, who maintained, quite justly, that nowhere in his writings did Paine advocate defiance of the law.[1] "He instructs me to admit," said counsel, "that, when government is once constituted, no individuals without rebellion can withdraw their obedience from it— that all attempts to excite them to it are highly criminal, for the most obvious reasons of policy and justice—that nothing short of the will of a *whole people* can change or affect the rule by which a nation is to be governed— and that no private opinion, however honestly inimical to the forms or substance of the law, can justify resistance to its authority while it remains in force." [2]

Enemies of the ministry said that every possible measure was taken to prejudice the trial. But it was Paine himself who made Erskine's task impossible by writing a letter warning the king and the attorney-general to be mindful of the fate of similar dignitaries in France. Erskine tried hard to have the letter set aside as a forgery,[3] but it was almost certainly genuine. False or genuine, an acquittal could not be expected in the circumstances, and the jury found Paine guilty without allowing the attorney-general to reply for the prosecution.[4]

"Constraint is the natural parent of resistance, and a pregnant proof that reason is not on the side of those who use it," said Erskine in a famous peroration that deserves repetition. "You must all remember, gentlemen, Lucian's pleasant story : Jupiter and a countryman were walking together, conversing with great freedom and familiarity upon the subject of heaven and earth. The countryman listened with attention and acquiescence while Jupiter strove only to convince him; but happening to hint a doubt, Jupiter turned hastily round and threatened him with his thunder. 'Ah! ah!' says the countryman,

---

[1] *S. T.* XXII. 416.   Paine was charged with seditious libel.
[2] *Ib.* XXII. 416.   [3] *Ib.* 419.   [4] *Ib* 472.

'now, Jupiter, I know that you are wrong; you are always wrong when you appeal to your thunder.' " [1]

During the next few months Government appealed very often to its thunder. A host of printers were convicted for selling the *Rights of Man* and other of Paine's writings; [2] amongst them Richard Phillips, a Leicester bookseller, originator of the Leicester Permanent Library, and founder and editor of an unfortunate Leicester newspaper called the *Herald*. Phillips was sentenced to eighteen months' imprisonment. [3] Whilst he was in gaol a disastrous fire put an end to his newspaper. Later in life he achieved considerable worldly success; he became Sheriff of London and received a knighthood. Perhaps a surer title to remembrance is that he came under the literary scourge both of George Borrow and "Christopher North."

Whilst reformers were thus harassed, it cannot be supposed that their cause prospered. [4] Stanhope thought that petitions for reform would do positive harm; [5] county meetings were now impossible, because of the "patriotic wave." [6] Few even amongst the reformers could be suspected of disloyalty; they, too, were subject to the influence of the patriotic wave. In his *Defence of the Reformers* Wyvill had maintained that the English republicans were few, that they could be increased only by persecution, but that the reformers "wisely preferred safe and progressive improvement to the doubtful event of a great but hazardous Revolution." [7] At the very end of 1792 Miles, the ablest informant of the French ministers, gave precisely the same account of the reformers, and insisted repeatedly that nothing was to be gained by any attempt to foment disorder in England. ". . . In the event of war," he said, "it will be rather a war of the English people than of the

[1] *S. T.* XXII. 471-2.
[2] *Add. MSS.* 27809, ff. 268-9. A number of cases are collected in Conway's *Life of Paine*, II. 27-8.
[3] In April 1793.—*Add. MSS.* 27809, fo. 268.
[4] *Life of Grey*, 22.
[5] Stanhope to Wyvill, Sept. 16, 1792.—*Wyvill Papers*, V. 80.
[6] *Ib.* 94, 96.
[7] A Defence of Dr. Price and the Reformers of England, 1792. Also *Wyvill Papers*, III, App. 13-89, where the pagination is faulty. cf. V. 70-1, 99.

Minister. Those who tell you the contrary, and who seek
to make you believe that England is ripe for revolution
against the Government, seek only to mislead and deceive
you." [1]

On the 1st of February, 1793, war broke out between
France and England. It was a calamity that Pitt had
tried hard to avoid. Now that war had come the catastrophe was personal as well as national. From the
economic and administrative reform, which he had found
a delight, he had to turn aside to tasks for which he felt
himself suited neither by talent nor inclination; he was
henceforth condemned to devote his energies to the
organisation of war and the conduct of diplomacy. But
the eyes of contemporaries were holden, and, failing to see
the tragedy that history has revealed, they were inclined
to impute bad motives. Thomas Hardy, for example,
expressed an opinion common among reformers when he
declared that ministers were wise in their generation, and
sought to turn the public mind from reform by "plunging
into a destructive war." [2]

This was not strictly fair. The execution of Louis XVI
and the growing excesses of the Convention frightened
even its friends.[3] George III, himself a lover of peace,
was deeply convinced of the moral justice of the war [4]—a
war, as Pitt had it, against "the tremendous consequences
of that ungovernable, that intolerable and destroying spirit
which carries ruin and desolation wherever it goes." King
and ministers did not stand alone. There is every reason
to believe that the opposition were as distrustful of the
spirit of proselytism as Pitt himself. On the day after the
declaration of war Sheridan, on behalf of Fox and his
friends, had an interview with an agent of the French
Government. "We desire a reform," he said; "we desire
it good, although founded on constitutional bases. We do

[1] Miles to Maret, Dec. 3; to Mourgue, Dec. 24; *Corr. of W. A.
Miles*, I. 367 and 420; Miles to Mourgue, Dec. 6, 1792, *ib.* 373; this
opinion is reiterated, 419.
[2] Hardy, *Mem.* 35. cf. Prentice, 18.
[3] Fraser Rae's *Sheridan*, II. 108-9; John Cartwright, "A Letter to
a Friend in Boston," Jan. 1793; *Life of J. C.* I. 195-7. See the change
in the views of the Bishop of Llandaff.—*Anecdotes of Watson*, 270.
[4] Geo. III to Pitt, Feb. 2, 1793; Stanhope, II. 429.

not desire a war with France, *if there is no aggression made against Holland;* and if this war is solely to take place to secure the opening of the Scheldt, we will even present the minister's desire to make war as a desire to prevent reform." They would attack Pitt, and if necessary go so far as to propose his impeachment. "But we at the same time tell you that we will make common cause with the ministry, and that we are assured that nine-tenths of the three kingdoms " will do the same, "*to repulse any idea of the assistance of the French in our home affairs.* We would regard it as just as prejudicial to the tranquillity of the country as to the courage and energy of the English. We have well understood how to give to France the example of revolution; we shall know also how to follow hers in our own fashion, and by our own strength to perfect our government and increase our liberty." [1]

In the face of every warning, in the face of plain statements to the contrary from French agents and English reformers, there were still those in France who believed that England was on the verge of rebellion. Collot d'Herbois told the Jacobins that French armies would march to London, and plant the tree of liberty under George's window. George would be sent to the Tower, from which he would set out on the same journey as Louis Capet. Then the two peoples would embrace each other.[2] A few days later another Jacobin spoke as if the English people awaited nothing but the encouragement of a few French troops to rise in rebellion. France and England were thereafter to form one republic, a single people.[3]

This was sheer nonsense. "Soon after and long after its commencement " the war was popular.[4] Whilst the trend of events made extreme reformers more extreme, moderate men grew wary, and the lukewarm stifled their opinions for a time.[5] Only Sheridan was so hopeful that

---

[1] Affaires étrangères, T. 515 ; pièce, 142, ap. Robinet, 271-2. I was unable to find this memorandum at the French Foreign Office. But Dr. Robinet was a careful historian, and as there can be no doubt that he actually saw the document, either there or in the Archives nationales, it may be accepted on his authority.

[2] Feb. 3, 1793, *A. J.* V. 15. [3] Feb. 13, 1793, *ib.* V. 26.

[4] Prentice, 18 ; cf. *Mem. of C. J. Fox*, III. 38-40.

[5] Hollis to Wyvill, March 8, 1793.—*Wyvill Papers*, V. 129. See

he was willing to lay two to one on the chances of a speedy reform; and his betting book probably represents rather the measure of his inebriety than the vigour of his optimism.[1] The English "Terror," as the reformers called it, had indeed begun. On the one hand, fear of invasion from abroad or from violence at home excited those whose interest was in the security of property;[2] on the other, the pressure of want[3] drove the poorer classes to excesses unthought of in better times. To many, even amongst moderate men, Jacobinism was now the enemy.[4]

---

also V. 135, 154. Letter to Pitt, Feb. 9, 1793, *ib.* III, App. 95. See the letters of Dr. Symonds, 8 April, and of Dr. Burney, May 12, 1793 ; *Auto. of A. Young*, 238 and 235.

[1] May 25, 1793 ; cf. Jan. 29.—Moore's *Sheridan*, II. 215.

[2] A lady, not named, to Hy. Erskine, July 6, 1793 ; *Henry Erskine*, etc., 345 ; Harriet Francis to Mary Johnson.—*Francis Letters*, II. 407-8.

[3] Palmer to Skirving, July 9, 1793, *S. T.* XXIII. 323.

[4] Windham to Mrs. Crewe, Oct. 5, 1793.—*Diary*, 291, cf. 299 ; *Mem. of Aikin*, I. 160, 162. Fox was not much better pleased with the temper of the times than Windham, *e. g.* Aug. 22, 1792.—*Mem. of C. J. Fox*, III. 47.

CHAPTER X

REPRESSION IN SCOTLAND

1792–1793

SCOTLAND could offer least resistance to a policy of repression; it was in Scotland, accordingly, that active repression began, and there that it was carried to its extremest lengths. "Politically Scotland was dead," we are told. "It was not unlike a village at a great man's gate. Without a single free institution or habit, opposition was rebellion, submission probable success." [1] Even Burns was told by the Board of Excise that his business was to act, not to think; and that whatever might be men or measures it was for him to be silent and obedient.

On the very eve of the French Revolution Scotland had nevertheless shown signs of returning life. Men whose opinions on other questions were widely different had united to propose a reform of those close corporations whose thirteen hundred members returned a third of the parliamentary representatives of Scotland. The immediate object of these reformers was a purification of the internal administration of the burghs : but no municipal reform that was worth the name could have failed to enlarge, either directly or indirectly, the share of the citizens in the election of the fifteen members who sat in Parliament for burghal constituencies. In 1788 petitions for reform were presented to the House of Commons from forty-six of the sixty-six burghs.[2] Sheridan, who had taken up the question, asked leave to introduce a Bill to redress the evil complained of "by as respectable a body of petitioners

[1] Cockburn's *Life of Jeffrey*, I. 77 ; cf. *Examination into the Trials for Sedition in Scotland*, I. 76.
[2] Friday, Feb. 8, 1788.—*C. J.* XLIII. 206-9 ; Monday, June 9, 1788, *ib.* 539.

as ever had approached the bar of that House." [1]   Pitt
gave a qualified support to the proposal,[2] but the promoters of the Bill were unable to overcome the determined
resistance of Dundas.[3]   In 1789,[4] in 1790,[5] and again in
1791,[6] Sheridan renewed his attempt, but without success.
At last, in 1792, the Lord Advocate, Robert Dundas of
Arniston, did agree that municipal officers should be made
accountable to a court of law for bad or dishonest management of the burghal revenues,[7] and he introduced, accordingly, a bill for "better regulating the Mode of Accounting
for the Common Good and Revenue of the Royal Burghs
of *Scotland*," [8] which passed a second reading; only, it
would appear, to be quietly strangled in committee.[9]   In
January of the same year an influential meeting of those
interested in reform appointed a committee, which included the Lord Chief Baron of the Exchequer, the Hon.
Henry Erskine, then Dean of Faculty, and the Lord Advocate, Robert Dundas of Arniston himself, to consider the
best way of improving the electoral system in the Scots
counties.[10]

Either a reform of the burghs, or an improvement in
the electoral system of the counties, would have gone some
way, though not a very long way, towards the needed
reform in the parliamentary system.   But in Scotland, as
in England, the reforming spirit of the times had not been
without its effect.   Zeal for reform was quickened by the
outbreak of the French Revolution.   How deeply the first
events of the Revolution stirred even moderate reformers
is shown by an address sent, in June 1790, to the President
of the National Assembly by the Whig Club of Dundee.
We have thought this address worth printing in an
appendix, not for its text alone, but because it bears the
signatures, styles and occupations of seventy-six "solid"

---

[1] *Parl. Hist.* XXVII. 632.   Bill introduced and read a first time,
June 17, 1788.—*C. J.* XLIII, 544.
[2] *Parl. Hist.* XXVII. 635.   [3] *Ib.* 634.
[4] *C. J.* XLIV. 114, 495, 500, 521, 550 ; *Parl. Hist.* XXVIII. 221-6.
[5] *C. J.* XLV. 548.
[6] *Ib.* XLVI. 654 ; *Parl. Hist.* XXIX. 636-41.
[7] *Ib.* XXIX. 1183-1203 ; *C. J.* XLVII. 696, 711.
[8] *Ib.* 793.   See also 750.   [9] *Ib.* 802, 831, 1024.
[10] Jan. 2, 1792.—*Wyvill Papers*, III. 36-40.

citizens. The signatories congratulate the National Assembly on "the triumph of liberty and reason over despotism, ignorance and superstition," and declare their "ardent wishes that liberty may be established in France in an unchangeable manner." They hope and believe that the re-establishment of constitutional government in France will result in an indissoluble union of France and England "to secure the peace and prosperity of the two Empires." They sketch the growing prosperity of Scotland—the increase of wealth and happiness in an ordered State. "Our sovereign, the Father of His People," is, they declare, almost the object of their adoration; and the nobility and clergy are "useful and illustrious members of a State where all is subordinated to the Law." But nevertheless all is not perfect, even in Britain, for the club, they say, has been "instituted with a view to the re-establishment of our liberty, to guarantee and to bring to perfection our political constitution." The means by which it is to be improved are not specified; probably the members of the Whig Club were in favour of some moderate measure of parliamentary reform. But it is clear enough that the Revolution had stimulated the desire for constitutional improvement amongst the burghers of Dundee.[1]

All over Scotland societies were springing up, in imitation of those in London, to promote a comprehensive reform in Parliament. At Glasgow the Lord Provost presided over a meeting at which resolutions were adopted in favour of equal representation, frequent elections and universal suffrage.[2] "The associated friends of the Constitution and of the People" demanded annual Parliaments which were to bring in their train not only the good things of which English reformers dreamed, but also benefits more particularly Scottish. "The right in the people to elect their own Clergymen most likely would be restored, and the law of patronage abolished." In November 1792 the society had already to complain that it had been assailed with falsehood and misrepresentation. "Associated in defence of, not to hurt, the constitution; and conscious of the purity and rectitude of their intentions, the Associated

[1] Appendix II.   [2] July 23, 1792.—*Wyvill Papers*, III. 41–5.

Friends of the Constitution and of the People at Glasgow are confident that, for their endeavours, they shall have the thanks of the good, the wise and the moderate part of their countrymen." [1]

A Society of the Friends of the People at Perth was in favour of a reform of Parliament in general, and of the Scottish burghs in particular. Dundas's informant, though credulous enough to believe that it was not uncommon to hear boys crying in the streets, "Liberty, Equality and no King," was scrupulously fair to the members of the society, whom he reported to be perfectly loyal. A proposal to raise a subscription for the purchase of arms had, indeed, been seconded, but it had been "almost unanimously rejected by the other Members present." Many people who thought the time unsuitable for agitation and disapproved of the society were nevertheless, said this informant, in favour of reform. [2]

On the 3rd of November, 1792, a society of the "Associated Friends of the Constitution and of the People" was formed at Kirkintilloch "to co-operate with the Association of the Friends of the People in London in all constitutional Measures, in order to restore an equal Representation of the People in Parliament and a shorter Duration of Parliament." It was resolved "that in applying to Parliament the Society shall know no other order than that of the Constitution," and "that any who may attempt to precipitate the People of Scotland into Riot and Sedition are the Enemies of the People, of Reform and of Freedom." [3] There were societies at Dalkeith [4] and Paisley,[5] at Anderstown [6] and

---

[1] A Few Facts and Remarks, Ordered to be printed by the associated friends of the Constitution and of the People at Glasgow for the information of those who wish to become Members of the Society. A foolscap page, closely printed in two columns. Endorsed "received from Mr. Dundas, Nov. 27, 1792."—H. O. $\frac{102}{2}$.

[2] David Smyth to Dundas, Nov. 24, 1792.—H. O. $\frac{102}{2}$.

[3] MS. report endorsed "Copied from the *Courier* of Nov. 14, 1792." —H. O. $\frac{102}{2}$.

[4] MS. report from an informer, Nov. 28, 1792.—H. O. $\frac{102}{2}$.

[5] A Declaration of Rights and an Address to the People, approved by a number of the friends of Reform at Paisley, Nov. 1792.—H. O $\frac{102}{2}$.

[6] The inhabitants of the village of Anderstown formed a Society of the Friends of the Constitution and of the People for more equal representation and shorter parliaments, Nov. 17, 1792. Newspaper cutting, probably from the *Glasgow Advertiser*. Annexed is a somewhat

Musselburgh.[1] Sixty gentlemen of landed property were present at the first meeting of a society at Strathaven,[2] and a society at Stirling was reported to have about six thousand members.[3] It is impossible to accept such a figure without question, but like the conventional numbers given by mediæval chroniclers, it is, no doubt, to be taken as evidence that the society had many members.

More important was the Society of the Friends of the People at Edinburgh. Its organisation was similar to that of the London Corresponding Society, with which it corresponded, though there is nothing to prove the allegation of an informer that it corresponded with the Jacobins.[4] Amongst its members were Major Maitland, Member of Parliament for the burghs of Roxburghshire, Colonel Dalrymple, Colonel Macleod and Captain Johnston, proprietor of the *Edinburgh Gazetteer*.[5] But the best remembered of them was a young advocate called Thomas Muir, the only son of a shopkeeper, who was also a small proprietor at Huntershill. Young Muir is said to have been an infant prodigy, and was sent to the University of Glasgow at the age of ten;[6] he was a member of the University during the Lord Rectorship of Burke,[7] and was rusticated, along with a dozen others, for writing squibs on the professors during the rectorial election in 1785[8]— an offence that will be excused or condemned according to the academic standing of the reader. Muir thereupon went to Edinburgh, where he studied law; in 1787 he was

---

indecent and altogether dishonest parody of the resolutions of a reform society headed, " Reform ! Reform ! "—also a newspaper cutting.—H. O. $\frac{102}{8}$.

[1] Report (Nov. 28, 1792) from an informer, of a letter read to the Glasgow Friends of the People.—H. O. $\frac{102}{8}$.

[2] *Ib.* H. O. $\frac{102}{8}$.   [3] *Ib.* H. O. $\frac{102}{8}$.

[4] So far as I know. There may, of course, have been correspondence between individuals.

[5] MS. report of an informer of a meeting of Aug. 28, 1792. If the informer is to be believed, some unwise expressions were used at a meeting of fourteen delegates on Aug. 29. But how did an informer get there ?—H. O. $\frac{102}{8}$.

[6] Peter Mackenzie, *Life of Muir*, 1. Muir was born at Glasgow, Aug. 24, 1765. According to legend his mother dreamed that he would one day be Lord Chancellor.—*Political Martyrs*, p. 8 note.

[7] *Life*, 2-3.   [8] *Ib.* 3.

admitted to the Faculty of Advocates,[1] and began to acquire
a lucrative practice at the bar.[2]   He seems to have sown
his not very wild "wild oats," as he became an elder of
the kirk and a speaker in the General Assembly.[3]   He
supported the movement for a reform in the burghs, but
he had greater faith in a wider reform of Parliament, and
outdistanced many advocates of the more restricted local
measure who were not in sympathy with the demand for
annual Parliaments and universal suffrage.   Archibald
Fletcher thought, indeed, that Muir was "an honest enthusiast," but an "ill-judging man," [4] yet even the reports
of his speeches which were supplied by Government informers show how moderate and careful was his language.
The friends of the people, he urged on one occasion,
should stand by one another "until a complete reform was
obtained," but "no rash measure should be taken to effect-
uate this."   An application should be made to Parliament,
and if the first failed, a second, and in this way they should
persevere until success was theirs.[5]   At a later meeting,
when it was decided to summon delegates of all the reform
societies in Scotland to arrange for a united petition to
Parliament, the speeches of Muir and Maitland, Dalrymple
and Macleod, "were chiefly directed to admonishing the
people with respect to their behaviour in the present critical
situation of affairs, and strongly enjoining temperance and
moderation—intimating that if any who had joined should
be concerned in promoting or being in any riot that they
would be expelled." [6]

In Scotland, as in England, the month of November
1792 was a month of alarm.   A soldier who gave his
direction, but not his name,[7] and who seems to have
desired employment in the secret service, wrote, possibly
to Dundas, saying that he had visited several places in

---

[1] *Life*, 4.   [2] Mackenzie, *Reminiscences of Glasgow*, Part I. 26.
[3] *Life*, 4.   [4] *Autobiography of Mrs. Fletcher*, 59.
[5] Copy of letter from William Scot to the Lord Advocate, Nov. 22,
1792.—H. O. $\frac{102}{6}$.
[6] Scot to the Lord Advocate, Nov. 22, 1792.—H. O. $\frac{102}{8}$. See also
John Pringle to H. Dundas, Nov. 24, 1792.—H. O. $\frac{102}{8}$.
[7] Address to " Mr. Robertson, care of Mr. Kerr, secretary of the post
office, Edinburgh."

Scotland and corresponded with others, and that he believed
"that all the lower ranks, particularly the operative Manu-
facturers, with a considerable number of their employers,"
"were poisoned with an enthusiastic rage for real liberty that "
would "not easily be crushed without coercive measures."
Haunted by "imaginary fears" of increased taxation, they
were "prompted by a newly started licentious newspaper
writer (who deserves to be hanged) to join One and All—
which admits of no construction amongst them but to join
in arms." "I cannot help thinking," he continued, ". . .
that the gentlemen and lovers of real liberty are cul-
pably remiss in not coming forward, and thereby demon-
strating to the people that every thing that is virtuous
and respectable in the Country will opose (*sic*) with their
lives and fortunes their diabolical attempts to pretended
reform. . . ."[1]

A Mr. James Mathison, an accountant at Edinburgh,
wrote to Pitt denouncing reformers and their meetings.
"Seven-Eighths of those persons who Join in these meetings are Tradesmen—many of them Members of Incorporations." He therefore suggests that if the members of
incorporations encouraged or attended illegal meetings
they should be punished by the opening of the trade of
the city to strangers. In Glasgow the progress of the
reformers had been extremely rapid. Within two months
some branches of their society had been compelled to
divide four or five times. "This is the time to put a stop
to it. . . . Though these meetings are apparently done
in a peaceable manner, yet their Conversation is far from
being proper. This I aver from experience."[2]

Sir William Maxwell of Springkell (Dumfriesshire)
wrote to the Duke of Buccleuch a most alarming account
of the activity displayed by the "emissaries of sedition,"
who fanned the peasant's ever-smouldering discontent with
the burden of taxation, and tried to persuade him that it

---

[1] Probably to Dundas, but it may be to Pitt, Nov. 9, 1792. " Sir,
I conceal my name from a timid diffidence . . ." etc. This writer
apologises for " addressing on politics so able a statesman."—H. O.
$\frac{102}{6}$.

[2] James Mathison, accountant, Edinburgh, to Mr. Pitt, Nov. 16, 1792.
—H. O. $\frac{102}{8}$.

was due to the expense of royalty. "Scots Peasants understand nothing of Parliamentary Reform, equal Representation and the other grievances of which the discontented in a higher rank of life complain, while they may be tempted to unite, to try their strength and to risk their Necks in the hopes of bringing about a Division of the landed Property, and of getting ten acres each which they have been told will fall to the share of each Individual." Paine's pamphlet was in the hands of "almost every Countryman," and could be purchased for twopence. Sir William added that he had employed "two or three sensible people" to learn the views of the lower orders in his neighbourhood, and to persuade them of the unreasonableness of discontent. "I have also desired it to be imprest on their minds that the French who were formerly Papists are now absolute Infidels, Ruffians, and Marauders," and "have no other object in view than to render all the rest of the World as wicked as themselves, by abolishing Christianity and every other Religion."[1]

These letters are not very satisfactory evidence of actual disaffection. There is a touch of wildness and exaggeration in the language of these correspondents which would throw doubt upon their testimony, even apart from the fact that they produced no evidence that could be submitted to a court of law.[2] These letters are written in exactly the same temper as the letters that the Marquis of Buckingham was writing to Lord Grenville at about the same date,[3]

---

[1] Copy of a letter of Nov. 19, 1792, from Sir William Maxwell of Springkell, to the Duke of Buccleuch, enclosed in a letter of Nov. 24, from H. Dundas to Nepean. Maxwell's appeal to the religious instincts of the peasantry might be compared with a curious half-fanatical letter of Dec. 18 from Thomas Milbank of Dundee, either to the Lord Advocate or to Henry Dundas. "I am delighted when Lords and Lairds come forward to *recommend the Scriptures.* This is indeed *a Revolution.*" Nine-tenths of them are infidels. "Blush at your impudence. Have not Lords and Lairds brought in Infidelity and Impiety like a Flood? Do you, my Lord, read the Scriptures and you will not dare to support that system of Bribery and Corruption by which our Government now stands. You will regard the Rights of Man and labour to correct abuses wherever they are found."—H. O. $\frac{102}{8}$.

[2] Cf. report from Kirkcudbright, Dec. 10, 1792, that, after diligent search, no seditious writings had been found to be dispersed in the Borough.—H. O. $\frac{102}{8}$.

[3] Cf. Buckingham to Grenville, Nov. 8, 1792, *H. M. C.* XIV. App. V. 327-8.

and they mean nothing more than that the local cobbler had read Tom Paine, that the village publican thought his quarrel with the excise might be assisted by universal suffrage, or that the driver of the nearest coach had heard political opinions which he could not understand expounded in the parlour of a house of call. Alarmist letters like Sir William Maxwell's[1] are really important because of the cumulative impression which they made upon the minds of responsible statesmen like Henry Dundas. "The letter struck me the more forcibly," he wrote, "as a Proof of the Rapidity with which these mad Ideas had made their progress, for I met the same Gentleman at the Duke of Buccleuch's house at Langholme on my way to Scotland, and he assured me that there was not a Symptom of any such Spirit in all that Country."[2]

Once Dundas caught the infectious alarm of the official classes he took steps to obtain more complete information. He gave orders for the letters of Colonel Macleod, Colonel Dalrymple of Fordel and Captain Johnston to be scrutinised at the post office.[3] Some one was already employed to report on the proceedings of the Friends of the People at Edinburgh.[4] Dundas now engaged a person called Watt, who had offered his services as an informer, and who for some months plied the dangerous but lucrative trade which brought him ultimately to the gallows.[5] No expense was spared to stamp out disaffection. The loyalist Press was liberally subsidised, and informers were rewarded with an open hand.[6] The consequences might have been anticipated. Men are prone to circulate slander for nothing; they will readily invent it for money, or the hope of gain. Dundas's trusted agent in Edinburgh was soon

---

[1] There are other letters of a similar sort in the Scots correspondence ; *e.g.* Prof. Richardson to Wm. Craig, Advocate, Edinburgh, Nov. 22, 1792 ; Mrs. Susan Bean, Montrose, to ——? Nov. 24, 1792.—H. O. $\frac{182}{6}$.

[2] H. Dundas to Nepean, Nov. 24, 1792.—H. O. $\frac{182}{6}$.

[3] The same to the same, Nov. 24, 1792.—H. O. $\frac{182}{6}$.

[4] The same to the same, Nov. 24.—H. O. $\frac{192}{6}$.

[5] *Ib.* One of Watt's reports is enclosed.

[6] £400 seems to have been paid to the " Principal Proprietor" of a newspaper called the *Herald.* R. Dundas to (?) H. Dundas, Dec. 12.—H. O. $\frac{182}{6}$. See also R. Dundas to (?) H. Dundas, Jan. 13, 1793, and Feb. 6, 1793.—H. O. $\frac{192}{7}$.

complaining that he was "pestered with false and exaggerated information," and that all his care had not saved him from being deceived.[1]

Prosecutions for sedition began with the year 1793. James Tytler, a chemist at King's Park, Edinburgh, was the first to be indicted. He had distributed an address "to the People and their Friends" which certainly advocated passive resistance, and might be interpreted as condoning an appeal to force. The object of the pamphleteer was parliamentary reform, of which he still hopefully counted Pitt a supporter. The doubtful points in the case were never cleared up as Tytler did not appear and was consequently outlawed.[2]

Three men, Anderson, Morton and Craig, were convicted, on very contradictory evidence, of having attempted to seduce the soldiery at Edinburgh Castle and of having drunk to "George the third and last; and damnation to all crowned heads."[3] The judges decided, before hearing the evidence, that the words, which possibly were never uttered, were of wicked and seditious design, and the prisoners were each sentenced to nine months' imprisonment and to find security for three years.[4] A newspaper proprietor called Johnston,[5] already mentioned as a member of the Society of the Friends of the People at Edinburgh, was committed for contempt for having published a report of the trial;[6] and later when, in quite a different connection, he acted in conjunction with reformers, whose zeal he did his best to moderate,[7] he was called up to answer to his bail. But even during the panic of the next few months Scots judges had some conscience, and they did not venture to declare his bail forfeit.[8]

---

[1] John Pringle to H. Dundas, Dec. 18, 1792.—H. O. $\frac{102}{6}$.

[2] Jan. 7, 1793.—*S. T.* XXIII. 1–6.

[3] Watt had reported (Nov. 2, 1792) that four Friends of the People had tampered with some soldiers, and had exclaimed "*Damn the King and none but the nation.*" Watt to H. Dundas, enclosed in Dundas to Nepean, Nov. 24, 1792.—H. O. $\frac{102}{6}$.

[4] Jan. 8, 9, 11, 1793.—*S. T.* XXIII. 7–19, 20–35 ; Cockburn, I. 95–108.

[5] " Mr. Johnstone, the publisher of the new seditious paper." Dundas to Nepean, Nov. 24, 1792.—H. O. $\frac{102}{6}$. The name is variously spelt Johnston and Johnstone.

[6] *S. T.* XXIII. 59 ; cf. 43 ; Cockburn, I. 118–27.

[7] See William Scot to the Lord Advocate, Nov. 22, 1792.—H. O. $\frac{102}{8}$.

[8] S. *T.* XXIII. 62–80 ; cf. 409.

John Elder, a bookseller in Edinburgh, and William Stewart, a merchant in Leith, had issued two medals, one bearing on the observe, "Liberty Equality and an end to Impress warrants ": on the reverse, "The Nation is essentially the source of all Sovereignty"; the other had on the obverse the legend, "Liberty of conscience, equal representation and just taxation ": on the reverse, "For a nation to be free it is sufficient that it wills it." [1] They also circulated a reprint, with some additional comments, of the French National Assembly's declaration of the abstract rights of man. But even the catalogue of the rights of man, which may constitute philosophic heresy, cannot fairly be interpreted as sedition; still less could such a construction reasonably be placed on the words in which these perfectly innocent reformers demanded equal representation and a reform of the Scots burghs. [2] Perhaps the impartiality of Scots judges and the temper of Scots juries, rather than the guilt or innocence of the accused, is to be gauged from the fact that Stewart, whom alone it concerned the authorities to secure, had not confidence enough to face his trial and fled from justice.

A most interesting pamphlet next excited the ire of Government. Its title was, "The Political Progress of Great Britain, or an Impartial Account of the principal Abuses in the Government of this Country from the Revolution in 1688. The whole tending to prove the ruinous consequences of the Popular System of War and Conquest—the World's Mad Business." [3]

Dynastic wars were the chief object of attack, but no small amount of scorn was expended upon "our most excellent constitution " as being "in practice a conspiracy of the rich against the poor." [4] "There is a cant expression in this country that our Government is deservedly 'the wonder and envy of the world.' With better reason it may be said that Parliament is a mere outwork of the court, a phalanx of mercenaries embattled against the reason, the happiness and the liberty of mankind. The

---

[1] *S. T.* XXIII. 30–1.
[2] *Ib.* XXIII. 29, 25 ; Cockburn, I. 108–14.
[3] *S. T.* XXIII. 81. See also supra, p. 17.
[4] *Ib.* 82.

game laws, the dog act, the shop tax, the pedlar tax, the attorney tax and a thousand others give us a right to wish that their authors had been hanged." [1] The author of the spirited, but perfectly defensible, political Jeremiad was called James Thomson Callender, and was described as a "messenger at arms and writer in Edinburgh." [2] Callender did not appear to answer to the charge against him and was outlawed. [3] He found a refuge in the United States, where he became a journalist and earned a reputation so little enviable that a modern historian has pronounced the Scots reformers well rid of him. [4] Callender's printer and publisher had been colonial loyalists during the war of American Independence, but their loyalty then did not save them now from prosecution for the publication of his pamphlet; and though the jury did not find the pamphlet seditious, but found the printer guilty of printing and publishing only, the publisher of publishing only, the accused were denied the benefit of their special verdict, which was tantamount to an acquittal, and were both sent to prison. [5]

In February 1793 Smith and Mennons, two reformers of Partick, were indicted for sedition. Smith was charged on the ground that on the 22nd of November, 1792, he had moved a series of resolutions in favour of the formation of an association called Sons of Liberty and Friends of Man, setting forth also the principles of the proposed society. With assertive mendacity the society as a body claimed to have attentively perused "the whole works of the immortal author of the *Rights of Man*." Smith put no trust in juries and, not appearing, was outlawed. As the principal offender could not be brought to justice the case against Mennons, who was charged with publishing the resolutions, collapsed. [6] So weak, indeed, was the case for the prosecution that it had to be bolstered up by citations from *Common Sense*, [7] a pamphlet written by

---

[1] *S. T.* XXIII. 81-2. [2] *Ib.* 83.
[3] Jan. 28, 1793, *ib.* 83-4. [4] Porritt, II. 5.
[5] Feb. 18, 1793.—*S. T.* XXIII. 115. The judgment seems to have been manifestly bad, but it was sustained on appeal to the House of Lords.—*Ib.* 116.
[6] Feb. 4, 1793.—*S. T.* XXIII. *ib.* 35-42 ; Cockburn, I. 115-17.
[7] *S. T.* XXIII. 36-7.

Paine in 1776 on the eve of the American Declaration of Independence, and a portion, therefore, of the complete works of the immortal author which the Sons of Liberty claimed that they had attentively perused.

Hitherto the law officers of the Crown had directed their attention chiefly to the offences of blunderers. Such men may or may not have deserved conviction; but, with the possible exception of Callender, they certainly did not deserve the compliment of prosecution. The Lord Advocate and his subordinates now stalked more worthy game. At the end of 1792 Robert Dundas had hoped "to lay Muir by the heels on a Charge of High Treason."[1] Muir was in France when the charge was actually preferred against him. His parents implored him not to return, but to go to America till the storm blew over. It is uncertain whether the letter of warning ever reached him.[2] After visiting Ireland he returned to make his answer to the charge. He landed at Stranraer, probably on the 1st of August, 1793, and was at once taken into custody. The letter in which the Lord Advocate announced the arrest to Henry Dundas shows how slight was the chance that any fair or reasonable interpretation would be placed upon his words and acts. "I have little doubt that though he avows his intention of coming home to have been [with] a view to stand Trial, that he is an emissary of France or the disaffected in Ireland."[3] The Lord Advocate did not dare, however, to indict him for treason. He was charged with sedition on the ground that he had formed political societies in support of parliamentary reform,[4] that he had urged three specified persons to buy and read Tom Paine's *Rights of Man*, and that he had circulated Paine's works,[5] and other pamphlets advocating reform, such as a perfectly innocent declaration of the principles of the society at Paisley,[6] and "A Dialogue between the Governors and the Governed," to establish the sovereignty of the people as sound political doctrine. "Nations," said this last, "cannot revolt; tyrants are the only rebels."[7] Also he

---

[1] Robert to Henry Dundas, Dec. 15, 1792.—H. O. $\frac{102}{8}$.
[2] *Political Martyrs*, 8–9.
[3] R. Dundas to H. Dundas, Aug. 2, 1793.—H. O. $\frac{102}{8}$.
[4] *S. T.* XXIII. 118.   [5] *Ib.* 119.   [6] *Ib.* 122.   [7] *Ib.* 123–4.

was alleged to have read aloud at a convention of delegates of the Friends of the People an "Address from the Society of United Irishmen,"[1] which, considering the fount of its origin, was almost scandalously moderate. "We will not," said the Irishmen, "buy or borrow liberty from America or from France, but manufacture it for ourselves, and work it up with those materials which the hearts of Irishmen furnish them with at home."[2]

Muir conducted his own defence. He had all the ability and eloquence that in happier circumstances might have won success, but he made a grave mistake when he declined the help of Henry Erskine, the able and sympathetic Dean of Faculty.[3] Probably no man pleads well in his own cause. It is of the essence of advocacy not merely that the lawyer should be able to see the case from the point of view of his client, but that he should also be able to appreciate it as it presents itself to the minds of other men. Muir knew how to make a brave and honest defence, a defence that must be held good at the bar of history, but he could not, as another lawyer might have done, read the minds of his judges and divine the thoughts of the jury.

Muir admitted that he had promoted parliamentary reform and popular instruction, but denied that his conduct was seditious, for he had urged people to adopt none but constitutional means to attain constitutional ends.[4] He had advised people to read books on both sides of the question—Blackstone's *Commentaries* and Erskine's *Institutes* were amongst those he had recommended—and the witnesses for the Crown admitted that this was true.[5] His conduct at the formation of popular societies was proved to have been uniformly constitutional, and his speeches not free from direct expressions of loyalty.[6] Of the three witnesses who had heard him read the "Declaration of the United Irishmen," only one could swear that he had

[1] *S. T.* XXIII. 124, cf. 154, etc.; *Life of Muir*, 8.
[2] *S. T.* XXIII. 125, cf. 155 *et seq.*
[3] Erskine was applied to by Muir, and offered to undertake his defence, if Muir would leave the case absolutely in his hands. Muir refused to accept the condition.—Letter of H. Erskine, *S. T.* XXIII. 806 note.
[4] *Ib.* 129, 138, 140, 144, 146.   [5] *Ib.* 129, 138, 139, 146.
[6] *Ib.* 138, 144, 146, 151, 153, 173, etc.

defended it,[1] and all three agreed that his language was
moderate. The Convention to which it was addressed had
no other object than parliamentary reform; and that by
lawful means.[2]

Much was made of the charge about Paine's *Rights of
Man*. Muir had declared the book "foreign to the purpose" of reformers,[3] had never really recommended it,[4]
had promised to take eighty or a hundred tickets for a
course of lectures to refute it,[5] and had even attempted to
dissuade one man from reading it on account of its doubtful tendency.[6] His interrogator's curiosity being still
unsatisfied, he had allowed him to take a copy from the
pocket of his great-coat; it was still uncut![7] Muir did
recommend the book to his barber as good for casual
readers—a mere jocular allusion to the notorious popularity
of the book of the hour, which, in any case, the barber
did not buy.[8] But if men are to be judged—as the prosecution would have had Muir judged—by the chance
remarks, the very shuttlecocks of conversation, tossed to
and fro between friends whilst one is being shaved and the
other awaits his turn,[9] then must our barbers have at once
the wit of Nello and the discretion of Oliver le Daim.
Muir also asked a friend if he had read the *Rights of Man*,
and learning that he had not, but that he would like to
borrow the book, remarked that he had no copy, but that
it could be bought; and thereupon sent the maid to buy it.
The witness "being interrogated if he would have purchased it," replied, with the traditional carefulness of his
race, that "he would not, if he could have borrowed it."[10]

This was an astonishingly weak case on which to base
a capital charge. Two circumstances, however, augmented
the force of it. At a meeting of reformers Muir had instituted an unlucky comparison between the finance of revolutionary France, at first erroneously believed to be brilliant,
and the finance of the United Kingdom.[11] In the face of
the evidence his prosecutors strove to enlarge the scope of
this comparison, and to interpret it as a eulogy of the

[1] *S. T.* XXIII. 159.   [2] *Ib.* 159–60.   [3] *Ib.* 139, 143, 144.
[4] *Ib.* 138–9.   [5] *Ib.* 178.   [6] *Ib.* 173.   [7] *Ib.* 143–4, 160.
[8] *Ib.* 151–2.   [9] *Ib.* 152.   [10] *Ib.* 153.   [11] *Ib.* 137 ; cf. 143, 182.

Government of France by way of contrast with the Government of England.   Secondly, Muir had gone to France in January 1793, whether to make representations against the execution of the king or to avoid prosecution is uncertain, and had stayed there apparently until April or May 1793 : [1] that is to say, until some weeks after the declaration of war between England and France.   These circumstances enabled the prosecution to appeal to the prejudices of bench and jury.[2]

Muir was, of course, convicted; as he said, "for having dared to be, according to the measure of my feeble abilities, a strenuous and active advocate for an equal representation of the people, in the House of the people; for having dared to attempt to accomplish a measure by legal means which was to diminish the weight of their taxes and to put an end to the profusion of their blood." [3]   Braxfield, the Lord Justice Clerk immortalised by Stevenson as Weir of Hermiston, a man whose arrogance was matched only by his brutality, replied "that the promotion of that measure, in the circumstances, was, of itself, sedition."   "No attention could be paid" by Parliament "to such a rabble" as the petitioners for reform.   "What right had they to representation?"   In this country "the landed interest alone has a right to representation." [4]

Muir was sentenced to transportation for fourteen years. No lesser punishment was seriously considered.   It was even debated whether it would not be better to condemn him to the semi-servitude of an indentured servant, and it was with manifest reluctance that one of the judges decided against the degrading punishment of whipping as "too severe and disgraceful" to inflict upon a man of Muir's rank and character.[5]   We are not compelled to accept the legend that Braxfield said to a juryman, "Come awa', come awa', and help us to hang ane o' thae daamned scoundrels," [6] but certainly no circumstance was neglected which might lend the colour of plausibility to such a story.

---

[1] *S. T.* XXIII. 165–7 ; cf. *Life*, II. 13–14.
[2] Apparently the prosecution was not above suborning witnesses against the prisoner.—*S. T.* XXIII. 141–3 ; *Life of Muir*, 14–15.
[3] *S T.* XXIII. 228.   [4] *Ib.* 231.
[5] For this, as indeed for the whole trial, see Cockburn, I. 144–83.
[6] Cockburn's *Memorials*, I. 102.

The subject of the next trial was an address to their fellow-citizens by the Friends of Liberty at Dundee, printed and distributed on their behalf.[1] Its argument was that liberty was waning, despotism dawning. "Is not every new day adding a new link to our chains? Is not the executive branch daily seizing new, unprecedented and unwarrantable powers? Has not the House of Commons (your only security from the evils of tyranny) joined the coalition against you? Is the election of its members either free, fair or frequent? Is not its independence gone, while it is made up of pensioners and placemen?"[2] ". . . Nothing can save this nation from ruin . . . but a reform in the House of Commons founded upon the eternal basis of justice, fair, free and equal."[3] The war—"the destruction of a whole people merely because they will be free"— resulted proximately in bad trade, scant employment and heavy taxes, and would ultimately suffice not merely to "form chains for a free people," but eventually "to rivet them for ever on yourselves."[4]

A charge first of composing this address, and then of causing it to be printed and distributed, was lodged against a divine of the Unitarian persuasion called Thomas Fyshe Palmer. Palmer, who was descended "from a respectable and opulent family in Bedfordshire," had been originally intended for the Church.[5] At Cambridge he seems to have had a distinguished career, for he obtained a fellowship at Queens',[6] but his resolution to take orders was broken by a change in his religious opinions. He became a Unitarian through reading the works of Joseph Priestley and Theophilus Lindsey,[7] and entered upon the work of the ministry at Dundee, where, according to one writer, he was misplaced, and according to another, was instrumental in forming a considerable society of Unitarians.[8]

---

[1] *S. T.* XXIII. 238–9 ; Cockburn, I. 186 ; cf. *Trials*, 305.
[2] *Ib.* 239 ; Cockburn, I. 187. [3] *Ib.* 239–40 ; Cockburn, I. 187.
[4] *Ib.* 240; Cockburn, I. 188.
[5] Belsham's *Memoirs of Theophilus Lindsey*, 351.
[6] B.A. 1769 ; M.A. 1772. *Graduati Cantabrigienses*, 354.
[7] Belsham's *Lindsey*, 351.
[8] *Ib.* 351 and 352 ; *Political Martyrs*, 20.

He was soon a political suspect. "Palmer, the Methodist Clergyman,"[1] wrote Robert Dundas to his cousin Henry, ". . . is strongly suspected" of composing the Dundee address, "and if he is the Man, I doubt not his being got hold of; which he was artful enough to keep clear of when watched last Winter."[2] There appears to have been a lull in the Scots reform campaign during the first months of 1793,[3] but as the summer advanced the activity of the reformers was renewed, and the fears of ministers rose accordingly. "You may rest assured, from the accounts I have received from Glasgow and from Perth and Angus," Robert Dundas had continued, "that these Rascals have laid a Plan for exciting this Country again to *Discontent* and Disorder, on account of the War; and that this is the topic on which they are to dwell." He hopes that the efforts of the "Rascals" will prove abortive, but "after the experience of last Winter, nobody can answer for the future."[4]

Palmer was not, as a matter of fact, the author of the Dundee pamphlet. He had, indeed, been requested by the society to write it and had refused.[5] In consequence, it was written by a certain George Mealmaker,[6] and was afterwards revised by the society. In this revision Palmer assisted, and his share seems to have consisted in the modification of its more violent expressions.[7] He discouraged the circulation of the pamphlet owing to the disturbed times,[8] was outvoted, and thereupon undertook to superintend the publication,[9] probably because he thought that the best security against excesses of mistaken zeal would be to undertake the responsibility himself. Mealmaker, the real author, maintained that the society had "no idea of sedition," and that its sole object was "to cause a reform."[10] There is nothing to show that the society had any more sinister end in view.

---

[1] Methodist means, I suppose, that he was neither an Anglican nor a Scots Presbyterian.
[2] R. Dundas to H. Dundas, July 29, 1793.—H. O. $\frac{1}{2}\frac{0}{2}$.
[3] Watt to the Lord Advocate, Feb. 9, 1793.—H. O. $\frac{1}{2}\frac{0}{2}$.
[4] R. Dundas to H. Dundas, July 29, 1793.—H. O. $\frac{1}{2}\frac{0}{2}$.
[5] *S. T.* XXIII. 311.   [6] *Ib.* 300, 313.   [7] *Ib.* 301–4, 306.
[8] *Ib.* 305–6, 318.   [9] *Ib.* 313.   [10] *Ib.* 375–6 ; Cockburn, I. 211.

The Lord Advocate had, however, made up his mind that Palmer was the source of all mischief, and Palmer, accordingly, he meant to secure. "I earnestly hope it will be in my Power," he told his cousin, "to make such a case to a Jury as will assure his Conviction. He is the most determined *Rebel* in Scotland." [1] Within the limits of decency, it is the business of a public prosecutor to be a partisan : it is equally the business of a judge to preserve, as far as the frailty of the human intellect permits, a calm and unbiassed mind. But as an avowed parliamentary reformer Palmer could rely on no such unprejudiced trial. Lord Abercromby told the jury that, as universal suffrage tended to subvert the Constitution, it was for them to consider whether agitation to promote it did not in itself constitute sedition. Clerk, for the defence, held that the Dundee address was couched not in the language of sedition, but in the language of legitimate controversy : "the language of freemen who had a right to complain of their grievances for the purpose of having them redressed.[2] The prisoner declared that a reform of Parliament and the equalisation of the representation were his only objects; calculated, as he thought, to "enhance the happiness of millions and establish the security of the empire." [3] In the view of the court this was little better than a plea of guilty. Palmer was convicted and sentenced to transportation for seven years.[4]

In Muir's case the jury which had found him guilty was astounded at the severity of the sentence, and there is little doubt that it would have petitioned the court for a mitigation of it but for an unlucky letter addressed to one of the jurors, in which he was threatened with assassination for his concurrence in the verdict.[5] Indignation spread when Muir and Palmer were treated like common gaol-birds; "their being hand-cuffed or obliged to work like other Felons" was, reported Robert Dundas, "made the handle of much Clamour," which, he feared, might have a bad effect. "If you think it proper to show them any

[1] R. to H. Dundas, Aug. 2, 1793.—H. O. ¹⁸².
[2] *S. T.* XXIII. 342.   [3] *Ib.* 375.   [4] *Ib.* 375–6.
[5] See Cockburn, I. 182.

distinction from the case of the other Convicts, it appears to me your doing so would be of service. If the Juries here take it into their heads that more is done to these Gentry than is absolutely necessary they may acquit where they would otherwise have convicted." [1] They were conveyed to London and were lodged upon the hulks to company with the offscourings of Petticoat Lane. In this horrible situation they were visited by many friends, who did what could be done to alleviate their miseries. [2] Palmer bore up with cheerfulness, but Muir's health, already feeble, was impaired by the rigour of his treatment, and a medical man reported that his condition "seemed to indicate the latent seeds of consumption." [3]

Powerful friends had already made an attempt to upset the sentences on the ground of illegality. Lauderdale, Sheridan and Charles Fox submitted a memorandum to Dundas, expressing a doubt as to whether the punishment for leasing-making, or verbal sedition, restricted by a statute of 1703 to "Fine, imprisonment or Banishment," could be made to cover a sentence of transportation. Was banishment meant to include transportation? [4] The Lord Justice Clerk was asked by the minister to take the opinion of the judges. [5] Braxfield replied that transportation was known in Scotland before 1703; that banishment was a generic term which covered transportation and that banishment and transportation were not considered distinct punishments; and finally that Muir and Palmer were convicted not of leasing-making, but of sedition proper, and that, according to the common law of Scotland, they were liable to transportation for the offence. [6] Thereupon Dundas declined "to take any steps for either preventing or retarding the regular course of Justice." [7] On the legal point,

---

[1] R. Dundas to H. Dundas, Dec. 11, 1793.—H. O. $\frac{1\,2\,2}{8}$.

[2] Theophilus Lindsey to Dr. Toulmin —Belsham's *Mem.* 352 note.

[3] Copy of letter from Nathaniel Hornsby, Surgeon, to Duncan Campbell, Esq., Jan. 6, 1794.—H. O. $\frac{1\,0\,2}{1\,0}$.

[4] Dec. 14, 1793.—H. O. $\frac{1\,2\,2}{8}$.

[5] Copy of letter, Dec. 15, 1793.—H. O. $\frac{1\,2\,2}{8}$.

[6] Robert McQueen (Braxfield) to H. Dundas, Dec. 27, 1793.—H. O. $\frac{1\,2\,2}{8}$. Encloses formal opinion of the Court.

[7] Draft letter (undated) of Dec. 1793.—H. O. $\frac{1\,2\,2}{8}$.

Lauderdale accepted the opinion of the judges,[1] but he disputed still the justice of sending Muir and Palmer to Botany Bay. Stanhope and he in the Lords, Fox and Sheridan in the Commons, tried hard, but in vain, to obtain a revision of the sentences.[2]

The Scots seditions trials were much reprobated even outside reforming circles. But a Whig like Romilly, who was present, was inexpressibly shocked,[3] and Fox, who was not present, declared that there was "not a pretence left for calling Scotland a free country, and a very thin one for calling England so."[4] Perhaps the worst feature of the proceedings was the application of a new "Morton's fork" to the case of the prisoners. Muir's case had been aggravated in the eyes of his judges by the fact that the people were in a state of frenzy at the time of the alleged sedition. It was held to be part of the wickedness of Palmer that he committed his acts of sedition at a time when "the country was quiet" and "all alarm had ceased."[5] There can be little disagreement, therefore, with judgment that a juryman pronounced thirty-five years later on bench and jury : "We were all mad."[6]

[1] Lauderdale to H. Dundas, Dec. 31, 1793.—H. O. 102/2.
[2] *Parl. Hist.* XXX. 1300 *et seq.*; 1550 *et seq.*; XXXI. 567 *et seq.*; Cockburn, II. 133–47. Cartwright made a personal appeal for the assistance of the Duke of Richmond.—*Life of J. C.* I. 198–9. See also Aikin, *Mem.* I. 161–2
[3] *Mem. of Romilly*, II. 23.
[4] *Mem. of C. J. Fox*, III. 263–4, cf. 60–2.
[5] *S. T.* XXIII. 371 ; Cockburn, I. 211–12.
[6] *Ib.* I. 183.

CHAPTER XI

REPRESSION IN ENGLAND

1793

IN England the Government constantly misjudged the situation. The harmless were prosecuted, whilst the dangerous escaped. *Political Justice*, the *magnum opus* of William Godwin, which appeared early in 1793, escaped condemnation, though it proved to be one of the most powerful solvents of tradition that appeared in Godwin's generation. "The period in which" this "work makes its appearance is singular," he wrote in the preface.[1] "The people of England have assiduously been excited to declare their loyalty, and to mark every man as obnoxious who is not ready to sign the Shibboleth of the Constitution. Money is raised by voluntary subscription to defray the expense of prosecuting men who shall dare to promulgate heretical opinions, and thus to oppress them at once with the enmity of Government and of individuals. . . . Every man, if we may believe the voice of rumour, is to be prosecuted who shall appeal to the people by the publication of any unconstitutional paper or pamphlet; and it is added that men are to be prosecuted for any unguarded words that may be dropped in the warmth of conversation and debate. It is now to be tried whether, in addition to these alarming encroachments upon our liberty, a book is to fall under the arm of the civil power, which, beside the advantage of having for one of its express objects the dissuading from all tumult and violence, is by its very nature an appeal to men of study and reflexion."[2]

Yet Godwin believed, and attempted to prove, that law and government were in their nature evil; though as

---

[1] Dated Jan. 7, 1793.   [2] *Political Justice*, Preface, x–xii.

he had to do "not with nations of philosophers," but with men of weaker mould,[1] he admitted that law and government were necessary evils, the regrettable incidents of an imperfect state of society. Burke said that the simple governments were radically defective. Godwin, on the contrary, held that, in government, every departure from simplicity was an evil to be deplored.[2] The reason, free, untrammelled and accessible to truth must, in the long run, prove omnipotent, for no reasonable being could knowingly reject the truth once it was set plainly before him. The human mind could no more offer resistance to truth than one billiard ball could prevent itself from being rolled against another. "Ten pages that should contain an absolute demonstration of the true interests of mankind in society could no otherwise be prevented from changing the face of the globe than by the literal destruction of the paper on which they were written."[3]

It followed that, since government contracted the sphere of private judgment, the less there was of government the better for mankind.[4] "Since government, even in its best state, is an evil, the object principally to be aimed at is, that we should have as little of it as the general peace of human society will permit."[5] Of governments, "that is the best which shall least impede the activity and application of our intellectual powers."[6]

Government "gives substance and permanence to our errors. It reverses the genuine propensities of mind and instead of suffering us to look forward, teaches us to look backward for perfection. It prompts us to seek the public welfare, not in innovation and improvement, but in a timid reverence for the decisions of our ancestors, as if it were the nature of mind always to degenerate and never to advance."[7] "Let us look back that we may profit by the experience of mankind; but let us not look back as if the wisdom of our ancestors was such as to leave no room for future improvement."[8]

As he attacked government and the unreasoning

[1] *Political Justice*, II. 732-3. [2] *Ib*. Pref. viii.
[3] *Ib*. I. 211 ; see also 75-6, 202 ; II. 577. [4] *Ib*. I. 193.
[5] *Ib*. I. 186. [6] *Ib*. II. 382 ; see also 578-9.
[7] *Ib*. I. 31-2. [8] *Ib*. I. 50.

worship of tradition which he thought it fostered, so also Godwin attacked law which is the expression of government. "Legislation, as it has been generally understood, is not an affair of human competence. Reason is the only legislator, and her decrees are irrevocable and uniform."[1] "Law tends no less than creeds, catechisms and tests to fix the human mind in a stagnant condition . . . ,"[2] and to attempt to secure an impossible uniformity. Godwin, therefore, appealed from the authority of law to the higher authority of reason and demanded "spontaneous justice."[3]

Many other opinions expressed in *Political Justice* might have been expected to alarm defenders of the established order and to confirm them in their distrust of the speculative politician. Godwin declared, for example, that monarchy was "founded in imposture,"[4] that it lived on the distortion of the truth, and that it made sincerity impossible. "There is a simplicity in truth that refuses alliance with this impudent imposture."[5] Again, Godwin thought a bi-cameral parliamentary system radically unjust and "the direct method to divide a nation against itself";[6] whilst he said of religious establishment that "the most malicious enemy of mankind could not have invented a scheme more destructive of their true happiness, than that of hiring at the expense of the state a body of men, whose business it should seem to be to dupe their contemporaries into the practice of virtue."[7]

Nor were these the only doctrines in *Political Justice* that were calculated to shock the lover of old ways and received opinions. Godwin was a democrat;[8] but he was also much more than a democrat, as the word was commonly used in his day, for, despite his apparent individualism, he held one of those numerous varieties of opinion which are described under the common name of socialism.[9] "Not a talent do we possess, not a moment of time, not a shilling of property, for which we are not responsible at the tribunal of the public, which we are not obliged to pay

---

[1] *Political Justice*, I. 166   [2] *Ib.* II. 770.   [3] *Ib.* II. 776.   [4] *Ib.* II. 423.
[5] *Ib.* II. 426.   [6] *Ib.* II. 552.   [7] *Ib.* II. 607.   [8] *Ib.* II, 489, 499, 548.
[9] It might be interesting to compare his views with those of his French contemporary, Babeuf.

into the general bank of common advantage." [1] "To whom does any article of property—suppose a loaf of bread—justly belong? To him who most wants it or to whom the possession of it would be most beneficial." [2] "Justice does not stop here. Every man is entitled, so far as the general stock will suffice, not only to the means of being, but of well being." [3] If this view of duty and of mutual obligation were established, then crime and human wrong might be banished from the earth. "If every man could with perfect facility obtain the necessaries of life, and, obtaining them, feel no uneasy craving after its superfluities, temptation would lose its power. Private interest would visibly accord with public good, and civil society become all that poetry has feigned of the golden age." [4]

Godwin's logic, relentless within its range, led him still further. Not merely did he forecast socialism, but he foreshadowed also the "internationalism" which has brought socialism into such discredit on the Continent. When the world is governed by reason, "there must in the nature of things," he says, "be one best form of government which all intellects sufficiently roused from the slumber of savage ignorance will be irresistibly incited to approve. . . . Truth cannot be so variable as to change its nature by crossing an arm of the sea, a petty brook or an ideal line, and become a falsehood. On the contrary, it is at all times and places the same." [5]

Godwin's premises are disputed by the philosopher and the biologist, whilst his conclusions find little acceptance with the practical statesman or the political theorist, yet the austere eloquence of his writing and the invigorating strength of his reasoning have an attractiveness which, in 1793, might well have been condemned as dangerously alluring. His immunity from prosecution needs to be explained.

In the first place, no doubt, the abstract nature of *Political Justice*, which may have made it most dangerous, was, in practice, Godwin's best protection. He said that

---

[1] *Political Justice*, II. 432 ; see also II. 101.   [2] *Ib.* 790.
[3] *Ib.* II. 791 ; see also 831. Godwin deprecates, however, "supererogatory coöperation," *ib.* II. 844.
[4] *Ib.* I. 34.   [5] *Ib.* I. 182.

he was a theorist; and he was believed. He appealed to reason, not to force; and what influence could an appeal to reason have upon the labourer or the artisan? He preached passive obedience, and for once the Government forgot what it was usually too prone to remember—that the hearer and the preacher may draw different morals from the same sermon. Godwin argued that "the true instruments for changing the opinions of men" were argument and persuasion;[1] that whilst violence was a game that two could play at, a game that could be played in order to promote wrong as well as right, reason was invulnerable and only truth could triumph by persuasion.[2] Even in urging reform caution was needed if it was to be directed by reason and not by violence.[3] "We must, therefore, distinguish between informing the people and inflaming them."[4]

Secondly, he disapproved of political associations, though he granted that they might have a certain limited usefulness. They spread restlessness, and there was danger in any premature attempt to anticipate the conquest of truth; and they were unnecessary, for truth was omnipotent, and, with or without them, would surely prevail.[5] As a means of spreading information and ideas they might be useful; as political machinery, devised to enforce a settled policy, they were necessarily bad. "Clubs, in the old English sense—that is, the periodical meeting of small and independent circles—may be admitted to fall within the line of these principles. But they cease to be admissible when united with the tremendous apparatus of articles of confederacy and committees of correspondence. Human beings should meet together not to enforce, but to enquire. Truth disclaims the alliance of marshalled numbers."[6]

Thirdly, Godwin was free from the prevailing delusions of his political associates as to the supposed social contract and the abstract rights of man. In his view men had not rights, but duties, and the one excluded the other. To talk of rights implied a distorted view of man's moral nature.[7] "My neighbour has just as much right to put

---

[1] *Political Justice*, I. 203.   [2] *Ib.* 203.
[3] *Ib.* 204; see also 221.   [4] *Ib.* 203.
[5] *Ib.* I. 211.   [6] *Ib.* I. 216.   [7] *Ib.* I. 113

an end to my existence with dagger or poison as to deny me that pecuniary assistance without which I must starve, or as to deny me that assistance without which my intellectual attainments and my moral exertions will be materially injured." [1] It followed that no consent of ours could divest us of our moral capacity. "This is a species of property which we can neither barter nor resign; and, of consequence, it is impossible for any Government to derive its authority from an original contract." [2]

Fourthly, *Political Justice* was not made the subject of a prosecution because Pitt believed that "a three-guinea book could not do much harm among those who had not three shillings to spare." [3] Godwin, for all his democratic theory and his belief in the power of right reason, had the contempt of an intellectual aristocrat for people who could afford less. But Pitt and Godwin were alike deceived. Workmen, who alone could not possibly have afforded such a purchase, formed clubs for the express purpose of buying and reading *Political Justice,* and its sale and influence were considerable.

In contrast with Godwin's immunity stand a number of futile prosecutions. At Cambridge, the cumbrous machinery of the Vice-Chancellor's court was brought into operation to punish an unfortunate tutor who had published a pamphlet entitled "Peace and Union recommended to the Associated Bodies of Republicans and Anti-Republicans." [4] For the monstrous crime of approving the early stages of the revolution, "when every good man rejoiced" [5] with him, he was banished the University [6] and deprived of his livelihood. As if to offer an ironic proof of his faith in order and security, he found a lucrative resource in the business of insurance.

John Frost, [7] an active reformer, was convicted of

---

[1] *Political Justice*, I. 112, cf. I. 89.   [2] *Ib.* I. 149.

[3] Mrs. Shelley is the authority for this statement.—*William Godwin and His Friends*, I. 80-1.

[4] May 3, 1793, *S. T.* XXII. 530.

[5] *Ib.* 576. It should be added that, coming from a man in holy orders, the theological views expressed were decidedly advanced.

[6] *Ib.* 640.

[7] Frost was the intimate friend of Horne Tooke, and was left in charge of his house during his imprisonment in 1794. He did not fulfil

sedition for having declared in the public room of a coffee-
house that he was for equality and no kings.[1] On the
6th of November, 1792, Frost, who had just returned from
France,[2] was accosted by the Crown witnesses as he was
coming away from dinner at the Percy Coffee-House, and
was provoked by them, against his will, to engage in the
conversation of which they complained—a conversation
which, in any case, was not public. Three days later
Frost had been commissioned, along with Joel Barlow, to
return to Paris and present to the Convention the address
of the Society for Constitutional Information.[3] Whilst
in Paris he learnt that a proclamation had been issued in
the *London Gazette*, offering a reward of £100 for his
arrest. He replied at once in an open letter to Pitt—which
appeared, somewhat expurgated, in the *Morning Chronicle*
—that he would return to stand his trial, and "afford an
opportunity to some fellow-citizen to profit by the proposed bounty of the Treasury."[4] Frost was tried in
May 1793, and defended by Erskine, who set up, with
some plausibility, but without success, the defence that he
was drunk, and therefore irresponsible, at the time of
the alleged sedition. He was, however, convicted and
sentenced in June to six months' imprisonment in Newgate, to stand in the pillory at Charing Cross, to find
sureties for five years, and to be struck off the roll of
attornies.[5] When the time came for him to stand in the
pillory at Charing Cross, handbills were distributed, announcing the hour.[6] A mob assembled, demolished the
pillory and released Frost, who coolly took the arm of his
friend Horne Tooke, whom he happened to meet, and walked
back to prison.[7] On his release, he was dragged about

---

the trust altogether to the satisfaction of Horne Tooke. Tooke's *Diary
Notes and Queries*, 1897. 8th series XI. 103. Frost had corresponded
with Pitt on the Reform Question in 1782. *S. T.* XXII. 492–4 and *n.*

[1] *S. T.* XXII. 473–4, 476.   [2] *Ib.* 476, 482.

[3] Nov. 9, 1792. Resolution signed " D. Adams, secretary," in
Archives nationales, C. 241 (Dossier, 278).

[4] Paris, Dec. 19, 1792.—*Morning Chronicle*, Jan. 1. 1793, Burney
Collection, 853.

[5] *S. T.* XXII. 521–2.

[6] See *Political Broadsides*, an unmanageable folio collection in the
B. M. 554, g. 31 s. sh. fol.

[7] Smith, *English Jacobins*, 165.

the streets in a carriage by a rejoicing mob.[1] In 1813 the Regent granted Frost a free pardon, but he was never restored to the roll of attornies, and his career was, therefore, ruined.[2]

Daniel Isaac Eaton, who drove a regular trade as the publisher of so-called seditious literature, was always in conflict with the authorities.[3] In June 1793 he was charged on account of a bowdlerised reprint of the Second Part of the *Rights of Man*,[4] from which all the passages cited in Paine's trial had been carefully expunged. His plea that the remnant might fairly be considered innocent[5] was accepted by the jury, which returned a special verdict of "guilty of publishing, but not with a criminal intent."

Next month he was again prosecuted for publishing the *Address to the Addressers*,[6] but, despite the great persistency of the judge, no more satisfactory verdict could be exacted from the jury.[7] In 1794, Eaton was found not guilty of publishing *Hog's Wash*, an unauthorised version of one of Thelwall's speeches, and another pamphlet called *The Reflexions of a true Briton*.[8]

Injudicious prosecutions of this character showed a

---

[1] *Ann. Reg.* 1793, *Chron.* 59.

[2] Frost died July 25, 1842. Obituary notices, word for word the same, are to be found in *Gent.'s Mag.* Oct. 1842, and *Ann. Reg.* 1842, App. to *Chron.* 279. Despite these authorities there is no evidence that Frost was ever secretary of the London Corresponding Society. There are some letters in the Record Office from a certain John Frost, who had been appointed Assistant-Solicitor to the Stamp Office in Aug. 1787, and who lodged a claim for £4400, in a letter to the Commissioner of the Stamp Office, Nov. 2, 1792 [R. O. *Chatham MSS.* 137]. This Frost seems to have nursed a grievance, for on June 14, 1796, a letter was sent t ʹ him by Pitt's order, saying that he had already been treated generously and that he could expect no further payment [R. O. *Chatham MSS.* 102]. It is not, however, established that this John Frost was the John Frost convicted of sedition. The life of Frost in the *D. N. B.* is full of errors, *e.g.* it is there stated that Frost was sent to France in 1793, instead of 1792, and it is assumed that the London Corresponding Society and the Society for Constitutional Information were founded simultaneously.

[3] Hardy was asked about Eaton in his examination of May 13, 1794. Asked if pains were taken to get friends on Eaton's jury, he said he believed there were. *Q.* Eaton is a good printer for you, is he not? *A.* Yes, he prints freely, too freely.—*P. C. R.* 33, Geo. III. 58.

[4] *S. T.* XXII. 755.   [5] *Ib.* 774.   [6] *Ib.* 785 *et seq.*   [7] *Ib.* 822.

[8] *Ib.* XXIII. 1014–1054 ; Mrs. Thelwall's *Life of Thelwall*, I. 107–11. At Newcastle-on-Tyne, one Alexander Whyte was, to the manifest disgust of the Court, found "not guilty" of publishing a seditious paper, July 17, 1793.—*S. T.* XXII. 1237–1250.

want of judgment more alarming and far more dangerous
than the sedition which they were designed to suppress;
for they showed that, whilst the adventurous publisher of
contraband pamphlets ran the risk of conviction, he stood
at least a "sporting" chance of acquittal, and they showed
also that the probability of conviction was by no means
proportioned to the seditious character of his publications.
Just as a bad tariff and a spice of danger attract bold men
to engage in smuggling, so the unequal enforcement of
the law tempted the adventurous or irresponsible publisher
to risk the publication of works which administration
regarded as contraband.

A dissenting minister called William Winterbotham,
tried at Exeter in July 1793, was not so fortunate as Eaton.
His alleged sedition was contained in certain passages of
a sermon preached at Plymouth on the preceding 5th of
November which, though unguarded in expression, does
not seem to have been seditious.[1] None of the Crown
witnesses were practised "sermon tasters," as they were
unable to recollect the text; several of them were not even
present at the beginning of the sermon.[2] Their intelligence may be gauged from the fact that one of them
understood an allusion to the Stuarts to refer to an officer
in the royal household like a gentleman's steward;[3] and
their keen scent for sedition from the fact that another
reported as a "highly dangerous and improper" observation, words to the effect that "every man in a land of liberty
had a right to know how his money was applied."[4] Witnesses for the defence proved to have more homiletic genius
or better memories, recollected the text, and denied that
many of the words reported were ever spoken.[5] Winterbotham had declared "that in this country we wanted no
revolution, and he deprecated the idea of a revolution,
because it would produce anarchy and bloodshed."[6] For
the rest, he appears to have held the usual creed of the
reformers. After prolonged deliberation the jury found
him guilty.[7]

On hearing the rumour that it was intended to prosecute

---

[1] *S. T.* XXII. 823-4.   [2] *Ib.* 832, etc.   [3] *Ib.* 830-1.
[4] *Ib.* 832.   [5] *Ib.* 849-50.   [6] *Ib.* 849.   [7] *Ib.* 876.

him, he had preached a second sermon to put right those parts of the first which seemed liable to misconstruction. This second sermon became the subject of a second prosecution. At the trial the case for the Crown really broke down, but Winterbotham, who had been involved in a local dispute with the corporation, would seem to have had many enemies, and, after a discussion lasting five hours and a half, the jury found him guilty.[1] He was sentenced to pay a fine of a £100, and serve a term of two years' imprisonment for each offence. On his release he was, furthermore, to find sureties for five years.[2] An anonymous gift of £1000 which Winterbotham received years afterwards was supposed to be a juryman's conscience money.[3]

Lambert, Perry, and Grey, of the *Morning Chronicle*, charged with publishing the seditious address of a reforming society at Derby,[4] which attacked, though in moderate terms, both the war and the state of the representation,[5] were acquitted, after the jury had deliberated for fifteen hours—the judge having refused to accept a special verdict.[6] Daniel Holt, a Newark printer, was charged with publishing Paine's *Address to the Addressers*, an old reforming pamphlet by Cartwright, and another tract of like character.[7] He was found guilty on two counts, and sentenced to pay a fine of £50 and serve two years in prison for each offence; afterwards he was to find sureties for five years.[8] Holt was ruined both in pocket and constitution, and died probably as a result of his imprisonment.

Ill-luck befell another reformer, Dr. Hudson, or Hodgson, who was accused of sedition for having toasted liberty and the French Republic, and for having, apparently under provocation, used contemptuous expressions about the king. For these offences, too trivial to have been worth taking seriously, he was fined £200 and required to find

---

[1] *S. T.* XXII. 906 ; cf. *D. N. B.* LXII. 222.
[2] *S. T.* XXII. 907 ; *Add. MSS.* 27809, fo. 269.
[3] *D. N. B.* LXII. 222.   [4] *S. T.* XXII. 960.   [5] *Ib.* 961.
[6] The whole is in *S. T.* XXII. 953–1023.   [7] *Ib.* 1189-1203.
[8] *Ib.* 1238 ; *Life of Cartwright*, I. 199-202 ; *Add. MSS.* 27809, fo. 269 ; cf. *Mem. of Gilbert Wakefield*, II. 433. See also *S. T.* XXIII. 63, 70.

sureties for two years.[1] Hodgson lived to a ripe old age, and achieved considerable literary and scientific success. He might, indeed, have consoled himself with Christopher North's dictum that "the Animosities only are mortal, the Humanities live for ever."

[1] Hudson or Hodgson appears in the B. M. Catalogue as three different Hodgsons. See Mr. G. F. Russell Barker's note, *Notes and Queries* Sixth Series, IX. 475. For the trial see *S. T.* XXII. 1019–32; *Ann. Reg.* 1793, *Chron.* 46–8. See *D. N. B.* under Hodgson, XXVII. 72; cf. Alger, *Englishmen in the French Revolution*, 45. Richter in his MS. Annotations to the First Report of the Committee of Secrecy [B.M., C. 61. b. 16 (1)], interleaf 6, opposite p. 14, says, "Dr. Hodgson, who had been a prisoner for Debt, and had been recently discharged, and was without any property, was fined £200 and [sentenced to] two years' imprisonment in Newgate for *words* spoken."

CHAPTER XII

THE BRITISH CONVENTION

1792–1794

ALL the skill of their leaders was needed to guide the popular societies in these troublous times. The London Corresponding Society had to avoid, on the one hand, the bravado of publishing the names and addresses of its members,[1] a course which would have invited proscription, and, on the other hand, knew better than to accept a motion for the free admission of soldiers,[2] which would have afforded a plausible excuse for the attacks which its enemies were eager to begin. The society wisely refused to meddle in extraneous affairs, and declined, for example, to publish either a pamphlet against imprisonment for debt,[3] or a defence of the execution of "Louis Capet."[4] A society at Norwich rashly inquired whether the generality of societies adhered to the Duke of Richmond's plan, or whether it was "their private design to rip monarchy by the roots, and place democracy in its stead."[5] The Corresponding Society replied that universal suffrage and annual Parliaments were their only object; "to this . . . they steadily adhere, and turn themselves neither to the right nor to the left to follow any other plan whatever."[6]

More care was now taken in the admission of members, owing to the fact of "several improper persons intruding

---

[1] Oct. 18, 1792.—*Add. MSS.* 27812, fo. 24.
[2] Jan. 17, 1793, *ib.* fo. 31 ; cf. also *Life of Thelwall*, by his wife, I. 149–50.
[3] Feb. 23, 1793.—*Add. MSS.* 27812, fo. 37.
[4] April 4, 1793.—*Ib.* fo. 39.
[5] *C. J.* XLIX. 669, where the S. C. I. is erroneously stated to have received the letter ; 701 ; *S. T.* XXIV. 392-3 ; cf. *William Pitt and the Great War*, 168.
[6] *S. T.* XXIV. 394.

and intriguing to get into the room as members, and afterwards endeavouring to disturb the harmony of the society
by their noisy and virulent declamation . . . that they
might become an easy prey to their evil designs." [1] The
society was much troubled with Bow Street runners [2] and
agents provocateurs, such as Lynam, a man who figured
prominently in the State trials as a witness for the Crown,
but who had actually been tried as a spy by the society,
had been mistakenly acquitted,[3] and had afterwards been
entrusted with important duties.[4] Veracity does not seem
to have been a distinguishing characteristic of these gentlemen ; certainly they created much more disaffectation than
they discovered.

The City magistrates, acting on the evidence of these
informers, sought to suppress the divisions of the society,
though Sir Sampson Wright, after examining two publicans, was satisfied of the honesty of its members, and
even agreeing to the necessity of parliamentary reform,
declared that he had been misled by his informants.[5] To
avoid "police officers, who were prowling about seeking
whom they might devour," the divisions had to change
their places of resort,[6] and even hire houses and auction-
rooms at great expense.[7] "Church and King" clubs
flourished, though the reformers consoled themselves with
the doubtful comfort that the meetings of these self-styled
loyalist clubs did not prove nearly so profitable to the
publicans as did their own.[8]

The divisions of the Corresponding Society, says
Thelwall, were occasionally hunted from house to house
by the threats and intrigues, and sometimes by the
tumultuary violence, of the police officers ; but the virtue
and energy of the society weathered the storm. "Composed almost entirely of the soundest part of the community, and led on by men who united transcendent
abilities with the most prudent circumspection and inflexible decision of character, they still persisted in the vin-

---

[1] *Add. MSS.* 27814, fo. 37.   [2] *Ib.* ff. 38-9 ; cf. 48.
[3] *Ib.* 27812, ff. 47-8.
[4] *S. T.* XXIV. 770.   As to spies, cf. 639-53, 707-8, 713-17.
[5] *Add. MSS.* 27814, fo. 39.   [6] *Ib.* fo. 48:
[7] *Ib.* fo. 43.   [8] *Ib.* fo. 43.

dication of their natural and constitutional rights, and, in spite of every effort to suppress them, the principle of their Association was at once so consonant to the universal justice and individual interest that it was found, and I trust ever will be found, powerful enough to triumph over every persecution, and to gather increasing strength from the infuriated attacks of usurpation and corruption." [1]

Whatever the moral triumph of the Corresponding Society, there is no doubt that repression did it practical harm. Some members, Hardy tells us, fled in alarm to the country, others to America. "Others," again, "who were great declaimers in the Society slunk into holes and corners, and were never heard of more; others of the violent orators deserted and joined the standard of the enemy." [2]

The fury of Reeves and his Association for protecting Liberty and Property against Republicans and Levellers was so particularly directed against the London Corresponding Society that a defence was thought necessary, in order to repudiate the doctrines of equality which were imputed to it. [3] "Whoever shall attribute to us (who wish only the restoration of the lost liberties of our country) the expressions of *No King! No Parliament!* or any design of invading the Property of other men, is guilty of a wilful, an impudent, and a malicious falsehood." [4] This address was issued as a poster, and the Crown, deeming it impolitic to attack its authors, adopted the less courageous expedient of prosecuting a harmless bill-poster, who was sent to prison for six months. [5] A copy of the pamphlet was sent to Dundas by registered post, with a demand for protection in "legal and peaceable methods" of attempting to secure reform. [6]

One of these methods was a great petition, which some thousands of people signed. Fox begged to be excused

---

[1] *Life of Thelwall,* by Mrs. Thelwall, I. 114–15.
[2] *Add. MSS.* 27814, fo. 43.
[3] Nov. 29, 1792. *Mem. of Hardy,* 26: in the separate pamphlet, p. 8 ; cf. *Add. MSS.* 27814, fo. 41 ; 27815, ff. 25–7 ; *C. J.* XLIX. 669–700 ; 702–3 ; *S. T.* XXIV. 404–6.
[4] Pamphlet, 7–8.
[5] *Add. MSS.* 27814, ff. 40, 43–4 : 27812, fo. 32, etc.
[6] Dec. 4, 1792, *ib.* ff. 27–9 ; *S. T.* XXIV. 771–2.

from presenting it, as the reform it asked for included universal suffrage, "to which he was an avowed enemy." Philip Francis therefore consented to carry it to Parliament.[1]

Besides maintaining an extensive correspondence with societies in various parts of the country, the society published various pamphlets of a constitutional and educative character.[2] On the 8th of July, 1793, it held a general meeting, at which seven hundred members were present,[3] to adopt an address in which were re-stated the objects of the society : "A thorough Reform in Parliament by the adoption of an equal Representation obtained by Annual Elections and Universal Suffrage." The society declared its abhorrence of the contumelious fashion, whereby every advocate of reform in general, and the critic of any place-man in particular, was "stigmatised as a leveller and an enemy to his King and Country." Twenty thousand copies of this address, which also contained an attack on the war, were ordered to be printed for free distribution.[4] It was intended to issue yet another protest against the war, but the first draft was considered "more spirited than judicious, and not calculated to effect any possible good," and a chapter of accidents prevented the publication of the second.[5]

In opposition to the war, in active correspondence and pamphleteering, the Society for Constitutional Information also joined.[6] But that society had less wisely involved itself, by correspondence and unconcealed sympathy, with revolutionists in France,[7] in a way that was becoming increasingly dangerous. If the report of a spy may be trusted, the society was equally unguarded at its annual dinner in April 1793.[8] But an address issued to the public

[1] *Add. MSS.* 27812, fo. 43 ; *C. J.* XLIX. 670–711.
[2] *Ib.* 713 ; *Add. MSS.* 27812, fo. 57.
[3] *C. J.* XLIX. 709, 711–12 ; *Add. MSS.* 27814, fo. 50.
[4] Address to the Nation . . . July 8, 1793.—*Add. MSS.* 27814, ff. 51–5 ; 27812, ff. 49–55.
[5] *Ib.* 27814, ff. 55–6 ; 27812, ff. 62–74.
[6] *C. J.* XLIX, 692, 693, 715, 709, 711 ; *S. T.* XXIV. 545–7, 550, etc.
[7] *C. J.* XLIX. 666–7 692 ; *S. T.* XXIV. 531–3, 558–9, 540–1
[8] *Ib.* 790.

in the previous December had no such faults. In it they disclaimed "the Idea of wishing to effect a Change in the present System of Things by Violence and Public Commotion." "The Intentions of this and of similar Societies," they continued, "have of late been grossly calumniated by those who are interested to perpetuate Abuses, and their Agents, who have been industrious to represent the Members of such Societies as Men of dangerous Principles, wishing to destroy all social Order, disturb the State of Property, and introduce Anarchy and Confusion instead of Regular Government;"[1] and perhaps the fact that they so boldly published the case against themselves is a sufficient refutation of it. They were afterwards accused of pursuing during this period "a settled Design" tending to the "Subversion of the established Constitution."[2] If this had been true, their task would have indeed been difficult. The annual income of the society was about £60, of which £50 was absorbed by standing expenses. Only the most robust of optimists could contemplate the possibility of overturning the British Government by the aid of a doubtful income of £10 per annum.[3] "They have magnified their numbers and their strength . . . very much beyond the truth," said Justice Eyre at the State trials. "It appears upon the evidence that the Constitutional Society had neither numbers, money, nor even zeal. . . ."[4]

The Friends of the People were still more moderate. They disliked the war and denounced official interference with public meetings, but they also disliked foreign correspondence and addresses to the French Convention. Circumspection is needed, they say, when "the most venial Indiscretion of the Friends of Reform" is converted into an argument against it.[5] And in one sense they were right. Addresses to French assemblies were a deviation from the main line of attack upon the evils of the representation and hampered constitutional measures for the reform of the English Parliament. The Friends of the

---

[1] *C. J.* XLIX. 692.   [2] *Ib.* 601.
[3] *S. T.* XXV. 85–6; cf. 154–5.   [4] *Ib.* 265.
[5] Letter to the London Corresponding Society, Feb. 15, 1793.—*C. J.* XLIX, 704–5.

People hoped again to bring the question of parliamentary reform to the notice of the House of Commons, and they were anxious that no false step on the part of the reformers themselves should spoil their chances of success. Moreover, there was even amongst themselves a right wing as well as a left; and it was important that the moderates of the right should not be alarmed into opposition by the Hotspurs of the left. "Reform of Parliament is much canvassed, and a moderate Reform will not now content the People," wrote Hollis, speaking for the left;[1] "I wish . . . that you and the other Friends of Liberty in London could see the dangers of a Revolution in as strong a light as I do," replied Wyvill, a more cautious leader of what may be called the right, who expressed a hope that the Friends of the People would "beware of going too far."[2]

Whatever the Friends of the People might do, there was little hope that the House of Commons would go far enough. This at once became plain when, in May 1793, the reformers began to renew their agitation by way of petition to Parliament. On the 2nd of May the House of Commons refused by a large majority even to receive a petition from Sheffield, which was held to demand a reform of Parliament in language of unbecoming violence.[3] During the next few days it rained petitions. One from the town and neighbourhood of Birmingham seems to have served as a model for many others. The petitioners attacked influence and corruption; denounced a system by which members were returned to Parliament who had no real warrant to represent the people; and declared that members of the House of Commons ought to be freely elected by the commons of England. Finally, "relying on the virtues of some and the prudence of all," they prayed for a reform of Parliament.[4] A petition, slightly modified, but in substantially the same terms, was sent up from Glasgow and Leven.[5] About twenty-five other petitions echoed the words of Glasgow and of Birming-

---

[1] To Wyvill, March 8, 1793.—*Wyvill Papers*, 129–30.
[2] To T. Brand Hollis, March 17, 1793.—*Ib.* 130.
[3] Yeas 29, Noes 108.—*C. J.* XLVIII. 724 ; *Parl. Hist.* XXX. 775–80.
[4] May 2, 1793.—*C. J.* XLVIII. 724.
[5] May 3, *ib.* 729.

ham.[1] Petitioners from Durham and neighbourhood declare that the state of the representation was such as to make them "apprehensive that its continuance" in its existing imperfection "would expose to real danger the constitution, which they feel it equally their duty and their interest to preserve."[2] "Upon the most mature reflection and diligent inquiry," petitioners at Derby feel assured that "the present system of representation is contradictory to the Rights of Man and unauthorised by the genuine principles of the British Constitution."[3] A number of petitioners from London and Westminster wished to see the fulfilment of the Duke of Richmond's plan of universal suffrage and annual Parliaments.[4] In a petition from Nottingham all the evils of the time are attributed to the imperfections of the representation. "Presuming that national disgrace and ruin are equally unacceptable to you as to us," they earnestly request at the hands of the members of the House of Commons that reform of Parliament which alone can restore the well-being of the nation.[5]

Between all these petitions there is a strong family likeness. They were, in fact, meant to support, or to prepare the way for, a petition entered in the Journals of the House of Commons for the 6th of May, as coming from "certain persons whose names are subscribed." This petition had been promoted by the Society of the Friends of the People, and was presented by Charles Grey. It was a lengthy and detailed summary of the case for reform. The Friends of the People complained that the House of Commons did not fairly represent the people, and that its unrepresentative character constituted a grievance which ought to be redressed; that the representation was disproportionate, and that a mere handful of electors returned

---

[1] May 3, from Alnwick, Campsie, Glasgow (a second set of petitioners), Hamilton, Kirkintilloch, *C. J.* XLVIII. 730-1 ; May 6, from Aldgate, Anstruther, Dundee, Dunfermline, Edinburgh, Galston, Huddersfield, Irvine, Kilmarnock, Kirkcaldy, Linlithgow, Montrose, Newmilns, Paisley, Perth (2), Poole, Roxburgh, Strathaven, Suffolk, Warwick.—*Ib.* 735-8.

[2] May 2, *ib.* 724.

[3] May 6, *ib.* 734.   [4] May 6, *ib.* 735.

[5] May 6, *ib.* 738. A petition from Norwich, which it was intended also to introduce on the same day had in contravention of the resolutions of the House been printed before presentation. The motion for leave to introduce it was withdrawn.—*Ib.* 738-9 ; *Parl. Hist.* 786-7.

the whole House of Commons; that there was no uniformity in the franchise, and that it was based on no
principle of right. When it was proposed that the petition
should be referred to a committee, the motion was rejected
by an overwhelming majority (282–41), which showed
conclusively how futile it was to waste energy and time
in promoting petitions which the House of Commons
would refuse to consider, and which it would jump at any
excuse to reject altogether.[1]

The Friends of the People refused to believe that
petitioning was futile, and shut their eyes to the fact that
the country, as well as the Commons, was turning against
them. A few weeks after the rejection of their petition
they decided to issue an appeal to the people calling upon
them to renew their petitions for reform. They believed
that the people were in favour of it, and that if they dinned
their grievances into the ear of Parliament all might not
be lost.[2] It was a delusive hope. If proof were wanting,
it was forthcoming on the last day of the month, when a
Whig member moved for a committee to inquire whether
the provisions made by the revolution settlement of 1689,
"for securing the responsible exercise of the executive
authority; for securing a real independent and faithful
representation of the commons in Parliament; and for
securing a fair and impartial administration of justice in
the courts of law," had been "by any means invalidated
or taken away." "The glorious revolution in 1688" to
which appeal was made, is still, on occasion, a trump card.
In 1793 it took no tricks. The proposer of the motion
could not muster a dozen supporters in the division lobby,
and the debate excited so little interest that not a quarter
of the ministerialists took the trouble to be present to vote
him down.[3]

[1] May 6 and 7, 1793.—*C. J.* XLVIII. 739–43, 749 ; *Parl. Hist.* XXX,
787–925. Authentic Copy of a Petition praying for a Reform in Parliament and presented to the House of Commons by Charles Grey, Esq.,
on Monday, May 6, 1793 ; and signed by the members of the Society of
the Friends of the People associated for the purpose of obtaining a
Parliamentary Reform ; also *Wyvill Papers*, III. 269–92.

[2] May 25, Authentic copy, etc. pp. 15–16.

[3] Friday, May 31. Mr. Wharton was the proposer of the motion.
Yeas 11, Noes 71.—*C. J.* XLVIII. 825 ; *Parl. Hist.* XXX. 961–5.

The political societies were now approaching the crisis of their history. On the 5th of March, 1793, the Norwich Society suggested to both the London Corresponding Society and the Society for Constitutional Information that, having in view the failure of petitions to Parliament and the doubtful policy of addressing the king, a convention of delegates from the reforming societies would be the wisest method of advancing their cause.[1] The reader is already aware that this plan was not borrowed from the French, but was the product of English political conditions, and had been adopted by the economical reformers when the French Revolution was still but a distant vision, seen of few. Both societies were inclined to look upon the suggestion with favour.[2] A similar suggestion came a few weeks later from Edinburgh,[3] and it was at a convention of delegates from all the Scottish reform associations that Muir had read the address from the United Irishmen for which he was indicted at his trial.[4] But for a time the movement for a larger convention lagged. The Friends of the People expressly disapproved of it, as "very improper in the circumstances, and likely to operate to the disadvantage of the cause."[5] On the 29th of October, 1793, however, there assembled at Edinburgh an association which called itself "The General Convention of the Friends of the People," but which afterwards took the name of "The British Convention of the Delegates of the People associated to obtain Universal Suffrage and Annual Parliaments."[6] "The landholder," ran the summons, "is called upon to coalesce with the Friends of the People, lest his property be soon left untenanted; the merchant, lest the commerce of the country be annihilated; the manufacturer whose laudable industry has been arrested in its progress; the unemployed citizen; the great mass of labouring and now starving poor; and, finally, all the rabble—are called upon by the remembrance

---

[1] *C. J.* XLIX. 706, 670.
[2] *Ib.* 670, 710, 601-2, 706-7; *S. T.* XXIV. 411-13, 548-9, 551-4.
[3] *Ib.* 36-9, 407-10; *C. J.* XLIX. 671-3, 708-9.
[4] *Life of Muir*, 8; *S. T.* XXII. 444-5.
[5] To Skirving, July 23, 1793.—*C. J.* XLIX. 672, 718.
[6] *Ib.* XXIII. 391.

of their patriotic ancestors who shed their blood in the cause of freedom, and to whose memories even the enemies of that cause are compelled to pay an involuntary tribute of applause." [1]   One of the leaders of the Scots reformers suggested to Hardy that the English reformers should join them.   Hardy was pleased with the idea, and asked for an official invitation,[2] which was therefore sent; [3] and the convention was adjourned to allow of the arrival of the English delegates.[4]

Several English societies sent representatives.   By universal consent the most brilliant of the band was Joseph Gerrald, a gentleman, a scholar and an orator, who was sent to represent both the London Corresponding Society and the Society for Constitutional Information.   The son of an Irish gentleman who had settled in the West Indies, Gerrald was born, it would appear, at St. Kitts, and he was certainly of the warm and enthusiastic temperament that the memory of Cumberland's *West Indian* tempts us to look for in his race.   At twelve he was left without parents, though not without resources, and he was brought up in the belief that he would be a wealthy man.   He was taught by Dr. Parr, and according to an anecdote which it would be cruel to condemn as apocryphal, Parr once told another brilliant pupil, Richard Brinsley Sheridan, that Gerrald was by far the cleverest fellow he had ever educated.   Somehow Gerrald's fortune disappeared, though it is not clear whether he squandered it himself in the first joy of possession, or whether, as is more likely, it was swallowed up by the greedy jaws of Chancery.   It is certain that Gerrald found himself in embarrassed circumstances.   He emigrated to America, practised at the Bar in Pennsylvania, seems by some rapid means to have restored his shattered fortunes, and returned to England a comparatively rich man.   He was now a young widower of

---

[1] *S. T.* XXIII. 511 ; Cockburn, I. 247–8.

[2] *C. J.* XLIX. 673, 713–14 ; *S. T.* XXIV. 39–40 ; 420–1.

[3] *Add. MSS.* 27812, fo. 73 ; *S. T.* XXIV. 421–2.

[4] The original convention seems to have adjourned on Nov. 1, 1793. Apparently the English delegates did not arrive till the next day.   But the standing committee endorsed the action of the secretary, who recalled the Scottish delegates to a second convention, which was opened on Nov. 19, 1793.—*Ib.* XXIII. 413–16.

perhaps rather more than thirty-two years of age, and was devoting himself enthusiastically to the advocacy of reform.[1]

Maurice Margarot, who was delegated both from the London Corresponding Society and from the society at Norwich, has already been mentioned as the author of the first published address of the London Corresponding Society. He was a man of much personal charm, an able writer and an eloquent speaker, but plausible rather than reliable. His whole history is a little mysterious, but it is clear that he was not free from charlatanry, that he was not always faithful to his colleagues, and that he was almost as dangerous a friend as William Godwin or Leigh Hunt.[2]

Brown, who arrived late, was the representative of Sheffield, but was afterwards commissioned to act also for the society at Leeds. Little is known of him beyond what may be gleaned from a letter sent to warn the Edinburgh authorities of his dangerous character by an irate master-cutler, whose name has unhappily been obliterated. According to this hostile witness, Brown was a strolling player who had married an Irish lady of considerable means. Her fortune he had long since dissipated, and finally he had found himself in prison for debt. He had been released through the liberality of "the Gentlemen in trade at Sheffield," but since his liberation he had been sowing sedition amongst the working mechanics and making trouble, said his angry critic, between master and man, to the great loss of the former. Beyond the fact, however, that a master cutler did not like him and regarded

---

[1] *Political Martyrs of Scotland.* 26–7. Gerrald, A Fragment : containing some account of the Life of the Devoted Citizen who was sent as a delegate to the British Convention at Edinburgh by the London Corresponding Society, for acting in which Capacity he is now transported to Botany Bay for Fourteen Years ! ! ! London : Printed for the Author, and sold by John Smith, Portsmouth St., Lincoln's Inn Fields ; who is just discharged from Newgate after having been detained there for SEVEN MONTHS on a supposed charge of *High Treason*. Entered at Stationers' Hall [Price Sixpence].—B. M., E. 2078.

[2] One obituary notice tells us that he was born in Devonshire. The *Examiner* declares that he was of a noble family, originally from Rome, and that he was educated at Geneva. These obituaries are preserved in *Add. MSS.* 27816, fo 221.

him as ungrateful to the gentlemen in trade at Sheffield, Brown's history is unknown.[1]

Of Charles Sinclair, who, along with Gerrald, represented the Society for Constitutional Information, even less is known. We learn from evidence given before the Privy Council that he was quite a boy. The witness was, indeed, surprised to see him at the meetings of the society, but would appear not to have questioned his title to be present, because he "considered him as a Friend and acquaintance of Lord Daer,"[2] a reforming Scots peer who corresponded with Thomas Hardy.

Thomas Briellat, a pump-maker in a small way of business in the Hackney Road, lent his field to the London Corresponding Society for the election of their delegates. Only by the greatest care on the part of the leaders of the society was it possible to avoid disorder, which the magistrates showed themselves inclined rather to provoke than to prevent. The delegates were peaceably elected, "to consult and deliberate on the best means of obtaining a thorough reform in Parliament."[3] Briellat was, however, proceeded against for sedition, and sentenced to twelve months' imprisonment and a fine of £100.[4]

The instructions to delegates of the Corresponding Society forbade them on any account to "depart from the original Object and principles of the Society, namely, the obtaining annual Parliaments and universal Suffrage by rational and lawful means." Payment of members was also admitted as an object, and it was declared permissible to resist any attempt "to prohibit Associations for the purpose of Reform."[5]

"The Delegates are instructed," said the Constitutional

---

[1] Sheffield, Dec. 24, 1793, apparently to the Procurator-Fiscal.— H. O. $\frac{182}{9}$.

[2] Evidence of Christopher Hull, May 30, 1794.—*P. C. R.* 33 Geo. III. 273 275.

[3] Oct. 24, 1793.—*Add. MSS.* 27812, ff. 76-8 ; 27814, ff. 56-60 ; 27809, ff. 269.

[4] *Ib.* 27814, fo. 59 ; 27809, fo. 269 ; *S. T.* XXII. 909-54 ; Richter's annotations to the First Report from the Committee of Secrecy, interleaf 6, opposite p. 14.

[5] *Add. MSS.* 27812, ff. 75-6 ; *C. J.* XLIX. 673 ; *S. T.* XXIV. 41-2, 423-4.

Society, "to assist in bringing forward and supporting any Constitutional Measure for procuring a real Representation of the Commons of Great Britain in Parliament. That in specifying the Redress to be demanded of existing Abuses the Delegates ought never to lose Sight of the Two essential Principles—General Suffrage and Annual Representation, together with the unalienable Right in the People to reform. And that a reasonable and known compensation ought to be made to the Representatives of the Nation by a National Contribution." [1]

Travelling expenses and three guineas a week were allowed to each delegate. The Corresponding Society found this a serious expenditure to face, and had to appeal to the public for help.[2] John Thelwall, orator, poet and man of letters, had recently joined the society, though it was not until months afterwards that he subscribed its full creed of universal suffrage and annual Parliaments.[3] Thelwall hired a room first in Southwark, and afterwards at the Three Kings in the Minories, in which he began a course of lectures, the first of which was "On the moral tendency of a System of Spies and Informers." Police officers were eavesdropping, but, to their great chagrin, found Thelwall too diplomatic to give them a decent excuse for interference. The profit of those lectures was devoted to the support of the society's delegates to the convention.[4]

Thelwall considered it a misfortune of the cause of reform that the name "convention," to which a popular stigma was attached, chanced to be the one selected for the meeting of delegates and "became the *war-whoop* of the tribe in power."[5] There is no evidence that the Convention had any other object than it professed. All the recommendations and decisions minuted are peaceable, though many are rash. Some members at least saw the

[1] *C. J.* XLIX. 602, 694 ; *S. T.* XXIV. 558, cf. 556-7.
[2] Address to the Friends of Peace and Parliamentary Reform.—*Add. MSS.* 27812, fo. 79.
[3] *Life*, by Mrs. Thelwall, I. 115-16.
[4] *Ib.* I. 122-5, 128, 130. 133-6 ; *Add. MSS.* 27812, fo. 79; *S. T.* XXIV. 734 ; Thelwall's printed "Lectures." Some of the small posters by which these lectures were advertised are still extant.
[5] *Life*, by Mrs. Thelwall, I. 116.

error of giving their enemies a handle against them,[1] but
this show of moderation was held to be the cloak of most
insidious designs against the established order.[2]

About fifty societies, most of which must have been
small, were represented at the Convention.[3] It lasted, in
all, fourteen days, and its total funds, most of which must
have been swallowed up by its known expenses, appear
on calculation to have been £44 4s. 3¼d.,[4] not by any
means a deep war-chest for an organised revolution.
Cockburn, who was a young man at the time, and was
powerfully impressed by the proceedings of the reformers
and their oppressors, devoted himself in later life to the
discussion of the case in one of those rare productions, an
interesting law-book. He had exceptional facilities for
gaining information, and yet could discover no other
design than the conventionals professed. They proposed
no other violence than discussion and agitation.[5]

The delegates of the London Corresponding Society
were forming plans of a great tour of propagandism in
favour of reform,[6] and offering other ambitious suggestions, when the Convention was broken up by the authorities. Only a nominal resistance was offered, and the
assembly dispersed without disorder, after making arrangements for the calling of a new convention if liberty were
further endangered.[7]

The second series of sedition trials at once followed,
and the charges in each case amounted substantially to
responsibility for the British Convention and its acts.
William Skirving, who had been a prime mover in the
Convention, if not its originator, was first tried. Skirving,
the son of a respectable farmer at Liberton, near Edinburgh, had been educated at Edinburgh University for
the Secessionist ministry, but had abandoned the idea of
becoming a minister; and after spending some time as a

[1] *C. J.* XLIX. 719-23 ; *S. T.* XXIII. 397, 403, 408-9, 410, 412, 430.
[2] *Ib.* 401-3, 407, 423 ; cf. 440, 465.
[3] *Ib.* 391-3, 413, 440 ; cf. 414, 394, 396, 413, 418.
[4] *Ib.* XXIII. 407-41, passim.
[5] Cockburn, *Examination of Trials for Sedition in Scotland*, I. 223-5.
[6] *C. J.* XLIX. 723-4 ; *S. T.* XXIV. 426-93, XXV. 206-9 ; *Add. MSS.*
27812, fo. 79.
[7] *C. J.* XLIX. 724-5; *S. T.* XXIV. 432-5.

tutor in the family of Sir Alexander Dick of Prestonfield, he had become a farmer. The theory of farming interested Skirving at least as much as the practice. He wrote on agriculture, published, in 1792, a *Husbandman's Assistant*, and once offered himself as a candidate for the Chair of Agriculture in the University of Edinburgh.[1] When societies began to be formed in and about Edinburgh to promote a reform in Parliament, Skirving became one of the leading reformers. But even a Government spy had to allow that Skirving and his fellows were well behaved, though he regarded their good behaviour as a most suspicious circumstance. ". . . The most conspicuous characters (Mr. Skirving for one) industriously circulate letters recommending moderation of Speech in the meetings as the most efficacious way of deceiving the Agts. (*sic*) of Gov^t. (*sic*) into a State of inactivity and false security." There was no escape from the dilemma which this informer proposed: did one advocate parliamentary reform, that was treason; did one keep silence, or set a watch upon one's tongue, that was the sly deceitfulness of "political expediency."[2]

Skirving certainly did not escape. His accusers, indeed, somewhat overreached themselves, as they imputed to him treason whilst formally charging him with sedition : a legal error which ought to have secured his acquittal. His judges assumed from the first that parliamentary reform and universal suffrage were treasonable objects; that the Convention was meant as a literal imitation of the French Convention; and that it was designed to rival the English Parliament. Conviction was, therefore, inevitable, if the jury could be persuaded to take the same view. It had been carefully picked, and was not even in need of persuasion. Skirving was convicted, and sentenced to transportation for fourteen years.[3] "My Lords," said the convict, "I know that what has been done these two days will be re-judged; that is my comfort and all my hope."[4]

[1] The Trial of William Skirving, Secretary to the British Convention . . . for Sedition, with an original memoir and notes. Glasgow, 1836.— B. M. 6573 a.a. 5 ; *Political Martyrs*, 21.
[2] Robert Watt to the Lord Advocate, Feb. 9, 1793.—H. O. Scotland, 1^2^2.
[3] *S. T.* XXIII. 391, etc. ; Cockburn, I. 222–92 ; cf. 124.
[4] *Ib.* 602 ; *Pol. Martyrs*, 1.

Maurice Margarot was also entitled to acquittal if the charges of the prosecution, substantially the same as those against Skirving, were just. He was charged with moving a resolution to persist in the consideration of ways and means of securing reform, "until compelled to desist by a superior force." [1] This resolution is not in the minutes of the Convention; it was not proved that it ought to have been inserted in any of the blanks in them; and the passage was taken from an unauthorised, though friendly, report. One of the judges objected that if people were allowed to point out the imperfections of Government and place them "in a strong light," no one could tell where it would end.[2] Having in view the conduct of the Scottish judges, there is reason to retort that they loved darkness rather than light, because their deeds were evil. Margarot was sentenced to transportation for fourteen years.[3]

Sinclair's case was the same as those of Skirving and Margarot, except in result.[4] He had gone home to England, but returned to Edinburgh to stand his trial,[5] amid the great enthusiasm of the reformers for their supposed martyr. But after some legal arguments the case dropped; Sinclair had, in fact, become a Government spy.[6] It does not seem probable that he intended treachery from the first. If he did, he could not have been more successful in hoodwinking his associates. Most likely he was a plausible but weak young man, who enjoyed the reputation of a martyr without daring to face the martyrdom.

The case of Joseph Gerrald was on all-fours with those of Margarot and Skirving. Gerrald was sufficiently well off to have discharged his bail, without returning to Scotland. He preferred to face the charge, and, indeed, made an eloquent defence; but this only provoked Braxfield to declare that he was "a very dangerous member of society,"

---

[1] On this point see Cockburn, II. 4.   [2] *Ib.* 22.

[3] *Ib.* II. 1-32. The London Corresponding Society seems to have done its best to render financial assistance to Margarot.—*S. T.* XXIV. 482.

[4] *Ib.* XXIII. 771-802.

[5] Manifesto of the Society for Const. Information to its Members.—*Ib.* XXIV. 204-5.

[6] It is so stated in Cockburn, II. 34-40, but there is little evidence as to Sinclair.

with "eloquence enough to persuade the people to rise in arms." [1] Like Skirving and Margarot, he was sentenced to transportation for fourteen years. Campbell, the poet, heard Gerrald's defence, and, stirred by his eloquent and moving peroration, turned round to a stranger standing near him, exclaiming, "By Heaven, sir, that is a great man!" "Yes, sir," answered the stranger; "he is not only a great man, but he makes every other man feel great who listens to him." [2]

Real treason was proved against Robert Watt, a most impudent and imprudent Government agent, in the pay of Dundas and the Lord Advocate, to whose reports the authorities owed, as we have seen, a good deal of their knowledge of the proceedings of the reformers in Edinburgh and its neighbourhood. With the conviction of the leading reformers and the collapse of the British Convention Watt found his occupation gone. Somehow he seems, however, to have got under his control a derelict committee of the British Convention, which he made the cloak of his endeavours to plot treason and to involve others against whom he might inform. He became responsible for the manufacture of a small quantity of arms, proposed to seize Edinburgh Castle, and drew into the conspiracy another man called Downie, though he failed to ensnare the real reformers. In his eagerness to prove treason against others, Watt had made plain his own guilt. Unfortunately, also, he put the price of his treason too high, and Dundas refused to purchase so extravagant a luxury.

Robert Dundas of Arniston, to whom it fell, as Lord Advocate, to prosecute Watt and Downie, misliked his task. He may have been intimidated by threatening letters. One such letter is amusing. The writer says that the Lord Advocate's unpopularity had been increased by his cruel treatment of Muir, Skirving and Margarot. A few more trials would render him "perfectly odious," and it would "then be reckoned honourable to deprive Society of such a *Pest*." Britain should not lack its Charlotte

[1] *S. T.* XXIII. 803 *et seq.*; Cockburn, II. 40-132; cf. *William Godwin and his Friends*, I. 125-8.
[2] Beattie's *Campbell*, I. 88.

Corday; "some Female hand will direct the Dagger that will do such an important Service." The letter has been taken seriously by a modern writer, but it was signed "Tabitha Bramble," and it can scarcely be imagined that in the eighteenth century a Scotsman failed to catch the allusion to *Humphrey Clinker*.[1]

But it is not really likely that the Lord Advocate shirked the prosecution through fear of pseudonymous correspondents. It is far more probable that he felt a twinge of conscience, and could not entirely absolve himself of blame for his early encouragement of Watt in the courses which led him to his doom. He would have liked an English barrister to take the case completely out of his hands, and he asked for a special commission to try the prisoners, and another judge, of less exceptional temper than the Lord Justice Clerk, to preside over the trials. ". . . *Entre nous*," he wrote to Henry Dundas, "I would prefer a Commission, were it only for the Reason that the President or Chief Baron would in that way fall to preside in place of the violent and intemperate Great man who sits in the Justiciary, and whose present state of Health and Spirits is such as to afford no chance of his being more soberly inclined in his Demeanour than he was last Winter." The Lord Advocate obtained part of his desire. Watt and Downie were tried by a special commission of oyer and terminer, over which presided Ilay Campbell, Lord Succoth, Lord President of the Court of Session, and John Anstruther, the English barrister for whom the Lord Advocate had asked, was sent down to assist in the prosecution, but Robert Dundas himself was compelled, after all, to lead for the Crown.[2]

Young Walter Scott came up to town specially "to be present at the trial of the Edinburgh traitors." It "dis-

---

[1] Tabitha Bramble to the Lord Advocate, Jan. 23, 1794.—H. O. $\frac{102}{10}$. The greater part of the letter is printed in Omond's *Lives of the Lord Advocates*, II. 196-7. Were Watt and his associates the unknown persons who tried to get financial aid from the French Government for the Scots reformers, or some pretended Scots reformers? See letter, enclosed in Francis Drake to Lord Grenville, dated Paris, Jan. 31, 1794.— *H. M. C.* Rep. XIV. App. V. 514.

[2] Robert to Henry Dundas (endorsed "private") June 20, 1794. —H. O. $\frac{102}{11}$.

played to the public the most atrocious and deliberate plan
of villainy which has occurred, perhaps, in the annals of
Great Britain." "It strikes me, upon the whole," he told
Miss Christian Rutherford, "that the plan of these miscreants might, from its very desperate and improbable
nature, have had no small chance of succeeding. . . ." [1]
Both Watt and Downie were found guilty, but Downie was
recommended to mercy : a recommendation which could
not be disregarded, said the Lord Advocate, though to
grant a free pardon would be equally inexpedient.[2] Watt
petitioned for mercy on the ground that all his acts were
performed with a single eye to the collection of information
for the Lord Advocate.[3] The Court made a report on the
case which was definitely against mercy to Watt and not
very favourable towards clemency to Downie.[4] Downie
was first reprieved and then pardoned, though opinion in
Edinburgh seems to have been against clemency to a man
who had plotted the assassination of the most distinguished
inhabitants of the city.[5] For Watt there was no mercy.
Walter Scott stayed a night in town to see him hanged.
The full and nauseous ritual of an execution for treason
does not appear to have been observed, but Scott reports
that "it was a very solemn scene." "The pusillanimity of
the unfortunate victim was astonishing, considering the
boldness of his nefarious plans." [6]

The fact that Watt had been a paid spy of the Government was not so evident then as it is certain now, and there
can be little doubt that his execution helped to inspire
terror. Though he had never been a trusted member of
the reforming party, the fate of Watt could be pointed to
as the inevitable end of all those who were so wicked as

[1] Scott to Miss C. Rutherford, Sept. 5, 1794.—*Lockhart*, ed. 1851, I. 308–9.
[2] R. Dundas to Portland.—H. O. $\frac{102}{11}$.
[3] John MacRitchie, Writer, to the Duke of Portland ; and petition of Robert Watt, Sept. 19, 1794.—H. O. $\frac{102}{11}$.
[4] Judges of the Commission of Oyer and Terminer to Portland, Sept. 25, 1794.—H. O. $\frac{102}{11}$.
[5] Lord Advocate to (?) H. Dundas, Oct. 13, 1794.—H. O. $\frac{102}{11}$; Walter Scott to Miss C. Rutherford.—*Lockhart*, I. 313.
[6] [Oct. or Nov.] 1794, Scott to Miss C. Rutherford, *ib.* I. 313 ; *Ann. Reg.* 1794, *Chron.* 28–9 ; *Mem. of Hardy*, 115, 120–1 ; A Vindication of the London Corresponding Society, 10–11.

to meddle with parliamentary reform. The reform movement in Scotland was put down by the sedition trials and
by the trials of Watt and Downie. The sentences on Muir
and Palmer, Gerrald and Skirving, "assured every man
that if he dared to show his thoughts, either by speaking
or writing in favour of good government, or of any
approximation thereto—Botany Bay would be his future
residence." [1]

The innocent suffered scarcely less than the guilty.
Muir and Palmer, Skirving and Margarot, were kept for
some time upon the hulks in the Thames, where they
suffered a good deal in health. They were visited by many
public men; every effort was made to save them; and it
was but slowly and reluctantly that their friends could
bring themselves to believe that the Government intended
to carry out the sentence of the Scots Courts. [2] Five or
six hundred pounds was raised for the service of Palmer,
Muir and Skirving, and also of Margarot, "who, as a joint
sufferer, was not to be overlooked, though his general
character was not so high as the others." [3] They were
taken down to Portsmouth, and at the end of April or
beginning of May set sail on the *Surprize* transport for
Botany Bay. [4]

Towards the end of the year rumours reached England
of disturbances on the *Surprize*. [5] Skirving, Palmer and
some of the other prisoners were charged with conspiring
to murder the master and crew. Margarot, who had formed
an intimacy with the captain of the ship, and had, in consequence, been shunned by his former associates, was
believed to be the real author of this monstrous accusation. [6]

---

[1] Place to Harrison, Feb. 15, 1842.—*Add. MSS.* 27810, fo. 91.
[2] See Theophilus Lindsey to Toulmin, Feb. 20 and March 8, 1794.—
Belsham, *Mem. of Lindsey*, 355 note.
[3] *Ib.* 353 note and 354 note.
[4] Lindsey to Toulmin, May 3, 1794.—*Ib.* 355 note.
[5] Lindsey to Toulmin, Nov. 8 and Dec. 15, 1794.—*Ib.* 357 note.
[6] Muir, Palmer, and Skirving to Jeremiah Joyce, Nov. 9, 1794.—
Narrative of the Sufferings, x–xii note. If the conspiracy was not
entirely imaginary I am inclined to suspect that Margarot himself was
the guilty person. See a memorandum of March 13, 1794 (enclosed in a
letter from Francis Drake to Lord Grenville, *H. M. C. Rep.* XIV. App. V.
543-4), which seems to show that his name was more familiar to the
French Government than were the names of his associates.

The most barbarous treatment was meted out to the alleged conspirators. "In the torrid zone," says Palmer, "when I could not bear the covering of my shirt, Mr. Skirving and I were shut up in a box six feet square, and not suffered to pass the threshold." Palmer paints a fearful picture of the colony of New South Wales as he first found it, but fortunately Governor Hunter arrived soon afterwards, and discipline was restored.[1] The country itself he found more pleasant than some of its inhabitants. "The soil is capital, the climate delicious. . . . I never saw a place where a man could so soon make a fortune, and that by the fairest means—Agriculture." [2]

Governor Hunter formed a favourable impression of at least three of his prisoners. "They seem, all of them, gifted in the powers of conversation," he wrote home to a friend in Leith. "Muir was the first I saw. I thought him a sensible young man, of a very retired turn, which certainly his situation in this country will give him an opportunity of indulging. He said nothing on the severity of his fate, but seemed to bear his circumstances with a proper degree of fortitude and resignation. Skirving . . . appeared to me to be a sensible, well-informed man. . . . He is fond of farming, and has purchased a piece of ground and makes good use of it, which will, by and by, turn to his advantage. Palmer . . . is said to be a turbulent, restless-minded man. It may be so—but I must do him the justice to say that I have seen nothing of that disposition in him since my arrival." [3]

The story that Muir interested Washington is little er than an improbable legend, but there seems no ,ubt that in 1796 some American sympathisers sent a vessel to aid his escape from Botany Bay.[4] Unfortunately he suffered shipwreck, and it was not till he had undergone terrible privations that he at last reached Havannah. When he sailed from Havannah for Spain the vessel in

[1] Palmer to Lindsey, Sept. 15, 1795.—*Mem. of Lindsey*, 522-5.
[2] To Jeremiah Joyce, *A Narrative of the Sufferings* . . . etc., vi-vii note.
[3] Governor Hunter to a correspondent in Leith.—*Political Martyrs*, 16.
[4] Margarot says the ship was the *Otter*, Captain Davies. Margarot to Citizen Lorimont Goddard, April 27, 1796.—*Add. MSS*. 27816, fo. 110.

which he had taken passage was boarded by the crew of a British frigate, and Muir himself was wounded in the cheek by a splinter, which destroyed the sight of one eye. By the kindness of one of the British officers, an old friend who fortunately recognised him, he was enabled to get to Spain. There he received and accepted an invitation from the National Convention to proceed to France, and lived in that country, on the pension which was granted to him, till his death at Chantilly on the 29th of September, 1798.[1]

Palmer was equally unfortunate. When his time was served he purchased a vessel and sailed for England. Unluckily, the ship, a prize of war, proved leaky, and by an awkward mischance Palmer was compelled to put into its port of registry in the Spanish island of Guam. The vessel was, of course, seized. Palmer was detained as a prisoner of war, and died a captive in Guam.[2]

Skirving did not long survive his arrival in New South Wales;[3] Gerrald landed only to die. "I die in the best of causes," he said shortly before his death, "and I die, as you are my witnesses, without repining."[4]

Margarot was more fortunate than his fellows. He was the only one of the convicts who ever returned to England. On his return he visited Edinburgh, found his judges dead and all his jurors dead or missing, except one, to whom he gave a supper. "By this time the juryman had become a Whig and the convict a Tory."[5] Margarot seems to have made himself something of a nuisance to his former associates. He passed the evening of his days in poverty; his misery was aggravated by failing eyesight, and he became a charge upon the generosity of his friends[6]—a charge which would have been borne the more willingly if he could have cleared himself of the suspicion of

[1] *Life of Muir*, 34–8 ; *Mem. of Hardy*, 51 ; Mackenzie, *Reminiscences of Glasgow*, 96.

[2] Cockburn, I. 220 ; *Mem. of Hardy*, 49.

[3] *Ib.* 49.

[4] "He died a martyr to the liberties of his country, in the 36th year of his age," is said to be the inscription on his tombstone at Fair Cove, near Port Jackson.—*Political Martyrs*, 1.

[5] Cockburn, II. 32–3.

[6] See Hardy to Godwin, Nov. 9, 1802.—*Add. MSS.* 27816, fo. 79.

treachery to Skirving and Palmer.[1] When Margarot died on the 11th of November, 1815, at the advanced age of seventy,[2] the reformers raised close upon two hundred pounds for the relief of his widow.[3]

In 1837 a proposal was made to erect a memorial in Edinburgh to the political martyrs of 1793 and 1794. Joseph Hume took the lead and gave £25 towards the cost. Many distinguished men subscribed—Brougham, Grote and O'Connell, for example, gave £10 apiece; so did the Dukes of Bedford and Norfolk; whilst the lesser lights of the reforming party, Francis Place and Richard Potter, Joseph Parkes and Perronet Thompson, gave £5 each.[4] Legal difficulties caused some delay, but in due time the monument, a plain obelisk in the style of Cleopatra's Needle, was erected on Calton Hill. When it was finished, in May 1846, Lord Cockburn, who thought that "nothing that sticks up without smoking" looked ill in Edinburgh, noted that the pillar added to "the general picturesqueness" of the mass of which it was a part. There was still some natural hesitation about the inscription, for a public monument ought not to be a standing offence to any one, and there were those alive whose relatives had taken part, as advocates or judges, in the trials of the reformers. Eventually safety was sought in simplicity. "The stone is engraven on one side with these words: 'To the memory of Thomas Muir, Thomas Fyshe Palmer, William Skirving, Maurice Margarot, and Joseph Gerrald. Erected by the friends of Parliamentary Reform in England and Scotland, 1844.' And on another side are these words: 'I have devoted myself to the cause of the People; it is a good cause; it shall ultimately prevail; it

---

[1] See Hardy to Joyce, Jan. 12 ; Joyce to Hardy, Jan. 13 : Hardy to Joyce, Jan. 18, 1811 ; Joyce to Hardy, Jan. 30, 1815.—*Add. MSS.* 27816, ff. 80, 81, 82, 97. Newspaper cutting in *Add. MSS.* 27816, fo. 90, about a meeting on Oct. 20, 1814, to raise a subscription for Margarot. Resolutions reprinted in a circular, *ib.* 91–2.

[2] Obituary notice from the *Examiner*, Dec. 1815.—*Add. MSS.* 27816, fo. 221.

[3] From an undated list published in the *Examiner*, it appears that £189 13*s.* had been received by Mrs. Margarot. Quite possibly this is not the most complete account.—*Ib.* 225.

[4] Circular letter, *ib.* 27816, ff. 441–2 ; newspaper cutting, *ib.* 444. Lord Holland subscribed ; how much I have not found out.—*Ib.* 443.

shall finally triumph.'—Speech of Thomas Muir in the Court of Justiciary on the 30th of August, 1793. ' I know that what has been done these two days will be re-judged ! ' —Speech of William Skirving in the Court of Justiciary on the 7th of January, 1794. That is all."

"A sparing inscription" is Cockburn's comment. "How the judges' names are omitted I cannot understand. For it is, in truth, *their* monument." [1]

[1] Cockburn, II. 252. Macaulay, then M.P. for Edinburgh, avoided a visit to his constituency at the time the foundation stone of the memorial was being laid (August 1844) lest he should be forced to be present at the ceremony. "Though I by no means approve of the severity with which those people were treated, I do not admire their proceedings, nor should I choose to attend the ceremony." But Macaulay apparently believed that the transported reformers were republicans. Macaulay to Macvey Napier, Aug. 10, 1844.—Trevelyan's *Life of Macaulay*, ed. 1908, p. 468.

CHAPTER XIII

THE POLITICAL SOCIETIES UNDER THE BAN

JAN.—NOV. 1794

IT is deplorable, though hardly surprising, that the first of the Scottish sedition trials drew from the Constitutional Society a most impolitic address; hardly less, indeed, than a threat that if Government continued its policy the people would resort to violence.[1] But the manifesto issued by the Corresponding Society when it was known that its delegates were to be brought to trial—a manifesto which the Constitutional Society subsequently adopted[2]—whilst no less trenchant, was a much more diplomatic document,[3] offering a sound constitutional argument against the policy of intimidation and repression, and announcing the intention of calling a new convention. At a great meeting of the Corresponding Society held on the 20th of January, 1794, it was resolved "that upon the first Introduction of any Bill or Motion inimical to the Liberties of the People, such as for *Landing Foreign Troops in Great Britain or Ireland,* for suspending the *Habeas Corpus Act,* for proclaiming *Martial Law or for Preventing the People from Meeting in Societies for Constitutional Information,* or any Other Innovation . . . the General Committee shall forthwith arrange to call a General Convention of the People. . . ."[4] In this resolution the Society for Constitutional Information joined them.[5]

[1] Jan. 17, 1794.—*S. T.* XXIV. 558–9; *C. J.* XLIX. 602, 694.
[2] *Ib.* 695; *S. T.* XXIV. 559–60; cf. 566–7.
[3] Address of the London Corresponding Society, united for the purpose of obtaining Universal Suffrage and Annual Parliaments, etc. (Jan. 6, 1794).
[4] *Ib.* 7; *Life of Thelwall,* I. 273–4; cf. *Add. MSS.* 27814, fo. 61–7, 69, 86; *C. J.* XLIX. 603–4, 694–5; *S. T.* XXIV. 26, 41–8, 441–6.
[5] *Ib.* 371–2, 561–5; *C. J.* XLIX. 605–6, 695–6; Proceedings of the Society for Constitutional Information, cf. also *C. J.* XLIX. 726–7; *S. T.* XXIV. 480–1.

On the 14th of April, 1794, the London Corresponding Society held a General Meeting on the green at Chalk Farm, afterwards the scene of Moore's comic opera duel with Jeffrey. John Lovett (or Lovet), a hairdresser, presided, and one of the chief speakers was John Thelwall. Despite the fact that a large crowd assembled, the meeting was perfectly orderly. The promoters of the gathering complained, however, that it was through no fault of the local magistrates that order was maintained. Bow Street runners, spies and even the magistrates themselves, it is alleged, sought to provoke the reformers by insults, and attempted to excite disturbances. Although it was a hot day and many of those present must have walked long distances to the place of meeting, the magistrates forced the innkeeper to shut his doors, and to supply refreshments to none but themselves, in the hope, as the reformers believed, that his refusal would create a disturbance and afford an excuse for calling in the military who were ready at hand. The reformers, no doubt, put the worst possible interpretation upon the actions of the magistrates. Those actions seem, indeed, to have been almost incredibly foolish, and forcibly recall the provocative stupidity of the Birmingham magistrates on the night of the 14th of July, 1791. If the magistrates hoped to see a disturbance their hopes were disappointed. Order was maintained throughout, and no excuse was afforded for an appeal to force.[1]

A large assembly, particularly in the open air, is apt to prove unwieldy, but the members of the London Corresponding Society had trained themselves in procedure and were able to get through a considerable amount of business. They voted an address to Joseph Gerrald, their "beloved and respected friend and fellow-citizen, a martyr to the glorious cause of equal representation." They denounced by resolution the recent proceedings in the Scottish courts, where the doctrines and practices of Star Chamber had been "revived and aggravated," and where sentences had been pronounced which must, they said, "strike deep into the heart of every man the melancholy conviction that Britons are no longer free." Not merely did they express

[1] *Add. MSS.* 27814, fo. 75.

agreement with the conduct of their delegates at Edinburgh, but in one sweeping phrase they declared that "the whole proceedings" of the British Convention were such as to claim their "approbation and applause."

They condemned "the late rapid advances of despotism in Britain," the invasion of public security, and "the violation of all those provisions of the Constitution intended to protect the people against the encroachments of power and prerogative." "Any attempt to violate those yet remaining laws" by which the security of Englishmen is preserved should, they declared, be considered as dissolving the compact between the nation and its governors, and as "driving them to an immediate appeal to that incontrovertible maxim of eternal justice, that the safety of the people is the supreme and, in case of necessity, the only law." It had been rumoured that foreign troops were to be used in "an outrageous attempt to overawe and intimidate the free spirit of Britons." One threatened danger, it would seem, had already passed. Hessians and Hanoverians did not "people the barracks which everywhere insult the eyes of Britons," and it was afterwards roundly asserted in the Privy Council that there had never been any intention to employ foreign troops in England. But the use which had been made of Hessian troops in the American war, and the further probability that foreigners who had taken refuge in England might be given military employment, lent some colour of plausibility to the rumour. It was therefore resolved that "with or without the consent of Parliament" no foreigners should be armed or drilled on British soil, and that "no pretence whatever ought to induce the people to submit to so unconstitutional a measure."

To many people, there can be no doubt, the whole of the proceedings at Chalk Farm seemed extremely alarming. In the protest of the reformers against the employment of foreign troops, and in their declaration that, in the last resort, the safety of the people was the only law, the Committee of Secrecy afterwards saw "a direct Invitation to the People to resist Measures then in the Contemplation of the Legislature, and expressly that they ought equally to be resisted, whether adopted with or without the Consent of

Parliament." The Committee plainly thought that the London Corresponding Society contemplated a resort to illegal measures of some sort. But there is no proof of any such intention. It is far more likely that it was illegal to employ foreign troops in England than that it was illegal to protest against their employment. And the last of the resolutions adopted at Chalk Farm makes it clear that the reformers appealed not to force, but to reason. It is a ringing profession of faith in the ultimate triumph of constitutional agitation for reform. "Whatever may be the interested opinions of hereditary senators or packed majorities of pretended representatives," "truth and liberty, in an age so enlightened as the present, must be invincible and omnipotent." [1]

Though both the Society for Constitutional Information and the London Corresponding Society faced the situation bravely, credit must be given to the Corresponding Society both for the greater clearness of ideas and greater vigour of determination; as well as for the less fallible discretion.[2] At the annual dinner of the Constitutional Society at the Crown and Anchor on the 2nd of May, 1794, three hundred persons were present.[3] The

---

[1] For the proceedings at Chalk Farm, see *Add. MSS.* 27814, fo. 70–5; *S. T.* XXIV. 50–3, 735–41; *C. J.* XLIX. 606–10. A number of draft resolutions, which were put in as evidence against Hardy, at his trial, were not put to the meeting at Chalk Farm. In Thelwall's *Life* it is stated that the drafts were definitely rejected by the committee of the London Corresponding Society. One of these resolutions called for a convention. Another declared the words " I declare it is not lawful upon any pretence whatever to take up arms against the King," to be no longer part of the oath of allegiance. This draft resolution is set forth in the Report of the Committee of Secrecy as evidence of the treasonable intentions of the society. But the statement was legally accurate. The declaration against the lawfulness of taking up arms against the king had been required by "*An Act for ordering the Forces in the several Counties of this Kingdom*" (13 and 14 Car. II. Cap. III. § 18), and by "*An Act for the Uniformity of Publick Prayers*," etc. (13 and 14 Car. II. Cap. IV. § 9), but these enactments had been repealed, at the Revolution of 1688, by "*An Act for the abrogating of the Oaths of Supremacy and Allegiance, and appointing other Oaths*" (1 Guill. and Mar. Cap. VIII. § 11). It was undoubtedly waste of time to protest against statutes that had already been repealed for a century, but it was not treasonable. See *C. J.* XLIX. 663–4; *S. T.* XXIV. 870–1; *Life of Thelwall*, I. 171–2.

[2] Cf. *S. T.* XXIV. 561; XXV. 206 with XXIV. 802.

[3] It is probable that many of those present at the dinner were not members of the society.

chair was taken by Mr. John Wharton, M.P. for Beverley, who must have been specially invited to preside, for this, he says, was the only occasion on which he was present at a meeting of the society. He thought, with reason, that some of the toasts were unwise, though from the knowledge he had of the members of the society he thought they should not be interpreted as disloyal. It may be admitted that, in May 1794, it was not wise to drink to the rights of man, with three times three, to toast "the armies contending for liberty," or to express the hope that the abettors of the war might be its victims; nor was it discreet of Horne Tooke to say that the society must either dissolve or change its name, since there was no longer any such thing as a Constitution in England. But Wharton answered rightly when he was asked what explanation was given of the toast, "The persecuted Patriots of England." "None," he told the Privy Council. "I did not think it required any, for I considered many of the persons alluded to in that Toast as persecuted persons." [1] The Constitutional Society seemed to flourish; [2] but this was, in fact, the last day of its vigour. It only claimed public notice again to protest, in 1795, against the extension of the law of treason and the restriction of the right of public meeting by the measures known as the Two Acts. [3]

Some time during the month of April a circular was sent to all the important societies for parliamentary reform asking them to join the London Corresponding Society in a Convention; [4] and there appears to have been a concensus of opinion in favour of the plan. [5] The Corresponding Society never concealed this design, and even after the arrest of its secretary maintained that it was legal, though no resolution approving of a convention was passed

[1] Evidence of John Taylor, May 17, 1794.— *P. C. R.* 33 Geo. III. 112–13 ; examination of John Wharton, May 22, 1794, *ib.* 163–8. The tickets for this dinner were sold at 7*s.* 6*d.—Ib.* 193.
[2] Proceedings, 9–12 ; *S. T.* XXIV. 571–2.
[3] Report . . . on the Treason and Sedition Bills.
[4] Undated, but April seems to have been the month of issue.—*C. J.* XLIX. 606 ; *S. T.* XXIV. 481–2 ; manifesto which begins, " The actual moment is arrived . . ."
[5] S. T. XXIV. 483–6 ; *C. J.* XLIX. 677–8, 727 ; cf. 660–1.

at the meeting at Chalk Farm on the 14th of April.[1] Gerrald, who was a member of the society, actually published a pamphlet in favour of a convention as the only means of saving the nation from ruin. The project was, at worst, an open secret, and would bear no possible interpretation of crime.

But in May 1794 what Hardy called the reign of the beast reached its height. A young barrister called Robert Plumer Ward, author of that once famous novel *Tremaine*, claimed long afterwards that it was he who, in 1794, gave the information which led the cabinet to determine at last upon the prosecution of the English reformers. According to the story, a watchmaker called Scott took Ward into his confidence and revealed to him a republican plot. No details are given, and no dates. Scott, so far as can be discovered, appears nowhere else in connection with the popular societies. If the supposed plot had a real existence, it had an existence which could not be proved, or the proofs would have been adduced at the coming trials, when they would have been an invaluable reinforcement of the slight amount of direct evidence that could be brought forward by the prosecution. Scott's recantation of his republican heresies reads, in fact, like an extract from a strained and artificial romance, and Ward's narrative, though based, no doubt, on information which he actually received, shows the hand of the creator of de Clifford and de Vere.[2]

The records of the Privy Council make it quite clear that it was, first, the meeting of the London Corresponding Society at Chalk Farm on the 14th of April; secondly, the annual dinner of the Society for Constitutional Information at the Crown and Anchor on the 2nd of May; and, lastly, the proposal to summon a convention, that precipitated the decision of the cabinet to prosecute the English reformers. At six o'clock on the morning of the 12th of May Thomas Hardy was arrested, and his house

---

[1] Specially *Life of Thelwall*, I. 171–2 ; *Add. MSS.* 27814, ff. 70–5 ; *C. J.* XLIX. 606–10; *S. T.* XXIV. 48–54, 735–9, 870–1. I admit, however, that this question might be argued.

[2] *Mem. of R. Plumer Ward*, I. 13–15.

and shop were turned upside down by the king's messenger and his subordinates in the search for incriminating
documents. "They ransacked trunks, boxes, drawers and
desk. Hundreds of letters and manuscript papers belonging to the London Corresponding Society were seized,
which they carried away in four silk handkerchiefs. And
many old and valuable private letters from kind friends
in America and other places. They were not satisfied with
letters and papers only, but they took books and pamphlets
which nearly filled a corn sack. Not a single article did
they *Mark*." Hardy's wife was in a delicate state of health
at the time, but the officers were afflicted with no inconvenient delicacy of feeling, and did not scruple to search
every nook and cranny of her sleeping-room whilst she
was still in bed. "When they had ransacked every place
in our bedroom that they thought fit, they then went into
the shop," says Hardy, "expecting, no doubt, to find
Treason Hatching among the Boots and Shoes." Later
they returned and made a second search for the Journal
of the Corresponding Society, but that they never found,
for it so happened that, by the merest chance, Hardy had
handed it, the night before, to the assistant secretary, in
order that he might make in it certain entries.[1]

An hour or two after the arrest of Hardy another
king's messenger arrested Daniel Adams, secretary of the
Society for Constitutional Information, and seized the
books and papers of that society, which he found stored
in two trunks. Adams "produced the Keys and unlocked
the Boxes himself."[2] He told the Privy Council, at the
examination, that he had no profession. "I live upon what
I have."[3] He had no interest in disorder and nothing to
conceal. He was perfectly frank, and gave the Council

---

[1] Hardy to Place, July 7, 1831. MS. letter prefixed to First Report
from The Committee of Secrecy, etc.—B. M., C. 61, b. 16 (1). Account
of the seizure of citizen Thomas Hardy.—*Mem. of Hardy*, 31-2 ; cf. *Life
of Cartwright*, I. 203. Hardy's wife died in child-bed whilst he was a
prisoner in the Tower. A letter from Hardy to Place, Aug. 17, 1831,
prefixed to the First Report, above mentioned, adds some details. The
messengers seized Hardy's pocket-book containing two bills of exchange,
one for £130, and another for £60, payable by G. Sutton, Esq., M.P., of
which Hardy was never afterwards able to obtain payment.

[2] May 12, 1794.—*P. C. R.* 33 Geo. III. 34-5.   [3] *Ib.* 35.

all the information he could.[1] But he was clear that the society was not in favour of calling an assembly of delegates by the odious name of convention, since "it was a Word not pleasant to the Ideas of People in general,"[2] and "as to Foreign Correspondence," "there never was any Foreign Correspondence."[3] Adams had nothing criminal to reveal, but he was a weak man and was anxious to placate his prosecutors, who, on their side, were anxious to get him to identify the books of the society. So, in July, a sort of bargain was struck. Adams swore an information authenticating the books of the Society for Constitutional Information, and by way of recompense he was released on bail and was never brought to trial.[4]

On the very day on which Hardy and Adams were arrested action was taken in Parliament. In response to a royal message declaring that certain societies intended to call "a pretended General Convention of the People, in Contempt and Defiance of the Authority of Parliament, and on Principles subversive of the existing Laws and Constitution, and directly tending to the Introduction of that System of Anarchy and Confusion which has fatally prevailed in France,"[5] the House of Commons ordered the appointment of a Committee of Secrecy to investigate the conspiracy.[6] The committee promptly reported that the proposed convention was intended "to supersede the House of Commons in its Representative Capacity, and to assume to itself all the Functions of a National Legislature."[7] A Bill giving the Government special power to detain

[1] May 12, 1794, *P. C. R.* 33 Geo. III. 35-37.

[2] *Ib.* 167. Confirmed by the evidence of John Pearson, *ib.* 183, and Thomas Thompson, M.P. for Evesham, *ib.* 160-3.

[3] May 19, 1794, *ib.* 122.

[4] July 3 and 7, 1794. Recognisances were entered into by himself in £1000 and by Susannah and Sarah Adams in £500 each, *ib.* 461, 473, 498-9, 499-500.

[5] *C. J.* XLIX. 586 ; cf. *Life of Thelwall*, I. 211-12.

[6] *C. J.* XLIX. 589, 594. This report was looked upon as an attempt to prejudice the trials.—Belsham, V. 150.

[7] *C. J.* XLIX. 609 ; cf. *S. T.* XXIV. 940. Lord Liverpool told Peel "that he had been a member of the Secret Committee of 1794, and that nothing came to light then which showed nearly so disaffected and seditious a feeling among the people" as existed in 1817.—Peel to Whitworth, Jan. 29, 1817, Parker's *Peel*, I. 237.

suspected persons was hurried through both Houses, and on the 23rd of May received the royal assent.[1]

A day was permitted to elapse after the arrest of Adams and Hardy, in the hope, it was believed, that there would be compromising attempts to escape;[2] but when it was found that the reformers showed no fear and intended to hold their ground, twelve others shared the fate of Hardy. Of these John Lovet, or Lovett, the hairdresser, who had been chairman of the meeting at Chalk Farm, and who "thought it a high honor to be in the Chair to so orderly and respectable a Company," was admitted to bail before any of the other prisoners were brought to trial, and no bill was returned against him by the Grand Jury which indicted the other prisoners.[3] Amongst the remaining eleven companions of Hardy there were all sorts and conditions of men. There was John Horne Tooke, who was personally acquainted with many of the political leaders of the day and occupied a foremost place in the eye of the nation, and there was Richard Hodgson, a Westminster hatter who was known as Hodgson the Jacobin.[4] John Richter and John Augustus Bonney, Matthew Moore and Thomas Wardle, were described as gentlemen, whilst John Baxter was a labourer.[5] Jeremiah Joyce was a Unitarian minister who lived with Lord Stanhope as tutor to his sons, and who was actually giving a lesson to his pupils at the moment of his arrest.[6]

Steward Kyd was a barrister-at-law of the Middle Temple,

---

[1] 34 Geo. III. Cap. LIV.—*C. J.* XLIX. 610-13, 622 ; *L. J.* XL. 203-6, 210 ; cf. *Add. MSS.* 27809, fo. 268.

[2] *Life of Thelwall,* I. 156-7.

[3] Examination of Lovet, May 16, 1794.—*P. C. R.* 33 Geo. III. 94. Admitted to bail, Oct. 10, 1794, *ib.* 34 Geo. III. 221-3. It is said that Lovett afterwards emigrated to New York, where he prospered.—*Add. MSS.* 27814, fo. 74.

[4] Gosling's evidence, *P. C. R.* 33 Geo. III. 123.

[5] *S. T.* XXIV. 232-3.

[6] Examination of Joyce, May 14, 1794, *P. C. R.* 61-4, 69 ; *Sermon* preached on . . . Feb. 23, 1794, by J. Joyce, Appendix 3-7. Rev. William Shepherd of Gateacre, was one of the friends permitted to visit Joyce in prison, July 3, 1794, *P. C. R.* 33 Geo. III. 460. The Rev. William Shepherd, LL.D., was ordained minister at Gateacre chapel August 4, 1791, and held the pastorate till his death, fifty-six years later, July 21, 1847. (Information kindly furnished by the present minister, the Rev. J. C. Hirst.)

the first volume of whose *Treatise on the Law of Corporations* had appeared in 1793. The last chapter of the second volume, which was published, with a dedication to Horne Tooke, whilst Kyd was a prisoner, was written in the Tower.[1] Kyd afterwards became notorious on account of his defence of the publisher of Paine's *Age of Reason*, but he was learned in the law rather than eloquent in speech, and though he made a good defence in that famous case, he was no match for a skilled pleader like Erskine, who persuaded the jury, in face of the contrary evidence of the pamphlet itself, that the *Age of Reason* was, in fact, blasphemous.[2] Thomas Holcroft had a recollection of the time when his mother dealt in greens and oysters, and he had himself been a stable-boy at Newmarket; but he had just caught the fancy of the town with his best-known play, *The Road to Ruin*, and was one of the popular playwrights of the hour.[3] John Thelwall has been mentioned before as a writer and lecturer. He was a man of eloquence and feeling, a poet and the friend of poets. "He is intrepid, eloquent and honest," wrote Coleridge a few years later. "Perhaps the only acting democrat that is honest, for the patriots are ragged cattle."[4] "We were once sitting in a beautiful recess in the Quantocks," wrote Coleridge in another passage which throws an interesting light on Thelwall's character, "when I said to him, ' Citizen John, this is a fine place to talk treason in.' ' Nay ! Citizen Samuel,' replied he, ' it is rather a place to make a man forget that there is any necessity for treason.' "[5]

[1] Examination of Kyd, May 29, June 4 and 6.—*P. C. R.* 33 Geo. III. 261–3, 301–2, 315–6, 322 ; Treatise on the Law of Corporations, by Stewart Kyd, Barrister-at-Law of the Middle Temple, 1793 and 1794.

[2] "The speeches of the Hon. Thomas Erskine in the Court of King's Bench, June 28, 1797, before the Rt. Hon. Lloyd, Lord Kenyon and a special jury on the trial, the King *versus* Thomas Williams for publishing the *Age of Reason*, written by Thomas Paine ; together with Mr. Stewart Kyd's Reply and Lord Kenyon's Charge to the Jury. London, printed for J. Debrett. 1797." Kyd was a friend of Erskine. A long account of the whole affair is given by Place in his Autobiography.—*Add. MSS.* 35143 ff. 34–52 ; especially ff. 38 and 43.

[3] Holcroft's *Recollections* are somewhat diffuse, but they can still be read with interest.

[4] S. T. Coleridge to Wade, 1797.—Cottle's *Reminiscences of S. T. C.* 148 ; *Early Recollections*, I. 255.

[5] *Table-Talk* (July 26, 1831), (ed. 1851), 105.

Such were the men who were now brought before the Privy Council to answer for their conduct, and who, later in the year, were put on trial for their lives on the charge of high treason. It is unfortunate that the minutes of Privy Council do not tell us who put the questions to the witnesses called before it. But some of the prisoners afterwards gave accounts of their examination, and these accounts, which agree in substance with the official record, sometimes tell us the names of the examinants. In one of them, for example, we catch a glimpse of Pitt behaving with the petulance of a spoilt child; [1] and another makes it clear that Dundas thought it no shame to bully a prisoner whose life, had he been less evidently innocent, might have been perilled by an incautious answer. [2] Many, indeed, of those who were brought before the council were subjected to a browbeating which was little short of nauseous. To get evidence against Thelwall, a simple youth of sixteen, whom he had employed as an amanuensis, was put through an examination by his rulers and governors which would have unnerved a case-hardened police witness. [3] A good deal of unjustifiable pressure was brought to bear upon Stewart Kyd in the hope that he might give evidence useful to the prosecution; [4] in the same way and with the same object a witness called John Pearson was badgered about from examination to examination, in a way which would have been impossible if the witnesses had been brought before a magistrate or protected by counsel. [5] In two cases these worrying tactics succeeded, for William Sharpe, an engraver, and John Williams, a wine merchant, were ultimately prevailed upon to lodge long informations. [6]

If ministers were determined to make out a case against the parliamentary reformers, the result of their endeavours might, perhaps, be held to excuse some loss of temper. Neither the prisoners nor their friends gave much satis-

[1] *Life of Thelwall*, I. 165–70.
[2] Bonney's examination in Appendix to Joyce's *Sermon*, 7–9 note.
[3] May 14, 1794, *P. C. R.* 33 Geo. III. 77–82.
[4] Examination of June 6, 1794, *ib.* 33 Geo. III. 315–16.
[5] *Ib.* 33 Geo. III. 319–21.
[6] *Ib.* 315–16, 349–53, 345–9.

faction to the hunters of treason and sedition. The Delphic Oracle itself could not have given less informing answers than were to be got from Dr. Joseph Towers, Price's old coadjutor, who for ten years had been a member of the Society for Constitutional Information.[1] John Pearce, an articled clerk, who was assistant-secretary of the Corresponding Society, declared in words that might almost have been echoed by Pitt himself, that "he had no view but that of Parliamentary Reform—he always thought the Society had nothing else in view, and if he had conceived that the society ever deviated from that he should not have consented to it."[2]

The prisoners, for the most part, declined to answer questions. Bonney asked to be committed so that the question of his guilt or innocence could be settled at once in a court of law; and no bullying on Dundas's part could get more from him than this.[3] A persistent attempt was made to entangle Joyce, whose only reply was that he was an accused person, and that he would answer no questions until he was protected by counsel.[4] Thelwall would not so much as tell the clerk how to spell his name. "I am bold in conscious innocence," he said, "and have nothing to answer;"[5] and his exasperated questioners had to abandon the interrogation in despair. Baxter was reminded that the members of the Corresponding Society "seemed to be persons of very inferior Station in Life, without any property," and yet they "voluntarily took great pains for reforming the State, as if what they thought or did could have any influence with the Nation," to which Baxter, though he was but a labourer, confronted by His Majesty's Privy Council, replied with honest bluntness, "that whatever they were, they were persons who thought they had a good right to their Opinions on public Matters."[6]

---

[1] June 14, 1794, *P. C. R.* 33 Geo. III. 366-9.
[2] June 2, 1794, *ib.* 295.
[3] App. to Joyce's *Sermon*, pp. 7-9 note.
[4] May 14, 1794, *P. C. R.* 33 Geo. III. 61-4 ; *Sermon*, 4-7.
[5] May 14, 1794, *P. C. R.* 33 Geo. III. 70-1.
[6] July 8, 1794, *P. C. R.* 33 Geo. III. 509. Baxter delivered a lecture in Nov. 1795, which was published as a pamphlet with the title " Resistance to Oppression, the Constitutional Right of Britons," etc.

Richter, a young man not yet twenty-five years of age, would probably have been flustered and scarcely able to find his tongue if a Cabinet Minister had stopped him in the street to ask the time of day. Not unnaturally he grew hot and excited when questioned before the Privy Council by Henry Dundas and the Solicitor-General. He begged for a glass of water. Dundas asked if he were alarmed. "No!" he replied. But, retorted the Solicitor-General—trying rather wickedly to snatch some advantage from his embarrassment—they had noticed that his voice failed him.[1] If he stumbled or hesitated in his replies it was from no sense of guilt. He had no object, he said, but a parliamentary reform, and if any of the society had any other object they had not his concurrence. "He understood"—it is the reporter, probably, who summarises —"that such reform would produce every sort of good." Asked if he had said that kings were useless, he replied that "it must be persons more hot than himself to say such things. . . . The society had no such object, nor any with whom he agreed personally." Asked if he had recommended strong measures in a speech which he had delivered on the night of Hardy's arrest, he replied that "he knew of none such but petitioning Parliament."[2] Pitt and Fox, Richmond and Sheridan, Wilberforce and Grey, Whigs in power and Whigs in opposition, could have answered no otherwise had they been catechised about their political faith.

With Tooke ministers felt themselves compelled to deal warily. When he was brought before the Council, Dundas told him in studiously diplomatic language that he was given an opportunity of explaining himself: "That the nature of the Treasonable Practices for which he had been apprehended, and of which it was conceived he was guilty, were that he had been a leading and active Member of Two Societies, the one the London Corresponding Society, and the other the Society for Constitutional Information; that the object of these Societies now evidently was to form a

---

[1] Richter's Narrative.—*Add. MSS.* 27816, ff. 473-87.

[2] May 16, 1794, *P. C. R.* 33 Geo. III. 95-7 ; cf. Richter's Narrative, *Add. MSS.* 27816 ff. 473-87 ; 501-16.

National Convention, in order to supersede the Established
and legal Government of the Country, and it was to this
point that it was intended to Examine him, and with a
view of giving him an opportunity of removing the
suspicions entertained on that head." [1]

In reply Tooke asked "if it could be imagined that it
was sufficient to justify the holding him in custody, the
taking possession of his House, and seizing his papers,
that it was conceived he had been guilty of Treasonable
practices. That if the Lord Chancellor, or Mr. Dundas,
or any other Member of the Privy Council, would upon
their Honour, assure him, that there had been any Information upon Oath against him for Practices full of Treason,
for that he understood Treasonable practices to mean, or
any one Act of Treason, He would not ask who the Informant was, or what the particular Charge was; He would
answer any Questions that might be put to him and be
Examined to the utmost extent Their Lordships pleased;
—Upon being told that no such assurances should be
given; but that he certainly was not obliged to answer at
all. He said that, in consequence of that refusal, he did
refuse to be Examined." Not another word, beyond some
complaints as to the manner of his seizure, could be extracted from the wily prisoner.[2] Dundas was foiled by his
neighbour from Wimbledon, whom he found an experienced political campaigner, as astute and as wary as
himself, and perhaps not less learned in the law.

The reformers were indicted before Chief-Justice Eyre
in September, but they were not actually brought to trial
until October and November. Meanwhile, in the month
of September, an attempt was made to prejudice the case
of the prisoners by an absurd alarm about what was called
"the pop-gun plot"—a Gilbertian plan to blow a poisoned
arrow at the king through an imitation walking-stick.
Several persons were taken into custody for their share in
the plot, and an unsuccessful attempt was made to trace
its origin to the London Corresponding Society. Robert
Crossfield, the only one of the prisoners who was ever

[1] May 16, 1724, *P. C. R.* 33 Geo. III. 93.
[2] *Ib.* 93–4. There is a thumb-nail sketch of this examination in Tooke's
Diary, Notes and Queries, Eighth Series, XI. 21.

brought to trial, was acquitted, and the rest were discharged without a trial. Upton, an *agent provocateur* like Watt, and the real inventor of the scheme, was never arrested, and the whole affair would have obtained no more than casual attention had it not afforded a convenient means of creating alarm, and of casting discredit upon the reformers in general and upon the London Corresponding Society in particular.[1]

The twelve apostles, as they were called, were now in the greatest danger. The inflamed condition of the public mind, the uncertainty of the law of conspiracy, the vast area over which the Crown ranged for its subjects of prosecution, made it possible for a man's life to be imperilled by an innocent word or action that he had utterly forgotten, or by some proceeding of his society that he had to the best of his ability opposed.[2] Prejudice against the reformers was much mitigated by a spirited reply of William Godwin to Chief-Justice Eyre's charge to the Grand Jury;[3] a pamphlet which made possible Erskine's difficult task of defending the prisoners.

Hardy was tried first. The minutes and proceedings of the London Corresponding Society and the Society for Constitutional Information, the publication of each and every pamphlet ever presented to either, the speeches of their honorary members, and every printed word that they had ever approved, were drawn upon to provide evidence against this single individual. What that evidence amounted to is already known to the reader. Sheridan and Lauderdale gave evidence in the prisoner's defence, which was conducted by Erskine. After a trial lasting nine days the prosecutors failed to convince the jury of his guilt, and Hardy was acquitted.[4]

[1] *Add. MSS.* 27808, ff. 123-31; *S. T.* XXVI. 1-222; *P. C. R.* 34 Geo. III. 119-94, *passim;* 414-21; 35 Geo. III. 1, 62-5; 37 Geo. III. 170-1, 181-3, 208-9, 211-14, 250-1, 561-2; 38 Geo. III. 171, 431, 554-5, 562. A pamphlet headed "Assassination of the King! The Conspirators Exposed . . ." giving an account of the affair, was published in 1795, B. M., E 2078.

[2] See Walker, Preface iv. and Thelwall, *Political Lectures*, No. II.; *William Godwin and His Friends*, I. 118-19; *Recoll. of J. Binns*, 43.

[3] *William Godwin and His Friends*, I. 129-34.

[4] *S. T.* XXIV. *passim;* see Erskine's remarks on the Trial as reported by Lord Broughton in *Recollections of a Long Life*, II. 169.

His acquittal was a blow to the Government. So confidently had a conviction been anticipated that the Law Officers are said to have had eight hundred warrants made out, of which three hundred were already signed.[1] These warrants may, for all one knows, still remain in forgotten pigeon-holes. There was probably truth in the words of a doggerel rhymer—

> "Twelve true-hearted men held the balance of fate,
> While these Shylocks were whetting their knife ;
> Of th' existence of thousands they lengthened the date —
> Their VERDICT was FREEDOM and LIFE."[2]

The unfortunate Hardy, though he escaped the Government, did not elude the mob. On the 11th of June, when Howe's victory of the glorious First was celebrated in London, although Hardy's house was illuminated, it was attacked by rioters, who broke the windows and endeavoured to force open the shop. Hardy's wife was so terrified that she made an imprudent escape, which resulted a few weeks later in her death.[3] Hardy's business was ruined by his prosecution, and though a temporary popularity on his release renewed his prosperity for a time, he never recovered the secure independence of former days.[4]

Horne Tooke, the only man among the prisoners of what was, in those days, called polite education, was so far from being guilty of treason or sedition that he had even declined to join the reformers in their more extreme demands. At the anniversary dinner held in 1790 to celebrate the fall of the Bastille he had persuaded the assembly to add to Sheridan's resolution in approbation of the Revolution in France, a second resolution, in which it was stated "that the English nation had only to maintain and improve the Constitution which their ancestors had transmitted to them."[5]

Tooke, unlike the other prisoners, interfered much in his own defence. Owing to his long imprisonment—he was arrested in May and tried in November—his health

---

[1] *Mem. of Hardy*, 42, 112.
[2] By John M'Creery, printer and poetaster.—*Ib.* 46.
[3] *Mem. of Hardy*, 36-8 ; cf. *Ann. Reg.* 1794, *Chron.* 16.
[4] From a circular issued to his customers, June 30, 1801, it appears that his business was then at 161 Fleet St.—*Add. MSS.* 27816, fo. 79.
[5] Supra, p. 150; *Mem. of Horne Tooke*, II. 113.

had been much impaired. "I come to you," he said, "but half a man; your lordship will expect a whole defence, and I do not doubt but I shall give you a whole defence, provided you furnish me with the necessary means of doing it."[1] Perhaps in consequence of this appeal he was allowed certain exceptional licences, which though no doubt in the interest of truth, certainly did not tend to sweeten the temper of the Crown lawyers.

"I attribute to the prisoner, together with others," said his accuser, "a conspiracy to depose the king, a deliberate plan to subvert the Constitution of the sovereign power as by law established, and to execute the plan by his own force, and by the force of those he hoped to draw to his assistance."[2] Tooke was a member of the Society for Constitutional Information, and on his connection with that society this charge was based. We have shown that the society had no wish to subvert the Constitution, and was without the money to do so even had it had the wish.[3] Justice Eyre quite disbelieved in its resources for revolution. Tooke, and apparently other members of the society, had even objected to the Edinburgh delegation,[4] the only episode in the history of the society which lent even the colour of reality to a charge of treason.

His clients, said Erskine, were prosecuted only because they had presumed to do what those who prosecuted them had done before them in other times; and from the doing of which they had raised their fortunes, and acquired the very power to prosecute and to oppress.[5] Horne Tooke actually called Pitt to prove this, and made him cut rather a sorry figure. After a lengthy trial the prisoner was acquitted,[6] and at a jovial dinner-party a little later the so-called traitor and his friends drank cordially to the health of the king.[7]

Tooke's acquittal excited general enthusiasm. "The burst of exclamation that took place *in the court*" when the jury gave its verdict, "and which the judges neither tried to repress nor reprove, was the signal of acquittal to the multitude *without*," says the *Morning Chronicle*. "A

[1] *S. T.* XXV. 10-11. [2] *Ib.* 28. [3] *Ib.* 85-6.
[4] *Ib.* 87-8. [5] *Ib.* 258. [6] *Ib.* 743.
[7] *Life of Cartwright*, I. 211.

sympathetic shout broke from the mass of the people, which was caught and echoed to every part of the metropolis in an instant. No telegraph—no artificial organ could convey the news with the electrical velocity of their enthusiasm. It was known at the remotest corners of the town in a minute after the event, and the satisfaction was as general as the interest which was felt in the cause." [1]

John Thelwall, whom Tooke called his political son, was the third and last prisoner brought to trial. He afterwards maintained that a new under-sheriff, who had recently entered office, found an officially prepared panel of jurymen awaiting him, and rejected it.[2] To this circumstance the prisoners probably owed their liberty if not their lives, as it is certain that jury lists were tampered with in the interest of the prosecution, whilst, on the other hand, men who desired to get their names upon the lists had, quite rightly, found it impossible to do so.[3] Once more the Government ventured to put a jury to the test.

It was more difficult in Thelwall's case than in the others to impute to him the acts of any society. But his lectures and speeches laid him open to charges more personal and more direct. Informers had been set to haunt his lecture-rooms. They reported much that might have been better unsaid, but foolish phrases are not treason, and there is reason to doubt whether the informers had always heard what they reported. An informer called John Taylor, for example, told how, in conversation over a glass of wine, Thelwall had reprobated the sentences of Palmer and Skirving, Muir and Margarot—which is likely enough —and had talked of attempting a rescue, which, except that their friends hoped to rescue them by invoking the clemency of the Crown, Thelwall was not in the least likely to suggest.[4] There are other strange mixtures of the probable and the improbable in the evidence of this witness which suggest that he spoke from faked memoranda. It is impossible to believe that a man who was not remarkably intelligent could carry in his head for three

---

[1] *Morning Chronicle*, Nov. 24, 1794, quoted in Joyce's App. to *Sermon*, 16.
[2] *Life of Thelwall*, I. 235–6.   [3] *Life of Paine*, I. 372.
[4] May 17, 1794, *P. C. R.* 33 Geo. III. 106.

or four months nine folio pages of evidence, full of names and dates. Any one who reads these pages in the minutes of the Privy Council and sees how this witness ran glibly through whole passages of his evidence without the prompting of a single question will realise that he must have spoken from notes; and no one who has studied the other evidence as to the behaviour of Thelwall will believe that those notes were untampered with and unedited.[1] One piece of Taylor's evidence we may believe. At a lecture on the 14th of February, 1794, he says, Thelwall "rejoiced to say" that "Tyranny and Despotism were on the eve of Dissolution all over Europe. The Undertaker was knocking at the Door and the Coffin already bespoke." Such was the bold but legal language of which, as his published lectures show, Thelwall habitually made use.

Every effort was made to blacken his character.[2] His attorney's clerk was tampered with, and knowledge obtained of his plan of defence.[3] Evidence was even manufactured by placing an unposted private letter from Thelwall in the pocket of Richter, who had never seen it, in order to prove publication.[4] Many witnesses spoke of Thelwall's high character and love of peace,[5] and though the judge summed up very much against him,[6] the jury found him "not guilty."[7] The Government gave up all hope of securing a conviction, and the other prisoners were discharged.[8]

About a month after his acquittal he was asked what he meant to do. "Do!" replied Thelwall; "continue to strain every nerve to gain reform in Parliament."[9] Certainly the failure to convict him assisted the cause and disheartened the repressionists. If one conviction had been

---

[1] May 17, 1794, *P. C. R.* 33 Geo. III. 105–13. We know from Gosling's evidence of May 19, that a person called Taylor was pointed out at a meeting of the L. C. S. as a spy.—*Ib.* 126. A good part of Gosling's own evidence must be dismissed as false, for he overdid his part and gave the impression that Thelwall defended a resort to physical force (*P. C. R.* 33 Geo. III. 114–15). Force was, in any case, alien from Thelwall's temperament, but he specifically maintained the contrary opinion.

[2] *Life of Thelwall*, I. 245.   [3] *Ib.* 247–8.
[4] *Ib.* 455; Cestre, 90–1.   [5] *Life of Thelwall*, I. 440–5.
[6] *Ib.* 440–5; Cestre, 99–102.   [7] *Ib.* 113.
[8] See *P. C. R.* Nov. 28, and Dec. 12, 1794, 34 Geo. III. 331, 369–72.
[9] *Life*, I. 290–1.

obtained it would have been the signal for proscription. "A system of proscription and terror like that of Robespierre," said Cartwright in announcing Horne Tooke's acquittal, "has been for some time growing up in this country, and had these trials been otherwise decided than they have been it would have been completed and written in innocent and virtuous blood." [1]

During their imprisonment, the treatment of the State prisoners was very various, but for the most part very bad, and often quite brutal.[2] Not the least part of their misfortune was that most of them were poor men, on whom their families were entirely dependent for support. The London Corresponding Society did its best to relieve them, and for this purpose over £300 was certainly collected.[3] The society also undertook Hardy's defence, which is stated to have cost £25,[4] though how this was sufficient, even if, as seems probable, Erskine gave his services, must remain a mystery.

A charge brought against the prisoners had been that they had accumulated arms in order to promote a rising.[5] Arms had certainly been manufactured to the order of Watt,[6] but then he also invented his own plot. These were the arms which were shown in London at the State trials. In London a young man called John Edwards, the son of a silversmith, did made a single pike for his own amusement; but it cannot have been very deadly since the pike-head was made out of an old mourning sword.

---

[1] *Life of Cartwright*, I. 210; cf. *William Godwin and his Friends*, I. 134–7.

[2] *Add. MSS.* 27809, ff. 202–61; MS. Diary of Horne Tooke extracted in *Notes and Queries*, 8th Series, XI. 21–2, 61–2, 103–4, 162–3; *Recollections of J. Binns*, 93–100; Cestre, 94–7; cf. *Life of Wakefield*, II. 149. The custody of the prisoners must have cost the nation well over £1000. One account for the detention of prisoners in Newgate amounts to £790 16s. 4d.—*P. C. R.* 41 Geo. III. 338–41. The trials also were costly. An account in the Home Office papers shows that the entertainment of Judges, Jury, Counsel, etc., on the trials of Hardy, Tooke and Thelwall cost £2411 11s. 7d. Gurney's reports of the trials of Hardy and Tooke cost £435 6s.; and their bill for the reports of the trials of Thelwall, Stone and Crossfield was £264 10s. Joseph White to W. Windham, Nov. 6, 1798.—H. O. ⅜.

[3] *Add. MSS.* 27813, fo. 143.   [4] *Ib.* ff. 6–9.

[5] Cf. *Bland Burges Papers*, 178.

[6] *S. T.* XXIV. 3–5; *C. J.* XLIX. 659, 662.

Some one in Sheffield also offered to sell pike-heads at a shilling a-piece, "money to be sent with the orders."[1] There is no evidence that he ever received either cash or order from London. A few pikes were certainly made in Sheffield,[2] where the risk of mobbing made an instrument of self-defence far from unnecessary; and at Manchester Walker had saved his premises, and probably his life, by scaring a Church and King mob with a few blank cartridges fired into the air. The Committee of Secrecy believed that the Corresponding Society had divisions for military drill,[3] but an attempt at the trials to fasten upon them responsibility for the acts of a peripatetic body called the Loyal Lambeth Association, which could alone be convicted of military exercises, proved entirely unsuccessful.[4] If all the reformers possessing arms had met in one place, and if they had all risen together, there is little doubt that a single company of infantry could have butchered them all within ten minutes. But the reformers do not seem to have felt the attraction of this plan.

Two trials took place in the provinces similar to those in London. Thomas Walker of Manchester, with nine others, was accused of sedition. Evidence was shamefully manufactured, the case utterly broke down, the Crown lawyers withdrew it, and their chief witness was convicted of perjury and sent to prison for two years.[5]

At Sheffield the reformers had long been active. Their pamphleteering had been more vigorous than prudent, but it showed some literary power.[6] The best-known of their leaders is James Montgomery the poet—to be distinguished from that Robert Montgomery of whose works nothing

---

[1] *S. T.* XXIV. 588–602, 608, 955; *Mem. of Hardy*, 33; *C. J.* XLIX. 657.

[2] *S. T.* XXIV. 655–78; XXV. 1016, 1050, etc.; cf. *C. J.* XLIX. 658–60, 656–7.

[3] *Ib.* 657–8, cf. 662–4.

[4] *S. T.* XXIV. 692–7, cf. 831–2, etc. There is a great deal about the Lambeth Association in the Privy Council Registers. It is perfectly obvious that it was a complete failure, and not worth getting frightened about. See also A Vindication of the London Corresponding Society, by James Parkinson.

[5] *S. T.* XXIII. 1055–1156; *William Godwin and his Friends*, II. 237.

[6] Cf. Holland and Everett's *Montgomery*, I. 148, 159, etc.

now lives but the portions immortalised by Macaulay. James Montgomery had already been convicted on an utterly ridiculous charge of sedition after the judge had refused to accept a special verdict.[1]

A large meeting in favour of reform had been held on Castle Hill on the 7th of April, 1794. Henry Redhead Yorke, an indiscreet young man who had made a flamboyant and extravagant speech, was charged with conspiracy.[2] Responsibility for the supposed arming was charged against him, but not proved;[3] and he was said to have spoken in favour of peace and against violence[4] and levelling principles.[5] He was found guilty, fined £200, and sent to Dorchester Gaol for two years.[6] He afterwards married the daughter of the governor of Dorchester Gaol, and ended respectably by being called to the Bar.[7] Even whilst he was still a prisoner Yorke changed his political views, became as zealous against reform as he had formerly been in its favour, and wrote a pamphlet in which he lectured the reformers on their political heresies. "Let us no longer be deceived by visionary projects of perfection, nor by the delusive promises of men who falsely call themselves philosophers. Let us not arrogantly mark out for ourselves a little Goshen of intellectual light; beyond which everything is to be deemed error, prejudice and slavery. . . . A moral reformation must, at all events, precede the political. Till this shall have happened, no real benefit can flow from the extension of the elective franchise or the limitation of the duration of Parliament. It might be appealing only from one set of corrupt men to another set of the same description; not from Philip drunk to Philip sober; but from Philip drunk to-day to Philip drunk to-morrow."[8]

[1] Holland and Everett's *Montgomery*, I. 190–203, cf. 252.
[2] *S. T.* XXV. 1007.   [3] *Ib.* 1061–2.
[4] *Ib.* 1034, cf. 1114.   [5] *Ib.* 1135.   [6] *Ib.* 1154.
[7] See *D. N. B.* and *E. H. R.* Oct. 1898, pp. 693–4.
[8] *A Letter to the Reformers*, by H. R. Yorke, Esq., Dorchester, 1798, pp. 85–6.

CHAPTER XIV

THE DECLINE AND FALL OF THE POLITICAL SOCIETIES

OCTOBER 1794—JULY 1799

THE London Corresponding Society was purged as by fire of all the unstable elements in its membership by the persecution of 1794.[1] But the attack on men like Thomas Hardy, "on whose inoffensive, upright character the breath of calumny has never breathed from the mouth of any one who ever knew him," awakened others to a just resentment of repression.[2] "Several persons," of whom Francis Place was one,[3] "considered it meritorious to join the society now that its founder and secretary was persecuted; those who did so were men who possessed something decided and energetic in their character, and they became very active members." "Vast numbers of the thinking part of the working people, as well as many who were better off in the world, joined the London Corresponding Society, as they did other reforming societies in various parts of England;" and in May 1795 it had a regular membership of 2000, dispersed in seventy recognised divisions.[4] Place became one of its most active members, and was for a long time president of its central committee.[5]

Valuable educational work was done by the society during these months. By means of a club, books were bought and read in rotation.[6] Meetings were held, in the homes of those who could provide the accommodation, for readings, conversation and discussion.[7] "This course of

---

[1] *Add. MSS.* 27808, fo. 3.   [2] *Ib.* 35154, fo. 25.
[3] *Ib.* 27808, fo. 3 ; cf. 28 ; 35142, fo. 236, 238 ; 35143, fo. 20.
[4] *Ib.* 35143, fo. 10 ; 27808, fo. 28 ; *Recoll. of J. Binns*, 41.
[5] *Add. MSS.* 27808, fo. 11.
[6] *Ib.* 35142, ff. 236–7 ; cf. 35143, ff. 93–4.   [7] *Ib.* 35142, fo. 237.

discipline compelled " the members "to think more correctly than they had been accustomed to do; it induced them to become readers of books, and the consequence—the very remarkable consequence—was that every one of them became a master, and permanently bettered his condition in life." [1] The society's business, in fact, "consisted in good teaching " and the formation of a "political public." [2]

Owing, apparently, to some doubt as to the constitution of the society, about which there had been many discussions, and to which it would seem that some members wished to apply experimentally Godwin's anarchic theory that the rule of law was degrading to freemen,[3] two divisions seceded and founded societies for themselves.[4] The Corresponding Society thought it desirable in consequence to demonstrate its vitality by a public meeting, which took place in St. George's Fields on the 29th of June, 1795.[5] The members soon experienced the danger of this policy, as it was necessary to rebut the charge of disorder in a pamphlet called *Reformers no Rioters*,[6] which is sufficiently described by its title; and in another pamphlet, written about the same time, they say that the reformer "can never employ means destructive to the end proposed and attempt to introduce peace by anarchy and war." [7]

In yet another pamphlet of about the same date the defence of the society assumes an ironic tone—"If to alleviate the sufferings of mankind and promote a reformation of abuses; to deliberate upon public measures and seek redress of grievances; to soothe the sigh of solitary wretchedness and speak comfort to the drooping heart; if these be treason and sedition, then am I content to suffer the imputa-

---

[1] *Add. MSS.* 35143, ff. 93–5 ; 27808, ff. 59–61 ; letter to Noble, *Life of Place*, 22–3.

[2] *Add. MSS.* 27810, ff. 91–2.

[3] *Ib.* 27808, fo. 27 ; 27813, ff. 51–2; I take this to be the meaning of the passage.

[4] *Ib.* 27808, fo. 27 ; 27813, fo. 50.

[5] *Ib.* 27813, fo. 50 ; cf. 75 ; cf. also *Bland Burges Papers*, 286–7; Account of the Proceedings.

[6] Printed by order of the London Corresponding Society.

[7] A Summary of the Duties of Citizenship written expressly for the Members of the London Corresponding Society, 12.

tion and to yield myself a willing victim; then may the Corresponding Society at once plead guilty to the charge, since with these attendant circumstances *libel* has been their morning's theme, sedition their evening's employment, and *treason their order of the day!*" [1]

Another meeting was held, on October 26, in a field near Copenhagen House, a tavern in the parish of Islington.[2] The resolutions carried at the meeting did not, it is true, go beyond the usual demands of the London Corresponding Society, but an address to the nation which was also adopted was extravagant in form, and another address to the king was somewhat taunting and disrespectful in expression.[3] Yet addresses and resolutions alike were far from being, as the Committee of Secrecy described them, "of the most seditious and inflammatory nature," containing "the most daring libels . . . against every Part of the Constitution." [4] Baxter, one of the members of the society who had been accused of sedition in the preceding year, argued in a pamphlet, published a few days after the meeting, that it was the desire of the reformers not to destroy the Constitution, but to preserve it. To say that resistance of oppression was wrong was mere nonsense, since history showed that time and again oppression had been resisted in circumstances which all men now applaud; but "we are not," he continued, "reduced 'to the awful necessity of opposing *Force* to Force," for "the horrors of a Civil War " could be avoided by "Association to obtain Redress of Grievances." He ends with the usual refrain,

---

[1] Sketch of a speech delivered at the Westminster Forum on Dec. 9, 16, 23, and 30, 1794 . . . by John Gale Jones, London 1795 [price one shilling]. Preface dated June 17, 1795. Jones had considerable eloquence, albeit of a somewhat frothy sort. See also " Substance of a speech delivered at the Ciceronian School, Globe Tavern, Fleet St., Monday March 2, 1795," on the following question : " At this awful moment of difficulty and danger, which best deserves the public confidence—Mr. Pitt or Mr. Fox?" By John Gale Jones, London, 1795 [price sixpence]. Preface dated Old Bond St., March 6, 1795. Jones decides for Fox.

[2] Kept at this time by a man called Orchard, according to Hone, who wrote an account of Copenhagen House in June 1825, when speculative builders were already encroaching upon the meadows that surrounded the old tavern. The Fives Courts of Copenhagen House were once famous. See Hone's *Every Day Book*, ed. 1826, I. 429–36.

[3] Account of the Proceedings, Oct. 26, 1795, *Add. MSS.* 27808, ff. 26–7, 31, 37–9   [4] *C. J.* XLIV. 334.

that universal suffrage and annual Parliaments will cure all the ills of the State; nor does he doubt that, "with the return of Liberty, Peace and Plenty will bless our Isle."[1]

Whilst the London Corresponding Society was bravely making head against the storm, the Society of the Friends of the People seems to have been scattered by its violence. In 1794, and possibly even in the beginning of 1795, the more ardent members of the society were still drawing up and discussing elaborate plans for a reformed House of Commons as if they had some hope that their schemes might be carried into law. The optimists were, no doubt, the most active members of the society, but it seems probable that they were few. The majority of the Friends of the People had lost courage, and early in 1795 their proceedings were suspended. At a meeting on the 30th of May, 1795, it was declared that the society still believed in a reform of Parliament, but that, rather than run the risk of disturbing public order, or of appearing to fail in the duty of presenting a united front to the foreigner, it would withdraw from interference in political agitation. The day of the society was over.

The Society for Constitutional Information was broken up by the State trials. The arrest of its secretary, the impounding of his books and papers, and his subsequent submission, put the machinery of the society completely out of gear. Probably the recognisances into which Adams was forced to enter were so drawn as to make it impossible for him to assist any longer in schemes of political organisation. But he was not a strong man, he seems to have been thoroughly frightened, and there is every likelihood that he lost his taste for political agitation when he realised what risks it involved. Leading members of the society, like Horne Tooke, continued, as individuals, to advocate reform as strongly as ever. But the real work of the Society was done. Its political force was exhausted. Of the chief organisations for the promotion of parlia-

---

[1] *Resistance to Oppression, the Constitutional Right of Britons,* asserted in a lecture delivered before Section 2 of the Society of the Friends of Liberty, on Monday Nov. 9 [1795]. By J. Baxter. Sold by J. Burks. No. 74, Sun St., and all Political Booksellers, Price One Penny. 8 pp.

mentary reform, the London Corresponding Society alone survived the prosecutions of 1794 in any effective strength.

Meanwhile, the war was unsuccessful, and the people were feeling the pressure of want. The king was met on his way to open Parliament, with cries of "No Pitt," "No War," "Bread," and may possibly have been shot at; on his return he was almost dragged from his carriage by "a miscreant in a green coat." [1] This outburst was attributed, with no show of reason, to the London Corresponding Society and its meeting at Copenhagen House.[2] Pitt himself was, as a matter of fact, as much disappointed as the crowd at being unable to announce a peace; [3] and it was to this failure, and to the dearness of provisions, that this outburst of disorder was due.[4]

Nothing could have been more fortunate from the point of view of the Government in power. The newspapers shouted treason. Loyal addresses—to the number of nearly six hundred, it is said—poured in upon the king. "The Loyal talked and acted just as they pleased." [5] It was thought necessary for the Corresponding Society to defend itself in a public address,[6] disavowing the attack on the king, and reaffirming their legal desire for a parliamentary reform. "Perhaps nothing has a greater tendency to inflame the irritation of the public mind," they said, "than the practice . . . of charging every accidental intemperance—every unpremeditated outrage" upon those who expose ministerial designs and are zealous for human liberty.

Late in the year, making the outrage on the king, and bread riots in the provinces,[7] their excuse, ministers

---

[1] *Add. MSS.* 27808, ff. 33–49 ; 35143, ff. 14–15 ; *L.J.* XL. 514–19, 521–2 ; *Recoll. of J. Binns*, 54–6.

[2] *Add. MSS.* 27808, ff. 49–50 ; *Life of Thelwall*, I. 381–5.

[3] Stanhope, II. 13.

[4] *Auto. of A. Young*, 254 ; *Life of J. Cartwright*, I. 269 ; *Mem. of C. J. F.* III. 116–17. See on the "dearth and discontent" of 1795, the passage in Dr. Holland Rose's *William Pitt and the Great War*, pp. 282–8, which is scarcely just to the London Corresponding Society, but which emphasises in a remarkable manner the seriousness of economic distress. See also J. L. and B. Hammond, *The Village Labourer*, 1760–1832, pp. 120–22. [5] *Add. MSS.* 27808, fo. 52.

[6] London Corresponding Society to the British Nation.— *Life of Thelwall*, I. 457–62, where it is misdated as Nov. 1793.

[7] For Manchester, cf. Reilly, 281–2.

extended their arbitrary powers by what are known as the "Two Acts."[1] The first made spoken and written words, although not followed by any overt act, a treasonable practice;[2] the second forbade all public meetings of which notice had not been given by resident householders.[3] Pitt seems to have shown genuine alarm. "My head," he said, "would be off in six months were I to resign."[4] But there was a tremendous outcry from the friends of reform and from many who, in ordinary times, were hardly to be called its friends.[5] The Constitutional Society awoke from sleep to make its protest.[6] At a great public meeting, numbering many thousands, the London Corresponding Society recorded its abhorrence of the measure in forcible but moderate and peaceful words.[7] Even at a second public meeting, after the Bills had passed, its language was still discreet, more discreet than that either of Fox or of his opponents.[8]

The Whig Club and the county meetings renewed their political activity in protesting against the curtailment of a liberty they had been in no recent haste to exercise.[9] There were petitions on both sides; in the main unfavourable to repression.[10] But the Two Acts were carried through both Houses by huge majorities, and were defended, once enacted, as "a temporary sacrifice of one of the means of Constitutional Security for the preservation of that Constitutional Security itself."[11] "Infamous as

[1] Even Thelwall, who was, it is true, out of office, thought this unnecessary.

[2] 36 Geo. III. c. 7.   [3] 36 Geo. III. c. 8.

[4] Stanhope, II. 114 ; cf. Windham's *Diary*, 336.

[5] *Mem. of C. J. F.* III. 124–5, 267–8 ; Moore's *Sheridan*, II. 256 ; *Life of J. Cartwright*, I. 231–3 ; 269–70 ; *Mem. of Parr*, I. 392 ; John Cartwright, Letter to the Sheriff of Lincoln ; Common Sence, "Ten Minutes' Advice to the People of England."

[6] Report of the Constitutional Society upon the Treason and Sedition Bills, price 1*d*.

[7] *Add. MSS.* 27808, ff. 54–6 ; cf. 27814, fo. 79 ; *Life of Thelwall*, 469–71.   [8] *Ib.* 471–77.

[9] *Wyvill Papers*, V. 323–7 ; 303–21 ; xxiv–xl. ; *Mem. of C. J. Fox*, III. 127–8.

[10] *Add. MSS.* 27808, fo. 52.

[11] Draft speech of Spencer Perceval ; Spencer Walpole's *Perceval*, I. 39. In the Lords a protest was entered against the Treason Bill as "founded on a false pretence," but only three peers set their names to it. Only nine peers signed the general protest against the Seditious Meetings

these laws were, they were popular measures," wrote Place years afterwards. "The people—ay, the mass of the shopkeepers and working people may be said to have approved them without understanding them. Such was their terror of the French regicides and democrats, such the fear that ' the throne and the altar' would be destroyed, and that we should be 'deprived of our holy religion' that, had the knowledge of their grand conspiracy been equal to their desires, they might have converted the Government into anything they wished for the advantage of themselves." [1] The situation was humorously hit off at Manchester by the formation of a Thinking Club. At its first meeting "there were three hundred present and silence prevailed for one hour." [2]

The Corresponding Society's constitution was revised in order to avoid the operation of the new Acts. Elaborate precautions were taken against the admission of undesirable members. Each division was normally to include no more than thirty people; when there were sixteen members more, these were to form a new division. Order was to be strictly maintained; even applause was to be expressed merely by uplifting the hand. "Persons attempting to trespass on order, under pretence of showing zeal, courage, or any other motive, are to be suspected. A noisy disposition is seldom a sign of courage, and extreme zeal is often a cloak of treachery." Over the president's chair at each meeting was to be inscribed, "Beware of Orators." [3]

Less wisely, perhaps, for their own safety, they sent certain of their members on missionary tours to spread belief in universal suffrage and annual Parliaments, to

---

Bill, though the Duke of Bedford, and three of the original nine, signed a second and more vigorous remonstrance.—Roger's *Protests of the Lords*, II. 283–7.

[1] Place to Harrison, Feb. 15, 1842 ; *Add. MSS.* 27810, fo. 91 ; cf. 35143, ff. 65, 68. Mr. Gladstone's first speech at the Oxford Union was "a strong oration much admired by his friends" in favour of the Treason and Sedition Acts of 1795.—Morley's *Gladstone*, I. 63.

[2] W. E. A. Axon, *Annals of Manchester*, 122.

[3] The Report of the Committee of the Constitution of the London Corresponding Society ; cf. Report of the Committee . . . to revise and abridge a former report of the Constitution of the L. C. S.—*C. J.* LIV. 344–51 ; *S. T.* XXIV. 575–83 ; *Add. MSS.* 35143, ff. 16–7 ; 27808, ff. 68–71.

encourage the formation of popular societies and to advise reformers as to the best means of constituting such societies so as to bring them into conformity with the Two Acts.[1] John Gale Jones, the first of these political missionaries, was an apothecary and surgeon, though it is doubtful whether he was fully qualified, and uncertain whether he ever engaged seriously in medical practice. He was a plausible and fluent speaker, more fervent than wise, but not without a certain gift of prudence, such as was an essential qualification of a political speaker after the passage of the Two Acts. Jones received elaborate instructions from the society. He was to "state precisely" that the sole object of the society was "a reform in the Commons House of Parliament." Whilst the Whigs were wasting breath in their efforts to secure the repeal of the Two Acts, the society preferred to accept them under protest and to confine itself to the constitutional agitation which the law still permitted. Citizens might still meet together to the number of forty-nine "to converse in an orderly manner on their constitutional rights," and, so long as they obeyed the law, the law would protect such an assembly. The delegate, who was to be himself "the example of sobriety, both of conversation and manners," was "to invite the society to guard against all persons who would introduce violent propositions or any illegal measure." "You are to strain every power of your mind to call upon our fellow-citizens to be ready with us to pursue our common object, if it must be to the scaffold, or rather (if our enemies are desperate enough to bar up every avenue to inquiry and discussion) to the field, at the hazard of extermination; convinced that no temper less decided than this will suffice to regain liberty from a bold and usurping faction." [2] Such desperate measures they did not believe would ever be necessary. Union would secure the parliamentary reform which they demanded. The cause was good; "we claim no more than the restitution of our rights." [3]

[1] *C. J.* XLIV. 333; cf. *Add. MSS.* 27808, fo. 71.
[2] Instructions to Gale Jones.—*Tour*, App. 102–7.
[3] J. Ashley, Secretary of the L. C. S., to country societies—letter of Introduction for Gale Jones.—*Tour*, App. 99–101.

Armed with these instructions, Jones was sent into Kent in February 1796, on a tour of which he afterwards composed quite a readable account. At Rochester he found parliamentary reform almost fashionable. The Recorder had written a pamphlet in favour of it, the Mayor was well disposed to it, and the reforming society consisted of nine or ten divisions. The spirits of the reformers in Rochester and Chatham had been somewhat damped by the repressive legislation, but Jones seems to have revived their drooping courage.[1] At Gravesend the aspect of affairs was less pleasant. The Mayor was a furious opponent of reform, and had hit upon a pretty method of venting his spleen and at the same time saving his pocket, by refusing to pay a just debt to a reformer because he had signed a petition against the Two Acts. Here again, however, Jones put new life into the reformers, and sixteen new members joined the society in consequence of one of his speeches.[2] After he had in like manner encouraged the faithful at Maidstone, where a new society was formed, Jones returned home to London in the beginning of March.[3] It had been hoped that, as a result of his tour, the London Corresponding Society might obtain some financial assistance from the societies in the provinces.[4] In this respect, however, it proved a failure, though as a political propaganda it was a complete success.

John Binns, a wordy young man, who afterwards became republican and prosperous in the United States, had been sent on a like mission to Portsmouth,[5] and afterwards he and Jones were together sent to Birmingham. They were explicitly instructed not to concern themselves with anything but parliamentary reform,[6] and seem, in the main, to have faithfully observed their instructions. They were, however, arrested in March 1796, and the London Corresponding Society had to send down Francis Place to try to extricate them from their difficulty.[7] When they were at last brought to trial in August 1797, no effort was

---

[1] *Tour*, 1–63.   [2] *Ib.* 63–9.   [3] *Ib.* 78–88.
[4] Section 12 of Gale's instructions.—*Ib.* 102–7.
[5] *Recoll. of J. Binns*, 64–6 ; *Add. MSS.* 27815, ff. 14–15, 29.
[6] *C. J.* LIV. 334, 351–2.
[7] *Recoll. of J. Binns*, 66–7 ; *Add. MSS.* 27813, ff. 35, 37, 47, 111.

spared to secure a conviction. Spencer Perceval prosecuted for the Crown, but Binns was defended by Romilly and was acquitted, and though Gale Jones was found guilty, no sentence was ever passed upon him.[1]

To the jury that acquitted Binns the London Corresponding Society sent a curious letter of praise and congratulation on a courageous verdict. "On your virtue depended not only the liberty of an Individual," it ran, "but in great measure the liberty of our common country." On the integrity of jurors depended "the political existence of the country." . . . "Be it their care to preserve this only remaining blessing degraded England enjoys. . . . If men like yourselves do not step forward we are a lost People, victims devoted to be immolated at the Shrine of Ministerial rapacity, or, as in Ireland, hunted down by human Butchers whose greatest recommendations are the number of innocent men they have murdered." The Corresponding Society, therefore, sends the Birmingham jurors its thanks for their verdict, thanks which are "honourable because they are the wages of virtue." [2]

In the middle of April 1797 a serious mutiny broke out in the fleet at Spithead; and in May a mutiny yet more serious and alarming broke out, under the leadership of a half-mad creature called Peter Parker, amongst the sailors at the Nore. There was a suspicion that the London Corresponding Society was, in some way, responsible for these outbreaks; and it must be admitted that the society had given some colour of plausibility to such rumours by sending its emissaries to naval towns like Chatham and Portsmouth. Two barristers, A. Graham and D. Williams, were sent down from London to take part in the prosecution of the mutineers at the Nore, and they were charged specifically to inquire into the truth of the report that the London Corresponding Society, and particularly two of its members called Beck and Galloway, had been in communication with the sailors.[3] In their reply, Mr. Graham

[1] *S. T.* XXVI. 595–652 ; *Add. MSS.* 35143, ff. 17–18 ; Letter of Binns to L. C. S., Aug. 19, 1797, *ib.* 27815, fo. 170 ; *Life of Perceval*, I. 41–3.
[2] Aug. 31, 1797. Signed: Thos. Goodwin, Pres., Thos. Evans, Sec.— *Add. MSS.* 27815, ff. 73–4.
[3] Copy (marked secret) of a letter of June 19, 1797, to A. Graham and

and Mr. Williams "beg leave to assure his Grace [of Port-
land] that they have unremittingly endeavoured to trace if
there was any Connexion or correspondence carried on
between the Mutineers and any private person, or any
society, on shore, and they think they may with the greatest
safety pronounce that no such connexion or correspondence
ever did exist. They do not, however, mean to say that
wicked and designing men have not been amongst the
mutineers; on the contrary, they have proof sufficient to
found a belief upon, that several, whose mischievous dispositions would lead them to the furthest corner of the
Kingdom in hopes of countenancing a disturbance once
begun, have been in Company with the Delegates [of the
mutineers] on shore, and have also (some of them) visited
the ships and by using inflammatory language endeavoured to Spirit on the Sailors to a continuance of the
Mutiny, without, however, daring to offer anything like
a plan for the disposal of the Fleet, or to do more than
insinuate that they were belonging to Clubs or Societies
whose members wished well to the cause, but from which
societies, Mr. Graham and Mr. Williams are persuaded,
no such persons were ever regularly deputed." Nor do
they believe that the men were moved by any such external
influence as that of a club; the mutiny was altogether too
wild and unorganised to have been fomented from without;
it was a spontaneous outbreak of aggrieved sailors, and
it was nothing more.[1]

The naval mutinies, and perhaps the first mutterings
of the storm of rebellion that was soon to break over
Ireland, account for the decisive defeat of Charles Grey's
motion for leave to bring in a Bill "to amend and regulate
the Election of Members to serve in the Commons House
of Parliament," which was rejected, by 256 votes to 91, on
the 26th of May, 1797. As reported in the *Parliamentary*

D. Williams, esquires, apparently from J. King, who was Under-Secretary
at the Home Office.—H. O. 42, vol. 41.

[1] Report enclosed in a letter from A. Graham, June 24, 1797.—H. O.
42, vol. 41. There was nothing to show that Parker had anything to do
with any one on shore. H. C. Litchfield to King, June 23, 1797 —*Ib.* 42,
vol. 41. On the Mutiny at the Nore, in general, see W. L. Clowes, *The
Royal Navy—A History*, IV. 172–9; J. W. Fortescue, *A History of the
British Army*, IV. 530–2.

History, Grey's speech was a bad one, tortuous in thought and clumsy in expression; though his plan was bold—bolder, indeed, than the Bill which his administration carried into law in the year 1832. He disavowed universal suffrage and dissociated himself from extreme reformers; but he would have made Parliaments triennial, and would, apparently, have insisted that elections should be carried out simultaneously throughout the country on a single day.[1] The representation of the counties was to be increased from 92 to 113—Yorkshire, for instance, was to have two members for each Riding instead of two members for the whole county; the counties were to be broken up into single-member constituencies, "in order to put an end to compromises," those "deals" between opposition and administration whereby one supporter of each was returned without the expense of contest, and in consequence of which, as Horne Tooke had bitterly complained, the constituencies concerned were virtually disfranchised; and, lastly, copyholders and holders of leases above a certain annual value were to enjoy the franchise hitherto monopolised by the freeholders.[2] The remaining four hundred members of Parliament were to be returned by new urban constituencies, constituted, in the main, in proportion to population, but with proper exceptions to guard against the imagined danger that the mere weight of population might give an undue balance of power to the most thickly peopled districts.[3] In the new constituencies there was to be one uniform franchise. Every householder was to have a vote, since the father of a family, "having given hostages, as it were, to society, as an assurance of his interest in its welfare, was not unworthy of a share in the legislation of his country."[4]

Pitt's answer to Grey was a most ingenious speech, in which he dexterously evaded the real questions and demolished the fictitious heresies of imaginary opponents. He expressly accepted Grey's disavowal of the advocates of universal suffrage, and then, by an adroit turn, proceeded, firstly, to fasten upon him, or to attempt to fasten

---

[1] *Parl. Hist.* XXXIII. 649–50.   [2] *Ib.* 649.
[3] *Ib.* 649.   [4] *Ib.* 650.

upon him, the responsibility for the policy which he had disowned, and, secondly, to argue that its advocates had "avowedly borrowed their political creed" from "that proud, shallow, and presumptuous philosophy which, pretending to communicate new lights to mankind, has carried theoretical absurdity higher than the wild imaginations of the most extravagant visionaries ever conceived, and practical evil to an extent which no age or history has equalled." [1]

The rest of the debate followed familiar lines. Grey's supporters urged the Government to set its house in order whilst yet there was time, to placate the discontented by a timely reform, and to meet the wishes of the moderate reformers by wise concessions rather than drive them into the arms of the extremists by obdurate resistance to necessary change. The ministerialists replied that a time of revolution was no time for constitutional experiments, that the moderate reformers were not likely to join the extremists in a moment of grave national peril, and that a moderate measure would satisfy none of the advanced reformers, since half a loaf would not be accepted as a boon by men who demanded the whole loaf as a right.[2] In vain Erskine argued that the condition of the country rendered a reform "most critically seasonable." [3] Many men felt that they might forfeit their last hope of dying peacefully in their beds if one sacrilegious finger were laid upon the rottenest of the rotten boroughs.

The country, in truth, was against reform. In place of the shoals of petitions that had once supported Pitt, there came, four days after the fair, one solitary belated appeal for reform and economy from the freeholders and assessed taxpayers of Boston, who bewailed a constitution "mangled and deformed," and declared that the condemnation of the parliamentary system was "written in the tears of the wretched and the blood of the slain." [4] The indefatigable Wyvill made an attempt in 1797 and again in

---

[1] *Parl. Hist.* XXXIII. 672.
[2] *Ib.* 644–735 ; also extract from a draft speech of Spencer Perceval, probably delivered, but not here reported.—*Life of Sp. Perceval*, I. 40.
[3] *Parl. Hist.* XXXIII. 670.
[4] May 30, 1797.—*C. J.* LII. 622.

1798 to rouse Yorkshire to protest, as it had done in 1780 and 1781 against the continuance of an expensive war and the denial of constitutional reform; but though he gathered together a committee at York, he and his supporters never ventured to put their opinions to the test of a county meeting. He had reluctantly to recognise that he would have been beating the wind.[1]

Debt was now pressing heavily upon the London Corresponding Society. The necessity of avoiding the Act against public meetings made it impossible to maintain the full democratic organisations of former times. Members felt that they did not share fully in the management of the society, interest declined, and many ceased to attend.[2] Against the advice of Place, the society started a magazine, which involved a steady loss, and which no persuasion could induce the members to abandon.[3] The money raised to defend Jones and Binns was swallowed up, and a second fund had to be raised to help them.[4] "We cajoled ourselves and each other," says Place, "with delusive expectations" as to the deputations to the country, "which prove us to have been very silly people."[5] The "Decline and Fall" of the society was recorded in a pamphlet; its epitaph even was written; its best members were leaving;[6] its debt increasing; and Hardy's great foundation was nigh unto death.

Less responsible men were now charged with the administration of the miserable remnant of the society. On the 31st of July, 1797, in defiance of the Sedition Act, they proceeded to hold a public meeting. It was proclaimed by the magistrates of Middlesex, who stopped the proceedings, and arrested the occupants of the platforms. These six men were bailed and were drawn through the streets by an enthusiastic populace. Though their proceedings were ill-timed, their papers of business were drawn up with talent and discretion, and no bill was ever found against them.[7]

---

[1] *Wyvill Papers*, V. 354, 367 note, prelim. pp. xlvi–xlix, VI. 1–31, 358, prelim. pp. i–ii.

[2] Cf. *Add. MSS.* 27808, fo. 69.   [3] *Ib.* 78–9 ; 35143, fo. 23.

[4] *Ib.* 25 ; cf. 27808, fo. 79.   [5] *Ib.* 72.

[6] Place resigned his offices in Aug. 1796 and his membership in June 1797. *Add. MSS.* 35143, ff. 19 and 25.

[7] *Ib.* ff. 25–6 ; 27808, ff. 80–2. Though there was no conviction, this

This meeting, however, was the death-blow of the real London Corresponding Society.

The disturbed state of Ireland, the mutinies in the fleet, and the fear of political organisation induced ministers to seek a further addition to their powers. An act was passed making it possible to inflict severe penalties on any one found guilty of inciting His Majesty's forces to mutiny; [1] and by a second act to prevent the administration of unlawful oaths, it was hoped to render impossible the formation of secret societies for political agitation. [2]

The remaining years of Pitt's administration were years of terror. "A disloyal word was enough to bring down punishment upon any man's head. Laughing at the awkwardness of a volunteer corps was criminal. People were apprehended and sent on board a man of war for this breach of decorum, which was punished as a terrible crime." [3] A harmless bookbinder was sentenced to stand in the pillory and to serve five years with hard labour for crying on Snow Hill, "No George, no war." [4] For damning the king, a blacksmith of Bourne, in Lincolnshire, was sentenced to silent and solitary confinement for twelve months. [5]

Huge sums of money were spent by the Home Secretary during 1797 in securing reports of the proceedings of a public debating society called the Westminster Forum, held at the Assembly Rooms in Beever Street, Golden Square. The price of admission was sixpence, and "no Political Remarks appertaining to this Country" were permitted. Subjects were discussed which can by no stretch of the imagination be regarded as political, such as the slaying of Jephtha's daughter, or the question, suggested by the Rev. A. M. Toplady, [6] "supposing a Mariner ship-

---

episode nevertheless seems to dispose of Dr. Hunt's statement that the Act against seditious meetings was inoperative.—*Political History of England*, X. 380.

[1] 37 Geo. III. c. 70. [2] 37 Geo. III. c. 123.
[3] *Add. MSS.* 27808, fo. 110 ; cf. *Mem. of Horne Tooke*, II. 237.
[4] *Recoll. of J. Binns*, 60–1.
[5] *Add. MSS.* 27808, fo. 110 ; cf. a similar case at Gosport, June 1797. —H. O. 42.
[6] Presumably this refers to the author of "Rock of Ages." But Toplady died in 1778, and the pleasant conundrum here attributed to him, must, I suppose, have been drawn from his writings.

wrecked with his Mother, Wife and Child: having Time and Power to save only one of the three, which ought to be the object of his Protection." The art of illustration, of course, knows neither law nor limitation, and a good deal of political matter may have been introduced to point a moral or demonstrate an analogy even during debates on such subjects as these. Other subjects, such as Paine's attack on Washington, lent themselves still more readily to the adroit extensions of an artful speaker. On the eve of his trial at Birmingham, Gale Jones, who was out on bail, and who had been one of the regular speakers at the Forum, delivered what he described as his farewell oration. In June, the Home Secretary took the opinion of counsel on the proceedings of the Westminster Forum. Randle Jackson,[1] the barrister first consulted, pronounced that the debates had been conducted throughout with great precaution, but admitted, rather cautiously, that Jones's farewell oration might form the subject of a prosecution. This reply was not, apparently, decided enough to warrant an attempt to bring Jones to trial, and in July a second opinion was sought from Sergeant Adair,[2] who thought that Gale Jones's farewell oration was the only actionable speech amongst those reported to him, and advised that no good could be effected by proceeding against him. A great deal of money was paid to shorthand writers for the reports of the debates in the Westminster Forum, but, to crown all, handsome fees had to be paid to the lawyers for advising the Government not to prosecute.[3] It is not surprising that the bill for rather more than a hundred and seventy pounds was paid without any effusive manifestation of delight.[4]

The money was, in fact, wasted, not merely because the orators at debating societies were harmless, but because the majority of Englishmen were as violent against the disaffected—as violent against many who were not disaffected

---

[1] Probably Randle Jackson (1758-1837), parliamentary counsel; counsel for the East Indian Company and the Corporation of London.

[2] The former Wilkite. Adair was one of those whom the French Revolution had made Tory. He was one of the counsel for the prosecution in the trials of Hardy and Horne Tooke. He died in 1798.

[3] H. O. ⅟₈, ⅟₇.   [4] See letter of Aug. 27, 1798.—H. O. ⅟₇.

—as were their rulers. If a spectator in the theatre failed to rise and uncover at the first strains of "God Save the King," his hat would at once be smashed over his head by scandalised neighbours. Sydney Smith relates that when he went to the play at Birmingham the audience insisted on two "Rule Britannias," three "God Save the Kings," and four other "songs about Britons," in the course of one evening.[1] Whilst the public remained in this temper, the force of opinion was more effective than the closest espionage. It is an old story, the proofs of which are in letters amongst the Home Office papers, that Wordsworth, Coleridge and Thelwall were roundly denounced as violent democrats by their neighbours at Alfoxton, whose suspicions were aroused by their habit of carrying camp-stools and of looking long and intently out to sea.[2] Not even in the depth of the country was Thelwall allowed to dwell in peace, but amateur detectives watched upon his slightest movement and sent their reports to the authorities in London.[3] There even came a time, in May 1798, when ministers, not content with the efficiency of this voluntary police, not content even with their supremacy, now almost unquestioned, in Parliament, even contemplated for a moment the prosecution of Fox himself.[4]

The written was no better protected than the spoken word. Fox believed that a final blow was given to the liberty of the press[5] by the prosecution and conviction of a harmless scholar, called Gilbert Wakefield, for a reply to the Bishop of Llandaff's defence of the administration.[6] A few years later, in 1800, at a dinner to celebrate the anniversary of his first election for Westminster, Fox toasted not the liberty of the press, but its memory.[7] In these circumstances the reformers were not to be blamed if they

---

[1] *Life*, I. 16-17.   [2] Aug. 1797.—H. O. $\frac{4}{4}\frac{2}{3}$.   [3] April 1798.—H. O. $\frac{4}{4}\frac{3}{3}$.

[4] Pitt to Dundas, May 5, 1798.—Stanhope, II. 276. Fox's friends realised his danger. In March 1798, the Prince of Wales, through the Duke of Northumberland, had tried to persuade Fox "to sign a declaration protesting strict adherence to the King and Government, in which declaration a specific reform might be stated."—*Journal of Elizabeth, Lady Holland*, I. 180.

[5] *Life of J. Cartwright*, I. 248-9.

[6] *Life of Wakefield*, II. 66-8, 115-47, 154; *Anec. of Bp. Watson*, 305-6; *S. T.* XXVII. 679-760, cf. 627-80; *Journal of Eliz., Lady Holland*, I. 179.   [7] Pamphlet containing his speech, 22.

believed that their cause was dead.   It needed all the robust faith of John Cartwright to cherish the sure and certain hope of resurrection.[1]

The repressive legislation of 1797 enabled the Government to suppress the feeble English and Scots compeers of the United Irishmen.   George Mealmaker, who had written the address for which Palmer had been convicted,[2] was the ringleader of the United Scotsmen.   The society was secret, and its oaths were presumably unlawful.   More terrible still, it had some success.[3]   The society does not, however, appear to have professed objects other than annual parliaments and universal suffrage,[4] and it expressed deep abhorrence of riot and tumult.[5]   But when sedition was found in the declaration that the will of the majority was not rebellion,[6] little mercy was to be expected for these associators.   Mealmaker was prosecuted and transported for fourteen years.[7]   David Black and James Paterson were proceeded against under the same act.[8]   Their chief offence was membership of the same society.   Black was outlawed for non-appearance, and Paterson was sentenced to transportation for five years.[9]   This would seem to have made an end of the United Scotsmen.

In England, what remained of the fabric of the London Corresponding Society, the mere shell and framework of the old organisation, fell under the influence of O'Coigley, an Irish priest, and member of the Society of United Irishmen.   Nursed, as Place at any rate believed, by the agents of Government, several weak-headed men tried to form a society of United Englishmen,[10] and were so far successful as to excite Arthur O'Connor to delusive hopes of a revolution.[11]   But even the Committee of Secrecy refused to believe that its numbers were ever large, and it is certain that several responsible reformers did their best to suppress it.[12]   An address to the United Irish, the chief object of

---

[1] *Life of J. C.*, I. 240.   [2] *S. T.* XXIII. 300, 313.
[3] *C. J.* LIV. 338–9.   [4] *S. T.* XXVI. 1160. [5] *C. J.* LIV. 359–61.
[6] *S. T.* XXVI. 1161.   [7] *Ib.* 1164.   [8] 37 Geo. III. 123.
[9] *S. T.* XXVII. 1179–90; Cockburn, II. 162–4, cf. a case, otherwise unreported, given in Cockburn, II. 159–61.
[10] *Add. MSS.* 35143, ff. 62–3, 65; 27808, ff. 91–2; *C. J.* LIV. 337; cf. *Recoll. of J. Binns*, 143–7.   They are sometimes, apparently, called "United Britons," though this may have been the name of a distinct society.
[11] *C. J.* LIV. 336.   [12] *Ib.* 336.—*Add. MSS.* 35143, fo. 62.

which seems to have been to exaggerate the importance of the United English, gives the impression that the new society had an organisation distinct from that of the old Corresponding Society, though it is extremely difficult to disentangle one society from the other. The "sedition" of the address to the United Irish depends entirely on the possible content of the "unlimited confidence" placed in the United Irish by the addressers, and it is impossible to say how far the United Englishmen were cognisant of the real designs of the United Irish.[1] "If to UNITE in the *Cause of Reform* upon the *Broadest Basis* be *Treason*," the London Corresponding Society had said in an address to the Irish, which betrayed no guilty knowledge of the brewing rebellion, "We, with you, are Traitors."[2]

Government affected to believe that the old organisation of the London Corresponding Society and the new organisation of the United Englishmen were being used to support a great conspiracy, and had branches all over England.[3] An end was put to the business by seizing the leaders of both—for the most part they were the same men. The alleged United Englishmen numbered only twenty-eight, of whom six were not members of that or any other society, but had gone to dissuade their friends from excesses. On the 19th of April, 1798, another thirteen were taken at a Corresponding Society Committee.[4] "This stroke extinguished the society, which never made any attempt to meet again."[5] The terror was so great that

---

[1] Jan. 5. 1798.—*C. J.* XLIV. 354-5.

[2] Jan. 30. 1798.—*Ib.* XLIV. 355-6. The address is said to have been post-dated more than a year by the Committee of Secrecy.—*Recoll. of J. Binns*, 143.

[3] The best explanation of the evidence, which is not very satisfactory, seems to be that certain sections of the London Corresponding Society changed their name and formed societies of United Englishmen. One witness says that there were seven sections ; one met at the house of Thomas Evans, 14 Plough Court, and another met at the Bull's Head, Rotherhithe. There was apparently a society of United Englishmen at Manchester.— *C. J.* LIV. 337-8, 357-9; secret information taken by Mr. Ford, March 12, 1798 ; deposition of John Scotson, March 12 ; examination of Thomas Evans.—H. O. $\frac{11}{6}$. There is also amongst the Home Office papers a certificate dated April 20, 1797, that a man called Thomas Cheetham was a member of the Society of United Englishmen at Manchester.—H. O. $\frac{11}{6}$. On the general question of the United Englishmen, cf. *Add. MSS.* 35143. fo. 63 ; 27808, ff. 92, 108-9. [4] *Add. MSS.* 35143, fo. 66.

[5] *Ib.* 35143, ff. 59-61 ; 27808, ff. 88-90, cf. 106; *C. J.* LIV. 337 ; cf., however, Wm. Stone (Strand) to Portland, April 26 1798.—H. O. $\frac{11}{6}$.

Place had great difficulty in getting a secretary or treasurer to collect money for the support of the families [1] of the supposed conspirators, who remained in prison until 1801.[2] In 1799 the Corresponding Society was included amongst the political societies which were suppressed by specific enactment; [3] but this was no more than a formal and legal slaying of the slain.

O'Coigley was captured at Margate, attempting to cross to France—itself a criminal offence—and was tried for treason, with O'Connor and John Binns.[4] O'Connor and Binns were acquitted. But O'Coigley was convicted and hanged.[5] He seems to have been an honest enthusiast, though of a sort that governments cannot tolerate.[6] Dr. Parr thought him worthy of defence. Mackintosh, who had by this time forgotten his old fervour for reform, had observed that O'Coigley deserved his fate. One could scarce conceive, he said, of a greater scoundrel. "By no means, sir," replied Parr; "for it is very possible to conceive a greater scoundrel. He was an Irishman—he might have been a Scotchman; he was a priest—he might have been a lawyer; he was a traitor—he might have been an apostate!"[7]

[1] *Add. MSS.* 35143, fo. 68.

[2] Letter from one of them, Alexander Galloway, to Portland, Oct. 11, 1798, is interesting.—H. O. $\frac{43}{5}$.

[3] The societies suppressed were: the United Englishman, United Scotsmen, United Britons, United Irishmen, and the London Corresponding Society. An Act for the more effectual Suppression of Societies established for Seditious and Treasonable Purposes, and for better preventing Treasonable and Seditious Practices (July 12, 1799), 39 Geo. III. C. 79.

[4] There is a letter from Binns to the Lords of the Privy Council, March 8, 1798, in H. O. $\frac{43}{5}$.

[5] *S. T.* XXVI. 1302; XXVII. 141-254.—*Recoll. of Lord Cloncurry*, 66-8; see also *Mem. S. T.* XXVII. 821-986; *Mem. of C. J. Fox*, IV. 342; Warrant for O'Coigley's execution found in the panels of the wall of an old inn at Dartford, is printed in *Notes and Queries*, Ninth Series, III. 327. There is little room to doubt that O'Coigley was, in fact, guilty of treason, though there seems to be a real doubt as to whether the evidence brought against him was technically satisfactory.—*Ib.* XI. 81, 198.

[6] *Recoll. of J. Binns*, 80-93. "Half-enthusiast, half-bigot," Lady Holland calls him in her *Journal*. Place, who liked him, describes him as "a tall, stout, good-looking man, of remarkably mild manners, kind and benevolent."—Place's Auto., *Add. MSS.* 35143, fo. 62. Cf. Fitzpatrick, *Secret Service Under Pitt*, passim, and the *Anti-Jacobin*, 233.

[7] *Mem. of Parr*, I. 394-5; slightly different version in the *Table Talk of Samuel Rogers*, 50.

CONCLUSION

"ALL the leading members of the London Corresponding Society," wrote Place in restrospect, with a strange,
but instructive, misuse of words, "were Republicans; that
is, they were friendly to a representative form of Government. But their leading men were none of them Anarchists,
none of them hot-headed revolutionists, but sedate men,
who sought for representation through the Government
itself, by such steps as might bring about the changes they
wished by degrees, and not more rapidly than an instructed
people could bear them." [1] This was the moderate attitude
of all those reformers whom Pitt repressed as traitors.
The revolution which they desired was, in the famous
phrase of the Duke of Wellington, "revolution by due
course of law."

It is not to be supposed that Pitt had any great liking
for his policy of repression, or that he cared in 1798, any
more than he cared in 1782, for the members of the great
family connections who battened upon an exhausted
treasury, but whose supremacy he thought it necessary,
for the sake of national stability itself, to maintain and
even to make day by day more secure. He was no believer
in the comfortable doctrine that all the first families should
have all the best offices, and there is a ring of unusual
sincerity in the words in which Lady Holland declares
her opinion that "not a man of the Corresponding Society"
was "more bitter against the aristocracy" than Pitt and his
disciple Canning.[2]

It was his sense of the magnitude of the dangers by
which England was threatened abroad that drove Pitt not
merely to resist change, but to repress the advocates of

---

[1] *Add. MSS.* 35143, fo. 90 ; cf. ff. 91–3, 88–9 ; 27808, ff. 59–60.
[2] *Journal of Elizabeth, Lady Holland,* Nov. 20, 1798, I. 206.

change at home. His policy of repression was supported by the majority of the nation, and supported so emphatically as to render it unnecessary. It was as if a nation of self-appointed policemen had turned out in force to keep guard over a handful of suspected pickpockets. Both Pitt and the nation were, in fact, over-anxious. Their fears were wasted, and they spent much rhetorical and legislative powder upon foemen who had neither the desire nor the strength to fight. But it is both just and easy to make excuses for the man, as for the nation, that erred in an hour of conflict when mankind was struggling with one of the darkest problems in its history, and when, in the words of Grattan, it seemed as if the fortunes of the world were in the scale, and the intellectual order in danger of kicking the beam.

If the historian finds it possible to make excuses for Pitt, he finds it still easier to do justice to those who were the victims of his policy of repression. Their sacrifices were not, after all, for nothing, and their efforts were not altogether spent in vain, for the Statute Book has become their justification, and no man would now condemn them. "When our ashes shall be scattered by the winds of heaven," Muir had truly prophesied to the court which tried him, "the impartial voice of future times will re-judge your verdict." [1]

The immediate future of the reformers seemed dark, but there were some who never lost courage. When Horne Tooke had told Major Cartwright, in a letter of 1797, that he thought the cause of reform "dead and buried," that incurable optimist had written in the margin : "But J. C. is a believer in the resurrection." [2] Cartwright's old friend Wilberforce met him in the street one day in 1801 and said he hoped they should meet in a better world. "I answered," said Cartwright, "that *I hoped we should first mend the world we were in.*" [3]

In 1801 few reformers were as hopeful as Cartwright,

---

[1] *S. T.* XXIII. 186.
[2] J. Horne Tooke to Cartwright, and Cartwright's endorsement.— *Life of J. C.* I. 240 and note.
[3] Cartwright to his wife, April 7, 1801.—*Ib.* I. 300.

but during the next few years others began to recover their courage. In Francis Place, the Radical tailor of Charing Cross, a great organiser had been born, and he had learned, in the popular societies and in trade clubs, lessons which were to have abundant influence upon social as well as upon political organisation—upon the development of trade unionism as well as upon the working of popular government.

In 1807 Place approached the question of parliamentary reform afresh, with the determination to make the best of the existing conditions. The wide " scot and lot " franchise of the city of Westminster afforded him just the opportunity he needed. At the dissolution of April 1807 he so organised the popular forces that Sir Francis Burdett,[1] an ardent parliamentary reformer, was returned for Westminster without cost to himself and without personal canvass. Burdett was "a fine-looking man " "of lofty stature, with a proud but not forbidding carriage," [2] who became a popular hero, and remained the idol and representative of Westminster for thirty years. He was no great politician, but his election gave the reformers what they most needed—a fearless spokesman in the House of Commons, a leader around whom advanced reformers might gather outside the walls of Parliament.[3]

In 1811, owing largely to the exertions of Major Cartwright, a new society of "friends to parliamentary reform " was established, with Sir John Throckmorton [4] as the chairman of its committee, and with nearly three hundred supporters, amongst whom were old reformers like Capell Lofft and Christopher Wyvill, reformers of the new generation like Henry Hunt, William Cobbett and Sir Francis Burdett, as well as that cut-and-thrust politician Lord Cochrane, and that accomplished party manager— the "King Tom " of the Whigs—Coke of Holkham. This

[1] Of Foremark Hall and Ramsbury Manor, Wilts, 1770–1844.
[2] Bamford, I. 21–2.
[3] There is a Memoir of Burdett, by Thomas Tegg, 1804. Also a " Sketch," published in 1810. See the account of him in Sheil's *Political Sketches*, II. 31–4, and the sketch of his character and abilities—perhaps too generous—in Hazlitt's *Spirit of the Age*.
[4] Of Congleton Court, Weston Underwood and Buckland (July 27, 1753—Jan. 3, 1819).

society became, in June 1812, "the Union for Parliamentary Reform according to the Constitution," and declared for annual elections and representation in Parliament on the basis of direct taxation. Already the more Whiggish members of the association would seem to have disappeared —perhaps a resolution excluding holders of pensions or places of profit under the Crown had been too much for them. But even when official Whigs no longer hampered it the society seems to have been too moderate and too respectable to accomplish much effective work. It is important chiefly as an example and because it shows that the reformers were retrieving their courage and seeking, however feebly, to revive their cause.[1]

Another association, the Hampden Club, first projected in May 1811, and formally constituted at the Thatched House Tavern on the 20th of April, 1812, was a dining society not altogether unlike the old Revolution Society.[2] It was to meet twice a year, in March and May, the expense of the dinners being met by the members attending. In order to become a member it was necessary to possess £300 a year in land, or to be heir to such a property; the annual subscription, in addition to the cost of the dinners, was two pounds. Peers, baronets and members of Parliament were among its early supporters. Doubtful characters like Cobbett and Hunt kept out of the way, and even Cartwright, who had helped to organise the new association, withdrew for a time when it was hinted that he scared away moderate reformers. The club declared itself in favour of "a reform in the representation of the people," though the declaration was expressed in vague phrases calculated to excite no unnecessary alarm in timorous minds. But reformers who were timid as well as moderate do not seem to have been induced to enter the club by these anxious endeavours to rob them of plausible excuses for staying outside. Cartwright returned to the fold, and the club laid down the same programme of reform as was

---

[1] *Life of John Cartwright*, II. 10, 24, 129, and Appendices XIII and XIV.

[2] Curiously enough, the most famous of all dining societies—Grillion's —began in the same year.

adopted by the Reform Union—annual Parliaments and the enfranchisement of all direct taxpayers.

Cartwright had hoped that the Hampden Club would be the heart and brain of a new and more vigorous movement for parliamentary reform. Its chequered career disappointed his hopes. It had its moments of energy. It carried on an extensive correspondence; it tried to "tune" the popular Press; in July 1815 it even sent a man called Thomas Cleary, a special pleader and conveyancer of the Inner Temple, who ultimately became its secretary, on a missionary tour to Wales. But these bursts of energy were fitful, and the reform propaganda was not carried on with the necessary persistence. Whenever the political sky was overcast fair weather reformers slunk away from the club, and in the dark days of 1817 it seems to have passed quietly out of existence.[1]

In their shining moments, no doubt, political societies like the Reform Union and the Hampden Club helped to sustain the spirits of the reformers during a period of discouragement and apparent failure. They also did much more; for though their record of directly effective work was not magnificent they were great exemplars. Up and down the country, especially in the industrial towns and manufacturing villages, there sprang up political clubs which took their names, imitated and developed their machinery and employed their methods. "It was they," says Place, "who gave the tone to many places, and revived the dormant desire for reform."

These clubs and unions were denounced as secret societies, though they were no more secret than the cry of the Watch. They were accused of plotting a total subversion of the Constitution—by the introduction of annual Parliaments and universal suffrage. They were even thought to be in league with the Spenceans, whose

---

[1] A Collection of the Reports of Proceedings of the Hampden Club. London, 1814–1822. This is not a published volume but a collection of printed papers, etc., made by Thomas Cleary with a view to writing the history of the society. It was afterwards presented by Cleary to Joseph Hume ("Penny Wise"), and Cleary's letter to Hume is fastened inside the book, which is now in the British Museum. See also *Life of John Cartwright*, II. 24–30, 72–3, 86, 119–20, 124–66, 163, and Appendix XV.

crude Socialism can have had little attraction for the sturdy individualists who were the strength of the reforming party. Committees of both Houses worked themselves into a frenzy of alarm. Even the cool and clear-headed Peel told a friend that the reform societies had in view "nothing short of revolution." [1]   If parliamentary reform was to Peel's mind—as it was to many minds—synonymous with revolution, this was strictly true.   In the provinces the clubs carried on a vigorous agitation for reform, and though they received temporary checks from the repressive enactments of 1817 and 1819 it may almost be said of them, as Falstaff said of the camomile, that the more they were trampled on the faster they grew.

Meantime another method of propaganda—the missionary tour—had been adopted by the reformers.   In 1795 Gale Jones had, as we have seen, been employed in this service by the London Corresponding Society, and had met, at first, with some success.   He and Binns had subsequently been sent to encourage the reformers at Birmingham, but the campaign had been abruptly terminated by their arrest, and their comrades did not renew it.   After long disuse this method of propaganda was revived by Major Cartwright and by the Hampden Club.   In July 1815 Cleary was sent on the missionary tour to Wales to which we have already alluded, and in January and February of 1813 Major Cartwright set out on a political campaign as arduous as any undertaken by the great platform orators of our own time.   He travelled 900 miles in twenty-nine days, and got as far north as Newcastle-on-Tyne.[2]   He visited thirty-five towns, including many of the great industrial and commercial centres of the north, the midlands and the west, and returned with 430 petitions for reform.   In July and August of 1815 he made a similar tour—and as he thought, a particularly successful one—through the great towns of Scotland.   Their opponents sneered at these "itinerant apostles," and Cartwright jokingly avowed that he had almost become a "field-

[1] To Gregory, Feb. 22, 1817.—Parker's *Peel*, I. 239.
[2] Probably the Hampden Club met the expenses of this tour.   But Cartwright paid the expenses of the subsequent tour out of his own pocket.

preacher." [1] Yet these propagandist tours were of real service to the cause of reform. They stirred up provincial reformers and confirmed them in the faith, and they were even more valuable as examples, for William Cobbett, more powerful than Cartwright on the platform as he was more effective in the Press, adopted his methods and followed in his wake. [2]

The reformers also found an ally, as powerful after his own fashion as Cobbett, in Jeremy Bentham. [3] At first sight the alliance might seem a strange one, for though English reformers had never paid much attention to abstract theory, yet as individuals their interest in politics had, as a rule, been stimulated either by the revolution in America or by the Revolution in France, and in both cases the revolutionists were inspired by the doctrine of the rights of man, which Bentham had begun life by demolishing in his *Fragment on Government.* But though his political theory was, for the most part, not theirs, Bentham found the measures of legal reform in which he himself was interested impeded by just those parliamentary conditions which the reformers attacked, and he became, on practical grounds, an advocate of the constitutional changes which they most desired. Around him there gathered the group of thinkers to whom, with their disciples, the name of philosophical Radicals came ultimately to be applied. Amongst Bentham's disciples was James Mill, to whom Francis Place had been introduced in 1808. In 1812 Mill introduced Place to Bentham; he was gradually admitted to the inner circle of the Benthamites, and he became, as it were, the link between the followers of Bentham and the followers of Burdett.

Bentham had composed, in 1809, his *Plan of Parliamentary Reform in the Form of a Catechism.*" [4] He advocated

---

[1] *Life of John Cartwright*, II. 45-50, 111-16.

[2] See, for instance, Carlyle's *Cobbett*, 187.

[3] On Bentham see Stephen's *English Utilitarians*, I. 169 *et seq.* He is the subject of one of the most interesting essays in Hazlitt's *Spirit of the Age.* Mr. H. A. L. Fisher has recently given us a charming picture of him in *The Republican Tradition in Europe*, 160-3.

[4] Place "edited" the work for publication in Wooler's *Black Dwarf*, a Radical newspaper speaking, in general, the opinions of Major Cartwright.

annual Parliaments, the suffrage for all who paid a certain amount of direct taxation—virtually, as he thought, universal suffrage—secret voting and as nearly as circumstances permitted, equal electoral districts. Bentham's pamphlet was published in 1817. His plan was afterwards discussed with Burdett, and together Burdett and Bentham drafted a series of resolutions in favour of universal suffrage, annual Parliaments and the ballot which Burdett introduced in 1818 into the House of Commons. Those resolutions marked the coalescence of the two divisions of the Radical army that was fighting for reform.

The official Whigs were still unconverted. Fox had never been an enthusiastic advocate of reform, and within a few weeks of his death he had discouraged proceedings which might have seemed to pledge him to it. In 1817 Lord Holland declared, "Parliamentary reform . . . . was not yet adopted as an indispensable article in the Whig creed." [1] In the same year he complained bitterly that the "cursed business of Reform of Parliament is always in one's way"—in the way, that is, between the Whigs and office—because one Whig leader will not hear of it and another Whig leader will hear of nothing else until it is accomplished. [2] Little could be expected from a party so divided. The party's tactics were, in the words of one of the Radicals, "to find good, whiggish, prudent, plausible reasons for procrastination," whilst amusing the reformers with delusive hopes. Activity and progress did not suit the Whig temper. It was the great Whig Lord Darlington—albeit the patron of the unquiet Brougham—who opposed the Stockton and Darlington Railway because it would interfere with the game. It was an advanced Whig, Lord Sefton, who put up another advanced Whig, Creevey, to denounce "the loco-motive Monster" "navigated by a tail of smoke and sulphur," and to oppose the projected railway between Manchester and Liverpool to which a Canningite Tory like John Gladstone gave his warm support. Not till an earnest parliamentary leader, convinced of the necessity of reform, arose from within the charmed

---

[1] *Further Memoirs of the Whig Party*, 254.
[2] Holland to Creevey (n. d. and June 24, 1817).—*Creevey*, Pt. I. 263.

circle of the great Whig families was the Whig party likely to brace itself to the effort of carrying a Reform Bill through the House of Commons.

One such leader the moderate reformers had had, but he had been banished from the Commons. In an evil hour Charles Grey's father had accepted a peerage. The death of the father in 1807 had deprived the Whig reformers in the Commons of the leadership of the son, and had buried Grey in the comparative obscurity of the House of Lords. There he was lost. As Wellington pungently remarked—"Nobody cares a damn for the House of Lords : the House of Commons is everything in England, and the House of Lords nothing." [1] For eleven years the moderate reformers in the Commons waited for a leader. But in July 1818 Lord John Russell, a former pupil, curiously enough, of Major Cartwright's brother, Dr. Edmund Cartwright, spoke on Burdett's motion for a parliamentary reform. He denounced wild and visionary schemes, condemned any inquiry "calculated to throw a slur upon the representation "—he sat himself for the family borough of Tavistock—or "to fill the minds of the people with vague and indefinite alarms." But at the same time he declared himself in favour of a moderate reform, and became from that hour the spokesman of the moderate reformers. The field was now set. The intellectual and political forces which were to fight the battle of reform, in and out of the House of Commons, were by 1818 fully marshalled under their chosen leaders.

Behind them were the dynamic forces of economic and social change. The country which emerged successfully from the struggle with Napoleon in 1815 was no longer the country that had entered in 1793 into the war against the Revolution. In the meantime the face of England had been changed. The country was still passing through a period of rapid and continuous transformation. Its separate parts were being welded more firmly together. Great bridge-builders and great road-makers had been, and still were, at work linking up the isolated fragments into one coherent and related whole. Apart altogether from the

[1] *Journal*, 1817–18, *Creevey Papers*, I. 287.

great improvements effected in the old roads, a thousand miles of new turnpike were laid in England and Wales between 1818 and 1829, an addition, within the short space of eleven years, of about a mile in twenty to the best roads in the country.[1] In Scotland the Board of Works constructed over 1200 miles of road and built over a thousand bridges during the first half of the nineteenth century. With the improvement in the roads the vehicles which travelled over them increased in number and were improved in quality. In the eighteenth century the driver of a fast coach was not ashamed of a speed of four miles an hour, but by the accession of Victoria the coaches had doubled their speed, and the best mail coaches could cover fully ten miles within the hour. "There are coaches of all varieties nowadays,"[2] Miss Mitford tells us in the charming sketches of *Our Village*—Three Mile Cross, near Reading—which she wrote between 1824 and 1832. "The macadamised roads, and the light open carriages lately introduced, have so abridged, I had well-nigh said annihilated, distance in this fair island, that what used to be judged a journey is now a drive; our neighbourhood has become, from a reverse reason to theirs, as extensive as that of the good people in the back settlements of America; we think nothing of thirty miles for a morning call, or forty for a dinner-party; Richmond is quite within visiting distance, and London will shortly be our market-town."[3] The nation was, in fact, being made "one and indivisible," was being gradually knit together in such fashion as to unite the dispersed elements of "public opinion" into a powerful and effective political force.

Public opinion was being influenced and educated by virile journalists, the ablest of whom were advocates of parliamentary reform. Between the opening of the century and passing of the Reform Act the circulation of stamped newspapers was more than doubled. Hone in the

[1] See, in the chapter of Miss Mitford's *Our Village* (1824–32), called " Another Glance at our Village," an amusing description of the adjustment of a road " on the plan of Mr. Macadam."

[2] Opening chapter of *Our Village*. It should, perhaps, be noted that these sketches began to appear in magazine form in 1819.

[3] Chapter in *Our Village* called, " A Visit to Richmond."

Reformer's Register, the Hunts in the *Examiner,* Wooler in the *Black Dwarf* chorused for reform. A greater than these, perhaps the greatest of all English journalists, William Cobbett, was at the same time carrying on a powerful reform agitation by means of his *Political Register.* The sixpenny stamp-duty on newspapers kept it dear. It cost a shilling and a halfpenny. But in 1817 he began to reprint his articles in an edition from which all news was omitted, and as he thus avoided the stamp duty he was able to sell the *Register,* in its new form, at twopence. Cobbett's "twopenny trash," as sneering opponents called it, was read on every cottage hearth in the manufacturing districts. Improved means of communications facilitated its distribution, and it became a powerful agent of parliamentary reform.

But not merely was the appearance of England transformed; its centre of gravity was shifted and its social texture changed. Edmund Cartwright's power-loom was proving a more effective agent of reform than his brother's pamphlets. It transformed the relatively barren and unproductive North into a prosperous hive of industry. In 1813 there were 2400 power-looms in use, and already the hand-loom weaver was being displaced. But so rapid was the increase of machinery that it was estimated that by 1829 there were about 60,000 power-looms in England and Scotland, and by 1833 a hundred thousand were in use. As home industries gave way before the conquering factories a teeming population crowded into the manufacturing districts. The population of Lancashire, for example, was, roughly speaking, doubled, the population of Manchester rather more than doubled between 1801 and 1831. In the same period the population of England and Wales, as a whole, which was rapidly increasing, rose about sixty-four per cent., at a rate, that is to say, which was relatively much slower than that of the industrial districts. Therefore, whilst the population as a whole was rising rapidly, it was rising in such fashion as to increase enormously the proportionate weight of the manufacturing districts, and to make daily more apparent the inequality of the parliamentary representation. An illustration will make this clearer. In 1801 the population of Lancashire was more than three times as great as the population of Cornwall; in 1831 it was more than four times as great, and Lancashire was assessed, for the purposes of the income and property tax, to between six and seven times as much, for the purposes of the poor rate to more than seven times as much, as Cornwall. Yet Cornwall as a whole, taking county and boroughs together, had more than three times as many representatives in the House of Commons as Lancashire. The contradiction was too obvious. Such inequalities were indefensible and called aloud for readjustment. The industrial revolution had made a Reform Act inevitable.

The agrarian revolution which had in part preceded the industrial revolution and which continued alongside of it, struck almost as crushing a blow at the comfortable doctrine of virtual representation. With the progress of enclosure the wage-paid class increased in the agricultural district as well as in the towns. With the decay of home industry the small man who had depended for his support in part upon his manufactures and in part upon his land, tended to gravitate to the towns. It could no longer be urged with even a show of reason that the interests of the great landowners who enjoyed direct representation were identical with the interests of the villagers, who no longer shared in the cultivation of common fields, or worked their separate holdings in the intervals of manufacture, and who were now, therefore, not even "virtually" represented. It is not necessary to believe that the enclosure movement took the monstrous forms of crime and pillage which it assumes in many minds. But it is plain that in the early years of the nineteenth century the labourers were nursing a sullen discontent, all the more dangerous because it was voiceless, which flamed out at last in 1830 in what has been called "the Labourers' Revolt."[1] That revolt had not political, but economic origins; it had not even, so far as it has yet been described, any political expression. But it might easily have become political, and the fear that the

[1] See the description of it, based on the Home Office Papers, in J. L. and Barbara Hammond's *The Village Labourer*, 1760–1832.

labourers of the village might join with the artisans of the towns in their demand for parliamentary reform was probably, almost certainly, one of the considerations which spurred on the Whigs to grapple with the problem oᶠ the representation when at last they entered office.

Time and change were fighting against the old parliamentary system. It had only to remain unchanged in order to grow gradually worse by comparison with what it ought to have been. The agitation for reform rose and fell in the country, answering, as a rule, to the fluctuations in the price of labour or provisions and to the consequent ease or misery of the working classes, the demand for reform rising to a scream when wages fell or food grew dearer, and falling to a murmur with better times. But agitation in the country had little effect upon Parliament. Moulded, as it was, by patronage, it was almost impervious to criticism. By 1830 the nation was probably as eager for parliamentary reform as it has been for any measure in its history—certainly much more eager than it had been for Catholic Emancipation, which had been carried in 1829 —but the reformers in the House of Commons had never yet done as well in a division as Pitt had done when he moved for a committee of inquiry in 1782. What was still needed was an exceptional opportunity to make the pressure of public opinion effective in Parliament, and such an opportunity was long in coming. "My opinion has long been," Cartwright wrote in 1823, "that reform, come when it will, will come suddenly"; and he was right.[1]

Three circumstances precipitated the crisis. The first— already mentioned—effected a breach in the defences of the party most strongly entrenched against reform. In January 1829 Peel and Wellington were out-generalled by O'Connell, and found themselves on the horns of a dilemma; either they must make the distasteful concession of Catholic Emancipation, or they must prepare for a constitutional struggle compared with which the Wilkes case would have been mere child's-play, a constitutional struggle which would, in fact, have been scarcely distinguishable

---

[1] To Colonel W. A. Johnson, April 3, 1823.—*Life of Major Cartwright*, II. 238.

from civil war. They chose to emancipate the Catholics, and they carried into law a measure of Catholic relief. But they broke their party. They exasperated those of their followers who were most tenacious in their conservatism. Weakened in credit by its surrender to O'Connell, and in solidarity by the strain which Peel and Wellington had put upon the loyalty of their most inflexible supporters, the Tory party was no longer capable of opposing an immovable barrier to all reform.

Secondly, George IV, who was another barrier to reform and would have used his influence against it, died in June 1830, and was succeeded by his brother William, who had no desire to set his personal wishes against those of his people, and who could even be persuaded to assist his ministers by using the powers of the Crown to overcome the interested opposition of the House of Lords. King George had not been dead three days, says Greville, before "everybody discovered that he was no loss and King William a great gain." William was not a great king. He looked like "a respectable old admiral," and putting a charitable interpretation upon the word respectable, so he was. Incapable of ruling by the light of his own intelligence, he yet had wit enough to know it. He was prepared to act as a constitutional king, on the advice of his ministers, and apart from some excusable vacillation during the unprecedented struggle over the Reform Bill, to that constitutional view of his position he faithfully adhered.

In the third place, the movement for reform received a final impulse from France. William was scarcely seated on the throne before the French Revolution of July overthrew the Bourbons. A wave of revolution swept over Europe and influenced the general election of 1830 in England. The French contagion at once turned many who before had been lukewarm into enthusiasts for reform, whilst others, on the contrary, took warning by the Revolution of July and supported reform as an insurance against the possibility of evil to come. So strong was the movement of public opinion that the change was reflected in a manner unknown before in the composition of the new

House of Commons, and for the first time since Pitt abandoned the cause it was possible to propose measures of reform with reasonable hope of success. When the Duke of Wellington made an uncompromising declaration against reform in the new Parliament he sounded the death-knell of his ministry.

The Whigs came into power under Grey, who was deeply pledged to reform and had advocated it when it was most unpopular. Now England demanded it, and Grey gave it in the Reform Act of 1832. That act had many faults. In enfranchised only the few, and left the many still unrepresented. But though, as was said by a great advocate of its improvement, the Reform Bill was not a good Bill, "it was a great Bill when it passed." [1] It was a first and necessary step in parliamentary reform. More than that, it was carried because public opinion demanded it, and the success of 1832 was, in that sense, a tribute to the men who had failed in the eighteenth century, for public opinion was roused by the aid of political machinery which they had invented, and educated by men whom they had inspired and taught.

[1] John Bright's Speech on the Progress of the Nation, Jan. 29, 1864.

APPENDICES

APPENDIX I

Aix (Bouches-du-Rhône): Society of the Friends of the Constitution.
Alais (Gard): Society of the Friends of the Constitution.
Amiens (Somme): Society of the Friends of the French Constitution.
† Apt (Bouches-du-Rhône [or Vauclause?]).
Arras (Pas-de-Calais): Society of the Friends of the Constitution.
Auxerre (Yonne), Patriotic Society meeting at.
Bayonne (Basses-Pyrénées): Society of the Friends of the Constitution.
Bergerac (Dordogne): Society of the Friends of the Constitution.
Bourdeaux (sic) (Gironde): Society of the Friends of the Constitution.
Club du Café National.
Bourges (Cher): Society of the Friends of the Constitution.
Brest (Finistère): Society of the Friends of the Constitution.
Calais (Pas-de-Calais): Society of the Friends of the Constitution.
Chalon-sur-Sâone (Sâone-et-Loire): Society of the Friends of the Constitution.
Chartres (Eure-et-Loir): Society of the Friends of the Constitution.
Cherbourg (Manche): The Society of the Friends of the Constitution.
Clermont-Ferrand (Puy-de-Dôme): Society of the Friends of the Constitution.
Cognac (Charente): Society of the Friends of the Constitution.
Cressey (sic). There is no letter from this society now extant, but the reception of a letter was minuted by the London Revolution Society [C. R. S. 105–107]. There are at least three towns in France called Creçy. Was it the famous scene of the battle, Creçy-en-Ponthieu?

Dijon (Côte-d'Or), Patriotic Society of.

Grenoble (Isère): The Society of the Friends of the Constitution.

Havre, Le (Seine-Inférieure): Society of the Friends of the Constitution.

Hieres (?): Society of the Friends of the Constitution.

Honfleur (Calvados): Society of the Friends of the Constitution.

Langon (Gironde): Society of the Friends of the Constitution.

†Laon (L'Aisne).

Lille (Nord: generally spelt Lisle in the English publications), Patriotic Union of the Town and Castleward of.

The Ladies of the Society of the Friends of the Constitution of Lille. The Lille Society, of course, changed its name on affiliation with the Jacobins, and was called Society of the Friends of the Constitution.

Limoges (Haute-Vienne): Society of the Friends of the Constitution.

Lisieux (Calvados): Society of the Friends of the Constitution.

L'Orient (Morbihan), la Chambre Littéraire de.

†Mâcon (Sâone-et-Loire).

Marennes (Charente-Inférieure): The Society of the Friends of the Constitution.

Marseille (Bouches-du-Rhône), Patriotic Club of.

Montargis (Loiret): Society of the Friends of the Constitution.

Montpellier (Hérault): The Friends of the Constitution and of Equality.

Nantes (Loire-Inférieure): Society of the Friends of the Constitution.

Nîmes (Nismes was the commoner spelling at this epoch: [Gard]): The Club of the Friends of the Constitution.

Orléans (Loiret): The Society of the Friends of the Constitution.

Paris: The Society of the Friends of the Constitution, called Jacobins.

The Young Friends of Liberty, Rue Dubacq, No. 231.

Poitiers (Vienne): Society of the Friends of the Constitution.

Pontoise (Seine-et-Oise): Society of the Friends of the Constitution.

Quimper (Finistère): District of Quimper. This was in the Rochefoucauld sphere of influence.

Rennes (Ille-et-Vilaine): Society of the Friends of the Constitution.

Rochelle, La (Charente-Inférieure): The Friends of the Constitution.

Rouen (Seine-Inférieure): Society of the Friends of the Constitution.

Saintes (Charente-Inférieure): Society of the Friends of the Constitution.

Saint-Servan (Ille-et-Vilaine): The Society of the Friends of the Revolution.

Strasbourg (Bas-Rhin): Society of the Friends of the Constitution.

Toulouse (Haute-Garonne): Club of the Friends of the Constitution.
    Young Friends of the Constitution at Toulouse.

Tours (Indre-et-Loire): The Society of the Friends of the Constitution.

Valence (Drôme): Society of the Friends of the French Constitution.

Versailles (Seine-et-Oise): Society of the Friends of the Constitution.

Vire (Calvados), Patriotic Society of.

Almost all the societies are known to have been affiliated to or in correspondence with the Jacobins of Paris, and in most of the other cases it is probable that a correspondence was carried on, though it has not been traced. Those societies of which the names are marked with a dagger (†) were only in correspondence with the Society for Constitutional Information; the rest corresponded with the London Revolution Society. In both cases the correspondence may be incomplete. The last known letter received by the London Revolution Society bore date December 27. 1791, and was from the Society of Honfleur, to whom the Revolution Society addressed its last known reply on February 6, 1792.

APPENDIX II

ADDRESS OF THE WHIG CLUB OF DUNDEE (JUNE 10, 1790) PRESENTED TO THE NATIONAL ASSEMBLY, JULY 31, 1790. IT IS TO THE PRESIDENT.

SIR,
    We, the Members of the Whig Club of the Royal Borough of Dundee, in the North of Great Britain, earnestly desire you to present to the National Assembly this humble Address, unanimously agreed to in our Assembly. The triumph of liberty and reason over despotism, ignorance and superstition, is an event interesting to the most distant spectators: but the regeneration of your kingdom becomes doubly so for Great Britain. Indeed the example of the abuses of your ancient form of government has, during the past century, done great injury to our own. It excited in our Princes and their Ministers a desire for power, often injurious and sometimes fatal to themselves, and which always injured the interests of the State.

Accept, sir, our sincere congratulations on the re-establishment of your ancient and free Constitution and our ardent wishes that liberty may be established in France in an unchangeable manner. We note for the homme [*sic*, ? honour] of the century and of your Nation, that your Revolution has been accomplished without civil wars, and that neither the useless Domains of the Prince, nor the estates of the Clergy have passed to greedy hands; but that they have been employed for the good of the State whose property they are. Some troubles, even some acts of violence may have accompanied this great Revolution; but far from finding that surprising, there is no politician who is not surprised that they have not been more numerous. We joyfully foresee that your example will be universally followed, and that the flame which you have lighted will throughout Europe consume the remnants of despotism and superstition.

Not only we hope but we firmly believe that the National Assembly of France and the Parliament of Great Britain will for the future unite in an indissoluble union to secure the peace and prosperity of the two Empires, and spread those benefits over the whole surface of the Globe.

We congratulate you on having an army of Citizens, and a wise Monarch, who in bending with such good will to the wishes of his People adds a new lustre to the House of Bourbon, and ensures the Crown of France to his descendants.

Be so good, sir, as to accept this Address from the obscure Members of a *Club* instituted with a view to the re-establishment of our liberty, to guarantee and to bring to perfection our political Constitution. We live in a Country the least favoured by nature : our climate is cold, our country mountainous; and yet, since the Revolution made us free, our Towns become from day to day more populous; our inhabitants more rich; our mountains less sterile, our country, in sum, more rich and more happy; and we have no reason to believe that the love of virtue and good order has declined amongst us. Our sovereign, the Father of his People, is almost the object of our adoration; our Nobility and our Clergy are useful and illustrious members of a State where all is subordinated to the Law.

We had wished to be shorter; but we could not forbear to express the sentiment of joy and admiration which an event so agreeable as the re-establishment of liberty in France inspires within us.

We conclude by addressing our prayers to the Sovereign Arbiter of Empires, that he may direct the efforts of your patriotism and guarantee it from corruption.

We have the honour to be, with the deepest respect, sir,

Your very humble and obedient servants,

The Members of the Whig Club of Dundee.

(*Signed*)

George de Dempttor (?Dempster) de Dunnichen, *President.*
William Stirling, Esquire, of Pittendick;

Patrick Stirling, Esquire, of Pittendick.
John Guthrie, Esquire, of Gaigie;
Alexander Thoms, Esquire, of Rumgalley;
Thomas Wemyss, Esquire, of Laurieston;
Patrick Scrymgeour, Esquire, of Rosemount;
Patrick Whitson, Esquire, of Balbrogie;
John Pilcairn, Esquire, of Merchunt;
James Robertson, Esquire, of Denork;
George Blair, Esquire, of Adamston;
The Revd. James Bluishall, D.D., Dundee;
The Revd. Robert Small, D.D., F.R.S. Edin., Dundee;
The Revd. David Davidson, Dundee;
The Revd. William Read, Dundee;
The Revd. James Thomson, Dundee;
The Revd. John Burch, Tannadice;
The Revd. John Gellately, Tealine;
The Revd. James Playfair, D.D., Historiographer to the
    Prince of Wales; [1]
The Revd. Samuel Martin, Monyoncal;
The Revd. Alexander Meldrum, Kincaple;
Robert Doig, Preacher, Dundee;
James Willison, M.D., Dundee;
James Stewart, Surgeon, Dundee;
James Johnston, Surgeon, Dundee;
John Rolle, Surgeon, Dundee;
The Revd. John Gilsen, Mains;
James Deck, Merchant, Dundee;
James Syme, Merchant, Dundee;
John Jobson, Merchant, Dundee;
Charles Jobson, Merchant, Dundee;
William Allisson, Merchant, Dundee;
Michael Lainke, Merchant, Dundee;
James Whright, Merchant, Dundee;
Thomas Crichton, Merchant, Dundee;
Andrew Jobson, Merchant, Dundee;
William Brissel, Merchant, Dundee;
Oliver Fairweather, Merchant, Dundee;
David Low, Merchant, Dundee;
James Ballingall, Merchant, Dundee;
George Gray, Merchant, Dundee;
George Barry, Merchant, Dundee;
Peter Kiel, Merchant, Dundee;
William Webster, Merchant, Dundee;
Archibald Nielson, Merchant, Dundee;
Gershorn Gourlay, Merchant, Dundee;
William Keith, Merchant, Dundee;
James Keith, Merchant, Dundee;
James Duncan, Merchant, Dundee;

[1] Elected Principal of United College, St. Andrews, in 1800.

William Anderson, Merchant, Dundee;
Patrick Crichton, Merchant, Dundee;
Patrick Smith, Merchant, Dundee;
Ebendser Anderson, Merchant, Dundee;
Alexander Pitcaturis, Merchant, Dundee;
James Dick, Merchant, Dundee;
David Jobson, Merchant, Dundee;
James Whright, Junior, Merchant, Dundee;
David Blair, Merchant, Dundee;
Patrick Maxwell, Merchant, Dundee;
Francis Suawright, Teacher of English;
James Walson, Rector of the Grammar School;
Robert Douglass, Mathematician of the Grammar School;
James Soory, Watchmaker, Dundee;
Samuel Bell, Architect, Dundee;
James Sanders, Writer to the Signet, Edinbourg;
John Craig, Baker, Dundee;
David Smart, Dundee;
Kinnaird Brown, Dundee;
Robert Nicoll, Stationer, Dundee;
Alexander Walt, Dyer, Dundee;
John Johnston, of Manchester;
Alexander Thomson, Writer, Edinbourg;
John McRitchie, Writer, Edinbourg;
John Kirkcaldie, Shipmenter;
Robert Mawer, Shipmenter;
Thomas Brown, Shipmenter;

An authentic list, attested by George Dempster of Dunnichen, Praeses, Dundee, June 10, 1790.

[*Procès-Verbaux de l'Assemblée nationale*, July 31, 1790, pp. 26-31. It is probable that some of the unfamiliar names were misprinted by the Assembly's printer.]

APPENDIX III

THE ADDRESS OF THE CONSTITUTIONAL WHIGS, DATED OCT. 25, 1791, AND PRESENTED TO THE NATIONAL ASSEMBLY DEC. 6, 1791.

Constitutional Whigs grand Lodge of England : President, the most noble *Briton*, in the chair.

The epitome of the French Constitution being read by the secretary, the following resolutions were agreed to unanimously—

Resolved, that the society do approve of the French Revolution and of the fundamental principles formed for the French Constitution by the National Assembly of France.

Resolved, that this society do congratulate the National Assembly, the King and the Nation, on the acceptation of the principles of the French Constitution by the King of the French.

Resolved, that the thanks of the society be given to the late National Assembly for their exalted patriotism and disinterested proceedings in constructing and maintaining until their secession the principles of the Constitution, the result of their wisdom and integrity, the basis of liberty, the annihilation of aristocracy, and the general emancipation of a brave, generous and hospitable people.

Resolved, that us (*sic*) Constitutional Whigs, the sons of liberty should any attempt power (*sic*), or be made by any despotic powers, to enslave the people of France, or diminish their liberties, that we will with our lives, interests and fortunes, oppose all such measures, until the destruction of slavery, usurpation and tyranny is compleated.

Resolved, that these resolutions be transcribed by our secretary from our register, and by him transmitted to the National Assembly of France.

The English is rather difficult to understand, but we do not think all its deficiencies are due to the French printers; some of them must have been equally apparent in the original.

[*P.-V.* of the Legislative Assembly, Dec. 6, 1791, pp. 287–89.]

This address is cited, with some verbal differences, by Sampson Perry. The difficult passage above he gives as follows: "Resolved by us, all constitutional Whigs, sons of freedom, that if one or more despotic powers, whoever they be, should make any attempt to enslave the French people, or even to infringe on the liberty they now enjoy, our lives, our fortunes, shall be employed in repelling their efforts, even to the total destruction of slavery, and the extirpation of tyranny."

[*An Historical Sketch of the French Revolution*, . . . II. 119–20.]

APPENDIX IV

ADDRESS OF THE FRIENDS OF THE PEOPLE AT NEWINGTON TO THE NATIONAL CONVENTION.

October 31, 1792.

FRENCHMEN AND CITIZENS OF THE WORLD,

United in order to obtain a fair and equal Representation of the People and a Compleat Reform of the Numerous Abuses which have crept into the Government of this Country, We observe with pain and anxiety, every attempt whether Secret or Avowed to disturb the *peace* and overthrow the newly acquired *Liberties* of *the French Nation*.

We congratulate you on the Defeat and total Expulsion of the combined Despots, and Savage Traitors who came to desolate your Plains, plunder your Habitations and destroy your innocent Inhabitants. The goodness of your cause deserved Success and your Wisdom and Bravery have assured it. Your wise Decrees have already enlightened Europe; and like the Rays of the Sun will shortly illumine the Four Quarters of the World. The grand Pillars of Human Liberty, are the Legislative and Judicial Bodies; by well organising the latter you have secured to yourselves the good Effects of the former; and you have given a further Specimen of your consummate Wisdom, by keeping the Legislative, Judicial and Executive powers totally distinct, and the two last respectively responsible to the Grand Council of the Nation. It is in France where justice is administered at an easy Expense. Commerce under your salutary laws, will be happily protected, and the Acquisitions of the Industrious everywhere defended.

Illustrious Senators, Enlightened Legislators, and dear Friends! With unfeigned satisfaction we are enabled to inform you that the unnatural Enmity, so long basely cherished in the Breasts of a generous people towards the *French Nation* by the insidious Arts and secret Engines of Court Despotism and Intrigue is now entirely dissipated except among those who benefit by the abuses; and we Hail with Joy the Auspicious Hour that shall join the two Nations in an indissoluble Bond of Union as the precursor of Universal Peace and Concord.

With the most lively sensibility we behold the brilliant success of your *Arms*, in emancipating from Slavery and Despotism, the Brave Nations on your frontiers. Happy humanity to dissolve your Neighbours' Chains!

JOHN FRED. SCHIEFER, Chairman.
FRANS. PEACOCK, Secretary.

[Archives nationales, C. 240 (275): French version printed as : Convention Nationale. Adresse Des Amis du Peuple de la Grande Bretagne de la ville de Newington, à la Convention Nationale de la République française.]

APPENDIX V

ADDRESS OF THE ALDGATE FRIENDS OF THE PEOPLE TO THE NATIONAL CONVENTION OF THE FRENCH REPUBLIC.

November 12, 1792.

ENLIGHTENED FRIENDS, PATRIOTS AND LEGISLATORS,

As Friends of the People associated for the purpose of cultivating and diffusing Political Knowledge we are united in holding sacred the Independence of Opinion, and an equal Participation of Rights amongst Men as the firm basis of *Liberty and Equality:* we therefore *Hail You* under the dignified name we are proud to recognise of *Citizens of the Universe—*

Protectors of the *Great Family* of the *Human Race*—whose liberal and benign views are to break the bonds of Slavery asunder and to give to Man *Political Life, Health and Strength* in every quarter of the Globe.

We receive the highest pleasure at the *Magnanimity* of *Your Resolves*, in declaring to reproachful Europe that you abjure conquest, and without regard to Clime, Situation, or Colour, wish to restore to Man the long lost Rights and indefeasible Privileges of his Nature, which the *Great Author of All Good* hath bestowed on him, and of which Man has long been bereft by the *Feudal Tyranny* of *Barbarous Despotism*.

Such are the Sentiments that claim the Testimony of *Our Regard* as Men and Englishmen devoted to the *Great Cause* of *General Liberty*, which the narrow and crooked Policy of Kingly Government, and the Pride and Profligacy of their vicious Offspring, have hitherto involved in frequent and fatal Enmities.

Therefore, Representatives of the French Republic, Brethren and Friends, for by those *Civic Names* we request to greet *You*, we have not contented ourselves with being idle, incurious Spectators of *Your Glorious and Effectual Struggles;—No*, we have combated (*sic*) prejudice * with increasing ardour and defied its frowns and we behold with peculiar satisfaction and delight, the *Sun* of *Liberty*, by the *Triumphant Progress* of *Your Arms*, dispelling the Clouds and Darkness of Fanaticism, Pageantry and Folly and with an *accelerated Force* driving before it the savage Ferocity of its invaders.

At the very moment in which we are assembled to transmit to you this *Heart-Felt Congratulation* on the prosperous Revolution in the Affairs of France, we receive the exhilarating news of the Success of the *Invincible Army* under the command of *Citizen General Dumourier* near Mons.—Language fails us to describe the lively emotions of Joy and admiration with which it hath inspired us; but the Sensibility of every *True Frenchman* may qualify him to judge of Our Transports by those which he himself must feel.—May the Blood of the *Brave Citizens* shed on this occasion, while it shews to Despots the Energy and Magnanimity which Liberty alone can give Spring up in an abundant *Harvest of Peace and Freedom* throughout the World and *Reason* supercede the necessity of *Military Conquest*.—May the Immortality of the French Republic be an *awful Lesson to Tyrants* of every Clime and Description!

Signed by order of the Aldgate Society of the Friends of the People.

JOHN HALL, President.
F. PAGE, Secretary.

* See the annexed Publications of *Our Sentiments* concerning the design of the Confederacy of Treacherous, Princely and Royal Incendiaries.

[The annexed publications are three printed papers, bearing dates May 28, 1792, July 9, 1792, July 14, 1792, which I have not found elsewhere.]
Dated Nov. 12 and presented Dec. 3, 1792.
[Archives Nationales, C. 242.]

APPENDIX VI

AUTHORITIES

(A) MANUSCRIPT

(i) *English*

British Museum—
Place MSS.

27808. (1) Notes respecting the London Corresponding Society.
(2) Remarks on the supposed origin of the Pop-gun Plot; 1817; by Paul Thomas Lemaitre.
(3) Collection for a Memoir of Thomas Spence and the Spenceans.

27809. Place's Collections on Political Societies—
(3) A full report of the Hampden Club; June 15, 1816.
(5) Narrative of John Oxlade; Feb. 12, 1837.
(6) "Political Societies and Occurrences;" 1792–1833.

27810. Account, Letters and printed Papers of the Metropolitan Parliamentary Reform Association; 1842; including Letters from Sir John Bowring, etc.

27811. Letter-book of the London Corresponding Society [L. C. S.]; Oct 27, 1791–March 23, 1793.

27812. Minute-book, and Letter-book of the L. C. S.

27813. Minute-book, and Letter-book of the L. C. S.

27814. Francis Place, Vol. IV. Sketch of the History of the London Corresponding Society, by Thomas Hardy, Secretary.

27815. Original Correspondence of the L. C. S.; July 2, 1795–Nov. 30, 1797.

27816. Papers, printed and MS., relating to Public Prosecutions in 1793, 1794 and 1798; including Richter's Narrative of his Arrest and Examination before the Privy Council, 1794.

27818. Hardy. Drafts of Letters.

27835. Papers, printed and MS., relating to Working-Men's Political Associations, etc., 1799–1842.

27837. Newspaper cuttings on Westminster Elections (1771–1807).

27838. Newspaper cuttings on Westminster Elections (1806–1809).

27839. Newspaper cuttings on Westminster Elections (1810–1812).

27840. Newspaper cuttings on Westminster Elections (1812–1817).

27849. History of General Politics; 1714–1784; and of Westminster Politics; 1790–1792.

27850. History of Politics; 1803–1818.

35142. Autobiography of Francis Place.

35143. Autobiography of Francis Place.

35152. Place's Correspondence; 1810–1816.

35154. Autobiography of Francis Place.

Place Papers (miscellaneous).

Also letter of Hardy to Place, July 7, 1831, prefixed to First Report from the Committee of Secrecy. Catalogue of Printed Books, C. 61. b. 16 (1).

MS. Notes by J. Richter to the Second Report from the Committee of Secrecy. . . . Fourth ed. 1794. Catalogue of Printed Books, C. 61. b. 16 (2).

Letter of Cleary to Joseph Hume, Feb. 10, 1854, fastened inside the cover of a Collection of Reports of Proceedings of the Hampden Club. Catalogue of Printed Books, 8135, f. 19.

Public Record Office—

Most useful are the Home Office Papers : H. O. Domestic, George III. 42, more particularly the following volumes :

40, Jan.–May 1797.
41, June–Dec. 1797.
42, Jan.–Mar. 1798.
43, April–June 1798.
44, July–Sept. 1798.
45, Oct.–Dec. 1798.

Similar papers relating to Scotland are to be found in H. O. 102. vols. 4, 6, 7, 8, 9, 10, 11.

A little can also be gleaned from the Chatham MSS.

Office of the Privy Council—

The Registers of the Privy Council (which I have cited as P. C. R.) yield a large amount of information, especially for the year 1794.

(ii) French.

Archives nationales. A. F. II. 49 (380); A. F. II. 63 (468); F. A. III. 57 (221); C. 28 (225); 42 (379); 238 (247); 241 (278); 242.

Archives du Ministère des Affaires Étrangères—
Correspondance d'Angleterre.

(B) PRINTED
(i) General

Memoirs and biographies will be found under the name of the subject; local histories under the name of the place. The

format is only stated when it is other than octavo, and the
place of publication when it is other than London. In many
cases I have not thought it necessary to give extended titles.

Aikin, Memoir of Dr. L. Aikin. 2 vols. 1823.
Aldgate. Friends of the People, pamphlet concerning.
A thing of Shreds and Patches, by an Association against
Levellers and to Procure the Restoration of the Rights
of the People.
Resolutions : March 11, 1793. 1793.
Alger, J. G. Englishmen in the French Revolution. 1889.
Almon, J. Anecdotes of Eminent Personages. 3 vols. 1797.
Annual Register.
Annual Register, the New.
Anson, Sir W. R. Law and Custom of the Constitution. 4th ed.
Anti-Jacobin, 1797-8.
Assemblée nationale, Procès-Verbaux (cited as *P.-V.*).
Assemblée législative, Procès-Verbaux (cited as *P.-V.*).
Athenæum, May 2, 1908. Article signed C. T. S., "A For-
gotten Early Prose Work of Coleridge."
Atlay, J. B. The Trial of Lord Cochrane before Lord Ellen-
borough. 1897.
Auckland Correspondence. 4 vols. 1861.
Aulard, F. A. Histoire politique de la Révolution française.
Paris. 1905.
La Société des Jacobins. 6 vols. 1889, etc.
Études et leçons sur la Révolution française. Première
série. 4th ed. Paris. 1905.

Bamford, S. Passages in the Life of a Radical. 2 vols.
Heywood. 1841–2.
Baxter, J. Resistance to oppression the constitutional right of
Britons asserted in a lecture delivered before section 2
of the Society of the Friends of Liberty . . . Nov. 9.
1795. 12°.
Bentham, J. Works, ed. Bowring. Edinburgh, 1843.
Binns, J. Recollections. Philadelphia, 1854. 12°.
Birmingham Life, A Century of, 1741–1841. J. A. Langford.
2 vols. 1868.
Birmingham, A History of. W. Hutton. 3rd ed. Birming-
ham. 1795.
Boswell, J. Letters . . . to the Rev. W. J. Temple, with an
introduction by Thomas Seccombe. 1908.
Bristol. The Annals of . . . in the Eighteenth Century. J.
Latimer. Frome. 1893.
Brown, P. Hume. History of Scotland. Cambridge. 1902–9.
Browning, O. The Dispatches of Earl Gower, English Am-
bassador at Paris, from June 1790 to Aug. 1792, to
which are added the dispatches of Mr. Lindsay and

Mr. Monro, and the Diary of Viscount Palmerston in France during July and Aug. 1791. . . . Cambridge, 1885.

Buchan, D. S. Erskine, Earl of. Essays on the Lives and Writings of Fletcher of Saltoun and the Poet Thomson. . . . 1792.

Buckinghamshire, the Duke of, editor. Courts and Cabinets of George III. 1853–5.

Buckle, T. H. History of Civilisation in England. 3 vols. 1873.

Burdett, Sir F. Memoir by T. Tegg. 1804. 12⁰.

Memoirs of. 1810.

Life of. 1810.

Burges, Sir J. Bland, Letters and Correspondence of, ed. J. Hutton. 1885.

Burke, Edmund. Correspondence of . . . between . . . 1744 and . . . 1797, ed. E. Fitzwilliam and . . . Sir R. Bourke. 2 vols. 1844.

Works. 8 vols. Bohn ed., various dates, 1877–1901.

Life of. Prior. Bohn ed. 1884.

Life of. J. Morley. E. M. L. ed. 1893.

Burney, Fanny. Diary. Ed. Austin Dobson. 1904–5.

Burns, Robert. A. Angellier. Paris. 1893.

Campbell, Life and Letters of Thomas. W. Beattie. 1849.

Cartwright, Major John. American Independence the Interest and Glory of Great Britain. 1774.

A Letter to Edmund Burke. . . . 1775.

Take Your Choice. Oct. 1776.

A Letter to the Duke of Newcastle. 1792.

A Letter to the Sheriff of Lincoln. 1795.

The Commonwealth in Danger. 1795.

The Constitutional Defence of England. 1796.

An Appeal on the Subject of the English Constitution. Boston. 1797.

Six Letters to the Marquis of Tavistock. . . . Harlow. 1810.

Reasons for Reformation. 1809.

A Comparison : in which mock reform, half reform and constitutional reform are considered. 1810.

The Life and Correspondence of Major Cartwright, ed. by his niece, F. D. Cartwright. 2 vols. 1826.

Cavendish, Sir H. Debates of the House of Commons [May 1768–March 1771], ed. Wright. 2 vols. 1841.

Cestre, C. La Révolution française et las poètes anglais. 1789–1809. Dijon. 1906.

Charlemont, J. Caulfield, E. of. Original Letters principally from Lord Charlemont . . . to Henry Flood. Ed. T. R[odd]. 1820. 4⁰.

Chatham, Wm. Pitt, E. of. Correspondence. 4 vols. 1838–40.

A History of W. P., E. of Chatham. F. Thackeray.
2 vols. 1827.

Chatham. His Early Life and Connections. Rosebery.
1910.

William Pitt, E. of Chatham. A. von Ruville. 3 vols.
1907.

Chesterfield, P. D. Stanhope, 4th E. of. Letters . . . to his
son. 2 vols. 1901.

Chuquet, A. (ed. and translator). Paris en 1790. Voyage
de Halem.

Cloncurry, Lord. Personal Recollections. Dublin. 1849.

Clowes, Sir W. L. The Royal Navy. A History. 7 vols.
1897–1903.

Cobbett, W., Memoirs of. H. Huish. 2 vols. 1836.
A Study of His Life as Shown in His Writings. E. I.
Carlyle. 1904.

Cochrane (Lord Dundonald). Autobiography of a Seaman.
1860.

Cockburn, Lord. Memorials of His Time. Edinburgh. 1874.
An Examination of the Trials for Sedition in Scotland.
2 vols. Edinburgh. 1888.

Coleridge, S. T. Table Talk. 1851.

Collection of Addresses transmitted by certain English Clubs
and Societies to the National Convention of France. . . .
1793. 4°.

Commons, Journals of the House of. [Referred to as C. J.]

Constitutional Information, Society for. Address of the
Society. 1780, fol.
Prospectus and List of Members. 1780?
Letter of Paine. 1792. s. sh. fol.
Proceedings. 1794.
Report on the Treason Bills. [1795.]

Constitutional Whigs, Society of. 1792.

Convention nationale, Procès-Verbaux. [Referred to as P.-V.]

Cooper, T. A Reply to Mr. Burke's invective against Mr.
Cooper and Mr. Watt, in the House of Commons on the
30th April. 1792.

Cottle, J. Early Recollections chiefly relating to the late
S. T. C. during his long residence in Bristol. 2 vols.
1837–39.
Reminiscences of S. T. C. and Robert Southey. [The
revised form of Early Recoll.] 1847.

Coventry, The History and Antiquities of the City of. W.
Reader. 1810. 12°.

Cowper, W. Correspondence. Ed. Wright. 4 vols. 1904.
Works. Ed. Southey. 1836–7.

Creevey Papers. Ed. Sir H. Maxwell. 1903.

Currie, Memoirs of the life, writings and correspondence of
[Dr.] J. W. W. Currie. 2 vols. 1831.

Danton. *See* Robinet.
Day, Thomas. Two Speeches of T. D., Esq., at the General
  Meeting of the Counties of Cambridge and Essex. . . .
  1780. Printed and distributed gratis by the Society for
  Constitutional Information. B. M. E. 2101 (18).
  Life of T. D. J. Blackman. 1862. 12°.
  Life and Writings of T. D. J. Keir. 1791.
Dicey, A. V. Lectures on the relation between Law and Public
  Opinion in England in the 19th Century. 1905.
Dodington, Diary of G. Bubb . . . [Lord Melcombe]. Ed. H.
  P. Wyndham. 4th ed. 1823.
Dowden, E. The French Revolution and English Literature.
  1897.
Dubois-Crancé. Analyse de la Révolution française. Paris.
  1885. 12°.
Dulaure, J.-A. Historie physique, civile et morale de Paris.
  Paris. 1825. 8 vols.
Dumont, Etienne. Souvenirs sur Mirabeau. 1832.
Durham, Life and Letters of the first E. of. Stuart Reid.
  1906.

Edgeworth, R. L. Memoirs. 1820.
Edinburgh Review, June 1816.
Eldon, Life of Lord. H. Twiss. 1844.
English Historical Review, vol. xiii. 1898.
Erskine, the Hon. H., Lord Advocate for Scotland, with notices
  of certain of his kinsfolk and of his time. Compiled from
  family papers. . . . Edinburgh. 1882.
Erskine, Lord T. A Short Defence of the Whigs. 1819.
  Speeches . . . reprinted from the . . . edition of 1810.
  With memoir of his life by S. Walford. 2 vols. 1870.

Fielding, H. Familiar Letters. Miscellaneous Works. Ed.
  Saintsbury. 1893.
Fisher, H. A. L. The Republican Tradition in Europe. 1911.
Fitzpatrick, W. J. Secret Service under Pitt. 1892.
Fletcher, Mrs. E. Autobiography. Privately printed. Carlisle.
  1874.
Fortescue, J. W. History of the British Army, vol. iv. 1906.
Fox, C. J. Memorials and Correspondence. Ed. Lord J.
  Russell. 4 vols. 1853–7.
  Life and Times. Lord J. Russell. 3 vols. 1859–66.
  A Political Study. J. L. le B. Hammond. 1903.
  Early History. Sir. G. O. Trevelyan. New ed. 1908.
Fox-Bourne, H. R. English Newspapers. 2 vols. 1887.
Frampton, The Journal of Mary, from . . . 1779, until . . .
  1846. . . . Ed. H. G. Mundy. 1885.
Francis Letters. Ed. Francis and Keary. N. D.
Freeholder, A. Hints to Juries in Trials for Libel. 1793.

Friends of the Liberty of the Press. Resolutions. 1793.
    Proceedings. 1793. fol.
Friends of the People, Society of the. Resolutions, etc., of the
    Society. [April 26,1792.] With the Declaration of the
    Society and an Address to the People of England [drawn
    up by Sir Philip Francis (?)]. 1792, 4°.
    Remarks on the Proceedings. 1792.
    Report of the Committee. [1792?] 4°.
    State of the Representation. 1793. 4°.
    Report of the Representation of Scotland. 1793. 4°.
    Proceedings . . . in 1792. 1793.
    Petition Presented by the Hon. C. Grey. 1793.
    Address to the Friends of the People. [1793?]
    Speech of Sir Philip Francis. 1794.
    Friends of the People, etc. 1794.
    An Address, etc. 1794.
    To the Inhabitants of Nottingham. [Address in Vindica-
    tion of the Friends of the People.] Notts. [1793?]
    See also Aldgate, Holborn.

Gentleman's Magazine.
Gerrald. A Fragment. B.M., E. 2078.
Gibbon, E. Private Letters. Ed. R. E. Prothero. 2 vols.
    1896.
    The Autobiographies. Ed. J. Murray. 1896.
    Memoirs. Ed. G. Birkbeck Hill. 1900.
Godwin, W. An Enquiry concerning Political Justice and its
    influence on General Virtue and Happiness. 2 vols.
    1793. 4°.
    [Projected May 1791. Begun Sept. 1791. Preface dated
    Jan. 7, 1793.]
    William Godwin : His Friends and Contemporaries. C.
    Kegan Paul. 2 vols. 1876.
Goldsmith, Lewis. The Secret History of the Cabinet of
    Bonaparte. . . . 1810.
Grafton, Autobiography of the D. of. Ed. Sir W. R. Anson.
    1898.
Gray's Poems, with Memoirs of his Life and Writings. W.
    Mason. Ed. 1827.
Grenville Papers. Ed. W. J. Smith. 4 vols. 1852–3.
Grey, Some account of the Life and Opinions of Charles,
    second E. Gen. the Hon. C. Grey. 1861.

Halifax. Union for Parliamentary Reform. An Appeal to the
    Nation. Halifax. 1812.
Hammond, J. L. le B. and Barbara. The Village Labourer,
    1760–1832. 1911.
    See also Fox.
Hampden Club, A Collection of Reports of Proceedings of the,
    1814–22. [A collection of papers and circulars relating

to the Club, collected by Cleary, its last secretary, and presented by him to Joseph Hume, Feb. 10, 1854. Autograph letter accompanying the gift prefixed. The volume seems to have come into the possession of the British Museum in 1872.]

Hardy, Memoir of Thomas. P. Mackenzie. 1832.

Hazlitt, W. The Spirit of the Age.

Historical Manuscripts Commission.
 Abergavenny MSS. Rep. X. App. VI. 1887.
 Dartmouth MSS. Rep. XI. App. V. 1887.
 Fortescue (Dropmore) MSS. Vol. I. Rep. XIII. App. III. 1892; Vol. II. Rep. XIV. App. V. 1896; Vol. III. 1829; Vol. IV. 1905; Vol. VI. 1906.

Holborn Society of the Friends of the People, instituted Nov. 2, 1792, for the purpose of Political Investigation.

Holcroft, T. Narrative of Facts. 1795.
 Memoirs of T. H., written by himself and continued to the time of his death from his diary, notes and other papers. Ed. W. Hazlitt. 3 vols. 1816. 12°.

Holland, Henry Richard, 3rd B. Memoirs of the Whig Party during my time. 2 vols. 1852–4.
 Further Memoirs of the Whig Party. . . . Ed. Stavordale. 1905.

Holland, Journal of Elizabeth, Lady. 2 vols. 1908.

Hone, W. Every Day Book. 1826.

Horner, F. Memoirs and Correspondence. Ed. . . . L. Horner. 2 vols. 1843.

Howell, Thomas Bayley (and T. J. Howell). A complete collection of State Trials. . . . 1809 et seq. [Referred to as S. T.]

Hunt, Frederick Knight. The Fourth Estate. 1850.

Hunt, History of the Public and Private Life of Henry. H. Huish. 2 vols. 1836.

Hunt, William. The Political History of England. Vol. X. 1760–1801. 1905.

Hutton, W. The Life of W. H. : including a particular account of the Riots at Birmingham. 1816. Another ed. 1818.

Jebb, John. Address to the Freeholders of Middlesex. Dec. 1779.
 The Works of . . . J. J., with memoirs of the life of the author. J. Disney. 3 vols. 1787.

Jeffrey, Francis, Lord. Lord Cockburn. Edinburgh. 2 vols. 1852.

Jephson, H. The Platform : Its Rise and Progress. 2 vols. 1892.

Jones, John Gale. Sketch of a Speech delivered at the Westminster Forum on the 9th, 16th, 23rd, and 30th Dec., 1794. [Preface dated June 17.] 1795.

Substance of a Speech delivered at the Ciceronian School, Globe Tavern, Fleet Street, Monday, March 2, 1795, on the following question : "At this awful moment of difficulty and danger, which best deserves the public confidence, Mr. Pitt or Mr. Fox?" 1795.

Sketch of a Political Tour through Rochester, Chatham, Maidstone, Gravesend . . . etc. 1796.

Jones, Sir William. The Principles of Government in a Dialogue between a Scholar and a Peasant, written by a Member of the Society for Constitutional Information. 1782.

Joyce, Jeremiah. A Sermon [on Mark xiv. 27] preached . . . Feb. 23, 1794, . . . To which is added an appendix, containing an account of the author's arrest for . . . treasonable practices . . . his examination before His Majesty's . . . Privy Council, his commitment to the Tower and subsequent treatment. 2nd ed., enlarged. 1795.

Junius, Letters. Bohn ed. 2 vols. 1850.
Ed. J. M. Good. 3 vols. 1812.

Kent, C. B. R. The English Radicals. 1899.

Kerviler, René. Cent ans de la Représentation Bretonne. 1re partie. États-Généraux. Paris. 1889.

Kyd, Stewart. A Treatise on the Law of Corporations. 2 vols. 1793, 1794.
The Speeches of the Hon. T. Erskine . . . on the trial, *The King versus T. Williams* . . . together with Mr. S. K.'s reply, etc. 1797.

Laprade, W. T. England and the French Revolution, 1789–97. The Johns Hopkins Press. Baltimore. Aug. Dec. 1909.

Lecky, W. E. H. History of England in the Eighteenth Century. 3rd ed. 1883.

Leicester in the Eighteenth Century. J. Thompson. Leicester. 1871.

Leicester, Glimpses of Ancient. T. F. Johnson. 1891. 4°.

Lewis, S. Topographical Dictionary of England. 3 vols. 1835. 4 vols. 1849.

Lindsey, Memoirs of Theophilus. T. Belsham. 1812.

Liverpool, Memorials of. J. A. Picton. 2 vols. 1873. 2nd ed. 2 vols. 1875.

Liverpool, Life and Administration of Robert Banks, 2nd E. of. C. D. Yonge. 3 vols. 1868.

London Corresponding Society.
Resolutions (April 2, 1792). 1792. s. sh. fol.
Address to the Nation (May 24, 1792). 1792.
Address (Aug. 6, 1792). 1792.

London Corresponding Society (*continued*)—
    Address (Nov. 29, 1792). 1792.
    Addresses, etc., reprinted. 1792
    Address to the Friends of Peace. 1793. s. sh. 12°.
    Address. 1793.
    Address to Francis. 1793.
    Address to the Nation (July 8, 1793). 1793.
    An Address to —— [name of society]. 1793. s. sh. fol.
    Report of a Meeting (Jan. 20, 1794). 1794.
    Address. 1794.
    General Committee (June 5, 1794). 1794. s. sh. 8°.
    Report of the Sub-Committee of Westminster (May 27,
        1780) to take into consideration all such matters relative
        to the election of Members of Parliament as may promote
        the purposes of the present Association. With a plan
        for taking the suffrages of the people . . . and the
        speech of Mr. Pitt on this subject (with the reply of Lord
        North . . . from the London *Courant,* May 7, 1783).
        1794.
    Citizens! etc. 1794 (?). s. sh. 4°.
    At a Meeting, etc. 1794.
    Report of the Committee of Constitution. 1794 (?).
    Report of Committee. 1794 (?).
    Seizure of Thomas Hardy. 1794.
    Report, etc 1794.
    Address. 1794.
    Account of Treason. 1794.
    Report of a Meeting (June 29, 1795). 1795.
    Account of a Meeting (Oct. 26, 1795). 1795.
    Report (Nov. 12, 1795). 1795. s. sh. 4°.
    Reformers no Rioters. 1795.
    Epistle to the L. C. S. [verse]. 1795.
    Remarks on the Principles. 1795.
    A Summary of the Duties, etc. [by Iliff]. 1795.
    Address and Regulations. 1796. 12°.
    Decline and Fall. 1796.
    A Vindication [by Jas. Parkinson]. 1796 (?).
Lonsdale, H. Worthies of Cumberland. 1867.
Lords, Journals of the House of. [Referred to as *L.J.*]

Macaulay, Life and Letters of Lord. Sir G. O. Trevelyan. 1908.
Mackenzie, P. Reminiscences of Glasgow.
Mackintosh, James. *Vindiciæ Gallicæ.* Dublin. 1791.
    Miscellaneous Works. 1851.
    Life of. R. Mackintosh. 1835.
    Macaulay. Critical and Historical Essays, II. Albany ed.
    1898.
Madden, R. B. The United Irishmen. . . . 7 vols. 1842–6.
    12°.

Maitland, F. W.   Township and Borough.   Cambridge.   1898.
Manchester, Annals of.   W. E. A. Axon.   1885.
May, Erskine.   Constitutional History of England.   1871.
Miles, W.   Correspondence on the French Revolution.   1890.
Minto, Gilbert Elliot, 1st E. of.   Life and Letters. . . Ed.
    Countess of Minto.   3 vols.   1874.
Mitford, Mary Russell.   Our Village.   [Began to appear in a
    magazine, 1819; in volume form, 1824-32; frequently
    reprinted.]
Moniteur.   Gazette nationale ou le Moniteur universel.   Paris.
    5 mai, 1789 et seq.   fol.
Montgomery, James.   Memoirs of . . . J. M.   Holland and
    Everett.   7 vols.   1854.
    Life, Times and Character of J. M.   Ellis.   Sheffield (?).
    1864.
Mozley, T.   Reminiscences.   2 vols.   1882.
Muir, Thomas, Life of.   P. Mackenzie.   Glasgow.   1831.

Newington   Convention nationale.   Adresse des amis du peupel
    de la Grande Bretagne, de la ville de Newington (Oct. 31,
    1792) à la Convention nationale de la République française.
    Paris.   1792.
Notes and Queries.
Nottingham Journal.

Oldfield, T. H. B. . . . History . . . of the Boroughs. . . .
    3 vols.   1792.
    Representative History. . . .   6 vols.   1816.
Orléans, Correspondance de Louis-Philippe-Joseph, duc d'.

Paine, Thomas.   Rights of Man.   Part I.   8th ed.   1791.
    Rights of Man.   Part II.   9th ed.   1792.
    Address to the Addressers.   n. d.
    The Writings of Thomas Paine.   Ed. M. D. Conway.
    6 vols.   1894-6.
    Life of T. P.   M. D. Conway.   2 vols.   1892.   3rd ed.
    1893.
Paley, William.   Principles of Moral and Political Philosophy.
    12th ed.   2 vols.   1799.
Pallain G.   Correspondance diplomatique de Talleyrand.   La
    Mission de Talleyrand à Londres en 1792.   Paris.   1887.
Palmer, T. F.   A Narrative of the Sufferings of T. F. Palmer
    and W. Skirving.   Cambridge.   1797.
Parliamentary History, Cobbett's.   Oct. 1806, etc.
Parr, S., Memoirs of the life, writings and opinions of.   W.
    Field.   2 vols.   1828.
Peel, Sir Robert, from his Private Papers.   Ed. C. S. Parker.
    3 vols.   1891-9.
Perceval, Life of Spencer.   Spencer Walpole.

Perry, Sampson. An Historical Sketch of the French Revolution. . . . 2 vols. 1796.
Pigott, C. The Whig Club. 1794.
Pitt, William, Life of. Stanhope. 4 vols. 1862. 3 vols. 1879.
    Rose, Dr. J. Holland. William Pitt and National Revival. 1911.
    —— William Pitt and the Great War. 1911.
    Lord Ashbourne. Pitt: some Chapters of his Life and Times. 1898.
    Rosebery. Pitt. 1906.
    Walter Bagehot. Biographical Studies. 1907. [Written 1861.]
Place, Life of Francis. Graham Wallas. Re-issue. 1908.
Political Broadsides. s. sh. fol. British Museum, 554, g, 31.
Political Martyrs of Scotland, Memoirs and trials of the. 1837.
Poole, Thomas, and his Friends. M. E. Poole, afterwards Mrs. H. Sanford. 2 vols. 1888.
Porritt, E. and A. The Unreformed House of Commons. 2 vols. Cambridge. 1903.
Porter, G. R. The Progress of the Nation. 1851.
Prentice, Archibald. Historical Sketches and Personal Recollections of Manchester. 1851.
Price, Dr. Richard. Observations on the Nature of Civil Liberty. 1776.
    Discourse on the Love of Our Country. 3rd ed., with additions. . . . 1790.
    The same, 4th ed. 1790.
    Additions to Dr. Price's Discourse on the Love of Our Country, containing communications with France. 1790.
Priestley, Life and Correspondence of Dr. Joseph. J. T. Rutt. 1831–2.
    Works. Ed. Rutt. 1817, etc.

Reeves, J. Thoughts on English Government. 1795.
Révolution Française. Ed. Aulard.
    Especially, Gallo. Les Jacobins de Cognac. Vol. XLIII.
Révolution, Revue de la. Ed. MM. Bord et d'Héricault.
    Especially, Philippe Muller (René Kerviler). Clubs et Clubistes du Morbihan. March 1885.
    Letters of Jean-René Boullé, deputy of Ploërmel, to the municipal officers of Pontivy. Published from the Archives of the Morbihan by M. Albert Macé. 1887.
Revolution Society in London. The Correspondence of the R. S. in London with the National Assembly and with various Societies of the friends of liberty in France and England. 1792. [Referred to as C. R. S.]
Robinet, Dr. Danton Émigré. Recherches sur la diplomatie de la République (An 1er, 1793). Paris. 1887. 12°.

Robinson, H. Crabb. Diary, Reminiscences and Correspondence. 1872.

Rockingham Memoirs. Ed. Albemarle. 1852.

Rodd, T. See Charlemont.

Rogers, Early Life of S. P. W. Clayden. 1887.
Recollections of the Table Talk of S. R. 3rd ed. 1856.

Rogers, J. E. Thorold. Complete Collection of the Protests of the Lords. 3 vols. Oxford. 1875.

Romilly, Memoirs of Sir Samuel, . . . with a selection from his correspondence. Ed. by his sons. 1840.

Rose, Diaries and Correspondence of George. L. V. Harcourt. 2 vols. 1860.

Russell, Life of Lord John. Spencer Walpole. 2 vols. 1889.

Schimmelpenninck, Life of Mrs. M. A. Ed. C. C. Hankin. 2 vols. 1858. Vol. I : Autobiography. Vol. II : Biographical Sketch and Letters.

Scott, Life of Sir Walter. J. G. Lockhart. 7 vols. 1837-8.

Sharp, Granville. A Declaration of the People's Natural Right to a share in the Legislature, which is the fundamental principle of the British Constitution of State. 1774.

Sharp, Granville. A Circular Letter to the several Petitioning Counties, Cities and Towns, addressed to their respective general meetings against the late Proposition for a *triennial Election* of REPRESENTATIVES. April 1780.

Sheil, the late Rt. Hon. Richard Lalor. Sketches, Legal and Political. Edited with Notes by M. W. Savage. 2 vols. 1855.

Shelburne, Life of. Ld. [Edmond] Fitzmaurice. 3 vols. 1875-6.

Sheridan, Life of R. B. Thomas Moore. 2 vols. 1825.
Life of. T. Fraser Rae. 2 vols. 1896.

Sidmouth, Life and Correspondence of. G. Pellew. 3 vols. 1847.

Skirving, William. The Trial of W. S., Secretary to the British Convention . . . with an original memoir [by David Stuart] and notes. Glasgow. 1836.
See also Palmer.

Smith, Edward. The Story of the English Jacobins. 1881.

Smith, H. Stooks The Parliament of England, from 1st Geo. I to the Present Time. 3 vols. 1844-50.

Sorel, Albert. L'Europe et la Révolution française. 8 vols. 1907-8.

State Trials [Referred to as S. T.]. See Howell.

Stephen, Sir Leslie. English Thought in the Eighteenth Century. 2nd ed. 2 vols. 1881.
The English Utilitarians. 3 vols. 1900.

Talleyrand. See Pallain.

Thelwall, John. Political Lectures. Vol. I. 1795.
Sober Reflections on the Seditious and Inflammatory Letter of the Rt. Hon. Ed. Burke, to a Noble Lord. 1796.
Poems chiefly written in Retirement. Hereford. 1801.
The Life of J. T. By his widow. Planned in 2 vols. Only Vol. I. published. 1837.
J. T. : a pioneer of democracy, etc. C. Cestre. 1906.
Tooke, John Horne. The Controversial Letters of John Wilkes . . . the Rev. John Horne, etc. 1771.
Two Pair of Portraits presented to all the Unbiassed Electors of Great Britain, and especially to the Electors of Westminster. 1788.
Diversions of Purley. 2 vols. 4°. Part I. 1798. Part II. 1805.
Memoirs of J. H. T. Alexander Stephens. 2 vols. 1813.
Diary of J. H. T. (May–Oct. 1794). Notes and Queries. Jan. and Feb. 1897. 4°.
Towers, Dr. Joseph. Thoughts on the Commencement of a New Parliament. (Appendix called : Remarks on the letter of the Rt. Hon. Edmund Burke on the Revolution in France.) 1790.

Valpy. The Pamphleteer. 9 vols. 1813–28.

[Wade, John.] The Black Book : or, corruption unmasked ! . . . 2 vols. 1820–3. In later editions "The Extraordinary Black Book." Corrected editions 1831, 1832, 1835.
Wakefield, Gilbert. Memoirs. 2 vols. 1804.
Walker, Thomas. A Review of some of the Political Events which have occurred in Manchester during the last Five Years ; being a Sequel to the Trial of Thos. Walker, and others, for a Conspiracy to Overthrow the Constitution and Government of this Country, and to aid and assist the French, being the King's Enemies. 1794.
The Whole Proceedings in the Trial of an Action for Libel brought by Thomas Walker, Merchant, against William Roberts. . . . Manchester. 1791.
. . . Correspondence . . . etc., relating to the Dispute between Mr. Walker and Mr. Roberts. Manchester. [1790.]
Walpole, Horace. Letters. Ed. Paget Toynbee. 16 vols. Oxford. 1903–5.
Last Journal, with notes by J. Doran. Ed. A. F. Steuart. 2 vols. 1910.
Memoirs of the Reign of George III. Ed. G. F. R. Barker. 4 vols. 1894.
Walpole, S. History of England. Revised ed. 1890. Impression 1905–9.

Ward (afterwards Plumer Ward), R. Memoirs. E. Phipps.
2 vols. 1850.

Watt, The Life of James, the Engineer, with selections from
his correspondence. Muirhead. 1858.

Watson, R. (Bishop of Llandaff), Anecdotes of the Life of.
1817. 4°.

Webb, S. and B.
English Local Government.
The Parish and the County. 1906.
The Manor and the Borough. 1908.
Problems of Modern Industry. 1902.

Westminster, Report of the Sub-Committee of. B. M., E. 2101
(19).

Wheatley, H. B. London, Past and Present. 3 vols. 1891.

Whigs, London Society of Constitutional. 1792.

Wilberforce, W., The Correspondence of. Ed. R. I. and
S. Wilberforce. 2 vols. 1840. 12°.

Wilkes, John. The Controversial Letters of J. W. . . . the
Rev. John Horne and their principal adherents. 1771.
Correspondence of J. W. . . . in which are introduced
memoirs of his life, by John Almon. 5 vols. 1805. 12°.

Windham, William. Diary. Ed. Mrs. Henry Baring. 1866.

Wollstonecraft, Mary. A Vindication of the Rights of Man.
1790.
A Study of M. W. and the Rights of Woman. E. R.
Clough. 1898.

Woodfall's Public Advertiser.

Wyvill, Rev. Christopher. A collection of . . . letters . . .
on . . . Parliamentary Reform. . . . 1783.
A Summary Explanation of the Principles of Mr. Pitt's
intended Bill. 1785.
A Defence of Dr. Price and the Reformers of England.
1792.
A Letter to the Rt. Hon. William Pitt. 1793.
Political Papers. 6 vols. York and Richmond. 1794–
1802.

Yorke, Henry Redhead. A Letter to the Reformers. Dorchester. 1798.

Young, Arthur. Autobiography. Ed. Betham Edwards. 1898.
The Example of France a Warning to Britain. 1793.

(ii) *Local Histories* (*French*)

Good local histories are few, and those that exist are not
easy to discover. A few only are cited, more or less useful.

Aix. Porte. Aix, ancien et moderne. Aix. 1863. In-8°

Alais. E. Rosbach Recherches historiques sur la ville d'Alais.
Alais. 1860. In-8°.

Amiens. M. H. Dusevel. Histoire de la ville d'Amiens, depuis
les Gaulois. . . . Amiens. 1848. (2ᵉ ed.). In-8°.
F. I. Darsy. Amiens et le département de la Somme
pendant la Révolution. Amiens. 1878. In-8°.
Arras. E. Lecesne. Arras sous la Révolution. Vol. I. Arras.
1882. In-8°.

Bordeaux. Camille Jullian. Histoire de Bordeaux depuis les
origines jusqu'en 1895. Bordeaux. 1895. In-4°.
Brest. Levot. Histoire de Brest. Vol. III. Brest. 1864.
In-8°.
Bretagne. Duchâtellier. Histoire de la Révolution en Bretagne.
Kerviler, René. Armorique et Bretagne. Tome III.
Bretagne pendant et depuis la Révolution. Paris. 1893.
In-8°.
See also under Kerviler in General Bibliography.

Clermont-Ferrand. Martin, Fernand. La Révolution au province. Les Jacobins au village. Clermont-Ferrand. 1902.

The Eure. L. Boivin-Champeaux. Notices historiques sur la
Révolution dans le département de l'Eure. Vol. I.
Évreux. 1893. In-8°.

Haut-Rhin. Véron-Réville. Histoire de la Révolution française
dans le département du Haut-Rhin. Paris and Colmar.
1865. In-8°.

Jura. Ant. Sommier. Histoire de la Révolution dans le Jura.
Paris. 1846. In-8°.

Lille. Victor Derode. Histoire de Lille. Lille. 1848. In-8°.

Marseille. Augustin Fabre. Histoire de Marseille. Marseille.
1829. In-8°.
Boudin. Histoire de Marseille. Paris. 1852. Gr.-in-8°.

Poitiers. v. the Vienne.

Rennes. Ducrest de Villeneuve. Histoire de Rennes, 1845.
Rennes. In-8°.

Vienne . . . L'esprit public dans le département de la. R.
Doucet.
Vosges. Félix Bouvier. Les Vosges pendant la Révolution,
1789, 1795-1800. Étude historique. Paris. 1885. In-8°.

A number of others which have been consulted proved
worthless.

(iii) *A Selection of Pamphlets published by or relating to French Popular Societies.*

Aix. Motion faite à la séance du 29 août, l'an second de la liberté, par Policarpe Constans, membre de la société des amis de la constitution, établie à Aix, département des Bouches-du-Rhône. Aix. 1790. In-8°. Bibliothèque nationale, Lb⁴⁰ 869.

Adresse de la société des amis de la constitution, séante à Aix, département des Bouches-du-Rhône, à l'assemblée nationale. Aix. 1790. In-4°. B. n., Lb⁴⁰ 868.

Amiens. Mémoire à l'assemblée nationale pour la société civique d'Amiens. Paris, n. d. In-8° B. n., Lb⁴⁰ 874.

Ancenis. Vie révolutionnaire des sans-culottes de la société populaire et régénerée . . . d'Ancenis. Nantes, n. d. In-8°. B. n., Lb⁴⁰ 875.

Auxerre. Liberté ou la mort. La société populaire d'Auxerre à toutes les sociétés populaires de la république.—La société populaire d'Auxerre à la convention nationale. Auxerre. An. II. In-4°. B. n., Lb⁴⁰ 883.

Billom. Egalité, Liberté. La société populaire séante à Billom, département du Puy-de-Dôme à la convention nationale. . . . Thiers, n. d. In-4°. B. n., Lb⁴⁰ 899.

Bordeaux. Adresse des amis de la constitution, établie à Bordeaux, à leurs concitoyens. Bordeaux, n. d. In-8°. B. n., Lb⁴⁰ 903.

Lettre de la société des amis de la constitution de Bordeaux à celle d'Angers sur la nécessité de donner aux hommes de couleur les droits des citoyens actifs (22 mars, 1791). Paris. In-4°. B. n., Lb⁴⁰ 904.

Discours prononcé, le 21 septembre, 1791, à la société des amis de la constitution de Bordeaux, par C. Reinhardt. . . . Bordeaux, n. d. In-8°. B. n., Lb⁴⁰ 906.

Mémoire présenté à la société des amis de la liberté et de l'égalité de Bordeaux le 25 oct., 1792. N. d. In-8°. B. n., Lb⁴⁰ 907.

La société républicaine de Bordeaux à la Convention nationale (8 mai, 1793). Paris, n. d. In-8°. Lb⁴⁰ 908.

Bourg. Circulaire de la société des amis de la constitution de Bourg aux sociétés affiliées . . . 4 mars, 1791. N. d. In-4°. B. n., Lb⁴⁰ 915.

Brest. Adresse de la société des amis de la constitution établie à Brest aux citoyens composant les equipages de l'armée navale (16 oct., 1790). Brest, n. d. In-8°. B. n., Lb⁴⁰ 917.

Procès-verbal de la députation chargée de présenter aux équipages de l'armée navale l'adresse de la société des amis de la constitution, établie à Brest. Brest. 1790. In-8°. B. n., Lb⁴⁰ 918.

Châlons (Marne). Adresse à l'assemblée nationale par la société des amis de la constitution de Châlons, département de la Marne. N. d. In-8°. B. n., Lb⁴⁰ 934.

Chalon-sur-Saône. Adresse de la société des amis de la constitution de France, à Chalon-sur-Saône, à la société de la révolution d'Angleterre à Londres. Chalon-sur-Saône. 1790. In-8°. B. n., Lb⁴⁰ 930.

Chartres. Adresse de la société des amis de la constitution séante à Chartres à l'assemblée nationale (11 juillet, 1791). Chartres, n. d. In-8°. B. n., Lb⁴⁰ 948.

Copie de la lettre écrite par la société des amis de la constitution séante à Chartres à l'assemblée électorale de Paris (9 sept., 1791). In-8°. B. n., Lb⁴⁰ 949.

Clermont-Ferrand. Motion de Jean-Henri Bancal à la société des amis de la constitution de Clermont-Ferrand les 23 et 24 juin, 1791. Clermont-Ferrand, n. d. In-8°. B. n., Lb⁴⁰ 952.

Laon. Adresse de la société des amis de la constitution séante à Laon, aux citoyens français à l'occasion des prochaines assemblées primaires et électorales. Laon. 1791. In-8°. B. n., Lb⁴⁰ 974.

La Rochelle. Le ministre de la Marine [Monge] à la société des amis de la liberté et de l'égalité républicaine à la Rochelle (31 déc., 1793). La Rochelle. 1793. In-8°. B. n., Lb⁴⁰ 975.

Le Hâvre. Les amis de la constitution du Hâvre à leurs concitoyens. Le Hâvre, n. d. In-8°. Lb⁴⁰ 970.

Lille. Discours militaire et patriotique prononcé dans la séance publique de la société des amis de la constitution des ville et district de Lille, le 13 jan., 1791. Par M. Vernoy. . . . Lille, n. d. In-8°. B. n., Lb⁴⁰ 982.

Lisieux. Adresse des amis de la constitution de la ville de Lisieux à l'assemblée nationale sur l'égalité des partages entre les frères et les sœurs. Lisieux, n. d. In-4°. B. n., Lb⁴⁰ 986.

Marseille. Adresse à l'assemblée nationale par les amis de la constitution de la ville de Marseille adhérée par les amis de la constitution d'Aix et de Toulon. Marseille, n. d. In-8°. (Lb⁴⁰ 991.)

Motion faite aux amis de la constitution de Marseille, séance du 25 . . . (jan., 1791). In-8°. B. n., Lb⁴⁰ 992.

Adresse à l'assemblée nationale. Marseille, n. d. In-8°. B. n., Lb⁴⁰ 993.

Melun. Réponse de la société des amis de la constitution séante à Melun, à une adresse ou pétition de la société de Bayeux à l'assemblée nationale. . . . (25 juin). Melun. 1791. In-8°. Lb⁴⁰ 997.

Metz. La société républicaine de Metz à ses frères de Nantes et de Bordeaux. Metz, n. d. In-fol. B. n., Lb⁴⁰ 999.

Nantes. Rapport des députés de la société des amis de la constitution, à Nantes, auprès de la société de la révolution à Londres; suivi d'un receuil de pièces traduites de l'anglais et relatives à la députation. Nantes, 1790. In-8°. B. n., Lb⁴⁰ 1020.

Les républicains de la société populaire et de la commune de Nantes à la convention nationale. Nantes, n. d. In-4°. B. n., Lb⁴⁰ 1021.

Nîmes. Adresse du club des amis de la constitution de Nîmes à l'assemblée nationale. Du 24 mai, 1790. Paris, n. d. In-8. B. n., Lb⁴⁰ 1034.

Discours prononcé le 20 juin, 1790 devant la société des amis de la constitution . . . par M. l'Abbé Caston de la Courtade. N. d. In-8°. B. n., Lb⁴⁰ 1035.

Vérités historiques sur les événements arrivés à Nîmes le 13 de juin et les jours suivants . . . (1790). N. d. In-8°. B. n., Lb⁴⁰ 1036.

Adresse présenté à l'assemblée nationale par le club des amis de la constitution établi à Nîmes. Du 28 sept., 1790. Nîmes, 1790. In-8°. B. n., Lb⁴⁰ 1037.

Réponse du club des amis de la constitution de Nîmes aux faits allégués par MM. . . . , officiers de la ville de Nîmes. . . . Paris. 1790. In-8°. B. n., Lb⁴⁰ 1038.

Lettre de la société des amis de la constitution de Nîmes affiliées à celle de Paris (25 fév., 1791). Paris, n. d. In-8°. B. n., Lb⁴⁰ 1039.

Discours prononcé par M. l'Abbé Mulot, au nom de MM. les commissaires du roi. . . . Nîmes (1791). In-8°. B. n., Lb⁴⁰ 1040.

Copie de la lettre d'Aubry, député à la convention nationale, addressée à la société populaire de Nîmes (14 déc., 1792). Réponse de la société à François Aubry. . . . N. d. In-4°. B. n., Lb⁴⁰ 1041.

Orléans. Statuts et règlements de la société des amis de la constitution d'Orléans. Orléans. 1790. In-8°. B. n., Lb⁴⁰ 1048.

Perpignan. Précis historique de ce qui s'est passé à Perpignan la nuit du 5 au 6 décembre, 1790, publié par la société des amis de la constitution. Perpignan. 1790. In-4°. B. n., Lb⁴⁰ 1055.

Rennes. Vivre libre ou mourir. Adresse de la société des amis de la constitution, établie à Rennes (12 déc., 1790). N. d. In-8°. B. n., Lb⁴⁰ 1066.

Rouen. Rapport fait à la société des amis de la constitution à
Rouen, le 27 juillet, 1790, et imprimé par son ordre.
Rouen, n. d. In-8°. B. n., Lb⁴⁰ 1069.

Société des amis de la constitution à Rouen. Adresse à
l'Assemblée nationale sur le projet de supprimer plusieurs
hôtels des monnaies, entre autres celui de Rouen, par la
société des amis de la constitution à Rouen (14 déc.,
1790). Rouen, n. d. In-8°. B. n., Lb⁴⁰ 1070.

Pétition des citoyens actifs de la commune de Rouen,
membres de la société des amis de la constitution, à
l'assemblée nationale, imprimée par ordre de cette société,
en juin 1791. Rouen, n. d. In-8°. B. n., Lb⁴⁰ 1072.

Strasbourg. Règlement de la société des amis de la constitution établie à Strasbourg, affiliée à celle de Paris (6 mars).
Strasbourg. 1790. In-18. B. n., Lb⁴⁰ 1103.

Toulouse. Les amis de la liberté et de l'égalité de Toulouse à
la Convention nationale. N. d. In-4°. Lb⁴⁰ 1111.

Tours. Réfutation de la lettre du ci-devant archévêque de
Tours, adressé au directoire du district de cette ville,
relativement au serment présenté par le roi, du 26 déc.,
1790. Tours, n. d. In-8°. B. n., Lb⁴⁰ 1113.

Lettre du ministre de la guerre (Duportail) à l'armée de
France. Tours, n. d. In-8°. Lb⁴⁰ 1114.

Règlement ou loi de la société des amis de la constitution
établie à Tours, affiliée à celle de Paris séante aux Jacobins (17 sept., 1791). Tours, n. d. In-8°. B. n., Lb⁴⁰
1115.

Vivre libre ou mourir. Lettre d'un prêtre fonctionnaire
public, membre de la société des amis de la constitution
de Tours aux prêtres et fonctionnaires publics du département d'Indre-et-Loire. Tours, n. d. In-8°. Lb⁴⁰
1116.

Valence. Rapport fait à la société des amis de la constitution
de Valence, par MM. Corbeau et Trie, de leur mission dans
le ci-devant comtat Venaissin . . . le 4 mars, 1791 . . .
N. d. In-8°. B. n., Lb⁴⁰ 1124.

Versailles. Discours prononcé à la société des amis de la
constitution pour l'engager à transférer au Jeu de Paume
le lieu de ses séances et pour lui présenter différents
dessins relatifs à ce projet, par le Sieur Guignet. . . .
Versailles. 1791. In-8°. B. n., Lb⁴⁰ 1134.

La société des amis de la constitution séante à Versailles
à M. Avoine, évêque du département de Seine et Oise
(4 avril, 1791). Versailles, n. d. In-fol. B. n., Lb⁴⁰
1138.

Lettre de la société des amis de la constitution séante à Versailles aux celles qui lui sont affiliées sur la manière dont les ordres ont été éxecutés à Bellevue le 5 mars, 1791, lors du départ des voitures de suite de Mesdames (25 mars). Versailles. 1791. In-4°. B. n., Lb⁴⁰ 1137.

Extrait du régistre des délibérations de la société des amis de la constitution, établie à Versailles. Du 24 jan., 1791 (Paris), n. d. In-8°. B. n., Lb⁴⁰ 1135.

Installation de M. Bassal, curé de la paroisse Saint-Louis de Versailles. Le 10 avril, 1791. Versailles, n. d. In-8°. B. n., Lb⁴⁰ 1139.

These pamphlets are of very unequal value, and the list is not complete, as I have omitted a large number which, when consulted, proved to have no value for the present purpose.

INDEX

387